The Irish and the Spanish Civil War

For the Fallen

Tom Hyde, Midleton – Jarama
Gabriel Lee, Tralee – Jarama
Mick Kelly, Ballinasloe – Brunete

and all those Irishmen
who died for their ideals in Spain

The Irish
and the
Spanish Civil War
1936–39

Crusades in conflict

ROBERT STRADLING

MANDOLIN

Published by Mandolin
an imprint of Manchester University Press
Oxford Road, Manchester M13 9NR, UK
and Room 400, 175 Fifth Avenue, New York, NY 10010, USA
http://www.man.ac.uk/mup

Distributed exclusively in the USA by
St. Martin's Press, Inc., 175 Fifth Avenue, New York,
NY 10010, USA

Distributed exclusively in Canada by
UBC Press, University of British Columbia, 6344 Memorial Road,
Vancouver, BC, Canada V6T 1Z2

British Library Cataloguing-in-Publication Data
A catalogue record for this book is available from the British Library

Library of Congress Cataloging-in-Publication Data applied for

ISBN 1 901341 13 5 *paperback*

First published 1999

05 04 03 02 01 00 99   10 9 8 7 6 5 4 3 2 1

Typeset by
Northern Phototypesetting Co. Ltd, Bolton
Printed in Great Britain by
Redwood Books, Trowbridge

Contents

Acknowledgements

During the wanderings which had this book as their main excuse, I blithely gathered gold apples of the sun and silver apples of the moon. Sometimes, lead apples and fool's apples fell into my lap, although they, too, tasted good to me. Sitting under an apple tree, I read a bit of Montaigne, whom I discovered was as good an assayist as essayist.

> Those clever chaps notice more things more carefully but are always adding glosses; they cannot help changing their story a little in order to make their views triumph and be more persuasive; they never show you anything purely as it is; they bend it and disguise it to fit in with their own views ... So you need either a very trustworthy man or else a man so simple that he has nothing in him on which to build such false discoveries or make them plausible. (Montaigne, 'On the Cannibals', in *Four Essays*, trans. by M. A. Screech (Harmondsworth, Penguin, 1995), pp. 6–7.)

Even – as the accountant might put it – after the necessary adjustments have been made, I still accumulated an enormous burden of debt, both material and intellectual. Two of these assume priority in my mind. The book would have been unimaginably poorer and weaker had it not been for the selfless collaboration of Leslie Ó Laoi. His indefatigable quest for source material has always been complemented by thoughtful scholarship, and – in the latter stages, when reading the complete draft – a critical response to my arguments. Only Leslie will know, by observing those few occasions where things are otherwise, how often his opinion has affected mine. To him go a hundred thousand thanks. The said wanderings, at least in Ireland, were largely made possible by my wife Helen, who has driven our car around the island several times in pursuit of some rare and elusive quarry. At first, mostly from her natural gregariousness, she took an increasingly lively interest in the subject matter, and much assisted in its maturation. Later, she developed an independent interest in Irish history and in the progenitors of her natural gregariousness (we are both out of Ireland via Liverpool).

I have innumerable memories of the fieldwork. Veteran *banderistas* (battalion members) Paddy Smith KSS, the late Bill Geraghty and the late Dennis Reynolds allowed me to make recorded interviews, as did close relatives of deceased Irish Brigade officers Tony Hyde and Tom Dalton. Bernie Boles retailed the adventures of his late friend Willie McGrath, and allowed me to make copies of other relevant material in his possession. James Kavanagh presented a copy of the reminiscences recorded by his late father and namesake on his deathbed. Tom Hyde explained his posthumous relationship with his exemplary uncle and also provided a copy of Lt Hyde's wartime commonplace-book. Ann Byrne donated copies of letters and other memorabilia of her late father, Patrick Hickey. Ann Neville did likewise on behalf of her late father, Leo McCloskey. Con Roche sent me a unique series of photographs taken in Spain by his late brother, Sean. Through the good offices of Liam Sheehan, I was put in touch with Dennis Hayes, who sent copies of a diary and other material left by his late father, Tom. Noelene Crowe allowed me to copy original documentary material pertaining to the XV *Bandera*, as the Irish Brigade was called, brought home from Spain by her father Matt Beckett, and provided me with a copy of an account of his experiences in Spain written shortly before his death. Thanks are also due to other relatives and friends of deceased veterans who have made useful contributions: George Breene, Brendan Ó Cathaoir, David O'Reilly, Tom Geraghty, Bridie Cunningham, and Jerry and Tom Fennell.

In compiling material for the book I have benefited from the help of fellow historians, librarians and archivists. In first place here is Des Ryan, who generously made available the results of his valuable work on the Limerick men who went to Spain. He has made a major contribution to the nomina of the XV *Bandera* – still, however, incomplete – which appears in Appendix A; and many other offerings from his store are scattered throughout my text. In a more actuarial sense, my debt to fellow hispanist Richard Robinson is also substantial. I am grateful to Roman Álvarez Rodríguez, Tom Buchanan, Gustav Klaus, Enrique Moradiellos, Patrick Long, Chris Ealham and Diana Sanchez for their help. In Dublin, Colette O'Flaherty extended timely assistance at the National Library of Ireland, as did Bernadette Chambers in connection with my work at the Irish National Archives. I thank Commandant Peter Young for his help at the Military Archive, Cathal Brugha Barracks. Once again, Dr Seamus Helferty assisted my research in the University College, Dublin Archive. In Tralee, I successfully sought the advice of Fr Kelleher and the local librarian Michael Costello. In Tuam, the staff of the local library patiently coped with excessive and urgent demands for photocopies. Also in Tuam, I was given privileged access to files of the *Tuam Herald* by the current proprietor David Burke. In a similar context, I gratefully acknowledge the permission of the Irish Minister for Foreign Affairs to consult certain confidential files held in Bishop Street. I would also like to thank Christy Moore for permission to quote from his song, 'Vive le Quinte Brigada'.

In the UK, I received invaluable help from Kate Johnson of the Imperial War Museum's Audio Records Department, and would also like to thank Tish New-

Acknowledgements

land at the International Brigade Association Archive, and Eddie Frow at the Working Class Museum and Library, Salford. The search- and reading-room staffs of the British Library, Colindale Newspaper Library, the National Museum of Labour History at Manchester and the Public Record Office at Kew were unfailingly courteous and helpful.

In Spain, I received expert guidance and help from Antonio Rubio Rojas, Municipal Archivist of Cáceres; Sargento Primero Francisco Quintero Martínez at the Archivo General Militar in Avila; Gregorio Redondo Bárbaro, Carolina González Recio and Antonio Checa Orta at the Civil War branch of the Archivo Histórico Nacional in Salamanca; María Begoña Ibanex Ortega, Director of the Centre for Documentation at the Archivo del Ministerio de Asuntos Exteriores in Madrid; and Carmén Soría and Carmén Sierra at the Centro de Información de Documentos y Archivos of the Ministry of Culture, also in Madrid. The staff of Madrid's Hemeroteca Municipal were tolerant and efficient in dealing with a novice in the field. I would like especially to acknowledge the kindness of Dr Dámaso Alonso, lately Head of the Cultural Office of the Spanish Embassy in London, for providing an infallible 'salvoconducto' for use in the Spanish repositories.

It was my ex-student, Richard Wynne, who first suggested to me that the O'Duffy Brigade might prove a rewarding subject for research. Since he is now one of Her Majesty's Senior Inspectors of Taxes, I sincerely hope he may have forgotten this occasion. As always, Meirion Hughes has been my frequent host and occasional companion on research trips, and a critical interlocutor in discussion of material and ideas. Anna Hearder also facilitated my London work and helped with some translations from Italian into the bargain. I am grateful to my cousin, Noel Cheevers, for his timely help with the location (and partial restoration) of General O'Duffy's grave. Once again, my friends Migi and Michael Reynolds of Moylough, exuded hospitality, interest, support, suggestions, and a stream of information – the last always fascinating (and sometimes even relevant!). Special thanks go to their son, Paul, for invigorating and expert assistance during some hugely productive days of research in Tuam. Good on yuz, Sham.

Finally, I remain grateful to the British Academy for once more subscribing to my research, as it has done consistently throughout my working life. On this occasion its award enabled me to make an invaluable visit to Spain in the spring of 1995.

Abbreviations, acronyms and glossary

Archives

AGM	Archivo General Militar (Ávila)	
	CGG	Sección del Cuartel General de Generalísimo
	EM	Estado Mayor, Primera Sección
	Org.	Organización
AHM	Archivo Histórico Municipal (Cáceres)	
AHN	Archivo Histórico Nacional (Civil War Department, Salamanca)	
	AR	Aragón
	MAD	Madrid
	PS	Sección Político-Social, Serie 'R'
	SM	Sección Militar
Carp.	Carpeta (file)	
Fol.	Folleto (folio)	
IBA	International Brigade Association (Marx Memorial Library, London)	
INA	Irish National Archives (Dublin)	
	DFA	Department of Foreign Affairs
IWM	Imperial War Museum (London)	
Leg.	Legajo (bundle)	
MAE	Archivo del Ministerio de Asuntos Exteriores (Madrid)	
	A de Ba.	Sección Archivo de Barcelona
	A de Bu.	Sección Archivo de Burgos
	A Ren.	Sección Archivo Renovado
NMLH	National Museum of Labour History (Manchester)	
PRO	Public Record Office (Kew)	
	FO Foreign Office Papers	
Reg.	Registro (bound papers)	
UCD	University College, Dublin (Fine Gael Party Archives)	
WCML	Working Class Museum and Library (Salford)	

Miscellaneous

africanista	member of the professional army normally stationed in Morocco
alférez	second lieutenant
bandera	battalion of the Foreign Legion (200–600 men)

banderista	member of a *bandera*
brigadista	member of the International Brigades
cabo	corporal
Carlists	political organisation in Navarre, strong Catholics and supporters of alternative claimant to Spanish throne
Caudillo	Franco's title as leader of the nationalist 'movement', and later as head of state
CNT	Confederación Nacional de Trabajo (anarchist workers' union)
CPGB	Communist Party of Great Britain
CPI	Communist Party of Ireland
CTV	Corpo Truppe Voluntaria
Cumman na nGaedheal	ruling party in the Free State before 1932
Dáil	parliament of the Irish Free State
Ejército Popular	the republican army, as reorganised in 1937, to which the International Brigades belonged
escuadra	squad (3–6 men)
Estado Mayor	high command (Brigade or Division level)
FAI	Federación Anarquista Ibérica (anarchist leadership group)
Falange Española	Spanish Fascist Party
falangista	member of Falange Española
FF	Fianna Fáil (governing party in the Free State after 1932)
FG	Fine Gael (main opposition party in the Free State)
GAA	Gaelic Athletics Association (state-sponsored)
Gaeltacht	Irish-speaking areas of Ireland (Republic)
Garda Siochana	Irish Police Force
generalísimo	Franco's title as supreme commander of nationalist forces
GOC	General Officer Commanding
IBA	International Brigade Association
ICF	Irish Christian Front
Intendencia	Army Supply Corps
IRA	Irish Republican Army
IRA Congress	splinter group of IRA (est. 1934)
Legión Extranjera	Spanish Foreign Legion (Nationalist army)
NCO	Non-Commissioned Officer
NCP	National Corporate Party (O'Duffy's political instrument after his split with FG)
OC	Officer Commanding
parte	official daily report on military situation issued to officers and (in censored form) to press
PCE	Partido Comunista de España (Communist Party of Spain)
POUM	Partido Obrero de Unificación Marxista (libertarian communist party, strong only in Catalonia)
PSUC	Partido Socialista de Unificación Catalana (Catalan Socialist-Communist Alliance Party)
pueblo	any settlement of a certain size and roughly 2–5,000 inhabitants
requetés	militia raised by the Carlist movement
RTE	Radio Telefís Eireann (Irish Broadcasting Network)

Saor Eire	proto-communist group in the Free State, 1930–33
Saorstát	Irish designation of the Irish Free State (1923–49)
soukh	open air stall or shop (Arabic)
tabor	battalion of Moroccan troops
Taoiseach	Irish designation of Free State prime minister after 1937
TD	Teachta Dála (Irish designation of member of Dáil)
teniente	lieutenant
Tercio	another name for the Legión Extranjera
TGWU	Transport and General Workers' Union
TUC	Trades Union Congress
UDC	Urban District Council
UGT	Unión General de Trabajo (Socialist Party trade union)

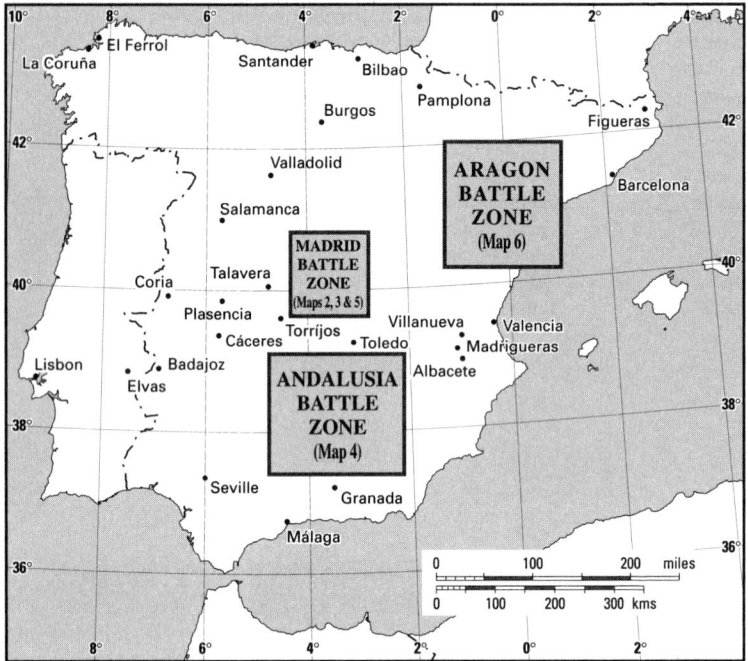

1   General map of Spain with places cited in text

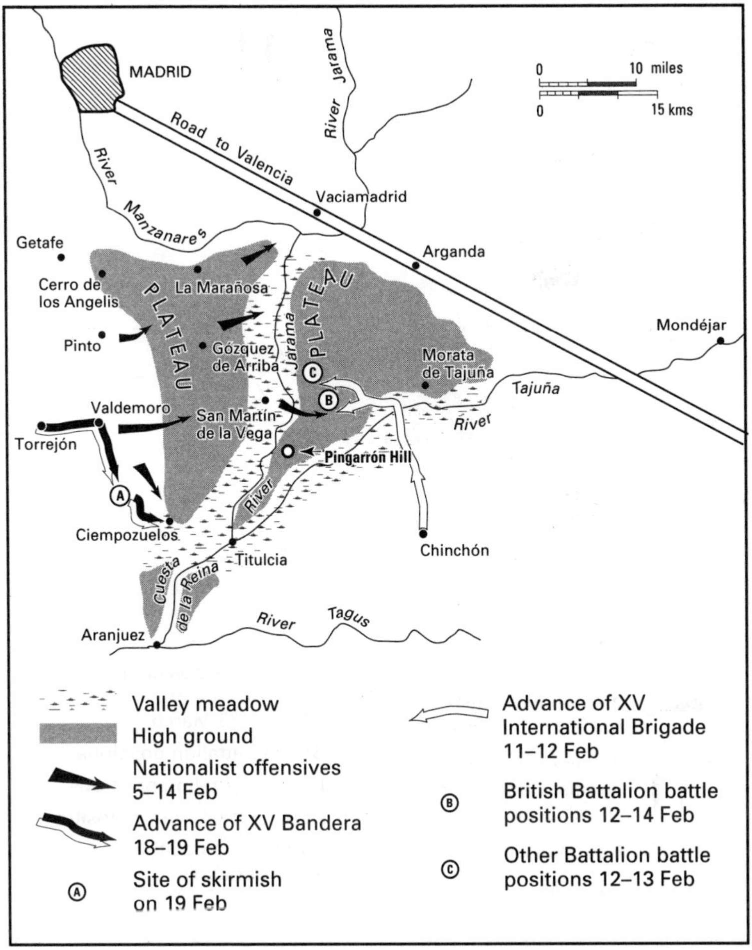
MADRID
River Jarama
0 10 miles
0 15 kms
Road to Valencia
River Manzanares
Vaciamadrid
Getafe
Arganda
Cerro de los Angelis
La Marañosa
PLATEAU
Pinto
Gózquez de Arriba
Jarama
Mondéjar
Morata de Tajuña
Tajuña
River
Valdemoro
San Martín de la Vega
Torrejón
Pingarrón Hill
River
Ciempozuelos
Chinchón
Titulcia
Cuesta de la Reina
River Tagus
Aranjuez
Valley meadow
High ground
Nationalist offensives 5–14 Feb
Advance of XV Bandera 18–19 Feb
Site of skirmish on 19 Feb
Advance of XV International Brigade 11–12 Feb
British Battalion battle positions 12–14 Feb
Other Battalion battle positions 12–13 Feb

2 Jarama – the battle (5–27 February 1937)

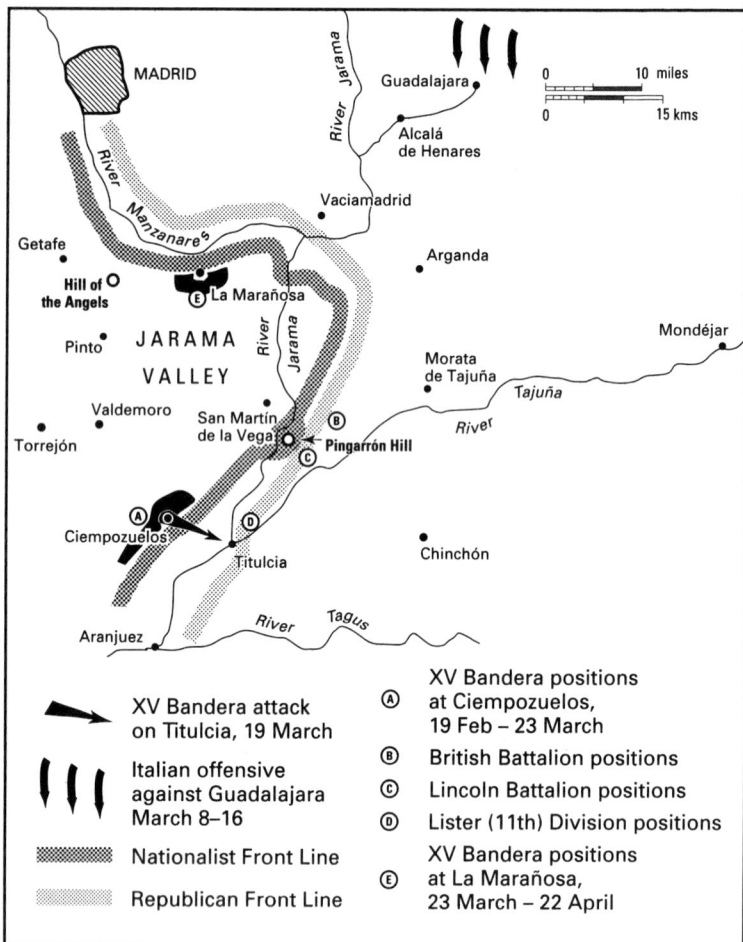

MADRID

Guadalajara

Alcalá de Henares

River Jarama

Vaciamadrid

Getafe

Arganda

River Manzanares

Hill of the Angels

La Marañosa

Mondéjar

Pinto

JARAMA VALLEY

Morata de Tajuña

Tajuña

Valdemoro

San Martín de la Vega

River Jarama

Pingarrón Hill

River Tajuña

Torrejón

Ciempozuelos

Titulcia

Chinchón

Aranjuez

River Tagus

0   10 miles

0   15 kms

XV Bandera attack on Titulcia, 19 March

Italian offensive against Guadalajara March 8–16

Nationalist Front Line

Republican Front Line

Ⓐ   XV Bandera positions at Ciempozuelos, 19 Feb – 23 March

Ⓑ   British Battalion positions

Ⓒ   Lincoln Battalion positions

Ⓓ   Lister (11th) Division positions

Ⓔ   XV Bandera positions at La Marañosa, 23 March – 22 April

3   Jarama – the front lines, spring 1937

4   (*facing top*) The International Brigade in Andalusia (December 1936–April 1937)

5   (*facing bottom*) The Madrid battles and Brunete (December 1936–July 1937)

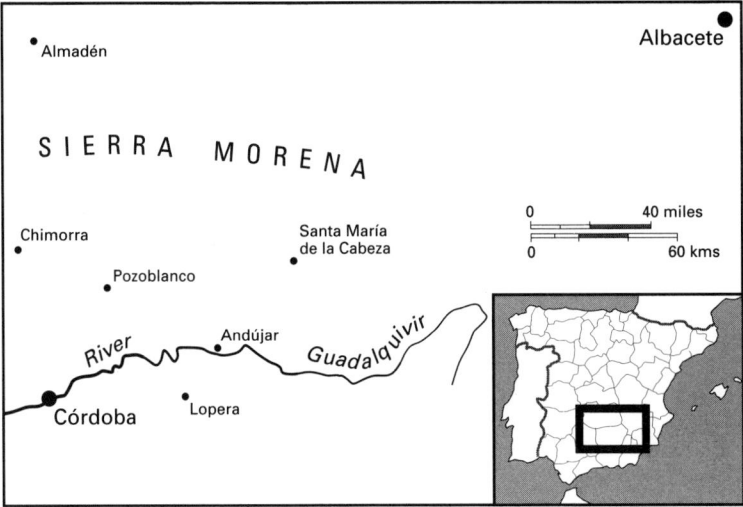

Almadén

S I E R R A   M O R E N A

Chimorra

Pozoblanco

Santa María
de la Cabeza

Albacete

0   40 miles

0   60 kms

River

Andújar

Guadalquivir

Córdoba

Lopera

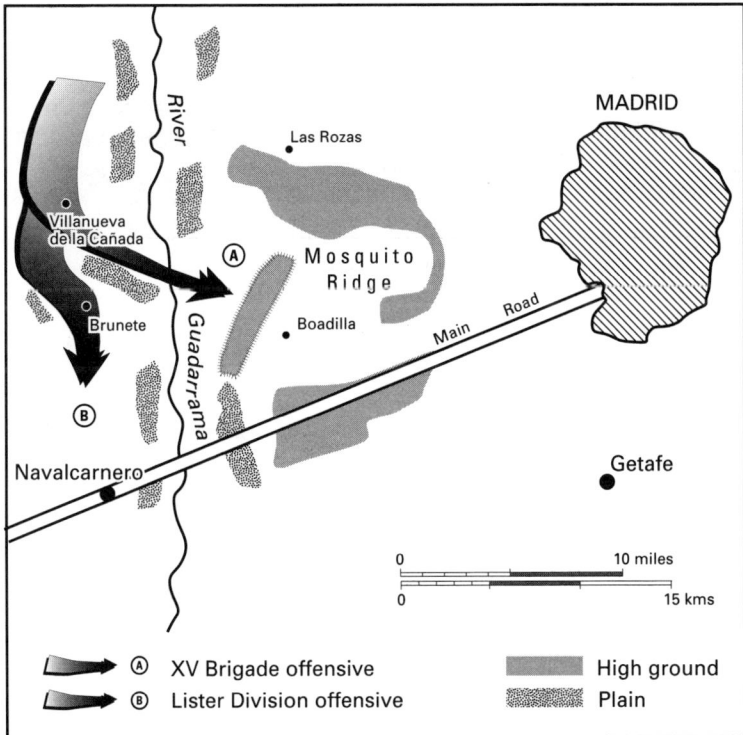

MADRID

River

Las Rozas

Villanueva
de la Cañada

Ⓐ

Mosquito
Ridge

Brunete

Boadilla

Main   Road

Guadarrama

Ⓑ

Getafe

Navalcarnero

0   10 miles

0   15 kms

Ⓐ XV Brigade offensive   High ground

Ⓑ Lister Division offensive   Plain

6   Zaragoza, Teruel and the Ebro (August 1937–October 1938)

Prologue: The war of ideals

Separated by only a few metres of ground, in the section of Glasnevin Cemetery dedicated to heroes of Irish independence, lie the remains of two celebrated members of that fraternity. One of these graves is often freshly decorated with flowers and other favours of public esteem. The other is overgrown with bushes, almost impossible even for the determined visitor to find. The men concerned had many things in common. Both were sincere, practising Catholics; dedicated fighters for Ireland during the wars of independence; supporters of Nazi Germany during the Second World War; and both died in 1944. In between, they fought against each other in the Irish Civil War, and led groups of Irishmen to fight on opposite sides in the Spanish Civil War.

The first of them, Frank Ryan, is famous in his own country and beyond; for the other, Eoin O'Duffy, the word 'infamous' seems more appropriate. The memory of the former is revered, that of the latter either ignored or execrated. Yet, politically, Ryan was prominent only in an obscure splinter group of the Irish Republican Army (IRA), which had a short lifespan and never once elected a representative to the Dáil, whilst O'Duffy was the first president of Fine Gael, one of the two governing parties in Irish politics. The explanation for this paradox lies almost wholly in the given cultural reaction to one word: fascism.

O'Duffy was the main founder of an Irish fascist movement, the Blueshirts, which in 1933–34 mushroomed into what was – in relative terms – the largest non-governing fascist organisation in the world. As such, he is virtually unspeakable in Irish historical discourse. The popular imagination is not capable of sustaining the shock which juxtaposing the adjectives 'Irish' and 'fascist' administers. Worse still, in the twentieth century's most resonant struggle for republican democracy against fascism, O'Duffy fought on the 'wrong' side. In Spain, he was least among Franco's foreign satraps, and was seen by his enemies as a miserable running dog of reaction. As such, he was firmly displaced from the main-stream of public memory.[1] The usual defensive strategy, invoked to pro-tect the self-esteem of the nation, is to exaggerate to slapstick proportions the amusing features in the behaviour (both in Ireland and Spain) of O'Duffy and the Blueshirts. Given the premium on wit in the national culture, they all too easily assume the role of a bunch of clowns sent by benificent destiny to enliven the introverted and colourless (if worthy) scenario of de Valera's Ireland. In this way 'Irish fascism' is shuf-fled off as a ritual joke, empty of meaning, sanitised and unthreatening.[2]

Neither in 1992, centenary of his birth, nor in 1994, fiftieth anniver-sary of his death, was any mark of recognition given to O'Duffy as one of the founding fathers of the Irish state. Not even a commemorative arti-cle in a national newspaper has come to my attention. In between these dates, a new history of Fine Gael appeared from the main party pub-lisher. Here, although O'Duffy was acknowledged *en passant* as its first leader, he did not figure among fifty-odd vignette biographies of party personnel, and whilst all the other leaders from Collins to Bruton were given photographic portraits, he appears only on the platform (back-ground) whilst Kevin O'Higgins is making a speech (foreground). It is as though Keir Hardie were to have been deliberately and systematically ignored by historians of the Labour Party.[3]

In contrast, Ryan was a socialist rebel in the conventional – almost stereotyped – image of Irish heroism. His own party was founded mainly to fight the Blueshirts, and he followed the logic of this – a process deeply appreciated today – by enlisting in the ranks of the 'volunteers for liberty' in Spain. He was captured, maltreated and sentenced to death by the Nationalists, and became the first 'prisoner of Franco' to receive wide-spread publicity outside Spain. With the single (if emphatic) exception of Michael Collins, he is now the most admired political figure of modern Ireland.

To seek redress of one reputation is not to seek to denigrate the other.[4] The two personalities are representative of the men they led to Spain and of the political attitudes this act expressed. They were both courageous soldiers, inspiring leaders and gifted administrators. Both had 'secondary' interests which are now recognised as deeply significant in terms of cultural politics, especially in the Irish nationalist context; O'Duffy in sport (above all, the Gaelic Athletics Association (GAA)), Ryan in writing (above all, in Irish). Each made a worthwhile contribu-tion to the sum of his people's endeavour in these respective areas. How-ever, this book highlights their common obsession, human freedom, above all freedom of political action and religious worship – ironically but equally true of men who hoped and worked for the victory of Hitler's New Order.

But however deeply symbolic, two men are not all. Tom Murphy and Phil McBride were both from the area of Newbliss, Co. Monaghan (not far away from O'Duffy's home village), born in the early years of this century (around the time of Ryan's birth). The latter, a farmer, went to Spain with the 'Catholic crusade'. He was overwhelmingly driven by the persecution of the Church in the Spanish revolution. His parish priest encouraged his enlistment, and told a like-minded friend in the confessional that 'you're doing a fine thing'. When a radio interviewer asked his reasons for meddling in a foreign people's problems, he replied: 'they were alright if they'd left the priests and nuns alone – I wouldn't have went there'.[5] The former's family moved to Belfast when he was a child, and he was brought up a Catholic in a working-class Protestant district. He was in the Irish Guards for six years, thereafter settling in London where he worked as a seaman and cook, before joining the 'Communist crusade'. On the Jarama front in March 1937, he found himself opposite the O'Duffy Brigade:

> Our trenches were maybe a few hundred yards away. Frank Ryan used to speak on the [loud]speaker, he says 'Irishmen go home! Your fathers would turn in their graves if they knew that you'd come to fight for imperialism. This is the real Republican army, the real, the real men of Ireland.'[6]

But Murphy and McBride are not all, either, even if imagined in the plural. The 1930s was an era of crusades. In Britain, the unemployed marchers carried banners reading, for example, 'Jarrow crusade'. In the USA, the term 'crusade' was used ubiquitously in the campaign propaganda of the New Deal. And (as John Keegan reminds us), western culture 'had always tended to depict war as a calamity … unless it could be represented as a crusade'.[7] This was the case with renewed emphasis in the context of the interwar years, when a dominant liberal-pacifist morality was challenged in international affairs by the rise of an intolerant national-ideological belligerence and the increasing development of modern systems of mass destruction. But whilst some communities saw no possibility of compromise between the crusades of the cross (on the one hand) and of the hammer and sickle (on the other), others felt instinctively that they were – or could be – the same crusade. The challenge of writing this book has been to study the intense perspectives which the complex obsessions of modern Irish history bring to bear upon that most complex and obsessional of twentieth-century conflicts, the Spanish Civil War. For understandable reasons which cannot be explored here, Spaniards have been reluctant to recognise that their civil war, unlike any other, is part of the history of all the nations of the modern world. This book will challenge certain Spanish sensibilities. Some will be disturbed that so many Irishmen saw the nationalist struggle as a good and great cause. Perhaps for some among the Catholic clergy, this is not the kind of international profile they would wish their country's history to project. Even a recent neo-Francoist account exhibits a certain embarrassment over the presence of Catholic Irishmen in the 'Cruzada' on the Madrid front.[8]

But we can never come to all. Other intriguing connections of Ireland with the Spanish War are so remote and hazy that they can only take the form of queries tossed into the void. I will mention two examples, both concerning outstanding exponents of modernism. When Joyce (in *Finnegans Wake*) named Bruno Nola, reconciler of Manichean opposites, after his original publishers, Browne and Nolan – who also published O'Duffy's *Crusade in Spain* – was he thinking of the Spanish Civil War? Was Christopher St John Sprigg (aka Caudwell), perhaps the most promising British intellectual of his generation, conscious of his Irish antecedents and influenced by Irish friends in volunteering for the crusade of which he became one of the most famous martyrs?

I am convinced that Spanish democracy, like Ireland's, can only derive further strength and plural flexibility from citizens' serious confrontation of issues represented by the equal and opposite crusades espoused so deeply by their forebears. But this book is more concerned with Irishmen than with Spaniards. Despite its intentions, and precisely because it strives for impartiality, it will outrage many, and will even be taken by some as a considered affront to all that is best in Ireland's history and national character. I hope not to succumb to the tempting delusion that the self-righteous condemnation it receives is commensurate with the extent of its success in achieving objectivity.

The
Catholic crusade

1

Origins of the Irish Brigade

The conspiracy

On 10 August 1936, three weeks into the military uprising in Spain, the *Irish Independent* carried what had become a normal ration of horror stories from what was by then a civil war. Readers were informed, for example, that in Barcelona 'bodies of nuns are left on the sidewalks of the principal streets'. By now the daily press had created a market of interest in Spanish barbarities. This time, however, the front page was split, in order to accommodate a fresh and highly newsworthy development. Under the headline 'IRISH BRIGADE FOR SPAIN – SUGGESTED BY GENERAL O'DUFFY', and supported by the dramatic sub-heading 'Anti-Red Crusade', appeared a letter from the leader of the National Corporate Party (NCP). General Eoin O'Duffy suggested that Irish volunteers might enlist in a Catholic Brigade to fight on the side of the Nationalists, and expressed his belief that 'there are thousands of young men here who would cheerfully answer the call to join the crusade'. He linked his idea with a political programme recommended by the Vatican, and which he understood as equally applicable to Ireland and to Spain: 'We cannot have a Workers' Republic, Farmers' Republic, or any other "class" Republic. Such is the form of Government which his Holiness warns the world against.'[1]

Elsewhere in the same issue, the general was reported as having delivered an address to local members of the NCP at Mullingar, in which he claimed that such a crusade might 'help in the restoration of a Christian Administration in Spain'. He answered a Galway opponent's assertion that the struggle in Spain was between democracy and fascism. 'Does this,' O'Duffy riposted, in one of his more effective rhetorical moments, 'interpret democracy by the massacre of priests and nuns …? If these atrocities are carried out in the name of democracy, then the sooner Fascism triumphs, the better.'[2]

It seems likely that the newspaper itself had participated at a primary level in the hugger-mugger negotiations which preceded this initiative. In an unpublished memoir of his leader written in the 1940s, O'Duffy's secretary, Captain Liam Walsh, paid tribute to the help provided by the *Irish Independent* in launching the Brigade. According to Walsh, they regarded O'Duffy as being 'actuated by sincere motives and … leading a band of missionaries to a country where the forces of evil were striking a deadly blow at the Catholic Church'.[3] Though no longer supporting O'Duffy's personal political aspirations within Ireland, the paper's proprietor, W. L. Murphy, and his editor, Frank Geary, were probably involved more deeply and clandestinely in the affair than Walsh's acknowledgement explicitly betrays. Indeed, the prospect of a band of pure young crusaders setting out to relieve the besieged city of God provided a perfect catharsis after a long build-up of suspense with scarifying daily episodes of 'Mother Church in Danger'. It would hardly be surprising if, as well as placing his paper at O'Duffy's disposal, Murphy gave some guarantee of financial support for the whole venture.[4]

Details of the arrangements to establish the Brigade still remain imperfectly clear. From one angle they seem a pale reflection of the military conspiracy which precipitated the actual war in Spain. Indeed, the former was a contingent outgrowth of the latter. Members of the same London-based ring of Spanish diplomats, businessmen and journalists who organised international financial support for the military rising, and (in particular) arranged for the airborne delivery of General Franco from the Canary Islands to lead Spain's only professional army in Morocco, were also *dramatis personae* in the weave of events which brought the Irish Brigade to Spain.[5]

The bare narrative outline relates that the idea was first mooted when a Spanish aristocrat with international credentials got in touch with the Irish primate, Cardinal MacRory in the first days of August.[6] Count Ramírez de Arellano was a Navarrese nobleman resident in London. He had contacts with disloyal elements within the Spanish embassy, but was also acting with the aid of a group of right-wing Spanish associates in the British capital, and with the approval of the main co-ordinator of the military rising, General Emilio Mola.[7] MacRory recommended an approach to General O'Duffy, whose name apparently occurred to the cardinal without a second thought. O'Duffy, he informed Ramírez, was a 'chivalrous, courageous, upright man and a good Catholic, and above all a good organiser'. Shortly thereafter, MacRory and O'Duffy met in Rosslare, and agreement in principle was reached.[8]

The Spaniard now addressed Eoin O'Duffy in terms the latter found irresistible: 'Do you think it might be possible to raise in Ireland a volunteer force to come to aid us – purely personally voluntary, so as to avoid all possibility of international complications? What a glorious example Ireland could give the whole of Christendom!'[9]

O'Duffy hesitated only briefly before drafting his letter to the *Irish Independent*. But a bizarre development followed. Having set the bandwagon rolling, the general's next move was to let go of the reins and leave for a previously arranged holiday in the Netherlands. Whilst he was away, various individuals and organisations reacted to his announcement. Some jumped on board the wagon, but others were more inclined to stick spokes in the wheels or to push heavy obstacles into its path. Not every supporter acted with straightforward motives. One or two may have leapt on board with the intention of hijacking the currently driverless vehicle. O'Duffy's main lieutenant in the south-west, Colonel Thomas Carew, appealed at Cashel (Tipperary) on 14 August for 'the formation of an Irish Brigade', revealing a few days later that he had received 'letters from all parts of Ireland and England' with offers to serve.[10] Bolstered by the personal support of well-known warriors like Major O'Malley and Lt-Col. Butler, Carew later told 'a company of Cashel recruits' that:

> it was a great and glorious thing to fight for one's country, but it was far more glorious and more noble to die for one's Faith … The fight for Christianity in Spain is our fight … Is it not much better for this country to sacrifice some of its sons on the battlefields of Spain now than to sacrifice, perhaps, the whole nation in a few years' time?[11]

Carew's move was matched in Tralee, where Eamonn Horan stated at a meeting of the Urban District Council (UDC) that he 'would personally organise a Kerry contingent'.[12] Later developments were to suggest that both these men viewed themselves as more qualified to lead the crusade than the self-appointed (but absent) incumbent. Meanwhile, in Cork city, the NCP director alleged that amongst the Spanish clergy suffering at the hands of murderous Reds 'many are of Irish blood and Irish descent' and a resolution urged the immediate 'formation of an Irish Brigade to help the Spanish people in their fight'.[13]

Preaching the crusade[14]

The only national newspaper based outside Dublin, the *Cork Examiner,* reacted coolly to proposals for a crusade. The newspaper supported the official opposition, and accordingly expressed its approval when Limerick corporation demanded an outright break in the Saorstát's (Irish Free State) diplomatic relations with the Spanish Republic.[15] But although reporting the work of his associates, and carrying a lively correspondence on the issue, the *Examiner* otherwise ignored O'Duffy's appeal for over a week, and thereafter paid him only scant attention. Keen to reflect the line of the newly reconstituted Fine Gael, which had ejected O'Duffy from its leadership (and, perhaps, suspecting the hand of his Dublin competitor in the whole business), the editor noted – somewhat sourly, but with prophetic realism – that 'if volunteers are willing to set out of the Free State and find their way to Spain it evidently must be at their own risk and responsibility. In all wars some foreigners join up ... but if their own country remains neutral they cannot subsequently claim its support if they get into difficulties.'[16]

In the wake of O'Duffy's initiative, de Valera and his cabinet hesitated to spell out a policy over Spain. Yet, with calls for an official break with the 'Red Republic' heard on all sides, de Valera's own view seems unequivocal. In the first week of August he communicated to the Madrid government his determination not to be overwhelmed by the clericalist furore.[17] He believed his Spanish blood and name made him the ideal mediator in the search for a compromise solution to the Civil War, but Madrid summarily rejected his offer to act in this capacity.[18] His government's position was further weakened when the Spanish ambassador, Señor Aguilar, who had assured Madrid of his 'absolute loyalty to the republican cause', resigned 'for family reasons' in early September. Spanish diplomatic staff followed their chief's example, leaving a junior (Irish) assistant in charge, and crippling communications between the Spanish Republic and Irish Free State.[19]

On 20 August, Eoin O'Duffy returned from vacation and immediately put his full efforts into the preaching of the crusade.[20] He was encouraged by widespread popular support which must have reminded him of the heady days of 1933. On 21 August, for example, the Corporation of Clonmel passed a resolution – which became a template for similar bodies – including an implied pledge of support for military intervention. Its wording offered help 'to any movement which might be established to safeguard the interests of Catholics in that unhappy country [Spain]'.[21] Though their town had never been a strong base for Blueshirts or Greenshirts (the NCP equivalent corps), the city fathers of Clonmel now, in effect, offered to act as O'Duffy's recruiting agents. The so-called 'Clonmel Resolution' was soon to become unlawful, and most of the other public bodies which adopted it were obliged to amend or delete this clause. Yet, all the same, the atmosphere in which it was so adopted was a perfervid one which often sanctioned a crude silencing of opposition and sent a powerful warning to the government.[22] O'Duffy had been humiliated in the local elections two years earlier; now he enjoyed a certain rehabilitation at the grass roots.

This phenomenon was undoubtedly fuelled by the work of the Church as well as that of the *Irish Independent*. It is true that in public the Catholic clergy – at all levels – restricted itself to vaguely approving noises. The clerical extremism acknowledged in de Valera's dealings with Madrid drew a line at the explicit recommendation of military intervention. In the literal sense, at least, there was little or no preaching of crusade. In private, however, parish priests all over the country extolled the names of the Church's fearless champions – Generals Franco and O'Duffy – and in the confessional many a young man was pointed towards an ideal penance for his sins. It was not until 9 September that Cardinal MacRory, who had acted as midwife to O'Duffy's enterprise, felt able to offer it a (deliciously equivocal) public endorsement. In a sermon at Drogheda he suggested:

> We should all pray for Spain, and if able to we should send all help from our purses ... to help her obtain war supplies – what I should say is medical supplies for her sick and wounded. I do not want to say anything about any other kind of help as Christians, where we are able, we should be prepared to render that help to her.[23]

Around this time appeared another vital contribution to the cause of the Brigade. Aodh de Blacam was a journalist working on the staff of de Valera's *Irish Press*. His pamphlet *For God and Spain* now stirred waters his chief would have much preferred to lie stagnant. However, its line on the question of military intervention marks it out as essentially a clerically inspired production:

> Were we to stand neutral or indifferent when this Last Crusade is being fought, we would deserve to go down to history as a shameless generation, helping by our silence and consent the new Crucifixion. We cannot give material aid, although we do not forget how Spain sent us ships and armies and gave colleges to educate our priests and leading laymen in our own dark hour.[24]

Thus far, the trumpet had sounded an uncertain note. One of those who perhaps appreciated the negative import thereof was Bishop Mac-

Namee of Longford who, preaching on an appointed 'Day of Reparation for Spain', referred to the crusading links between Ireland and Spain in terms calculated to convey a sense of duty to many men who were susceptible to the call of history: 'Spain … has intimate relations with our own Ireland. She supported us against religious persecution in the days of Elizabeth. She afforded a home to our exiled princes; she trained our greatest Catholic Captain, the hero of Benburb. So let us pray for Spain.'[25] The somewhat bathetic conclusion here seems to mark the point beyond which few clerics would step, at least in public. Yet Irish Brigade veteran Patrick Smith recalls seeing one bishop's appeal in the *Irish Independent*:

> First he explained that General O'Duffy was organising a group to go to Spain. And he said that they were going to fight for Catholicism against atheistic communism … He said that any single unattached young man who would go out there with the right intentions … should they fall should 'in my honest opinion be a Christian martyr and therefore have a place in heaven'.[26]

Another seeming exception to the rule was Fr Leonardo Bello, a member of the religious order which had in former days fought, sword in hand, alongside the 'Wild Geese', for the Catholic cause. From the pulpit of the Franciscan church at Waterford, he relayed what was reportedly a message from Pope Pius XI himself, offering guidance on the current political crisis: 'The burden of the message was that they should strengthen their faith so that they might withstand whatever trials were before them in the universal troubles of the present time, and, more important still, that they might be ready if called upon to make the supreme sacrifice.'[27]

Yet voices more contrarious were also heard. The Jesuit organ *Social Justice* commented acidly on the fact that 'one of our metropolitan dailies is giving prominent space to a proposal to send an Irish Brigade to Spain, on the principal [*sic*] apparently that if there is a fight going on "the fighting race" should join in'.[28] In Galway, a town councillor (Mr Healey) criticised his colleagues' support for intervention, suggesting that 'word be sent to O'Duffy stating that if he is going to form a brigade, the brigade is needed in Belfast more than in Spain'.[29] More central and more effective opposition than this lone Sinn Feiner was now emergent. After a week of reflection, O'Duffy's ex-lieutenant, Eamonn Cronin – veritable 'inventor' of the Blueshirts and now head of its much-weakened successor body, the League of Youth – issued a statement highly critical of O'Duffy: 'Some of those who are indulging in those mock heroics know only too well that an Irish Brigade has as much prospect of reaching Saragossa as it has of reaching the moon.' In Cronin's view, 'the only effective course is to establish a fund for medical aid'. Indeed, it seemed the Brigade might yet be stillborn, for it came under pressure from other directions too. The O'Duffyite enthusiasm of W. B. Yeats had long since cooled, and now Maud Gonne McBride made a speech in Dublin referring sarcastically to the story that 'General O'Duffy was taking 2,000 Irishmen to help the Moors to Christianise Spain'.[30]

A whole new dimension to the issue of Spain was meanwhile opening up. On 28 August, a meeting in the Dublin Mansion House produced a tactical confederation of lay Catholic organisations which – neatly expropriating the enemy's vocabulary – called itself the Irish Christian Front (ICF). Ostensibly, the new movement had nothing to do with Spain, but aimed to initiate and co-ordinate anti-communist activity in the Free State. Yet the ICF's creation was obviously precipitated by the 'Red persecution' in Spain, and its first public undertakings were focused on this and contingent issues. The holy hand of the hierarchy was behind this initiative, and the ICF quickly received the strong support of the *Irish Independent.* Though the inaugural meeting was convened by Alfred Byrne, the (Fine Gael) Lord Mayor of Dublin, the opposition party remained officially aloof.

General O'Duffy was not invited to (or at any rate did not attend) this convention. It soon became clear that the new group did not approve O'Duffy's project, though it refrained from explicit condemnation. The ICF's main spokesman, opposition Teachta Dála (TD) Paddy Belton, could not be persuaded – even by MacRory – to set aside his personal antipathy towards O'Duffy in the common cause. Instead, Belton announced that the proper way for the Irish to help their persecuted coreligionists would be with humanitarian aid – food, clothing and medical supplies – which his movement would accordingly organise. Belton's move effectively upstaged both O'Duffy and Cronin. The ICF rapidly moved to occupy the publicity spotlight. It did so partly by appealing for a sensible and moderate response, thus evoking the silent majority who, although anxious to help Spanish Catholics, drew short of risking Ireland's embroilment in another war – especially another civil war. Such sympathisers were now offered a chance to demonstrate both their religious loyalty and their humanitarianism by contributing money to a central fund for non-military aid. But even here, the primary source of inspiration and charity – also, in this instance, the primary object thereof – insisted on its precedence. The Irish hierarchy's own national collection for Spain was announced quite independently of all the competing lay leaders. A Sunday collection was to be held outside all the Catholic churches of the Free State. It was surely not accidental that the event was scheduled to take place on 25 October, the Feast of Christ the King, a day which was the main feast in the Carlist religious calendar.[31]

Despite this reference to Irish-Navarrese solidarity, the net effect of the new activity encouraged many to revert to a picture of O'Duffy as an extremist, who lacked the sense of responsibility of his more mature political rivals. This view seemed consistent with (what was often portrayed as) a violent past as instigator of the so-called 'Blueshirt War' and with his more recent record as an isolated self-seeker. The general had to respond quickly to this fresh attempt to marginalise him from the mainstream of events. His answer was to enlist the shade of his own warrior-hero and mentor, Michael Collins. Then, as now, Collins was a figure of Leninist resonance in the politics of the Irish revolution. Above all, his equivocal political heritage represented almost the only nucleus around which the otherwise irreconcilable sides of the Irish Civil War might be able to gather. On 30 August, O'Duffy held a meeting at the monument erected on the site of Collins's death at Beal Na Blath in Cork. If the NCP could be said to have had a heartland, it was in the general proximity of rural Cork. Even the *Examiner* felt obliged to give the event prominent coverage, and its photographs rather belie the reporter's cool estimation of 'a fairly large gathering'. In his speech, O'Duffy alleged that Collins had 'left behind a message for the Irish people that should he fall, Eoin O'Duffy would carry on'; and he followed up with the assertion that if this tragedy had never come to pass, Collins himself, and not O'Duffy, would have been leading the Irish Brigade to Spain. In a disingenuous move he expressed his disappointment that 'West Cork was very low down the list' of volunteers, declaring that 'we should have a couple of hundred thousand volunteers ready to fight for the faith and for the country whether they went to Spain or not.'[32]

If the *Examiner*'s report is accurate, the general's oration – made, as was his custom, extempore – also committed howlers. For example, he explained that the Spanish Church had not felt able to give a lead in the 'national' uprising 'because the government of Spain was elected by the people'. Whilst this kind of tactical slip offered hostages to fortune, the general also made long-range strategic errors at the planning stage. Much is revealed by his initial failure to set up an appeal fund for support of the Brigade. This oversight later had serious political as well as financial consequences. Perhaps, indeed, O'Duffy felt, like Christian warriors of old, that God would provide for His cause. But it seems equally plausible that his complaisance derived from the assurance that his enterprise was already underwritten by powerful financial interests both of Spanish and Irish origin.[33] In any case, by the end of August, political developments outside Ireland towards an agreed framework on 'non-intervention' were imposing limitations on his enterprise which could hardly have been fully foreseen three weeks earlier.

While the general himself had no direct access to its medium of publicity and enthusiasm, the campaign of meetings and marches, open-air services and fund-raising events organised by the ICF put tremendous pressure on the government. This was directed at achieving a definitive break between the Free State and the Spanish Republic, and was bound to work broadly to O'Duffy's advantage. It brought home to de Valera that his room for manoeuvre was circumscribed. Dozens of his own Fianna Fáil delegates at Leinster House (not to mention hundreds of local councillors nationwide) made clear to 'the chief' the risk to their positions should the government resort to any action that might be successfully projected by political rivals as 'anti-Catholic'. This may not have deflected the premier from his determination to adopt official neutrality, along with its diplomatic medium of non-intervention, in terms of the nation's official stance on external affairs; but it made him hesitate to offer overt and repeated challenges to the domestic tide of Catholic populism generated by the ICF. The potential for extremists to dominate the issue at local and street level was great. Just like his old rival chieftain O'Duffy, 'the chief' knew he had to tread carefully and avoid either public provocation or outright confrontation on the issue of Spain.[34]

Non-intervention intervenes

The stance adopted by the government towards O'Duffy and the Brigade was studiously neutral, despite the fact that little sympathy for either existed in government circles. Yet virtually all 'inside' accounts of the process of recruitment make some reference to petty harassment and general obstructionism by police and other authorities. Given that many of the former were men who were specifically unsympathetic to the O'Duffy interest, drafted in after the general's dismissal by de Valera as Garda Siochana Commissioner, these complaints are not hard to credit – at least on the face of things. Whilst, on the one hand, it did not want to be heavy handed in the matter, on the other, the government was sensitive to international opinion and to its legal responsibilities. In the last week of August the *Cork Examiner*, not without a certain smugness, revealed that 'the question is being asked whether General O'Duffy would be allowed to leave the country with such a force ... A well-known constitutional lawyer ... was of opinion that unless the government agreed, recruiting would be illegal.'[35] Nevertheless, it soon proved that the question was not as cut and dried as this report suggested. De Valera responded favourably to the initiatives of the French government aimed at establishing an international basis for non-intervention.[36] On 25 August, the Saorstát adhered to a joint preliminary declaration prohibiting 'the export of arms and ammunition to Spain and Spanish possessions'.[37] Within a month, the institutional apparatus of the Non-Intervention Committee had been set up in London. Throughout this body's stormy and controversial existence the Free State was to behave with impeccable loyalty to its principles and decrees. This course was maintained by de Valera only with considerable difficulty, and his resolution often came under severe attack. Nonetheless, his reading of the political situation was in the highest degree acute and apposite.

De Valera wished to maintain flexibility of action. Keenly aware of popular strength of feeling against the Spanish Republic, he also knew that this feeling had no necessary implications in terms of party politics. Perhaps he anticipated that the Non-Intervention Committee's decision to suspend the (otherwise lawful) international practice of providing arms to a constitutionally elected government would blunt the edge of clerically inspired criticism. In terms of public opinion, it was true that negative distaste for the Republic was more in evidence than positive support for the Nationalists. Like Blum's government in France, if for different reasons, de Valera saw non-intervention as a way of reducing risk of conflict at home. He wanted, above all, to avoid a renewed clash between ex-Blueshirts and IRA hardliners (many of both still secretly armed), and was worried that coping with such disturbances might lend more credence to critics who already believed his government to have too many powers of arbitrary detention. The need for the government to play a more open role in the affair seemed reduced when, after several weeks' deliberation, the attorney-general concluded that as things stood:

> I do not think that any offence is committed by persons joining or encouraging others to take part on the side of Insurgents in Spain. The [British] Foreign Enlistment Act of 1870 even if it applies here, which is doubtful, does not prohibit persons from taking part in a civil war such as this. It was effectively passed for the purposes of preventing Englishmen joining either side in the Franco-Prussian War. It deals

altogether with wars between two States … If it is desired to prevent
Irish citizens from taking part in the Spanish Civil War, legislation
should be passed.[38]

Indeed, in Whitehall itself, officials lacked confidence in the validity of
invoking the 1870 Act, whilst Foreign Secretary Anthony Eden specifically
decided 'in the present case, to avoid any reference to the question of
enrolment in the Dominions'.[39]

As long as this state of productive confusion prevailed, both O'Duffy
and his Red opponents were able to proceed with impunity. As time wore
on, however, regulations issued by the Non-Intervention Committee
became more numerous and restrictive. There was a growing awareness
of major intervention on the parts of the USSR, Italy and Germany.
Before 1936 ended it was clear that member states would soon be called
upon to pass detailed prohibitive legislation.[40]

For the Free State government this was easier said than done. With a
slender majority, it had to fight a daily battle on the floor of the Dáil
against an opposition whose demands ranged from the banning of all
trade with the Republic to immediate recognition of the Franco regime
as defenders of the faith against the Bolshevik hordes. In the midst of the
storm, de Valera remained firm, with a superb sense of opportunism in
dividing or wrong-footing his rivals. Though he was a devout Catholic,
his position was potentially weakened by the fact that he had never fully
repaired the breach with the Church caused by his defiance of their influence in the quarrel over the 1921 Treaty. He was prepared to offer some
sops to Cerberus. For example, he allowed his newspaper, the *Irish Press*,
to display over Spain a moderately pro-Catholic – but not pro-Francoist
– sympathy. Perhaps his stand against the populist-clerical tide came
more from natural obstinacy than visionary statesmanship. At any rate,
the first real crisis arrived in early November. In his secondary capacity
as External Affairs minister, de Valera received a note from the senior permanent official, Joe Walshe, warning him that 'it seems fairly certain that
General Franco's forces will succeed in capturing the Spanish capital at
an early date. Franco's government may be expected to claim the de jure
right to govern all Spain.'[41]

Later in the month, indeed, Radio Castile, the nationalist station in
Salamanca, announced that 'In Dublin the president of the chamber has
submitted to it a proposition asking for official Irish recognition of the
government of General Franco.'[42] In fact, the frontal assault on Madrid
had already failed, and fears were growing that the capital's resistance

might even provide the foundations of ultimate victory for the Republic. Meanwhile, '*no pasarán*' ('they shall not pass') might well have been de Valera's watchword as he rode the crisis with the Olympian bearing and style which were soon to become his trademarks.

Tying the ends

Thus, in a political context where the public was favourable and political authority not overtly hostile, O'Duffy was able to initiate the process of recruitment. Once assured that this was progressing satisfactorily, he again left Ireland, in order to finalise details by liaison with the nationalist representatives. His primary aim was to tie the Irish and Spanish ends of the operation together. It was not to prove an easy task. Up to this point O'Duffy had not perceived any equivocation in the status of his 'gentleman's agreement' with Ramírez de Arellano. In practice, however, the situation was less simple. General Franco had emerged as the outstanding candidate for leadership of the Nationalists.[43] Even before his final appointment as sole leader in the last days of September, it was becoming obvious that without Franco's approval the whole notion of an Irish Brigade might as well be abandoned. Franco was an unknown quantity – not just to foreigners such as O'Duffy. As several actors in the drama discerned, the ground between the two men demanded careful advance preparation.

It was probably not until O'Duffy and Ramírez met for the first time in London (in early September) that the former was apprised of the significant alteration in his circumstances caused by the rise of Francisco Franco. He became dimly aware of a darker mass lying underneath the sunlit summit of the original crusading vision. The complex political nature of the nationalist cause began to reveal itself to the general, like the first layers of an onion peeling away. (Perhaps he later regretted that he did not rub his watery eyes a little harder.) Ramírez's original invitation had set out not only the basic ideological rationale of the Brigade but also a key detail of its conditions of service.

> This heroic movement in Spain was really started by the party to which I have the honour to belong – the Carlist-Traditionalists, essentially the most Catholic movement in Spain, whose headquarters have ever been in Pamplona, the capital of Navarra ... We Carlists have up to now placed in the field 30,000 armed men, and we hope to raise as many more. If your brave, noble Irish came to our help they should be placed in the Carlist command.[44]

It was now evident that the approval of General Mola, Franco's main rival in the leadership contest, did not provide sufficient guarantee of the project's realisation. The Carlist invitation would have to be ratified by Franco, and any contingent details could only be finalised by a personal meeting between Franco and O'Duffy. Indeed, the latter soon understood that even Mola, despite being overall commander of the *requetés*, was neither himself a Carlist nor necessarily a supporter of any specific item on the agenda espoused by Ramírez.[45]

His encounter with Ramírez was bound to have introduced doubts into O'Duffy's mind. It now seemed all the more important to find powerful allies outside the little sphere of Ireland, and thus he took the opportunity of his London trip to sound out the leader of British Catholics, Cardinal Hinsley. Through an intermediary, O'Duffy 'sought the Archbishop of Westminster's sanction for appeals in the English Catholic Press'. Though the intention was not to preach enlistment in the crusade, but merely to evoke financial help from British (above all Irish immigrant) sources, the request was coldly rejected. Hinsley's secretary replied that the archbishop's 'position precluded him from having anything whatever to do with military or political activities with regard to Spain. His position would be different were it a question of providing an ambulance to succour the wounded and sick no matter to which side of the struggle they belonged.'[46]

Undeterred, once back in Dublin O'Duffy prepared a memorandum to form the basis of his negotiations with the insurgent leaders. This was sent for advance perusal, and on 20 September the general received instructions to travel to Spain for the necessary meetings. The next day he left Ireland again, this time bound for Spain via London. By now, Whitehall – perhaps alerted by Westminster – had begun to take an interest. The Non-Intervention Committee had been equipped – as was only proper – with a British chairman, secretary and supporting staff. With furious accusations and counter-accusations flying between the totalitarian-interventionist powers, it was important that His Majesty's Government's own hands were seen to be clean. Accordingly, a Special Branch agent observed O'Duffy's disembarkation at Holyhead and his onward journey by train. From Euston Station two detectives tailed the reception committee's car to the Grosvenor Hotel, Victoria. PC Johnson's detailed report on the next few days informs us that the general had several meetings with Ramírez de Arellano and Juan de la Cierva in their Mayfair homes. Unfortunately for historians, these were the days before effective listening and recording devices, and the substance of the consultations is unknown. However, one important development took place. O'Duffy's London-Spanish associates were fluent in English, but once in Spain he would need his own, reliable Spanish-speaking aide. This need was met by the recruitment of Thomas Gunning, an old associate of O'Duffy's, who had recently been in Nationalist Spain fulfilling a journalistic commission. After four days in London, O'Duffy and Gunning flew to Bordeaux from Croydon airport.[47]

Their arrival at Pamplona on 26 September was a triumph.[48] The general was greeted as a crusading hero, 'veteran of the World War', and accommodated in the private suite of the Navarrese regional council (*diputación foral*). At a Mass in the cathedral to celebrate the Holy Alliance of Ireland and Navarre, O'Duffy was presented with a *boina roja*, traditional headwear of the *requetés*.[49] Accompanied by his new aide, Gunning, the general travelled by car to Burgos, the Castilian city most closely linked to the historic crusade against the Moorish infidel (*reconquista*), and now established as the administrative capital of 'National Spain'. Here their reception was less enthusiastic. They met the crusty General Cabanellas, acting head of the rebel junta – in effect the provisional government. Cabanellas was firmly anti-monarchist, and in particular loathed the Carlists, devotees of a species of monarchy both absolute and dynastic. To their bemusement, the two would-be crusaders were brusquely informed that 'we do not want foreigners to collaborate in the work of liberating the fatherland'.[50]

Elation must have given way to doubts and confusion in O'Duffy's mind as he drove further south and west to Valladolid for the meeting with his main patron.[51] General Emilio Mola had been the chief co-ordinator of the military conspiracy, but now – though unchallenged head of the rebel armies in the north of Spain – he was already taking a back seat to his junior colleague, who commanded the victorious professional army advancing rapidly towards Madrid from the south. Whatever the Irish apprehensions, this encounter proved a success. Mola agreed that the zealously Catholic *requetés* were the most suitable body in which the Irish Brigade should serve. Given the heavy losses being suffered by his army (still mostly comprising volunteer militias from various rightist sources), Mola was also doubtless impressed by O'Duffy's assurances about the strength of potential Irish recruitment, based on the figures then current in the NCP offices. For his part, O'Duffy was quite overcome by his interlocutor's familiarity with the historic military links between Spain and Ireland, and references to the descendants of chieftains-turned-grandees, who had brought lustre to Spain's armed forces ever since the seventeenth century.[52]

During this conversation, which took place on the evening of 27 September, Mola's desk telephone rang. Franco was on the line, with the news that his men had relieved the Alcázar (castle) of Toledo, where a small force of rebel officer cadets and right-wing civilians had been besieged by republican militias since the first days of the war. The siege had received such intense publicity around the world that this action provided the Nationalists with their biggest propaganda coup to date. Though Mola shared in his colleague's jubilation, he must have realised the implications of his success. The very next morning, the nationalist junta met in Salamanca for a series of tense meetings; before the day was out – though only just – Cabanellas grudgingly signed the decree appointing Franco as *generalísimo*.[53]

Though no juncture could have been ideal in the midst of war's alarms, O'Duffy's visit to Spain proved to be singularly badly timed. These days were among the most critical in the politics of the war and in the career of General Franco. The new dictator spent the following week negotiating with representatives of his powerful peers in Berlin and Rome, whose support was vital to his plans. He had no time available to interview a minor Irish adventurer. Nevertheless, Mola – who had supported Franco's leadership claim, if more reluctantly than the latter knew – flew to his new chief's headquarters in Cáceres, 'and' (as the official press release put it) 'after a conference of the two leaders the joyful acceptance of General O'Duffy's offer of an Irish Brigade was announced'.[54]

The change of emphasis noticeable here was important for the new relationship between the partners, and for the purposes of nationalist propaganda and self-esteem. The position was no longer that Ireland had magnanimously responded to Spain's appeal for help, but rather that Nationalist Spain had graciously agreed to a request from the Irish to be extended the honour of joining their crusade. It was understandable that O'Duffy, ignorant of the political background, should be slow to grasp the full significance of the events surrounding his visit. He shared in the ecstatic celebrations in Valladolid for the relief of the Alcázar. He appeared on the Town Hall balcony alongside Mola, whilst the latter made a speech to the crowd in the Plaza Mayor – the ancient square where the Inquisition had once burned dozens of heretics in the presence of Philip II. He even made a radio broadcast to acknowledge the people's acclamations of *¡Viva Irlanda!* Not surprisingly, the general returned to Ireland in the comfortable illusion that all had been settled.[55]

In fact, the Irish learning curve about Spain had still hardly got off its base, and many more enlightening revelations were to come. After the disastrous last-minute cancellation of the Waterford troopship in mid-October, O'Duffy immediately left for Spain to discover what had gone wrong.[56] He met Franco for the first time in Salamanca. The meeting lacked warmth on a personal level, but this was not unusual, given the *generalísimo*'s natural demeanour. O'Duffy was reassured, and felt that all was well.[57] He left on a tour of various towns and frontal commands which lasted for two weeks. This was potentially of tremendous use, but, dependent as he was on interpreters, it is doubtful he learned much from his experiences.

One encounter, however, was crucial. At Toledo, he visited the primate of Spain, Cardinal Gomá.[58] From Gomá, O'Duffy received his first instruction concerning the Basques and the paradoxical nature of their resistance to the nationalist movement. Thus he grasped the utter impossibility for any Irish brigade to serve in the northern zone, where action against the zealously Catholic Basques, whose regiments marched to war behind their priests, would be inevitable. On returning from his tour, he again met Franco in Salamanca. Both at this and the earlier meeting between the principals, Juan de la Cierva was present. He was a man with an international scientific and business reputation who had earned Franco's respect. La Cierva was probably responsible for the ultimate success of the negotiations; he acted both as interpreter and advocate for O'Duffy.[59]

As a result it was agreed that the Irish (who at this juncture were expected to muster a full brigade of four or even five thousand men) would serve as part of the Foreign Legion – also known as the Tercio – the core units of Franco's own professional army. Each of the seven expected *banderas* (battalions) would be commanded and staffed by Irishmen. However, Spanish liaison officers would be integrated into each *bandera*, and a certain number of native non-commissioned officers would serve alongside their Irish *compadres*; all these personnel would be English-speaking. O'Duffy himself was to hold the rank of Brigadier-General, and to act as Inspector-General of the *Bandera*. In the latter capacity, he was to be responsible directly to the *generalísimo*. O'Duffy was assured that the Irish would never be called upon to serve against the Basques. Finally, 'the period of service would be for the duration of the war or for six months – whichever was the shorter'.[60]

The allocation of the Irish to the Legion was on the face of things a compliment, since the latter units were undoubtedly the elite of the nationalist army.[61] Perhaps Franco had been regaled with stories of Irish military accomplishments by Mola and La Cierva. On the other hand, although the Tercio was not designed originally for foreigners, foreign individuals and small groups who volunteered for service with the Nationalists were normally assigned to its ranks. Most of this force, currently much reduced by constant use as spearhead attack formations, was part of the army of the centre. Indeed, even as O'Duffy took his leave of Franco, these doughty and ruthless fighters were poised for their great assault upon Madrid. The watching world expected this onslaught to be decisive in bringing about the collapse of republican resistance, and an end to the Civil War. O'Duffy left Salamanca determined that he would bring his men over in time at least to take part in the victory parade.

2

Motivation and mobilisation

Weaving the strands

The socio-political environment in which Eoin O'Duffy implemented plans for recruitment was a broadly sympathetic one. Most Irish Catholics who were not committed to the policy of the governing Fianna Fáil were moved, in some part of their being, by the appeal he articulated. Of course, for those to whom the experience of the Civil War of 1922–23 was the first (or only) principle of political reasoning, nothing that O'Duffy espoused could ever be acceptable. There were thousands of sincere Catholics who would never have followed his lead, even had the Archangel Michael in full crusading armour been commonly observed at the general's side on his public appearances. On the other hand, there is evidence that various Fianna Fáil stalwarts, and even some Republicans, were prepared to set party politics and the past aside – if only temporarily and provisionally – in response to a higher vocation.

Although the main NCP offices in Pearse Street were utilised as headquarters, and many of the party's regional officials acted as recruiting agents, collaboration in the enterprise went much wider than this. For example, it seems that various lay Catholic bodies were clandestinely involved. Two veterans recalled being summoned to the offices of the popular magazine, *The Catholic Record*, at Standard House, Dublin, where they underwent medical examination before final enlistment.[1] By 1936 the NCP had become little more than a fringe party in which General O'Duffy himself, although its focus and *raison d'être*, took a gradually diminishing interest. It seems unlikely that on its own it could ever have mustered the resources necessary to embark on the grand design.

This latter phrase is hardly a hyperbole, since the general and his Spanish mentors seem to have envisaged a total Irish force of no fewer than twenty thousand men – by Spanish reckoning, a division.[2] To this end, O'Duffy was hoping to launch (in terms later used by another political general) a *ralliement* or *rassemblée* of the Blueshirts, with the possible addition – reaching further back – of Treatyite army veterans. The recent political context suggests that this was not as sanguine as it may appear today. The pool of potential for volunteers was vast. Recent estimates place the total membership of the Blueshirts at the height of their influence under O'Duffy in 1934 at nearly fifty thousand.[3] If reliable, these dimensions help to explain the general's confidence in being able to raise not just a battalion but a small army for the service of Nationalist Spain. Other evidence confirms his calculations. The successive and diametrically opposite reactions of Commandant Eamon Cronin are of equal moment in illustrating his fear that the ranks of the League of Youth might crumble overnight as its members were seduced by the O'Duffyite renaissance.[4] In government circles, too, the general's powers of persuasion and organisation were by no means underestimated.

With benefit of hindsight, a sense of scepticism intrudes, and we remind ourselves of the modest reality of the force which actually materialised. However, the successful mobilisation and maintenance of such an army – which was well beyond any powers O'Duffy and his helpers could ever hope to mobilise – would have brought portentous implications in its train. For a start, it would have placed the forces behind what might be called the 'Brigade Movement' almost on a par with Fascist Italy and Nazi Germany in terms of the politics of intervention. Yet, though we only have vaguely expressed internal sources to rely on as regards planning figures (both for men and materials), some important later developments simply do not make sense unless we accept them as broadly accurate.

At any rate, if O'Duffyite sources are to be believed, in the fortnight which elapsed after his *Irish Independent* letter, offers of help in all aspects of the work flooded in to Pearse Street and to the general's private residence in the Dublin suburb of Blackrock. Two days after returning from his continental holiday, and only twelve after publication of his original initiative, O'Duffy gave a press interview at which he claimed 'over two thousand' applications had already been received.[5] It was now emphasised that the Brigade project was not merely a Catholic one, but that it should unite all varieties of Christian opinion – an important factor in view of the fact that the 'non-intervention' movement was the work of the French prime minister Leon Blum, a 'freemason, Jew and Socialist'.[6]

Newspaper correspondence columns, even in the *Irish Independent*, reflected differing shades of opinion, most of them vigorously expressed.

Though happy to include contrary contributions for the sake of debate, the *Independent* was particularly anxious to sport a mailbag from Fianna Fáil voters and Republicans who had revised their former opinion of General O'Duffy. Such was K. Fitzgibbon, who now urged him to make all haste to get to Spain and save the Church.[7] One correspondent of the *Cork Examiner* (M. J. Buckley) stated that the Brigade 'should be supported by all loyal Catholics [because] our government does not have the courage to stand up against communism'. An ex-captain in the National Army (S. Keane) registered abhorrence of O'Duffy's 'fascist ideas', yet felt moved to express appreciation of his ruthless combatting of communism and offered his personal support.[8]

Dozens of men like Keane, who were among the disaffected officers compulsorily retired from the army as a result of the so-called 'mutiny' in 1924, looked on the Brigade as a way of redeeming lost or tarnished reputations. Patrick Dalton of Waterford, who had been cashiered as a result of this still-obscure affair, later became commander of the Dublin branch of the Blueshirts, and in October 1936 was nominated by O'Duffy as second-in-command of the Brigade.[9] Several dozen such men saw themselves primarily as career soldiers. Along with a group of police officers who had left the force on their leader's summary dismissal, they had feelings of personal loyalty to O'Duffy and naturally craved renewed tasks of command and action.

There was no shortage of men ready to be trained and commanded. On 27 August it was reported that no fewer than five thousand letters had been received from men wishing to volunteer. Eighteen Youghal men enlisted as a group, whilst in Clonmel thirty had already signed up.[10] In this same week the *Cork Examiner* reported the results of an official census which returned the population of the Saorstát at just under three million.[11] No special statistical skills are needed to realise that Ireland's response to the perceived need for military intervention in Spain had assumed a greater dimension than that of any other nation – at least in pro rata terms, and whether or not one regards the forces placed in the field by Germany and Italy as being composed of 'genuine' volunteers.[12]

Those to whom the general liked to refer as his 'key men' were now working round the clock to collect names, issue instructions and tackle a plethora of organisational problems. From Dublin, an application form was sent to every volunteer: 'on the return of these forms, records were prepared by counties, showing the name, address, references, age, nationality and particulars of the applicants, military, professional and educational qualifications, whether married or single, [or] having dependents.'[13]

An insight into the local dimensions of the operation is provided by a file of documents which later came into the hands of the Dublin government.[14] It concerns recruitment in Carlow-Kilkenny, where the leading agent was Padraig Quinn, O'Duffy adherent and former Blueshirt officer who had served a term of imprisonment in 1934 for being found in possession of firearms. This particular 'key man' was assisted by a trio of brothers named Dunphy. Amongst others, the group recruited Patrick Smith and his best friend, Jim Morrissey, in Thomastown.[15] Quinn instructed J. C. Dunphy that 'a number of Blueshirts here [in Gowran] and throughout the counties of Carlow and Kilkenny have volunteered their services' – which, the latter is reminded, are always to be represented as being 'for THE GLORY OF GOD AND THE HONOUR OF IRELAND'.[16] The Dunphy brothers in turn contacted other volunteers who were willing to help in further recruitment, among them Joseph Doyle of Castlecomer.

A virtual news blackout was imposed in September and October whilst the network of operations was quietly extended and strengthened. Late in October, however, the network was damaged by the consequences of the abortive attempt to embark a large number of men at Passage East (Waterford). Quinn urged Doyle to be resolute: 'we must not be upset by men withdrawing their names from membership'.[17] Quinn soon arranged a meeting with his sub-agents in order to restore morale.[18] Shortly afterwards, J. C. Dunphy announced to Doyle that Madrid, capital of Spain and main bastion of the Republic, had fallen to Franco – but added, in order to anticipate any waning of enthusiasm, that 'the war is by no means over'. The latter was ordered to procure a passport – the cost (12s 6d.) to be refunded by General O'Duffy. In fact, it seems he never obtained one and was obliged to get to Spain via the steerage class trip from Galway in December.[19]

Of the approximately 670 volunteers of the Catholic Brigade who reached Spain, as part of its original contingent, during the last seven weeks of 1936, details have come to light of nearly 440.[20] The data include (in some 320 cases) an indication of geographical origins. These, in turn, demonstrate that a majority of the recruits came from small-town, rural Ireland. This is hardly an unexpected result. In such places, allegiance to the Church was relatively unalloyed by the complications of modern society. Indeed, the Church's power in such communities might be generally characterised as 'feudal'. Success in recruitment here is a testament to the eager determination to enlist of many remotely located individuals, but also to the energetic activities of the NCP organisation, sometimes in areas where it enjoyed little indigenous support in terms of national politics.

The figures show a distinct pull to the south-west. Rural Kerry, Tipperary and Cork were perhaps the most fertile areas for O'Duffy's harvesters. Munster was easily the most impressive province (providing over 47 per cent of the total number of the Brigade). Within Munster, Limerick city (twenty-five recruits) and Tralee (twenty-three) were outstanding – in relative terms rating far higher than the populous capital. The former was traditionally Ireland's most active centre of revivalist Catholicism. From Tralee, Eamon Horan brought over 7 per cent (compared with Dublin's 12.5 per cent) of all the volunteers who successfully reached Spain – an amazing response from a town of less than fifteen thousand people. No fewer than four of the six men to be killed in action were natives of Tralee. (However, in the town whose approach road is dominated by the Ballyseedy monument, it is doubtful if any public mark of this fact will ever be made.)

Though Leinster contributed nearly a third of the overall total, this was largely derived from urban Dublin; the other eastern counties showed a poor response, with the south-east least impressive of all. Connacht, too, contributed only meagre pickings, though totals here are more understandable in terms of population density – and Co. Mayo was a clear exception to the rule. The Ulster contribution is almost wholly explained by the West Belfast contingent, men who often reacted against negative attitudes prevalent amongst the Protestant community, combined with the clannish personal support for O'Duffy (a local hero) which came in from the Free State counties of Cavan and Monaghan. Outside the larger towns, the most prominent communities were Clonmel (Co. Tipperary), Bandon and Midleton (Co. Cork), and Westport (Co. Mayo). Of the thirty-two counties, only Laois and Down made no contribution which has so far emerged into public record. All in all, though we can never ultimately verify the claims made concerning the strength of the original response, it is clear that the organisers were able to mount a reasonably co-ordinated nationwide operation.[21]

Many are called

I said you are endangering your lives. They said … we've come to fight for Spain and religion and we remember all we have suffered in the persecutions … In the past the Spaniards helped us, and came to Galway and were defeated by the English, but we will have our revenge now … We're going to shoot every damn Red in Spain. … Spain has always been a Catholic country like Ireland. We are for religion and we don't want the Reds to conquer Spain.[22]

These words, spoken with such fervour sixty years ago, and mistily recalled forty years later, vividly convey the motives which inspired the volunteers of the Irish Brigade. To our minds, burdened by the intellectual elaborations endowed by hindsight, some of these can seem inconsistent and even contradictory. At the time, however, the inward representation of their objectives pictured by most men was a convincing unity. Of the twenty or so veterans whose reminiscences survive, the great majority nominate the religious factor as the overmastering reason for volunteering.[23] At the same time, many admit that they had some yearning for adventure, the factor that George Timlin – a lone voice in this arrangement of priorities – stated from his experience was the leading motive.

In Bandon, Co. Cork, Michael O'Connell left his job as a hospital porter to enlist with the Brigade. He was among those left waiting at the quayside at Passage East in mid-October, and was consequently obliged to apply for help to the Board of Assistance. 'He has resigned,' said one councillor; 'let General Franco look after him now.' But O'Connell protested: 'I have done nothing out of the way. As a Catholic I would fight for my faith at any time.'[24] James Kavanagh, a Dublin slum kid whose later memories displayed the disillusionment of maturity, nevertheless remembered that his religious feelings were dominant at the time. Another volunteer, Ivan O'Reilly, had Blueshirt elder brothers and resented having been too young to join them in the paramilitary ranks (and pranks). In later life, he looked back on this episode with little satisfaction, yet grudgingly confessed to being attracted, as a young man, by the idea of 'fighting for your faith'.[25] Denis Reynolds recalled that religious feeling and a wish to fight coexisted equally (and appropriately) in his crusading breast: 'I always had an interest in soldiering', as he put it.[26] Paddy Smith was sickened by the anticlerical persecution in Spain, and gladly accepted the risk of death in return for the assurance of a martyr's place in heaven. Reynolds and Smith had both been Blueshirt rankers, whilst Dalton, Tom Hyde and Quinn were senior commanders. All had left the Blueshirts in sympathy with O'Duffy when the general resigned its leadership (1934), but only Dalton had joined him in the NCP.

On the other hand, most working-class city lads had not been Blueshirts. One such Dubliner of socialist inclinations, John Corway, joined the Brigade with an overwhelming sense of outrage at religious persecution in Spain.[27] Another Dublin working man, Bill Geraghty, had perhaps the most culturally complex experience. He had opposed the Blueshirts and was a supporter of Fianna Fáil, joining the party's Volunteer Reserve militia, where he served with de Valera's son, Vivion. As a firm Catholic, however, Geraghty was susceptible to the anti-communist propaganda which had 'softened up' so many sensibilities in the period prior to 1936. His fears were not too distant from those of Paddy Smith and Denis Reynolds, who saw the troubles in Spain as being part of a worldwide Soviet conspiracy. The *Irish Independent* regularly devoted space to this theory, a tactic which reached its culmination when it ran the famous headline – in more than one sense a banner – 'IRELAND DECLARES WAR ON COMMUNISM' in October 1936.[28] Only a month after the uprising it reported that Spanish Reds were being trained in Moscow and that 'chekas modelled after those of Soviet Russia are slaughtering the citizens wholesale'. Soviet military instructors had arrived in Spain, whilst 'members of the "People's Front" are being armed in a similar way to that of the Bolshevik revolution in 1917'. Churches were being converted into 'Lenin' or 'Dimitroff' houses to store Russian weapons. Meanwhile – most imaginative of the revelations – Moscow radio was broadcasting instructions in Spanish on how to make a revolution.[29]

None of this was enough to push Bill Geraghty into enlistment, until, one night at the cinema, he saw the image of General O'Duffy appearing on the screen to appeal for volunteers. The item formed part of the newsreel magazine projected in the interval between feature films. The general eloquently extolled the history of religious-military empathy between Ireland and Spain – and Geraghty was hooked. Aspects of a certain sub-romantic sensibility were part of the broad cultural background to volunteering (on both sides). Teenage imaginations had been stirred by schoolteachers' stories or by reading the history of Ireland (an object of desire already seductively draped in the myths of nationalist sacrifice and heroism). Many youngsters were increasingly attracted by the beckoning of a silver screen towards escapist adventure. At the age of eighteen, Bill Geraghty was by no means the youngest volunteer. Some were undoubtedly younger, and at least one was only fifteen. In Tuam, Co. Galway, Paul Reynolds, chief engineer in the local beet-sugar factory, lost a promising apprentice, a boy of sixteen who decamped to join O'Duffy. Reynolds's chagrin was all the greater since he himself was a regional IRA commander.[30]

Tom Hyde, whose business was that of owner-manager of the local cinema in Midleton, may have advised O'Duffy on the potency of a film-star medium, and was well placed to observe the effect upon young audiences of films like *The Crusades* and *Castles in Spain* – which happened to be on general release in the Free State in the autumn of 1936.[31] Like O'Duffy himself, many who followed him were in thrall to the pied piper of history. Perhaps this was particularly true of the adolescents – technically 'minors' – whose number, the general asserted, ran into three figures.

> The Minstrel Boy to the war is gone,
> In the ranks of the dead you'll find him;
> His father's sword he has girded on,
> And his wild harp slung behind him.[32]

In the popular and magazine press, romantic exotica also seemed to enjoy a sudden currency. One remarkably early feature in the *Cork Examiner* Magazine Supplement was devoted to 'Old Toledo': 'Against the blue sky gleams the spire of the glorious cathedral … Long may it continue to be held in reverence by the people and escape the ruthless destructive fury of the Communists who have already laid low so many churches and convents in this old Catholic land.'[33] Equally well timed was a story about the 'Wild Geese' in Spain, which appeared just as the campaign of recruitment for the Irish Brigade was getting into its stride. The author painted in glowing romantic colours the fabulous glory and rewards won by Irish warriors in the service of Catholic Spain.[34] Other publications chimed in with resonant peals, underlining the message that 'Spain has many legendary attractions for the Irish'.[35] Given the circumstances obtaining in Spain, such publicity can hardly have been intended to encourage tourism, nor yet pilgrimage to its celebrated shrines. But for young imaginations nurtured on films such as *Beau Geste* and stars like Douglas Fairbanks and Rudolf Valentino, the prospect of visiting the land of the Cid and Al-Andalus might serve as a magic enhancement of religious duty.

But religious feeling (*pur sang*) remained central. Indeed, we do not even need to leave our cinema seats to recognise its primacy. In the summer and autumn of 1936 newsreels regularly transmitted pictures which horrified Irish audiences far more than any other cinema-goers in the Hollywood-colonised world. They watched footage of burning churches, of religious objects being defiled by mobs, of militiamen lined up to 'execute' a towering statue of the Sacred Heart of Jesus; above all, they witnessed the hellish spectacle of nuns' corpses exhumed and exhibited to public gaze. To state that such scenes were calculated to arouse maximum outrage in the Free State is to put things mildly.[36]

Though most single men wrote to O'Duffy, signed up and left home without consulting parents, priests or politicians, they had little doubt – mothers' natural reservations apart – of the elemental approval of all concerned. Upon discovering the truth, parents often wrote to the *Irish Independent* to express their pride. Bishop Gilmartin of Galway merely announced in public that 'the Rosary is the strongest weapon against Bolshevism' – having won many crusades in the past, including the campaign of Lepanto (1571) when Spain had saved Europe from the Turks; but his private support for the Brigade was well known.[37] One Fine Gael TD asserted in the Dáil that Franco was 'fighting to save Christendom just as surely as Don John of Austria fought to save Christendom at Lepanto', adding for good measure that there was no difference between 'the young Irishmen who at present go to fight for Christianity in Spain and the Crusaders who went from all over Europe to fight for Christianity in the Holy Land'.[38]

Whilst religious feeling was paramount, emotions connected with comradeship – often in a military or paramilitary context – also provided a common denominator amongst the largest fraction of the volunteers (probably over 70 per cent). Whilst such agglutinates might be characterised under currently fashionable categories – as (for example) 'male bonding' – they had also a more mundane social aspect. There are several references to men making a pact with their best friends to sign up as crusaders for Christ. Geraghty, Hickey, Smith and Reynolds all behaved according to this familiar custom. In the village of Oughterard, Co. Galway, where eight youngsters initially came forward, doubtless too in Youghal, Midleton and elsewhere, the peer-group pressure mentality was strongly in evidence. In Dundrum, Co. Dublin, four pals, including Paddy Hickey, enlisted as a group. Indeed, the organisers were conscious of the potency and importance of this phenomenon, and even sought to introduce it artificially.[39] On 13 March 1937, childhood friends from the same street in Tralee were to be killed by the same shell in the Jarama valley.[40]

But few are chosen

The first logistical plan for transport of the Brigade to Spain was relatively straightforward. With the support of Nicholas Franco, the *generalísimo*'s brother and secretary, Juan de la Cierva conducted negotiations with Spanish shipowners for the commissioning of a transport ship. This vessel was to make a series of voyages to various points in order to ferry several thousand men to a suitable port in nationalist-held Galicia (north-west Spain). A Spanish pleasure-steamer, the SS *Domino* – according to O'Duffy, ideally furnished for the purpose – was chartered in early October.[41] The deal was probably underwritten by la Cierva and members of his London-based lobby – who (moreover) had some call on the patronage of the millionaire Francoist, Juan March.

Various problems were contingent on the proposed operation. Above all, O'Duffy had to ensure that places chosen for embarkation were suitable. They needed to be fairly remote, so as to avoid attention, yet accessible to motor vehicles, and attainable in no more than six hours' journey – preferably in the hours of darkness – from any part of the Free State.[42] Local authorities had to be relied on to turn a blind (or at least a sleepy) eye to proceedings. It was physically impractical and legally impossible for large transport vessels even to enter such harbours, let alone tie up at the quayside, so that numbers of small boats had to be available to tender men out to the ferries.

On Wednesday 14 October, word went out from Dublin for a gathering of volunteers in the fishing village of Passage East, near Waterford, two days later. Each agent was given a prescribed route to follow, and assured that 'men carrying ash plants in their right hands' would be placed to act as guides at key points.[43] Contingents were to arrive in time to embark at 2.00 a.m. on Friday 16 October. After supervising the dispatch of these instructions, O'Duffy left for Blackrock in order to pack his bags. He was interrupted by the arrival of a messenger. Franco had decided that the international situation was unfavourable and had postponed the sailing of the *Domino*. The general immediately returned to Dublin, and with Liam Walsh's help worked through the night to get the bad tidings through to local agents. Outright public humiliation was thus forestalled, but the damage-limitation exercise could only be partially successful. Confused and annoyed, O'Duffy left for Spain via London in order to confront Franco and demand an explanation.[44]

Hindsight knowledge of Franco's reservations over the Brigade encourage the supposition that his action had been an opportunist attempt to suffocate the project. Although such a hidden agenda cannot be ruled out, the *generalísimo*'s ostensible reasons were convincing on their own terms. Franco explained to O'Duffy and la Cierva that Stalin had threatened to send more troops and supplies to the Republic for every piece of evidence (produced to the Non-Intervention Committee) that the Nationalists were drawing on outside help. The military situation was dominated by the need to capture Madrid, whilst Franco's assault forces were now markedly weakening in number and battle-readiness. O'Duffy accepted Franco's explanation and assurances that another attempt would soon be made, with use of privately chartered transports which could not be traced back to Burgos.

By the time O'Duffy got back to Ireland in early November, the battle for Madrid had begun in earnest, and had revealed the presence of substantial Soviet aid to the Republic. Not long afterwards (around the time the International Brigades first went into action) he received official notice to initiate his operation once again. This time, a two-tier plan was adopted. Volunteers who possessed passports were to leave Ireland via normal scheduled routes. This was a minority fraction, mostly comprising those who were potential members of the officer corps. A ferry-boat to Liverpool left Dublin every day, and was able to accommodate modest numbers. A private shipping company, the Yeoward Line, operated tourist cruises from Liverpool to the Canary Islands, sailing every Saturday during the winter months. The fleet bore the Spanish names of various birds – though not including the wild goose.[45] At any rate, very conveniently for the enterprise, liners made Lisbon their first port of call. For the normal traveller, the cruise offered an escape from a dull winter in depression-ridden Britain. Doubtless, some were engaged in escapades as clandestine in their ways as that of the Irish crusaders, and staff had learned to exercise suitable discretion.

Like his rival crusaders of the left, who also utilised the first-stage B & I ferry service, O'Duffy had contacts in Liverpool – but with the important differences that several of the latter's friends were influentially placed among the local police force and Catholic clergy.[46] In this way, safe houses were made available for parties of men crossing the Irish Sea on the weekday ferries in advance of a Saturday cruise departure. In addition, at least a dozen Irish expatriates joined up with various units of the Brigade as they passed through Liverpool.

Despite leaving Dublin on Friday 13 November, the first operation went smoothly. Ten members of the 'advance guard' boarded the SS *Alondra* at Liverpool and went ashore at Lisbon three days later.[47] One of the passengers, on his way to spend Christmas in the Canary Islands, was a Welsh landowner, Evan Morgan, Lord Tredegar. A dilettante scholar of strong Celtic interests, he found the presence of the Irishmen intriguing, and they shared their secret with him. A letter Morgan later addressed to a friend in Ireland has survived and provides observations on the party.

He admired as a 'tough bird' the leader, Tom Carew, whom he had met for the first time many years before; but his overall view was more cynical. Despite his own Catholic background, he failed to empathise with the men he spoke to, including 'a certain Connolly [who] had to leave a £12 a week job at Dagenham' in order to enlist: 'He was attempting to work himself up to a bloodthirsty mood by studying the poems of Thomas Davies [*sic*]… placing the Spanish rojos in the position of the so-and-so Saxons. This was a fine young fellow too good to be wasted on that affair.' According to Morgan, a posse of Irish priests, waiting at the Lisbon dockside, informed Portuguese immigration that the men had come in order to study for the priesthood. 'The official looked very hard at some rather villainous faces and was left scratching his head whilst the godly youths went off in military formation.'[48]

On three further occasions this service was utilised, each more intensively than the last. On 21 November, a party of fifty men, headed by O'Duffy himself, left Liverpool on the SS *Avoceta*. A week later the contingent aboard the SS *Aguila* was eighty-six-strong. Lastly, after a longer interval, a complement of more than a hundred men reached Lisbon aboard the SS *Ardeola* on 17 December. Meanwhile, protracted delays, culminating in the Passage East incident, had excited public speculation about the Brigade's attempts to reach Spain in defiance of the Non-Intervention Agreements. Not surprisingly, the *Alondra* expedition was known to the government in advance. On the day before the 'advance guard' left Dublin, the *Irish Press* revealed its intentions in detail, adding that an additional 'several hundred' planned to leave soon afterwards by means of 'a cargo vessel': 'The vessel will stand out to sea after having cleared the port and the whole contingent, who will have gathered secretly at some adjacent points on the coast, will then be taken on board off small boats from the shore.'[49]

Government intelligence had evidently penetrated the NCP organisation. In itself this was hardly remarkable, but de Valera's decision to leak the story to his own newspaper was a clever stroke. It had the effect of alerting police commanders and other unsympathetic elements who were willing and eager to act on their own initiative in order to disrupt O'Duffy's plans, yet at the same time it obviated the need for official government intervention. De Valera and his ministers could truthfully claim that no decision to prevent or impede the Brigade's leaving Ireland had been taken. Thus the premier hoped not so much to appease the parliamentary opposition as to defuse criticism which might surface within his own party.[50]

Though some of its details were awry, the large-scale enterprise anticipated by the *Irish Press* story was certainly in preparation. Funds were not available for the universal purchase of passports, and various delays – not all of them 'inspired' by official attitudes – were experienced by many who did apply. Moreover, even had the budget extended to mass purchase of tickets, the space and frequency provided by the Canary Islands cruise service were not sufficient for the numbers involved. A large-scale sailing had to be arranged to cope with the surplus. O'Duffy was faced with a major headache over this urgent and complex logistical issue. At some point in the latter part of November, the general decided that the port of Galway offered the best prospects as a *point d'appui*. No primary evidence is extant to throw light on the selection of Galway for this honour; thus the analysis which follows is largely circumstantial in basis.[51]

On the face of things, the choice was surprising. As a whole, Co. Galway had never been sympathetic to O'Duffy. It had a small-scale agronomy, based on middling-to-poor quality land farmed by hard-working but often indigent peasant families. Thus, strong sociological and economic factors predisposed the population to support Fianna Fáil, to which party the majority of voters duly transferred their allegiance in the wake of its establishment in the late 1920s. Galway town (with a population of about twenty thousand) had a core of Cosgraveites among the business community and its dependants, enabling Fine Gael to hold on to its Dáil seat in 1933. But the constituency was under threat – and the opposition was to be ousted in a by-election early in 1937.[52] It is true that the UDC had adhered to the Clonmel Resolution, calling for a break in relations with the Spanish Republic. However, when one councillor had mentioned the name of General O'Duffy, the chairman (M. J. Cooke) had intervened in order to pass the withering comment that 'we ignore him altogether'.[53]

Yet Galway had several advantages. It was on a good, straight road across the waist of Ireland from Dublin, and a direct railway link also existed. At the same time, it was central enough to be accessible from most parts of the island. O'Duffy may have recalled a successful (if typically turbulent) Blueshirt rally held in Galway in 1934, and since his men would need to assemble in the very centre of the town he surely reckoned on the protective interest of some influential local backers. Furthermore, on 22 November a triumphant Christian Front meeting was held in Galway – which 'pledged the I.C.F. to bringing about an economic system based on the Papal Encyclicals'.[54] Since this programme was one which

O'Duffy himself advocated, and was the official policy of his party, the NCP organisers must have derived encouragement from this news.[55]

This time, O'Duffy was determined to maintain close supervision of transport arrangements. On 20 November he accompanied a second party of volunteers who travelled to Spain via the Liverpool–Lisbon route. After checking on developments in Salamanca, he returned to Dublin, only to leave again within a few days for consultations with la Cierva in London, held on or about 5 December. The go-ahead was now given for the voyage of a German-registered merchant ship to Galway.[56] The 'key men' were instructed to concentrate their forces in the town on the night of Saturday 12 December.[57] The operation was carried out with remarkable efficiency. In Dublin, best mates like Bill Geraghty and Danny Farrell, larger groups of pals such as that to which Patrick Hickey belonged, and single individuals like James Kavanagh, turned up at a central collection point. The last-named of these recalls reporting to the offices of the *Catholic Recorder*, where he found 'a couple of hundred' men already arrived. As volunteers came in they were given medical checks and had their baggage examined – each man had been told to bring only one item, manageable with one arm or slung over the shoulder. Kavanagh was then taken to the lobby of the Beresford Hotel and treated to tea and sandwiches, whilst waiting for transport. Others spent much of the day at the Midland Hotel, Dominic Street, owned by the O'Duffy supporter, Captain Hughes. The men were told to behave as though they were off on a works or parish 'outing'. Some hours after dark, and with most of the registered names checked in, motor coaches (or 'charabancs' as then popularly called) pulled up outside and the lads piled in for the four-hour drive to Galway.

When the appointed day arrived, Dennis Reynolds and Phil McBride walked several miles into Cootehill, the nearest town to their farmsteads, near the border with the North. Here, several cars were waiting to pick up local volunteers, organised by the NCP agent, John Martin. Reynolds recalls that the Garda duty sergeant loitering in the High Street seemed unsure of his position. After Reynolds's return home, the policeman admitted that he should have arrested them, but felt that affected uncertainty was the better part of valour.[58] Similar scenes were played out in numberless small towns and villages during the day. Not all the volunteers were mobilised by O'Duffy's organisation. Three Limerick men reached Dublin under their own steam in the middle of that week. Reporting to the Christian Front offices, they were installed in Iveagh House (Dublin's equivalent of a Salvation Army hostel) and later taken to Galway in cars belonging to 'business people and doctors'.[59] Later in the day, as witnesses and newspaper reports attest, brogues from all corners of Ireland could be heard among the excited babble in Galway's Eyre Square.

Eyre Square, conveniently enough, is a large open space situated in Galway town centre but only a few hundred yards from the harbour walls. Perhaps it had not been sufficiently considered beforehand that the square would be filling with crusaders at the same hour of the night that local bars were emptying – and on a Saturday night at that. Stories of challenges, scuffles, ambushes with hurley sticks and other escapades entered local folklore, and over the years were fortified with communitarian political correctness in a city which has no desire to recall any sympathetic connection with the Irish Brigade.[60] Though there was a substantial police presence, any hostile intention was offset and even immobilised by that of protective clergymen, led by the authoritative figure of Archbishop Gilmartin himself. At one point, the archbishop stood on a lorry and addressed the Gardai, implying grave risks to their souls were they to arrest any who were bound on such a holy mission. According to Dennis Reynolds, Gilmartin got the policemen to join in a rendition of the evocative battle-hymn, 'Faith of our Fathers':

Faith of our Fathers, living still
In spite of dungeon, fire and sword;
Oh, how our hearts beat high with joy
Whene'er we hear that glorious word!
Faith of our Fathers, holy faith,
We will be true to thee till death.

In retrospect, it seems more likely that the force (which included plain-clothes officers) was on duty primarily to maintain a degree of public order and glean useful information, rather than to chain the crusaders – this, in any case, being hardly a realistic course of action in the circumstances. Perhaps of critical influence in their successful discharge of the former task was the fact that it rained steadily throughout the night in question.

The Kerrymen were the last to turn up, having been delayed by a vehicle breakdown.[61] Around 480 volunteers had managed to reach Galway in time.[62] A crowd of onlookers had gathered, sufficiently composed of family and neighbours to represent a basically friendly audience. One eye-witness recalls a band which led renditions of a sacred repertoire familiar to all Catholics.[63] A few hours before dawn the men marched around to the quayside to board the waiting tender, the Aran Islands ferry-boat *Dun Aengus*, whose task was to get the men out to the troopship, expected to be riding at anchor in the bay, under shelter of darkness. The accompanying chorus recited the rosary, its decades punctuated by last goodbyes and tearful embraces. As one witness later recalled, 'it was an atmosphere which is etched in my mind, and makes me understand why people join armies'. Indeed, at the very last moment, three local men rushed spontaneously up the gangplank to join the crusaders.[64]

The weather was now deteriorating rapidly. Such was the wind that handkerchiefs sodden with tears and rain were nearly ripped out of waving hands on the quayside. As the *Dun Aengus* got out into deep waters, the swell was daunting even for experienced sailors. As ill luck would have it, the first collective experiences of the Brigade – or its majority – were to represent the worst ordeal that most of its members were ever to face during its whole existence. The storm which raged around the coasts of Connacht and Clare that weekend was one of the most destructive in living memory. The men's excitement, after months of standing by for the orders which would take them to Spain, rapidly gave way to fear, and (in quick succession, for many) to violent seasickness. Some idea of the conditions obtaining is conveyed by a local newspaper report:

> The gale warning was hoisted at Galway docks on Sunday morning [13 December]. The wind had been rising during Saturday night, and it rose to gale force on Sunday morning ... South Galway suffered severely as a result of the rain, and several areas in that part of the county lie under water ... The Galway Bay Steamship Company's vessel, *Dun Aengus*, which was out on Galway Bay between 3.30 a.m. and 5 p.m. on Sunday, with over 700 volunteers for the Spanish civil war, received a severe pounding from the waves when she ventured outside the mouth of the bay. She took shelter under Black Head while awaiting the foreign vessel which was to take aboard the volunteers.[65]

When dawn broke with no sign of the transport ship, profound depression set in. Most men were conscious of little beyond the acute misery prevailing in their stomachs. Many must have recalled the failure at Passage East, convinced they were victims of an even worse calamity. Yet, somehow, Captain Coggins was prevailed upon, first to head south in the hope of making quicker contact; and when this stratagem failed, to wait at anchor for some hours. At last, at around 10 a.m., the desired object was sighted – SS *Urundi*, a German-registered cargo vessel of some

14,000 tons. But this by no means signalled an end to the men's ordeal. The operation of transferring them to the *Urundi* now had to be conducted. In a storm-force gale, with the vessels lashed crudely together so that bumping was added to the uncontrolled pitching and rolling of the ships, two rope ladders were let down to the *Dun Aengus*. The volunteers were required to shin up some thirty feet to the deck of the larger ship, and safety. It was a manoeuvre which even today might be relied upon to reduce numbers at any passing-out parade of the SAS.[66] Not surprisingly, around fifty men felt unable to complete this crucial stage of the adventure. After the painful transfer of men and baggage was completed, well into the afternoon – but with no serious mishap to man or beast – this group returned to Galway with the *Dun Aengus*.[67]

Watched from shore by several groups of observers, the *Urundi*, swastika flapping wildly from its mainmast, turned south-west towards the open North Atlantic and Biscay. The journey which lay before it was neither short nor sweet. The ship was poorly equipped for its allotted task. Men were crowded into open holds and lashed to girders in order to prevent injury in the steep pitching which, Dennis Reynolds remembered, tossed the vessel around like a cork. Tom Hayes's diary jottings became ever more illegible: 'Sunday: slept on top of one another and slept on coal bed … very sick today … weather very bad, ship travelling slowly, five knots, a lot sick one man broke leg others scalded when ship swayed.' A volunteer doctor attending to sick men was thrown so badly he broke several ribs. Things were no better in Biscay, where (according to James Kavanagh) 'the waves were mountains high'. As the ship at last made port at General Franco's home town of El Ferrol, sirens were sounding for an air raid. In dock nearby lay the SS *Domino*, which was now able to atone for its earlier failure. The Brigaders – at worst already afflicted with injuries or illnesses from which they never properly recovered, at best exhausted and bruised – were transferred to this vessel for a hot meal and a good night's sleep in regular bunks.

As in any given slice of life, whilst the steerage class suffered the miseries of cattle, tourist-class crusaders enjoyed quite a different experience. When the party destined for the SS *Avoceta* sailing, led by O'Duffy himself, left Dublin, the *Irish Press* again scooped the story. Though its report was not unfavourable, O'Duffy rejected an attempt to interview him, with the comment that 'this is no time for words but actions'.[68] Once aboard, however, we had the ship almost to ourselves, for there were not more than a dozen other passengers ... Captain Gunning taught two Spanish classes daily, we had military lectures, deck games, whist drives and an Irish ceilidhe each night ... The captain and staff and the other passengers entered into the Irish atmosphere of the ship and altogether we had a very happy journey indeed.[69]

One week later a third party set out for Lisbon. The SS *Aguila* carried eighty-six volunteers, drawn from seventeen counties of Ireland, along with expatriates from Manchester and London. This group was led by Charles Horgan and Eamon Horan, and by the Brigade's official chaplain, Fr J. Mulrean of Westmeath. Perhaps because of the chaplain's presence, the *Aguila* party attracted some of the strongest public support for the Brigade yet expressed by senior clergy. The volunteers were cheered to the echo as they boarded the Liverpool ferry, and packed a veritable armoury of rosaries and other objects of piety donated by the diocese of Waterford which Monsignor Ryan, Dean of Cashel, described as 'more powerful than weapons of war'.[70] Landing at Lisbon on 2 December, this party, like the others, was looked after by the staff of the Irish Dominican church in the Portuguese capital. Despite support for the Nationalists provided by the dictator, Alonso Salazar, Portugal had kept up appearances by bowing to British pressure to join the Non-Intervention Committee.[71] Its partisan operations had to remain clandestine, and although in practice this meant little more than a thin veil of deception, a certain care had to be taken over the next stage of the Irishmen's journey to the Spanish frontier.

For most of the volunteers who passed this way (some 250 in all), negotiation of these difficulties afforded a few days' relaxation in Lisbon. Accounts from the 'inside' present a picture of this stage of the journey as little differing from a pilgrimage. The days were apparently spent attending church services, and sightseeing was dominated by visits to other religious establishments.[72] At one of the latter, the rector of the Irish National Church (St Patrick's) delivered a long and lurid sermon intended to fill his audience with the spirit of warrior-martyrdom. This particular cleric in no way felt himself bound by the diplomatic limitations of his colleagues at home.

> You are fighting in God's holy name ... to save the world from the fiendish atrocities which have been perpetrated in Russia, in Mexico, and now in Spain ... Never before were sweet young girls stripped in the public streets, flogged and beaten, inhumanly violated and mutilated and subjected to such unspeakable torments ... You are going to

fight those monsters, who are more like demons let loose from Hell than mortal men ... Why wait to see our churches burned, our priests and nuns butchered, our women – your mothers and wives and sisters – violated and mutilated by those fiends in human form ...?

Having worked up his audience of young males to a state of high (if confused) emotional excitement with repeated references to torments which were evidently all too speakable, the preacher went on to adjure them thus: 'Let no malice or hate, no political bias or miserable ambition mar your motives ... Neither let any indiscretion or bad conduct, any act of impetuosity or indiscipline ... call a blush of shame to those who are watching you at home.'[73] Perhaps it was just as well that Lisbon in December is often as cold and damp as any Irish location. The nearest an occasion of sin approached was when certain officers visited a hotel where they had been 'set up' to meet some female company. Whatever the chevaliers were expecting, their ladies turned out to be exiles from Red Barcelona, who entertained them with more stories of atrocities, taking over where the priests had left off.[74]

The last contingent to travel this route was also the largest – a body of more than 100 men who landed at Lisbon on 17 December under the command of Captain T. Smith and arrived at the general Brigade HQ in Cáceres, amidst much jubilation, a few days before Christmas. Though the whole affair had been fraught with difficulty, and extended over nearly three months of anxious labour, in the circumstances O'Duffy and his backers must have been pleased with their achievement of transporting more than 650 men to Spain without serious mishap. In particular, publicity had been kept to a minimum, and any negative encounter with the rapidly augmenting surveillance network of the Non-Intervention Committee had been avoided. This had certainly been General Franco's main area of concern, and the congratulations he conveyed to O'Duffy on the first formal muster of the Brigade in Cáceres were sincerely meant.[75]

One last episode of this chapter must have provided the general with even greater personal satisfaction. His ex-colleague and now bitter adversary, Eamon Cronin, who earlier had poured scorn upon the whole idea of an Irish Brigade, had attempted to enter Spain in order to offer Franco a second Irish Brigade under his own command. Cronin sailed on the *Aguila*, and (according to one witness) even tried to suborn some of the volunteers to defect to his leadership.[76] However, Cronin was prevented from making further progress. O'Duffy's chief aide, Thomas Gunning, got wind of his plans and alerted Portuguese customs, who seized

Cronin's passport on arrival. Cronin contacted Salamanca and volunteered personally to serve in the Foreign Legion. The nationalist authorities referred him to General O'Duffy. He attempted to cross the border at Elvas, but was refused entry. Cronin's humiliation was complete. He was obliged to return to Dublin, where he told the *Irish Press* (the Fianna Fáil paper) that O'Duffy lay behind alleged orders to shoot him if he tried again to enter Nationalist Spain.[77]

Vigil in Cáceres

Arrivals and receptions

The veterans of the battle of Galway Bay and the *Urundi*'s voyage still had a long way to go before embarking in earnest on the struggle to defend the faith of their fathers. Like thousands of unknown predecessors three hundred years earlier, they had been dumped for convenience at the nearest geographical landfall from Ireland, in Galicia.[1] The province occupies the north-western corner of the Iberian peninsula. The actual port of arrival of the men discharged from the bowels of the *Urundi* was El Ferrol, naval base and native town of General Francisco Franco y Bahamonde. Few of the volunteers felt well enough to be conscious of the honour. Galicia has a dimly recorded Celtic prehistory, but this, too, was a feature unlikely to have been noticed by the Irish Brigades. More importantly, Galicia – like Ireland – had traditionally been a nursery of soldiers, and was even now providing the *caudillo* with some of his most dedicated new regiments.

In any case, the men were given little chance to savour Galicia. The morning after disembarkation they entrained on the third stage of their journey, towards the town of Cáceres, nearly six hundred kilometres to the south, selected as their headquarters. Their first stop was Salamanca, which lay directly athwart the rail route to the south. This city was the military control centre of the Nationalists (Burgos acted as civilian capital), and thus some senior Spanish commanders had an ideal opportunity to inspect the Irishmen and judge their quality. The first impression can hardly have been favourable. As they marched from the railway station to Salamanca's celebrated Plaza Mayor, the men were still suffering from the debilitating effects of their voyage, which a twenty-four-hour train journey had not alleviated. Most wore civilian suits – for some, this meant their Sunday best – though others sported the blue or green shirts of paramilitary affiliation. The men were provided with lunch by the municipal authorities, and addressed in Spanish by the Archbishop of Salamanca. The sermon was interpreted for the men by Fr Alexander McCabe, rector of Salamanca's Irish College, a seminary which at that time had enjoyed a continuous history in the city since the early seventeenth century.[2]

As he spoke, McCabe's compatriots were sampling (Spanish) wine for the first time. For the great majority this meant, quite simply, their first experience of this exotic (and in Ireland, hieratic) beverage. At first, not many were impressed. One veteran remembers that the archbishop's sermon made reference to the role of wine, apparently in the context of the prevailing difficulties of a clean water supply at the front. The archbishop announced a general dispensation to all volunteers who had taken the 'pioneers' pledge of temperance.[3]

> O my Dark Rosaleen
> Do not sigh, do not weep!
> The priests are on the ocean green,
> They march along the Deep.
> There's wine ... from the royal Pope
> And Spanish ale shall give you hope.[4]

However, other evidence suggests that the Church's sanction may have been ill-considered. Peter Lawler was an Irish-Australian who, after service with the British army in the Great War, had gone on to fight against Britain in the Irish War of Independence. One of the few officers to accompany the Galway group, he later described how his men were overcome by their reception in Salamanca:

> I knew it was going to be sheer bloody murder with the boys drinking all that wine on empty stomachs. I tried to see if I couldn't get them some food, but it was no use. Sure enough, when the time came to get back into the train the boys were so drunk it was all we could do to push them into it.[5]

A fortnight earlier, the Irish-born journalist Frank McCullagh had been on his way from Salamanca to Badajoz.[6] Though evidently apprised in general terms about the coming of the Brigade, he was not privy to O'Duffy's plans. By coincidence, he was held up in Cáceres by the fractured railway timetable. The first railway porter he addressed naturally assumed he was looking for the Irish Brigade, and directed him to the Hotel Álvarez in the Calle de la Cruz. There, McCullagh found Major Paddy Dalton, Captain Diarmiud O'Sullivan and a dozen other officers. They took him to a nearby barracks, 'an imposing new building as large as the Wellington Barracks in London'. Here he met another twenty men – the other ranks – in good health and spirits. Dalton and O'Sullivan entertained Captain McCullagh to dinner, at which (remarkably, the reader may feel, for an Irish journalist) he found there to be 'too much liquor for my taste'.

The next day McCullagh travelled on to his destination. In Badajoz, he noted that the Majestic Hotel had run up the Free State flag alongside those of Spain, Italy and Germany. The day after his arrival 'a company of green-shirted men' marched into the lobby. These were the leaders of the third Yeoward Line contingent, commanded by Eamon Horan. McCullagh journeyed on to Lisbon, where he met Captain T. F. Smith, 'an Ulster Protestant', who had been sent from Cáceres to liaise with the fourth and last Liverpool group. This group of more than a hundred men soon arrived, singing 'Faith of Our Fathers' as the SS *Ardeola* came into dock.[7] Despite his religious affiliation, Captain Smith was apparently not over-sensitive to the triumphalist sentiments of a Catholic hymn that was rapidly becoming the unofficial battle-song of the Irish Brigade.

The delights of Salamanca behind them, the main (Galway) contingent arrived in Cáceres a week before Christmas. A few days later they were joined by the *Ardeola* group. With this final substantial increment, the Brigade was officially mustered at 663 total members fit and reporting for duty.[8] The military barracks allocated for their use were on the northern outskirts of the town. As McCullagh observed, it was a new, purpose-built installation, having been constructed under the military dictatorship of Miguel Primo de Rivera in the 1920s for accommodation and training of the (mainly conscript) garrison attached to the local Captaincy-General. The Irish settled into these relatively comfortable quarters for a lengthy period of acclimatisation, organisation and military training. Also, as McCullagh had discovered, O'Duffy and his staff took over the Hotel Álvarez, a modest-sized establishment situated just behind the main square and close to municipal buildings.

Over a year after the Irish had finally moved out of the town, Cáceres was visited by the young English aristocrat, Pip Scott-Ellis, who was serving as a nurse in the nationalist medical corps. She recorded the experience in her diary:

> Wednesday 7 September. Tonight we are once more in a place we did not expect to be in. The Hotel Álvarez in Cáceres. It is a beastly dirty hotel, sort of large low-class with bad food and the service done by grubby little boys … Thursday 8 September. We set out from our gloomy hotel at 8 o'clock after a filthy breakfast that made me feel sick.[9]

The setting

Then, as now, Cáceres was the administrative capital of its own province, which in turn forms part of the region of Extremadura (today being one of the autonomous regions of Spain). Extremadura is a vast rural area, lying to the west and south of the central province of Madrid. On the map, it may be seen to occupy the middle fraction (about one-third) of the long Portuguese frontier which runs roughly north to south. Like many settlements of ancient origin, Cáceres is built on an extensive and flattish mound, which rises gently to less than one hundred feet at its highest point. Its core comprises a largely medieval group of buildings sheltered within a curtain wall. Even by the standards of ancient Castile, this virtually pristine conjunction of narrow passages crammed with town houses, convents, churches and tiny squares, is of surpassing historical interest and architectural beauty. The walls look out on to the undulating plain of Extremadura, an empty agricultural vista which in 1936 had not altered significantly in aspect for many centuries.[10]

In recent times, and at a quicker rate since the coming of the Second Republic in 1931, the landless labourers of the surrounding villages, who scratched for a living in primitive social and economic conditions, had been radicalised by labour-union activity and especially by the anarchist Confederación Nacional de Trabajo (CNT).[11] Though many *pueblos* seethed with pre-revolutionary enthusiasm, Cáceres itself, a market town dominated by prosperous commercial families, remained more conservative in temper. All the same, they had accepted a socialist mayor (Antonio Canales) in 1931, and another Partido Socialista de Obreros Españoles man (Antonio's brother, Miguel) later became Civil Governor. In February 1936 the capital was swept along with the Popular Front tide, Cáceres province electing seven out of its nine delegates on the left-wing ticket. In reaction to this, and the leftist programme of the new Madrid government, many hundreds of bourgeois, right-wing citizens (especially younger males) abandoned the democratic parties altogether and joined the local Falange.[12]

The officer commanding the local garrison, Colonel Álvarez Díaz, was not privy to the military conspiracy. In fact, only a few days before the uprising in Morocco he assured the Civil Governor of the absolute loyalty of himself and his men to the Republic. However, several junior officers were in the know and, having enlisted the co-operation of the Falange, were ready to act when the signal arrived from General Mola. On 18 July, they confronted their commander, who – wisely, and without undue hesitation – threw in his lot with them. Before effective resistance could be organised by their opponents, the rebel troops seized key points of the town and declared martial law. Thus Cáceres passed decisively under nationalist control. Antonio Canales and other Republicans were imprisoned. Luckily for Cáceres, it was Badajoz, some forty kilometres to the south-west, which the local revolutionary militias selected as their primary centre of resistance. Cáceres thus escaped the fate of the latter town, ravaged and ruined by the onslaught of Colonel Yagüe's Legionaries in mid-August.[13]

As the main thrust of the nationalist offensive passed through the province on its way to Madrid, 250 kilometres distant, Franco made Cáceres his headquarters. It was here, in the Palacio de los Golfines, that he took the decision to relieve the Alcázar of Toledo instead of pressing on to Madrid; and here that he received news of his nomination as *generalísimo* on 29 September. Meanwhile, a new military governor of the province, Colonel Luis Martín-Pinillos, was appointed, and the Falangist leader, Luciano López Hidalgo became *alcalde* (mayor). The latter was a mere puppet of the military authorities. On all important matters, O'Duffy and Dalton had to deal with Martín-Pinillos, who in turn kept Franco informed of relevant developments.[14]

Martín-Pinillos was an anxious and harassed man. The province of which he was viceroy was a prime target for enemy guerrilla activity, and by the early weeks of 1937 this had become a problem of urgent concern to Franco. Though no longer on the front, the security of this zone remained vital for communications with Cádiz and Huelva. Following Franco's failure to capture Madrid in November, substantial military supplies from Nazi Germany were now flowing towards the front from Andalusian ports. As Franco planned his next great offensive, in the valley of the Jarama river to the south of the capital, the Condor Legion, with its associated armoured and mobile artillery batteries, was moving into place behind his assault forces. Any negative incident involving these units would have been unwelcome to the *generalísimo* for political as well as military reasons. Yet in January alone, a supply train was derailed by a bomb on its way to Talavera, and several ambushes of troop convoys were reported, all taking place within the jurisdiction of Cáceres province.[15] Gangs of partisans were holed up in the remote *sierras* (mountain ranges) which fringed the province, and a regime of repression was imposed upon its population by the nationalist authorities. At the end of the month Martín-Pinillos was warned by Burgos that 'Espionage may be carried out in Cáceres, Salamanca and other places in the following fashion. Women stand near the road exits of cities soliciting lifts from troop-carrying vehicles to nearby villages, and take note of any military indiscretion of the occupants that they may manage to overhear.'[16]

Cáceres province quickly became the scene of a large-scale anti-terrorist campaign and its capital a centre for detention and 'justice'. In the course of January 1937, one guerrilla group mounted a sabotage operation concentrated in the sensitive zone lying between the town and the Madrid front, leaving a trail of destruction before being hunted down. In addition to the town's native Republicans, the prisons had already been used for hundreds of other 'unreliables' in the province. Dozens of guerrilla suspects were also now rounded up.[17] Regular interrogations and executions took place in Cáceres. A favoured place for the latter was the northern wall of the army barracks, conveniently situated not far from the municipal cemetery.[18] The most prominent victim of a series of reprisal exercises was ex-mayor Antonio Canales, who was taken out and shot on Christmas Day 1937, following an alleged Red conspiracy in the area.[19]

The Foreign Legion

Although they had originally been destined for the ranks of the Carlist *requetés*, various factors had persuaded Franco instead to incorporate his Irish volunteers into the Foreign Legion (the Tercio). On the face of things, this was evidence of high expectations of their fighting quality. For a start, Franco himself had been the co-founder of the Legion, designed as a professional force to overcome a long-standing rebellion in Morocco. Unlike the more famous French outfit, the Spanish Foreign Legion (*Legión Extranjera*) was not usually made up of foreigners but, rather, Spaniards dedicated to the army as a career, as distinct from mere conscripts. Nonetheless, thousands of non-Spanish volunteers joined during 1936, coming from backgrounds, and acting for motives, just as varied as those of the International Brigades. Legionaries enjoyed privileged status in terms of pay and conditions, but lived under a hard disciplinary regime. Their icy courage stemmed from a military rather than an ideological ethic. Officers and men regarded themselves, first and foremost, as soldiers. These units, operating virtually without the assistance of mechanised transport, had conquered the whole south-western quadrant of Spain for the insurgents in little more than eight weeks. Until the latter stages of the war, their presence and that of their Moorish auxiliaries was a prerequisite for any important nationalist offensive.

However, late in 1936 it became policy in Burgos to require all foreign volunteers who came forward as private individuals to enlist in the Legion.[20] In part, political motives were present, for Franco – though he admired the *requetés* more than all other militia units in the insurgent army – had no wish to strengthen the hand of the Carlist faction in advance of the exercise he was preparing in order to 'unite' the various competing elements of the nationalist cause.[21] But in addition, sheer military necessity obliged the *generalísimo* to reconstruct the Tercio as quickly as possible, replacing the appalling losses it had suffered, especially during its attacks upon Madrid. At this point, Franco's forces were outnumbered by more than three to one on the Madrid front. He needed, above all, assault infantry battalions who would fight with the special dedication of volunteers. Apart from some sturdy Galician regiments and the fanatically Catholic *requetés*, few units outside the ranks of the *Africanista* professionals (the army previously based in Spanish Morocco) had (thus far) offered convincing evidence of capacity in this department.

The *Cork Examiner* had already taken note of the peculiar, even sinister, qualities of the Tercio:

> The death-hymns of the Foreign Legion and their cry of 'Viva la Muerte' ('Long live Death') are now most popular throughout northern Spain and are sung and shouted by men, women and children ... Legionaries who arrived in Salamanca from Tetuán, Morocco, on August 12 ... had excellent up-to-date war material. Their flag consists of a white skull-and-crossbones on a black background.[22]

Parents back home who may have remembered this item would have had equivocal feelings about the organisation which their sons had now joined. Many volunteers were below the age at which they could legally enlist, and the anxiety of their nearest and dearest can only have been sharpened by a later report which developed its points with considerable relish: '[The Legionary] must attack at the cry, whether the attack is right or wrong; whether it has any chance of success or is doomed to failure ... "Bridegrooms of Death" might sound a bit flamboyant to the Celt ... but that it is now the credo of nearly a thousand Irishmen must imprint it on the memory.'[23] Indeed, members of the Legion were expected to obey orders without question in the very face of death. Regulations made constant reference to the 'need for self-sacrifice' and 'scorn of death', and to 'the spirit of abnegation and sacrifice which must be pushed to its very limit'.[24] They were widely referred to in nationalist lore (and in the words of one of the songs referred to by journalists) as 'The Bridegrooms of

Death' (*Novios de la Muerte*). The metaphor was by no means inappropriate, as their casualty rate eloquently testifies.[25] Franco may have been expressing confidence in the military potential of the Irish Brigade by welcoming them to his own regiment. But, at least as important, in so doing he also signalled his natural and literal acceptance of O'Duffy's reiterated claim that his men had come to fight and die for the Christian cause.

Organisation and training

Fighting units of the Legion were organised into autonomous *banderas* (battalions), normally comprising around eight hundred men (including fifty officers and Non-Commissioned Officers (NCOs)), and commanded in the field by a *teniente-coronel* (the equivalent of the British major). There were four companies: three were composed of riflemen, and the other a machine-gun company, and each was led by a captain. In turn, companies were subdivided into three sections (*teniente* or *alférez*) and each section into two platoons (*sargento*).[26] More important was that the XV *Bandera* (as the Irish Brigade was designated) should be rigorously instructed in the codes and training practices of the Tercio. Colonel Yagüe, its overall field commander, selected Captain Manuel Capablanca for this task. Though Capablanca could not speak English, he was assisted by other Spaniards (some of Irish descent) who joined the new *Bandera* as interpreters.[27] The addition of a team of Spanish liaison officers and other personnel who had either volunteered or been seconded for the purpose, meant that the total number of men in the XV *Bandera* was now edging towards seven hundred.

A large minority of the new *banderistas* – perhaps one-third – already had experience of military life. Officers like Carew and Lawler, for example, had fought in the British army in France, and had subsequently joined the IRA in the War of Independence. It may be estimated that one in five of the Brigade's members had some kind of battle experience, and perhaps one in ten regarded themselves as hardened veterans. In addition, most of the remainder had received some military or paramilitary training.[28] Many were – as one Spanish liaison officer recalled forty years later – proficient at general infantry drill and already expert riflemen.[29] Yet this was a mixed blessing, and probably not an advantage to the corps as a whole, since learning Spanish army techniques was inevitably regarded by older men as both tedious and unnecessary. The superior attitude of Great War veterans was to be justified in practice, because as things worked out the prevailing circumstances in which they were to find themselves were those of trench warfare. Yet, on the other hand, younger men found the training schedule to be of positive use when put to the test by subsequent events.[30]

To begin with the *Bandera* was divided into the regulation four companies, designated as 'A' to 'D', the last of these being the machine-gun company.[31] Every morning except Sunday they were up at six and after a simple breakfast went on parade, followed by six hours of intensive training. Some of this took place in the barracks compound itself, but 'twice a week, at least', the men were marched to a hilly terrain a few kilometres outside the town to engage in field manoeuvres. For most men (Companies A, B and C), instruction included work with trench mortars, light machine-guns and grenade-handling in addition to normal rifle practice. The last of these, in addition to their dedicated task, sufficed for the machine-gun company.[32] At first, the rifles issued consisted of the many varieties of ancient and antiquated which are ubiquitously described by veteran volunteers on both sides of the Spanish Civil War. Indeed, relevant stories told by Irish Brigaders and the International Brigaders are not just similar but identical in content and comment. Some weapons were so ancient that they blew apart on firing, others had crooked barrels or no appropriate ammunition. After only a short wait, however, the whole corps was issued with new German automatic rifles of a state-of-the-art design and efficiency.[33]

A less unmixed cause of satisfaction was that with the weapons came German uniforms – which, in this case, actually were leftovers or reclamations from the Great War. Here was, surely, a subject of irony for those Irish ex-Tommies who had once looked out across no man's land in Flanders, and who had now assumed the appearance of the 'Fritz' they had watched out for twenty years before. They would perhaps have been less amused had they known the role that these markings were to play in their future.[34] However, most other ranks, who had hardly been able to pack a full change of outer garments, welcomed the issue with few complaints. One observer somewhat equivocally noted that:

> the Germans wore well-cut, well-fitting uniforms of sturdy German material, and it was some of these that fell to the lot of the Irishmen. As Germans have unusually large hips and Irishmen are slenderly built about the hips, the result was frequently unhappily baggy for the Irishmen. However considering the shortage of material for uniforms (the Reds are in possession of the industrial provinces) ... the Irish Legionaries looked remarkably well[35]

Each company was to carry a pennant decorated with the historic emblem of the Tercio – the crossed ragged staves; in the case of the XV *Bandera* the cross was of red on an emerald green background.[36]

In addition to the four fighting companies, the superstructure of command staff and the infrastructure of service units had to be organised. O'Duffy, his aide-de-camp (Gunning) and his personal interpreter (Meade), along with Dalton (appointed as General Officer Commanding (GOC)), twenty-four Irish commissioned officers and five Spanish liaison officers made up the former body. Most of these were lodged in the Hotel Álvarez, whilst NCOs were billeted with the other ranks in the barracks. In the latter building, Irish cooks were struggling to come to terms with Spanish food and rations – if not with the radically different Iberian hours of repast – whilst a quartermaster's stores supply and ordnance service (with seconded staff for each company) were also established.

During the training period, O'Duffy and his immediate entourage were present in Cáceres only for special occasions. Routine responsibility for training, discipline and all relations with the municipality and local military personnel fell to Dalton and his company commanders, Captains O'Sullivan (A), Smith (B), Quinn (C) and Cunningham (D). During this first period of billeting in Cáceres, at least, it seems that their task was a fundamentally happy one.

Irish and Spanish in Cáceres

In the last week of January 1937, the XV *Bandera* was visited by the *Irish Independent* special correspondent in Spain, Gertrude Gaffney. At this point, most of the men had been in Cáceres for four or five weeks. Gaffney submitted three reports, devoting many paragraphs to the conditions and morale of the unit. Not surprisingly, given the newspaper's special commitment to the enterprise, the content of these dispatches was upbeat, both about the *Bandera* and the nationalist cause generally. Their author dutifully (if skilfully) reported, for example, that:

> I went to Cáceres expecting to find the Irish Brigade composed largely of adventurers – an opinion shared, I know, by many of my neighbours … I do not deny that there were among them men and boys who had joined up and gone purely in the spirit of adventure, or because they could not find jobs and were 'fed up' with life; but what astonished me was that these appeared to be such a small percentage. I should say that 85% of them went because they thought it was up to them to fight for the Faith.

In this crusading context, Miss Gaffney made it her business to enquire about the social behaviour of the volunteers. She concluded there was little excessive drinking, since the wine was not popular and the beer too expensive. She also noted that the local women were completely resistant to smiling Irish eyes, adding that in any case they were not especially attractive.[37]

As these observations suggest, informal social contact between the *Bandera* and the citizens of Cáceres was not encouraged, and was in any case made almost prohibitively difficult by linguistic divisions. As one soldier put it, 'the people out here are very nice only they can't speak English we do have right sport trying to make them understand what we want'.[38] All the evidence indicates that few or none of the Irishmen who had no Spanish before they arrived made any serious attempt to grapple with the language. Though strong cultural barriers also existed to any warm general understanding, in theory at least there should have been one powerful antidote to this – the common Catholicism of visitor and native. In practice, however, this spiritual communion of peoples, even given the special emphasis placed on it by the conditions of crusade, proved unable to provide any channel of communication.

The *Bandera* was allocated its own place of worship, the parish church of San Domingo. The church was located not far from the barracks, in the middle of a busy, densely populated area. Every Sunday the whole *Bandera* marched there to attended Mass.[39] O'Duffy was not the only witness to observe that the locals were astonished at the sincere piety of the soldiers. There seems little need to doubt that the average Irishman's degree of spiritual observance was in excess of that imposed by the collective routine. Of course, not all men were equally zealous, and perhaps amongst the officers there was a tendency to slackness. As early as 29 December – admittedly during the religiously demanding Christmas and New Year period – Dalton noted that 'it is necessary to draw attention to the fact that ALL ranks not detailed for Fatigues, special employment, etc., must attend Church Parade'.[40] Nevertheless, the feeling of surprise was mutual (as between *cacereños* and *banderistas*) since for their part the Irishmen were disappointed by the meagre evidence of religious enthusiasm shown by the very people for whose religious liberty they believed themselves to be fighting. Religious practice in many parts of southern Spain – especially Andalusia and Extremadura – was statistically unimpressive if compared with Ireland (or, for that matter, with Navarre). Though only a minority of males outside the wealthy and landowning classes would normally have attended church, a tendency to absence was exacerbated by the demand for men to fill the ranks of the nationalist army. Yet appearances were to some extent deceptive, since all this helps to explain why families may have tended to avoid attending services in San Domingo – especially families with unmarried daughters or young women with husbands at the front.[41]

Partly as a consequence, nowhere in the primary sources can convincing evidence be found for a single example of even a passing social intimacy between members of the *Bandera* and those of the host community. To my knowledge, at least, no witness has ever been able to recall the name of a single citizen of Cáceres, nor do any appear to have so much as caught sight of the interior of any (occupied) private dwelling. The conclusion suggested by these observations goes for any context – and can be even more confidently assumed as applying to sexual relations. For Irishmen, this was no change from the norm, their own domestic customs being at least as sexually prohibitive as those current in rural Spain. Of course, there were temptations. Even at home, all save the most pious (or poorest) young people increasingly indulged in the godless – nay, almost communistic – pastime of attending organised occasions of sin, where 'jazz music' inflamed passions and dancing took place with members of the opposite sex.[42] Soldiers will be soldiers, and the occasional daring venture was made, in predictable circumstances and with predictable results, to sling hooks. 'We would sometimes try to chat up the local señoritas but they would only laugh at us as our Spanish wasn't very good', remembers Bill McCormack.[43]

One immature young crusader was so eager to rid his mother of fears for his body and soul that he must have succeeded in giving her an impression exactly contrary to that intended. 'The girls out here are no good,' he protested, adding as if to make things even worse, 'I would like to bump them all off.' In the same excessively chaste missive, addressed to his 'dear mother and dad', Hickey adds that 'I never touch the drink now, it is only a cod getting drunk, out here you need your head where I am.'[44] In contrast, Sean McKee (or his leftist ghost-writer) alleged that 'our time [in Cáceres] was spent drinking in the cafés and visiting the bordellos, and there was no lack of them'.[45]

Whilst sex, commercial or otherwise, was out of bounds and the virgin soldiers remained exactly that, alcohol was less – that is to say, more – of a problem. Pay rates in the Legion were good: for private volunteers, three pesetas a day – which represented thrice the average in the nationalist army. In practice, nearly half this sum was withheld to pay off the costs of uniforms and food, and the men were paid eleven pesetas each week.[46] This was still a goodly sum and could only be expended on food, drink and gambling. The last of these pastimes was, if only by default, by far the most popular – especially once the *Bandera* arrived in the trenches.[47] Drunkenness was an inevitable and perennial accompaniment to leave in town. Combined with homesickness, it could sometimes lead to individual acts of indiscipline, and several anecdotes have this scenario, including one or two relating to officers, and even to *banderistas* who later took Holy Orders.[48]

Within the *Bandera*, punishment was relatively light and rarely exceeded more than a few days' jankers. Perhaps the most feared fatigue was cleaning the latrines, especially during the early period, when the soldiers' physiological reaction to Spanish food and wine was at its most uncontrolled. However, outside the walls – quite literally – things were much grimmer. According to McKee, the barracks resembled 'a large concentration camp surrounded by barbed wire. At night, volleys of rifle firing disturbed our sleep. And it seemed to us as if firing squads were busy shooting people who did not appreciate the blessings of Franco rule.'[49] On this subject, for once, McKee was not exaggerating. Several other veterans remembered witnessing executions. Jim Kavanagh climbed on to trees which grew inside the barracks's walls and saw a squad of Civil Guards shooting a group of prisoners who were taken out of covered lorries and afterwards carted across to the cemetery. Bill McCormack and his mate Christy O'Sullivan witnessed a similar incident:

> Going across the barracks square Bill heard what sounded like a motor cycle engine. He climbed up a nearby wall; what he saw shocked him. Eight republican prisoners were being executed. Their hands were tied behind their backs and there were white markers on chests. After they were shot by the firing squad an officer went around and finished them off.[50]

Paddy Smith saw men executed 'in scores', and vividly recalled being allocated to guard the cell where an English-speaking Spanish army officer was being held the night before his execution.[51]

The six weeks of acculturation were a difficult period. Severe postal problems meant that the corps received no letters or packets from home for over a month. When O'Duffy's personal intervention managed to break the dam (which had occurred in Lisbon) many men were unhappy with their domestic news.[52] This accentuated existing boredom and frustration, inculcated by lack of military action, and despond was deepened by the continually poor weather. In this situation, men simply could not be kept cooped up in barracks. Yet there seems to have been little or no organised football, boxing or other sporting competition within the *Bandera*. This is all the more perplexing given the long association of its leader with the GAA and his more recent links with athletics; after all, he had been manager of the successful Free State team at the San Francisco Olympics (1932).[53] Even had this not been the case, the neglect of such an obvious deterrent to boredom, regarded as healthy and beneficial in almost every other army of the day, would remain puzzling. Perhaps O'Duffy feared that competition in such spheres would breed (or exacerbate) internal rivalries too powerful to be fully subordinated to the common good in the all-important context of military action. If true, such an attitude would have been so contrary to received wisdom as in itself to provide some indication of the latent potential for division within the *Bandera*.

Instead of the leather and the ash, the Irish devoted themselves to organising concert parties, and every Sunday and feast-day evening the main canteen was given over to home-brewed entertainment. The staple fare comprised Irish rebel songs and 'folk music', renditions of the sentimental ballads of Moore and Balfe, and the bloodily heroic odes of Thomas Davis, in particular his 'Fontenoy' in praise of the Wild Geese and 'Battle Eve of the Irish Brigade', with its irresistible exhortation:

> They fought as they revelled, fast, fiery and true,
> And, though victors, they left on the field not a few;
> And they who survived, fought and drank as of yore,
> But the land of their heart's hope they never saw more.[54]

Attendance at these parties seems to have been required almost as keenly as Mass parade duty. As for popular Spanish pastimes – the cinema and the bullfight – only one was acceptable to the Irishmen. Cáceres boasted two picture-houses (in addition to a theatre), where a seat could be had for fifty centimos. Hollywood films were occasionally on offer and attracted a big Irish audience.[55] In contrast, the *fiesta nacional* evoked one of the rare negative comments which the general permitted himself on the whole expedition:

> Many volunteers looked forward to seeing a bull-fight and a special performance was arranged for us … It was evident from the outset that this form of pastime did not appeal to the Irishman's sense of sportsmanship … When the volunteers returned to their barracks for tea, a unanimous wish was expressed that Franco would abolish bull-fighting as a national pastime in the new Spain.[56]

Much more appealing to O'Duffy were the formal occasions in which the *Bandera* participated. Various parades and special church services were held during the festive season, in which the *Bandera* received the public approbation of the citizen onlookers. As the time for action approached, various nationalist top brass came to inspect the Irishmen: Moscardó, hero of the Alcázar, whose eyes glistened when he shook Denis Reynolds's hand with the words 'you are too young to be at the front'; the less emotional Yagüe, GOC of the Legion came late in January, and Franco himself turned up early in February. But even more satisfying to O'Duffy were the many receptions and dinners held in the *Bandera*'s honour, and to which only he and (usually) certain selected officers of his staff were invited. Such occasions were offered by the municipality of Cáceres, by various other *ayuntamientos* (town councils) in the vicinity, by the Bishop of Coria, and by the military and civil governors of the province. These were the moments when he relished his role to the full, when he was fêted by grandees of Spain and princes of the Church, when the conversation was dominated by talk of crusade and duty, of Spain and Ireland and their joint historic destiny. It was then that the general could imagine himself a paladin of Charlemagne, standing shoulder to shoulder with Franco, Hitler and Mussolini against the infidel Red Horde – and putting Eamon de Valera to shame. No wonder that tediously repetitive accounts of these events dominate several chapters of his book.[57]

For the culminating example of this genre, however, we have an extraordinary alternative source. On 31 January, following notice to place itself on stand-by for the front, the *Bandera* held a grand public cere-mony to mark the unveiling of a commemorative plaque – which still decorates the wall of San Domingo – paid for by fund-raising events and subscription among the volunteers. Yet another concert party followed, but whilst the men were expected to meet the usual lights-out time of 11.00 p.m., their officers went on to a farewell banquet, given in honour of Martín-Pinillos, this time with themselves as hosts. Lieutenant Tom Hyde, perhaps the most generally popular man in the whole unit, pos-sessed a souvenir autograph-book, one of several that officers appear to have had specially made in Cáceres.[58] During the banquet he made his way from table to table soliciting signatures and suitable epithets. Many of the latter made reference to the sacrosanct nature of the XV *Bandera*'s undertaking:

> I warmly greet the brave and heroic Irish battalion which has united with our beloved Spain for the defence of its liberty and religion.
> (Capt. Botana, Liaison)

Long live the brave Catholics who fight with the Legion. (El Conde de
La Unión, Second Lieutenant)
My cordial greetings to a volunteer for the Faith. (Miguel Achender-
reta, Paymaster)
For faith and country you came to Spain – as you did I will do. (Anto-
nio Miracle, Second Lieutenant)
To the knights who came to Spain to fight this new Crusade. (Alfonso
Bustamente, Second Lieutenant)

Readers can decide for themselves whether these effusions, made on a
convivial evening sixty years ago, were sincere expressions of motivation
and spiritual confraternity. Less equivocally poignant is the fact that
Hyde himself harboured no shadow of doubt concerning the spiritual
nature of his commitment; and that with perfect aptness, he was to be the
first Irish 'martyr' of the crusade. Liaison officer Pedro Bove, destined to
die in the same moments, signed 'to Lieutenant Hyde with whom I hope
shortly to leave for the front'. 'Long live Tom Hyde!' added Major Paddy
Dalton. And finally, inscribed to a man who was already veteran of many
battles, but never to be a veteran of the XV *Bandera*, was Captain Capablanca's 'earnest desire that the *Bandera* will quickly become veteran
legionaries'.

4

On the Madrid front

Rites of passage

The farewell celebrations, full of cameraderie and good spirits, provided a suitable morale-booster. But no marching orders were immediately forthcoming, and the Irishmen had plenty of time to recover before needing to be on their mettle. The first demanding duty did not confront *Teniente-Coronel* Dalton until a week later, when General Franco made a surprise visit to the barracks at Cáceres.

The *generalísimo* arrived in Cáceres from Seville, where he had been auditing preparations for an advance on Málaga.[1] Meanwhile, on the evening of Friday, 5 February 1937, General Orgaz launched an attack in the southern Madrid sector, opening the major offensive at first called the 'battle for the Valencia Road', but which entered history as the battle of Jarama. This operation was long-planned but (and thus the premature farewells in Cáceres) had been held up for two weeks by poor weather conditions. The object of the first move was seemingly a mere pawn – the small town of Ciempozuelos, fifteen kilometres north of Aranjuez. In fact, its capture provided Orgaz's army with an axial point on which the whole offensive could swing, in a furious sweep to the north-east. The first-phase strategic target was Arganda, close to the south-eastern perimeter of Madrid; but the ultimate goal was the complete surrounding, and thus inevitable fall, of the Spanish capital itself.

Once he was sure that all was going well in Andalusia, Franco returned north to supervise the rapidly developing situation on the Madrid front. He flew out of Seville at first light on 6 February. It seems he was obliged to make a stop-over at Cáceres, perhaps for refuelling or because of nearby enemy air activity. The Irish had little advance notice of his intentions, and officers had to act frantically to assemble the men on parade. O'Duffy himself was (characteristically) absent, but eye-witness reports claim that Franco was not dissatisfied.[2] Doubtless he took the opportunity to check with Capablanca and liaison staff that training had gone according to plan, and that the unit was battle-ready. Before Franco left to resume his journey, the Irish officers were issued with their operational instructions. The XV *Bandera* was to form part of the second wave of the offensive across the Jarama Valley.[3]

On the morning of 17 February, shortly after O'Duffy had re-joined his men, the *Bandera* entrained at Cáceres station. There was a considerable delay before things got started, since the train driver was found to be missing and had to be replaced. To his passengers, it seemed that the new operative was incompetent, or simply lunatic. Within a few miles the engine seemed to go out of control, hurtling along at a pace which threw the men around like beans in a box. Suddenly, and with equally painful results, the train jerked to a complete stop – as if the buffers had been hit. Another substantial wait ensued before the journey restarted. When they arrived at Plasencia, the station area was in chaos following an air attack, and further delay supervened whilst bomb-damaged track was repaired.

Though no one seems to have explained what was happening, several men were later given to understand that a sabotage conspiracy had been foiled. Maurice ('Moss') Fennell recorded that 'seemingly the driver was a "Red", and was planted there to ensure that we would reach our first stop before the scheduled time … When we got to our scheduled first stop, at Plasencia, the whole area of the station had been bombed by enemy planes, during an air raid which had been meant for us.'[4] Not until the late afternoon of 18 February did the *Bandera* arrive at the rail junction of Torrijos. Here they changed to a minor line as far as Torrejón de la Calzada. Next, they were marched in the gathering gloom along a winding road which led twelve kilometres further forward, to Valdemoro. This township, marking what – before the battle – had been the front line, was reached at midnight, many hours later than planned. The men were already disorientated and exhausted. Only two servings of weak coffee had been made en route, and many were seriously hungry, but no rations were on offer in Valdemoro. Men were crowded into a few buildings which enemy artillery and aviation had left standing in order to get some rest. But General Orgaz needed them to relieve the occupying force in Ciempozuelos as soon as possible – preferably before dawn.

To O'Duffy's dismay, at Valdemoro orders awaited him to move on to Ciempozuelos at 6 a.m. the next day. He immediately got back into his car and drove to operational HQ, well behind the lines at Navalcarnero, to protest that his men needed a good night's sleep. Having apparently obtained Orgaz's permission to delay the next stage of advance, he returned to Valdemoro, only to leave again an hour later to report his arrival to the Military Governor in Toledo. When he got back to Valdemoro again at 11 a.m. on 19 February, the *Bandera* had left on its march to Ciempozuelos – indeed, unknown to the chief, his men had already undergone their baptism of fire.[5]

Ciempozuelos lies seven kilometres to the south-east of Valdemoro. It was a medium-size *pueblo* which, before the outbreak of the war, had been home to some four thousand citizens. Basically a market town, it served a local agronomy dependent on the production of olives, which grew on the hilly surrounding plateaux, and kidney beans, which flourished in the irrigated soil of the nearby Jarama valley proper. The two main institutions were a Carmelite convent and one of the country's largest asylums for the mentally ill, staffed by the nuns, along with the brothers of St John. It was by no means isolated from the world, lying as it did on the main railway line from Madrid to Aranjuez, Toledo and on to Andalusia. In the Popular Front elections of February 1936, Ciempozuelos elected a communist mayor and was known as a centre of radical political activity. However, in the course of the previous October, as General Varela's nationalist columns drove northwards following the capture of Toledo, the civilian population – like hundreds of others before them – had abandoned their homes for the security of Madrid. Since the nationalist line (in effect the right flank of the corridor opened to enable their advance on Madrid) ran so close, Ciempozuelos remained occupied by only a token republican force of militiamen, who constructed makeshift trenches and other strongpoints in the vicinity.

In late January 1937, these men were replaced by fresh regular army units. This infantry brigade (the 18th), trained in Madrid during the winter months and comprised three battalions and about two thousand men. Along with many other units, they were due to take part in a major offensive in the Jarama area. However, at dusk on 5 February, this force was hit by the sudden onslaught of a battalion of some six hundred Moroccan fighters. It was the first blow in a nationalist offensive which completely upset republican plans. According to a republican military news-sheet, 'The enemy mounted intense attacks on three points; Marañosa, San Martín and Ciempozuelos. Our brave troops resisted heroically, hanging on until the arrival of the enemy tanks drove them from their positions.'[6] The facts were less heroic. The defenders of Ciempozuelos were overwhelmed and literally annihilated by an infantry unit only one-third their numerical strength. The Moors carried out their work more with the knife and bayonet than with bullets. No tanks or other modern hardware were needed. Surprise, gained by the stealthy infiltration of dozens of small groups, taking advantage of the fading light and of the myriad random folds of the local landscape, was of the essence. No prisoners were taken, and accounts suggest that only a small minority of the garrison escaped. On 8 February, the official nationalist *parte* (military situation report) noted brusquely that 'on the Ciempozuelos sector, they have buried some 800 bodies as a result of the fighting on day 5 of this month'.[7] The carnage received more ample treatment in the Salamanca press a few days later.

> One thousand three hundred and six bodies have been recovered from the Red trenches at Ciempozuelos. Our charitable work in burying these men goes forward with active zeal, but the dead left on the field of battle are so numerous that several days of this work still lie ahead. In many cases the enemy have been buried where they died, in their own trenches. This provides more evidence that our forces have completely destroyed the second and third battalions of the enemy's 18th Brigade.[8]

The whole nationalist offensive likewise swept aside early resistance, and within three days had occupied some 150 square kilometres of territory in the junction of the Manzanares and Jarama valleys. Thereafter, the defence stiffened. Though their fighting qualities were far superior to those of most republican units, the attackers, largely comprising North African and Legionary *banderas*, were outnumbered in most sections. They, too, began to take heavy losses, casualties which – unlike those of their adversaries – could not be replaced. On the fourth day of the general engagement, in the north-east 'corner' of the battlefield, Franco's main thrust, towards the Arganda Bridge and a vital intersection of main roads, was held up by the XII International Brigade less than a kilometre from its target. The turning point came in the second week of the battle (12–14 February), when an attempt was made to punch a hole through hastily improvised republican lines. This was launched from San Martín de la Vega, a village situated in the very centre of the battlefield, some ten kilometres north-east of Ciempozuelos. Following initial success, the attack was stopped in front of Morata de Tajuña, by the XV International Brigade, reinforced in the nick of time by the 11th Division under Enrique Líster. After ten days of a combat hugely expensive in casualties, Orgaz had simply run out of assault troops, and the initiative switched to the republican leadership, Generals Miaja and Rojo, in Madrid.

The latter lost no time in organising counter-attacks.[9] On 16 February, an operation to mine nationalist positions in the Madrid suburb of Carabanchel was initiated. Republican units broke out behind the lines of the besiegers, whilst simultaneously a frontal attack was launched on Orgaz's left flank, across the Manzanares. For a few days, nationalist commanders struggled to stabilise the front. On 17 and 18 February, they reported major International Brigade attacks in the La Marañosa sector.[10] Meanwhile the republican press – understandably if prematurely – celebrated victory.[11]

Thus it was that on the morning of 19 February, as the XV *Bandera del Tercio* advanced on Ciempozuelos, Orgaz's field commanders were expecting further enemy movement on the flanks, and were not wholly certain of their lines.[12] It seems that shortly after leaving Valdemoro, the Irish took the shortest route, along a shallow valley where, in the winter months, a so-called 'sheep-track stream' (*Arroyo de la Cañada*) trickles south to join the Jarama.[13] After a while, artillery activity – always rumbling in the background – assumed a more threatening character. On the advice of his Spanish aides, as a prophylactic measure, Dalton ordered the adoption of attack formation. This meant that the unit spread out ten feet apart in line abreast, advancing at walking pace along both slopes of the valley. By now, the prevailing weather conditions had turned fine; the thin morning mist was clearing under the sun's rays, when a detachment of troops was spotted coming towards the Irish at a distance of some 600 yards.

Neither side had been advised of the possibility of such a conjuncture. Nobody knew what was happening. The leading company (A) halted. As they passed the word back, their commander, Captain O'Sullivan, went forward with his Spanish liaison officer, Lieutenant Pedro Bove, two other Irishmen and a Spanish interpreter. At the same time a party of similar size detached itself from the opposing line. When they met, Bove – who, for his part, had quickly established that there was nothing to worry about – saluted with a statement which included the words '*Bandera Irlandesa del Tercio*'. Almost at that instant, and apparently without reply, the other commander drew his revolver and fired wildly at Bove. As the group turned back in a mad scramble for safety, general fire was opened and both Spaniards in O'Sullivan's party were killed. However, the three Irishmen managed to reach their own lines safely, and their compatriots began to return fire.

A desultory action followed – desultory at least by the standards of the war in general and the Jarama battle in particular – lasting for something less than an hour. The opposing force was not much smaller than the XV *Bandera*, but seems to have been equipped with a trench mortar. Having no orders, unsure of the local situation, and faced with the possibility that the visible 'enemy' was the first wave of a major offensive tide, both sides merely went to ground and held their positions. Each soldier sought cover amongst olive trees, scrub and the odd hillock, whilst shooting at any feasible target. During the engagement, O'Sullivan's subaltern, Tom Hyde, and one soldier of A Company, Dan Chute, were killed, and another legionary was wounded. On the Irish side, it is claimed that once the heavy machine-guns of D Company were deployed, they took a much heavier toll of the 'enemy'. A combatant on the opposing side later confessed to a comrade – 'between clenched teeth' – that the fault for the disastrous encounter clearly lay with the opposing battalion, and that they had paid for it with thirteen dead.[14] At any rate, it was the latter who broke off the confrontation, withdrawing from the field to the heartfelt relief of their adversaries. Prudently, Dalton resisted the temptation of pursuit. The Irishmen carefully regrouped and reconnoitred before moving forward to their destination, which was reached in mid-afternoon.

After sixty years, a comprehensive explanation of this incident remains difficult. The only certainties are the (approximate) geographical location and time of the skirmish, the number and identity of the *Bandera* casualties, and the affiliation of their opponents – a nationalist battalion recruited from the Canary Islands. The official story on the Irish side states that, as a result of a full enquiry, the entire blame was later allocated to the Canary Islanders, and the unit was accordingly disbanded – presumably because it could not morally subsist with such a burden of humiliation. The records of the relevant tribunal are still undiscovered (or at least unrevealed) and it is not possible to corroborate O'Duffy's claims.[15] However, there seem to be no grounds for supposing that any fault lay with the XV *Bandera*. The fateful first shot was fired in a moment of panic by an opposing officer. The Irish were victims of the confusion which obtained behind the lines at that juncture of the Jarama battle, combined with a cruel coincidence of timing.

However, a conjectural reconstruction may be attempted, based on a range of witness and other circumstantial evidence. The Canary Islanders (as it proved, a Falangist battalion) were moving northwards in haste, probably as the crow flies, from the area of Toledo, in order to stiffen defences around the La Marañosa sector, on the left flank of Orgaz's salient, which was currently – as we have seen – under severe pressure from republican counter-attacks. In so doing, they crossed between Ciempozuelos, on their right and the Irish, advancing in attack formation to their left. The Falangist commander, having been issued with the daily reports, was aware of the immediately volatile situation – and, in particular, the involvement of the International Brigades – but not of the local movement of a friendly unit. Through his binoculars, he could see that the unidentified troops, spread out in attack formation, were attired in unfamiliar uniform, which certainly bore no resemblance to that of the famous Tercio. Thus, when Lieutenant Bove announced the presence of a Legionary *bandera*, his interlocutor was immediately on his guard. When O'Sullivan introduced himself in English – or, worse still, in broken Spanish – all doubt disappeared. The Canary Island officer was confronted with some trick manoeuvre by an infiltrating party of International Brigaders, or had even blundered into a full offensive spearheaded by these already notorious alien enemy. Either way, he did not fancy a pitched battle, and as soon as the cover provided by his mortars seemed effective, carried out a withdrawal, doubtless as relieved to have escaped as Dalton was to see the back of him.[16]

If the German uniforms were the immediate occasion, the fundamental cause of the disaster was a multiple failure of logistics. In the first place, the Irish were supposed to have completed their journey to Ciempozuelos some twelve hours earlier, and the necessary adjustments to orders had not been made and/or distributed by dispatch riders from General Orgaz's field HQ. Though O'Duffy reported details of his arrival to two different control stations, his claim to have had his orders amended by General Orgaz in person seems invalid. The latter directed the battle not from Navalcarnero, well behind the new front lines, but from the more advanced point of Gózquez de Arriba, a complex of farm buildings on the meseta of La Marañosa, ten kilometres north-east of Valdemoro. Now that the weather had improved, and although neither side had outright superiority in these departments, planes and artillery meant that the hours of dusk and darkness were utilised for troop movements. By the time O'Duffy arrived at Toledo the Canary Islanders were already on the march, and no messenger could overtake them before the fateful encounter near Ciempozuelos.

As with virtually every accident, imponderable factors were compounded by human misjudgement. In this case, two may be identified. First, it seems certain that permission to rest his men at Valdemoro should not have been given to O'Duffy. Second, the adjusted orders were to leave Valdemoro at 11 a.m. but in fact the *Bandera* left well before the appointed hour – possibly in order to take advantage of the cover provided by the morning mist.[17] Assuming that O'Duffy was telling the truth (even if not the whole truth) then neither of these errors was the responsibility of the Irish leaders themselves.

A week after the Ciempozuelos skirmish, a prominent nationalist daily carried a front-page notice of the death of Tom Hyde, under the headline 'A chief of the Irish "Blue Shirts" gives his life for the cause of Spain': 'From Dublin it was reported yesterday that one of the best-known chiefs of the Irish "Blue Shirts", Thomas Inder [*sic*], has fallen on the Madrid front, fighting in the ranks of the national troops. This news was given out over Nationalist Radio which afterwards broadcast, in honour of the Irish hero, the hymn called "I had a Comrade".'[18]

Since no Irish *caoin* (lament) was available, the broadcaster had recourse to a well-known German marching song ('*Ich hat ein kamerad*') – a record which had doubtless already become scratched from over-use. Nonetheless, the tribute was deserved and appropriate. Hyde went to Spain ready to give his life for a cause synonymous with his deepest personal values. A veteran of the War of Independence and the Irish Civil War, he was respected by fighters on both sides of that tragic conflict, and by those of all ranks of the XV *Bandera* who knew him in Cáceres. Pedro Bove, who had written in Hyde's autograph-book of looking forward to going into battle at his side, had died only minutes before his new comrade. On the penultimate page, O'Duffy now added: 'To Tom in Heaven: You were the first to join the Irish Brigade. You were the first to give your life for the cause which the Irish Brigade is fighting for. Intercede now for the glorious success of that cause.'[19]

Frontline routine

As the Irishmen approached Ciempozuelos, the town came under heavy artillery bombardment. But having (as many believed) scored an outright victory in their first engagement, confidence was high. Forty years later, Moss Fennell recalled a 'feeling of elation' akin to the final moments of a close-fought rugby match as they neared their objective. But, suddenly:

> I dived into a shell-hole … as four mortar bombs almost simultaneously burst around me. Then, after the dirt and stones showered down, and the smoke cleared away, a new and sickening sensation gripped me. It was the stench of rotting human flesh. I opened my eyes, there were three dead and decaying bodies, partially covered, one only inches away, and seemingly looking straight at me with glazed and sightless eyes.[20]

Fennell had found not a shell-hole but one of the shallow trenches-cum-catacombs of the doomed republican defenders of Ciempozuelos. Extricating himself from this ghastly situation, he advanced with his comrades – exercising the greatest circumspection – into the town's precincts. As Sergeant George Timlin described it:

> The day was well advanced when A Company entered the town ... Shells were coming screeching through the air, ploughing up the roads and knocking the sides and tops from already partly-demolished buildings ... I entered several houses on a tour of inspection. It required no great stretch of imagination to visualise the haste and terror in which some of these houses were vacated. Children's toys were trampled on, babies' shawls and bottles scattered about – one could almost hear the wailing of the mothers ... The [railway] station building was the guard-house and soon a machine-gun post was taken over from the Moors. In front of the station was a plateau and twin hills separated the Reds from our position. There were machine-gun and observation posts on the top of the hills, and we took these over also from the departing Moors.[21]

Bodies and bits of bodies were to be seen amidst the revolting wreckage which littered the streets of the town. For several days after taking over from the Moroccans, and despite their exhaustion, the Irishmen were kept awake at night by the sound of the dogs, gone to the wild after owners' abandonment of farms and villas, which roamed around the edges of the town to feast on the corpses. This happened in spite of the meticulous, Christian care in the burial of the enemy dead to which the Salamanca press had drawn attention.[22] So troublesome did the canine packs become that the off-duty Irishmen went out shooting the dogs, which one of them later recalled as being good training in sniping skills.[23]

But before this relaxing pastime could be indulged, the *Bandera* needed to establish a sound military routine for the defence of the sector of the front which had been entrusted to them. This meant not only the garrisoning of Ciempozuelos itself, but also the permanent manning of forward and reserve positions extending some five kilometres southwards towards the republican-held town of Aranjuez. The defensive system was not based on a single unbroken line of trenches. The Irish inherited – amending and developing where necessary – a patchwork of trenches, one or two partly fortified outlying farm buildings, sandbagged machine-gun posts, foxholes and a variety of other emplacements. These were designed, however crudely, to exploit their immediate topography.

Opposite the Irish position, less than two kilometres away on the left bank of the Jarama valley, was the republican strongpoint of Titulcia, situated where the west-facing cliffs which loom over the river-bed rise to their highest point. But between the two *pueblos* there protrudes the narrowing end of a line of low hills. This feature, described well enough by George Timlin in the above quotation, is in effect, the tail of the triangular, kite-shaped *meseta* of La Marañosa. Its presence meant that one enemy town could only be descried directly from the highest buildings of the other. As an early and heavy detail, the Irishmen needed to construct, on the forward slopes of these hills, a defensive position which would enable them both to protect Ciempozuelos itself and give a clear view across the valley to enemy positions to both north and south.[24]

As good luck would have it, the Irish defences were never to be tested. Franco's decision to call off the Jarama offensive coincided almost exactly with the Irish arrival at the front. One consequence was that the Moorish *tabor* (battalion of Moroccan troops) they relieved as garrison of Ciempozuelos – which, if freed for assault duty a little earlier, would have been worth its weight in gold to General Orgaz – actually remained in the town for a few days after the handover. The Irish were able to benefit from the extempore *soukh* which the Moroccans invariably established in any place from which immediate military action had receded.[25] On sale was nothing less than the plunder of the town, a promiscuous assortment of abandoned but portable commodities which had not been disposed of by the enemy; a store improved by personal possessions stripped from the bodies of the latter. By far the most sought-after items were tobacco and hard liquor. Both Moors and Legionaries were officially permitted to plunder a town for a strictly limited period (usually a few hours) following its capture. But since it was almost invariably the former who were sent in first, opportunities for the latter were limited.

In any case, Legionaries – as their code insisted – were 'gentlemen', *caballeros*, to whom such vulgar capitalism (the sale, I mean, rather than the plunder) should have been anathema. As things worked out, these particular businessmen were soon moved on. They were needed in their primary capacity to help defend the key nationalist position on the heights of Pingarrón from a sequence of enemy counter-attacks which began on 23 February and continued sporadically for four days.[26] After the failure of these desperate onslaughts, immensely costly in human lives as they were, the Republicans also acknowledged that the Jarama contest had ended in a draw. Indeed, until the end of the war in April

1939, there was to be no major change in the respective positions held by the two sides in the Jarama valley.

Although unsuspected by them at the time, the XV *Bandera* had been definitively spared from the normative slaughter imposed upon each other by the warring sides in Spain's Civil War. Nevertheless, the random tides of battle had left their position dangerously exposed. From Titulcia, the enemy lines extended on the Irish right towards Ciempozuelos, curving around to approach within five hundred metres of its southern perimeter. Attack from this quarter – especially at night – had to be regarded as a constantly impending event. To the north, the Nationalists occupied the centre portion of the Vega del Jarama, thus dominating both banks of a wide, fertile plain which spreads out as the river, replenished by the Manzanares, flows due south from Madrid. But, for their part, the Republicans had held on to the right bank of the river in a sector further downstream, where it pushes through a much narrower gap in the hills towards Aranjuez – a defile known as the Cuesta de la Reina.

With the enemy in such close proximity, the dangers of sniping were added to regular – sometimes heavy – bouts of shelling. Most accounts of life in Ciempozuelos mention the ever-present fear of snipers, and regular operations were mounted against them. Full protection was impossible, for any number of semi-ruined buildings on the outskirts of town provided potential nests for enemy sharpshooters. However, the only actual casualty sustained was Tom McMullen, who had his leg shattered, allegedly by an explosive bullet. A further harassment came with the occasional incursions of an enemy-armoured train into no man's land. This unusual vehicle of armoured assault was a major weapon in the republican armoury.[27] Fitted with trench mortar and heavy machine-gun, it was a constant nuisance, running out from the Tajuña valley, its approach hidden by random folds of hills or the unharvested vegetation in the valley.[28]

By now, a duty rota had been established whereby the *Bandera*'s four companies shared the manning of defensive positions. Each company spent two days on duty in each of the lines – front line, secondary line and rear (i.e. the town itself). They moved forward in sequence from the last of these duties to the first; the seventh was a rest day.[29] Even without contingencies arising and other extra fatigues, this was a demanding routine. The strain and discomfort of line duty was exacerbated by the fact that the weather had broken again. Central Spain was enveloped in one of the wettest springs in living memory. More than four weeks of intermittent and often heavy rainfall seems to have been linked to a huge meteorological depression affecting the whole of Atlantic Europe in February–March 1937. One republican news-sheet, exploiting the opportunity for an ironic reference to the policy of non-intervention, remarked on 'bad weather in England; storms in Wales; downpours in Ireland; heavy tides on the coasts; fog in everyone's eyes'.[30]

While the folks back home imagined their boys (at least) to have escaped the bad winter in sunny Spain, in practice the *banderistas* led a miserable existence in the sodden clay trenches. Little weatherproof protection was available and, given that both the quality and quantity of food rations was poorer than all but the poorest volunteer's normal diet, the hospital list mounted steadily.[31] If the men had been bored in Cáceres, many must have wished those relatively diverting days would come again. Legionaries exhausted after their six-day stint of duty had at least the opportunity to spend the seventh day in the scripturally appointed manner, and in the relatively comfortable billets provided by those domestic dwellings intact enough to offer shelter against the rain. However, this was also the only period when alcohol was freely permitted. In the lines, the wine ration was mixed with water, since the immediate area – as the name Ciempozuelos ('a hundred little wells') poetically indicates – was rich in natural water supply. But the seventh days saw little exploitation of these latter riches by the Irish garrison.

As the XV *Bandera* dug in at Ciempozuelos, and the whole nationalist army did so along the line, the German auxiliary force moved one of its batteries of 88-millimetre guns into a wooded depression between Ciempozuelos and Valdemoro. After a visit to the Irish quarters and negotiations with O'Duffy, General von Thoma, the unit's commanding officer, formally requested Franco's agreement that the Irish provide a regular guard for the gun site. A platoon was constantly assigned to this duty thereafter. Although the request was accompanied by a certain amount of flattery concerning Irish fighting qualities, this was appreciated more by the officers than among the rank and file who actually had to discharge this unwelcome extra responsibility.[32]

The horrors of Ciempozuelos

The presence of nuns in Ciempozuelos, and thus of an officiating priest, meant that regular religious services were soon available for the *Bandera*. The official chaplain, Fr Mulrean, was rarely to be seen in the line.[33] Nevertheless, the sanctions of religion and its relationship to the task in hand were never far from the minds of many volunteers. The section on 'Divine Service' was always placed at the head of the day's routine orders, which Matt Beckett typed out for Pat Dalton or his adjutant, Diarmuid O'Sullivan, to sign for distribution to the companies. Mass was given every day in the convent chapel.[34] This ground must have been re-sanctified at some point, since all the town's churches had been desecrated and were found to be in a shambles when the Irish arrived. Extant witness is unanimous in recording a sense of disgust at the sight of familiar objects of reverence and devotion found half-destroyed amongst the scattered filth. Sean Roche of Bandon set up a shot of a group of comrades who displayed to the camera some of this sacred detritus. Paddy Smith took home to Ireland a piece of burnt priestly vestment as evidence of communistic evil. Even young Paddy Hickey, who evidently found the act of writing home painful, was moved: 'well, mother, it is terrible to see the way the Reds smashed up the chapels here, it would make your blood boil.'[35] In a similar response to what smacks of an officer's coaching, J. O'Brien wrote home to the supportive press that 'it is terrible to see the churches desecrated, the altars torn down ... The faces in the holy pictures are riddled with bullets. We passed through one town where ten nuns and twelve priests had been executed.'[36] In another similar missive, Sean Roche's colleague in the ambulance corps, Leo McCloskey, commented, 'you should see the chapels here; their altars torn down and burned and the graves dug up and the skulls of the nuns all about the place. It's awful. It would make your blood boil.'[37]

There was little sign of the citizens themselves. Local inhabitants occasionally appeared, members of the better-off families who had managed to escape during the revolutionary terror which had raged the previous summer. They came back hoping to salvage some property or searching for a loved one; but the Moors had made off with anything portable among the former, and the latter had vanished without trace. People were allowed to undertake these fruitless expeditions (it seems) on condition that they exaggerated stories of their sufferings at the hands of the Reds. Irish duty officers listened to interpreters' versions of these tales; these were duly passed on down the line, and subsequently occur, with variations of detail, in a dozen extant accounts.[38]

The town had another presence, even more bizarre and tragic. Since neither side had given much priority to dealing with the problem, the lunatic asylums continued to subsist in the midst of the garrison. Coincidentally, the fate of these institutions had come to the notice of no less a person than the President of the Republic, Manuel Azaña, who was composing a dramatic dialogue about the Civil War and its origins. He makes one of the disputants tell the following parable:

> You all know the little town of Ciempozuelos, near Madrid. There are (or were) two madhouses there. When the enemy attacked Madrid, the town ended up between the lines. One side was unable to hold onto it, and the other unable to capture it. It was isolated in no-man's-land. (I don't know if this situation has changed now.) Someone I know got into the town and found that all its inhabitants had fled. The place was empty – except for the inmates who had broken out of their asylums and were wandering around aimlessly. Nobody but the mad. It seems unnecessary to explain in detail how this sums up our tragedy, but let us extend fact into fantasy for a moment. If the town is taken by the rebels, having heard that the idiots are enjoying their liberty, they will shoot one-half plus one of them and bury the rest alive. If it is taken by the government, they will convene a meeting of the mad, and a representative of the Popular Front will make a speech, explaining that they must be locked up again. But they won't want to be locked up again. So a committee is formed in which the idiots have their delegates, and in due course they agree to allow one-quarter of their number to be locked up. The rest remain at liberty, and in order to safeguard this, the idiots have two seats on the new Town Council. When the time comes to elect a mayor, the councillors quarrel so fiercely amongst themselves that the idiots soon think better of their desire for freedom. They retire with dignity from the proceedings and seek refuge in the asylum.[39]

The town was, as we know, captured by the 'rebels'. The fate of the male inmates is unknown, but it is difficult to ignore Azaña's adventitious assumption. Perhaps, indeed, their bodies provided extra material for the charnel house on the night of 5–6 February. As for the females, ex-Sergeant Joseph Cunningham later recalled the eerie sound of their screams mingling with those of shells during the regular bombardments from enemy batteries. On one occasion it was alleged that a girl had signalled to the enemy 'from an upper room of the psychiatric home attached to the convent … Some women … were evidently active in the interests of the enemy. Female suspects had their hair closely cropped … One morning several lorry loads of these doughty Amazons were seen to leave town, whether for internment camps or execution squads could not be ascertained.' In an aside which may be regarded as curious, Cunningham ascribed the inmates' condition of 'cretinous degeneracy' to 'the natural outcome of the unrestrained circulation of lewd literature during the Azaña regime'.[40]

Thus Ciempozuelos's recent history was one of unrelieved horror, from the beginning of the military rebellion and the social revolution sparked off by it in July 1936, until the moment of its occupation by the Irish. Perhaps the revolutionary killings in the town had not been drawn to the attention of President Azaña: after all, they were by no means unique. A modern authority records the names and professions of the victims of forty-three arbitrary killings which took place in the town and its environs in the summer of 1936. These certainly include some of the clerics in charge of the care of mental patients.[41] On the other side, the nationalist authorities were sensitive about the slaughter involved in its capture, possibly because of the inclusion of psychiatric patients among the victims. When two pro-Franco British journalists visited the Madrid front some time in 1937, they were given the full propaganda treatment, in which the case of Ciempozuelos seems to have been deliberately high-lighted. In a book published in 1938, they dutifully communicated this version to the world:

> The details of the campaign are too voluminous for us to deal with them here: but we must once more relate what they found at the small town of Ciempozuelos ... [This] was one of the small places where Largo Caballero and his friends had created one of the ten thousand Red cells which he boasted they would create throughout Spain. Naturally, the mayor ... was the leading Red of the village ... They were the leaders and instigators ... directly responsible for the atrocities.

According to the scenario elaborated here – fantastic even by the known standards of that summer – events in Ciempozuelos included the hand-ing over of priests 'to lunatics in an asylum who had been given knives' and old men being 'thrown into the bullring to be gored to death'.[42] One of the *Bandera*'s own officers, Lieutenant Noel Fitzpatrick, could have related an equally fantastic story. He had been seconded (apparently against his will) from another Legionary *bandera* and had been present at the fall of Toledo to the Nationalists the previous September. In a writ-ten memoir, consulted in the 1950s by the historian Hugh Thomas, Fitz-patrick recalled seeing the main street of the Imperial City literally running with the blood of republican militiamen who had been unwise enough to surrender to the Moors. Doubtless, he was wise enough to keep his own counsel on such matters, at least outside the officers' mess.[43]

At any rate, it seems reasonable to conjecture that, in order to counter negative feelings among the Irish volunteers, sustained attempts were made to bring home the pitiless brutality of the local Red terror. Perhaps O'Duffy himself complained in Salamanca about the unburied cadavers and the treatment of asylum inmates. It was known that many members of the *Bandera* had already witnessed executions in Cáceres, and none can have failed to notice the bodies littering the streets of Ciempozuelos. Luis Bolín, Franco's head of propaganda, was aware that (like reporters) the Irish would eventually be going home. If the evidence of their eyes could not be fully effaced, at least an attempt could be made to 'set things in context' – that is, to explain and justify them by implicit reference to a Mosaic law. Thus the men were more or less systematically exposed to atrocity propaganda, leading (in addition to the examples already cited) to press copy of the kind which must have made Bolín's task seem worthwhile:

> I have seen a statue of Our Lady with the Infant in her arms and the eyes of both riddled with bullets. I have also seen the cellars of the town full of the dead bodies of priests, nuns and others who were shot for their religion. Most of the girls in this town are in the Asylum after the treatment they got from the Reds.[44]

In Ciempozuelos today, few of the inhabitants have any memory of those dreadful months. The restored main square, which in the year of Franco's death (1975) still bore the *caudillo*'s title, has now been renamed the Plaza de la Constitución. Here, in 1995, I watched well-dressed and well-fed children playing happily with their expensive modern toys in the spring sunshine. The mental institutions, still in clerical care, have been restored and modernised. In contrast, in a side-street, the Church of Our Lady of the Immaculate Conception appears still in a rather poor state. A notice appealed to the passer-by: 'We are not able to continue with our restoration because of lack of funds. Can you help us?' All the same, the main parish church was full for mid-day Sunday Mass.[45]

The March attacks

After a long and uneventful month, the Irish were suddenly alerted for imminent action. On 8 March, the battle of Guadalajara had begun. It was intended as an offensive conducted exclusively by the Italian expeditionary force sent by Fascist Italy to help the Nationalists. The *Corpo Truppe Voluntaria* was a self-sufficient force which by this time had been built up into an army group of more than forty thousand men. Franco had succumbed to Mussolini's insistence that his men should have the glory of the main breakthrough to the north-east of Madrid, but the overall plan included a simultaneous move by General Orgaz on the

Jarama front, the aim being for the pincers to meet in the general area of Alcalá de Henares. In the event – for reasons which remain imperfectly clear – Orgaz failed to move at the appointed time. Attacking in appalling weather conditions, yet largely dependent on motorised elements, Roatta's army bogged down, and the Republic counter-attacked. The following week provided the latter with its first unequivocal victory of the war, and brought outright humiliation to the Italians.

On 12 March the nationalist Army of the Centre belatedly entered the fray with the first of a series of attacks on the Jarama. All these operations, although heavy in places, were intended as diversionary or, at best, as exploratory. Their main objective was to persuade the enemy not to send reinforcements to the Guadalajara sector.[46] On 12 March, the XV *Bandera* received orders to attack in full strength at dawn the following day, apparently with the stated objective of taking the village of Titulcia on the opposite heights. Few accounts of the operation, even those given many years later, betray suspicion that they were engaged in a merely diversionary attack.[47] All concerned accepted that Titulcia was a 'hard' objective and (implicitly) that they were involved in an autonomous and open-ended offensive. But even had this been the case – and even by the high standards of the Tercio – the capture of Titulcia would have been an amazing achievement. Apart from its physical location on the crest of a cliff which towered 150 feet above the river bank, the place had been heavily fortified, was bristling with machine-guns (some posts being mounted in caves on the cliff-face), and garrisoned by elements of the elite communist 11th Division.[48] Even had the Irish realised the chance to fulfil their vow of fighting against the Reds, it seems doubtful that they would have properly appreciated the honour. Not far behind the enemy positions, in the valley of the Tajuña, and ideally sighted from positions in Titulcia, were the main republican artillery batteries for the southern Jarama sector.

Two other factors must be mentioned before the events of the day are narrated. About a week before the attack, the *Bandera* had lost its Commanding Officer. Major Dalton was taken ill, and within a remarkably short space of time returned to Ireland. He was replaced as acting Officer Commanding (OC) by Captain Diarmuid O'Sullivan. The weather conditions on the day of the operation were as bad as any prevailing during the watery weeks described above.[49] The required advance lay across a waterlogged valley floor, in which physical movement was difficult. Between the starting point and the heights extended a mile of open terrain, crossed by two separate waterways – a canal, and the swollen river Jarama itself.

On 13 March, Alec Cummings, a Welsh officer in the British Battalion of the International Brigade, recorded in his diary: 'We are flooded out. [We] shout slogans [and] sing. Heavy fire, specially on [our] left flank.'[50] The gunfire he heard was republican artillery pasting the Irishmen as they attempted to cross the valley some eight kilometres south of the British positions. The engagement had been opened, as usual, by a detachment of Moors. On this occasion, however, it was not the fearful infantry but a cavalry company which swept around the Irish right and into the Tajuña valley – probably with the aim of reaching the gun batteries.[51] The valley opening was veritably a mouth of death. The *spahis*, their mounts struggling for a footing in the sodden ground, were scythed down by machine-gun defences. The few survivors were straggling back as the first two companies of the XV *Bandera* (about 350 men) went over the top.

'It rained all day like I never saw rain so heavy,' as Frank Fitzgerald put it – a powerful testament coming from a Limerick man.[52] To observers, it seemed that the enemy barrage was even more saturating and, as the day wore on, the watching O'Duffy resigned himself to a dreadful casualty list. Progress on the ground was meagre. Most men seem to have crossed the canal, and sections of A and D Companies got as far as the river bank. One witness claims to have been amongst a group which gained and crossed a bridge over the Jarama before it was blown up by mines.[53] In addition to several less credible adventures from the day, Fitzgerald apparently helped to save a man named Whittle from being swept away in the river.[54] Moss Fennell's experiences seem more typical, and his comments, made in cool reflection many years later, are both sensible and plausible.

> We were caught out in the open. We did manage to cross over the canal, in spite of heavy enemy fire. Between the canal and the River we had to cross heavy marshy ground, covered with reeds and high grass. We made the best of this cover by crawling forward unseen by the enemy who estimated we were retreating under their fire and kept up a creeping barrage to our rear. We took a fair hammering, but the fact that the rain poured down all day, and had turned the ground into a quagmire helped instead of hindering us. The shells and mortars went deep into the ground before they exploded, and consequently the fragmentation, to a great degree, was buried deep into the earth.[55]

A German artillery officer, Major Recke, who watched events alongside O'Duffy, asserted he had never seen such accurate shell fire. Indeed, an enormous artillery battle now began to develop, taking some pressure off the infantry. As Sergeant Joe Cunningham recalled:

The enemy barrage was so intensified that advance through the rushes of the Grove was veritably funereal. By 10.30 a.m. the more resonant rumble of the German guns, seven miles away in Valdemoro thundered in support of the attack. Chinchón roared its reply by shelling the German base. In all, five batteries were now engaged, three of the enemy and two of our own.[56]

Helping to pin down the attack, the armoured train now trundled out from behind Titulcia. This time, however, its intended victims were prepared. The previous night had been spent by a volunteer party working out in the valley to mine the railway track. Though the plan worked imperfectly, failing to destroy the train itself, the explosions on the line frightened the enemy into premature retirement from the fray.[57] This success brought little benefit. The whole *Bandera* had become literally bogged down, encumbered by extra equipment, such as makeshift boats and material for pontoon construction; the mules were useless in the mud; they were unable to bring heavy machine-guns to bear, even had they been brought up; the situation was hopeless. Once darkness supervened, O'Sullivan ordered a carefully phased retreat. That night, the Republicans claimed victory: 'Today has been completely felicitous for the fortunes of our arms. On the Jarama front our artillery has pounded into defeat the enemy concentrations which tried to break our lines. Today has written a glorious page in the defence of our cause.'[58]

Indeed, so many shells fell in the Jarama valley on the day that (perhaps in compensation for their failure) the Irish later made much of an alleged enemy claim that they had destroyed the XV *Bandera* completely. However, as the platoons were counted back into the shelter of Ciempozuelos, it emerged that casualties were unexpectedly light. At the end of the day of battle itself only one man had been killed outright, with nine others wounded; though during the subsequent week three of the latter also died.[59] Much worse seemed to be impending. As the men tried to dry themselves, clean equipment and get some rest, orders arrived that the attack upon Titulcia must be renewed without fail at dawn the next day.

At a council of war held during the night of 13–14 March, General O'Duffy, if with reluctance, seems at first to have been inclined to carry out his orders. However, it soon became clear that several Irish officers disagreed. Among the dissenters, Captain Thomas Cahill (who had succeeded O'Sullivan as OC of A Company) stood out for his outspoken opposition to any renewal of the offensive in the conditions prevailing. Faced with this feeling, O'Duffy spent the night and early morning attempting to ascertain whether his men would be guaranteed the air and flank assistance that had not been forthcoming the day before. In this quest he was (presumably) assisted by the chief staff liaison officer, the Duke of Algeciras. No satisfactory assurances had been received by the time the attack was scheduled for renewal, and accordingly General O'Duffy called off the whole operation.

However, both the general's published account and his personal comportment were strongly questioned in the memoir later published by Sergeant Joseph Cunningham. According to O'Duffy, he and all his officers (Irish and Spanish) were from the first unanimous in their opposition to the unwelcome order. He nevertheless instructed the *Bandera* to be readied to attack as ordered, whilst he drove to the headquarters of his nearest superior officer, General Saliquet, fifteen miles away. This officer duly authorised O'Duffy to ignore the earlier orders and abandon the operation. Within the week, at Navalcarnero, he met Franco in person, on which occasion the *generalísimo* appeared to endorse Saliquet's decision.[60]

The countervailing submission runs as follows. Following the retreat on the night of 13 March:

> it was early apparent that all was not well with the higher commands. Dissension was rife and acrid speculation was indulged in as to the issue of the trouble. Lieutenant Tom Cahill … was animatedly objecting to leading men on what must certainly be a fruitless expedition. Cahill, from the arrival of the Brigade in Spain, had shown himself to be the soldier's friend … His objections on March 14th were actuated by no self-interest but from a fine assessment of the position around Titulcia. His arguments were seemingly too much ad hominem for two days later Tom was removed from the lines (or else resigned his commission). The 'Irish Independent' later reported his return to Ireland as due to 'sickness'. We know it was due to over-strength.[61]

Cunningham himself, as quartermaster-sergeant of C Company, seems not to have participated in the attack, and neither would he have been present at the officers' council of war. He thus heard Cahill's story from the man himself or from a third party. However, whilst Cahill's role may be exaggerated in this version, he is not even mentioned by O'Duffy in connection with these events. As leader of A Company, Cahill would have been in the thick of things on 13 March. Perhaps he had been confronted with the moment when (according to a hostile witness) 'our ranks hesitated and wavered when men began to fall'; a moment that quickly turned into 'a mad scramble [as] panic seized the *bandera*'.[62] Cahill certainly vanished from the scene soon afterwards; he had either been cashiered or had resigned.

Other interrogatives may be posed against the leader's account. It seems unlikely that the *Bandera*'s Spanish officers would have advised in the sense O'Duffy implied. On the contrary, they could hardly have failed to urge the Irishmen to obey orders. By retreating to previously held positions, the *Bandera* had already offended against a fundamental principle of nationalist strategy, stemming from the *generalísimo*'s personal order, that no ground, once gained, should be given up under any other conditions than imminent annihilation. This approach was subscribed to a *fortiori* by the Tercio. In many other engagements throughout the war, Legionary *banderas* suffered casualties in excess of 75 per cent in taking or holding positions, and had to be ordered from the lines in order to avoid actually being wiped out. So axiomatic was this commitment that (on one reading) it seems the nationalist *partes* for the 13 March simply assumed that the advance positions reached along the river had indeed been held: 'In the Jarama sector, despite the storms, we have carried out an interesting advance, occupying enemy positions in the Pingarrón area, the enemy lines being pushed back more than three kilometres. Many enemy have been captured along with munitions and armaments.'[63]

Finally, one must read between the lines of O'Duffy's account. He never actually states that his refusal to obey orders issued for 14 March was sanctioned by either Saliquet or Franco. Arguably, both men merely accepted that, in the circumstances which its leader had (both consciously and inadvertently) brought to their attention, any further action by the XV *Bandera* was likely to be counter-productive.[64]

With the Irish Brigade now standing by, diversionary attacks continued in other sectors of the front for several more days. On 14 March itself, slightly to the Irish left, a Moroccan *tabor* stormed the enemy trenches. They hit on a section of the line manned by fresh conscripts, who (not surprisingly) beat a hasty retreat. Elements of the Lincoln Battalion, including the Irish company led by Bostonian Paul Burns, plugged the gap – at an appalling cost in casualties.[65]

On 17 March, Franco paid his second surprise visit to the Irish Brigade. Although the moment was carefully timed, he had not chosen the date in order to join them in celebration of their national day. The *generalísimo* was engaged on a rapid tour of the whole front, but he seems to have swooped on Ciempozuelos in the knowledge that O'Duffy was not present, hoping to avoid any embarrassment in carrying out his mission. He needed to discover for himself what had happened on 13–14 March, and to assess the future battle-worthiness of the XV *Bandera*. He obviously interviewed the Spanish liaison staff and (though this is undocumented) may also have spoken to some or all of the Irish officers – probably at a separate meeting. Matters could hardly have been worse to the *caudillo*'s eyes. *Banderistas* present in the town were marking St Patrick's day with an appetite sharpened by recent efforts in the field. Whatever he said to O'Duffy when they met shortly afterwards in Navalcarnero, it seems unlikely that Franco remained as impressed with his Irish adherents as he had been when he reviewed them in Cáceres.[66]

In sight of Madrid

> I suppose you saw in the papers about some of our fellows being killed it was pretty tough as they were very nice chaps, our Company was leading the attack that day and not one was hurt, we are up beside Madrid now we can see it in the distance it look very big from where we are.[67]

Early on 23 March, less than a week after the *generalísimo*'s inspection, the Brigade was pulled out of Ciempozuelos. The forward trenches were formally handed over to an Italian infantry unit by Captain Padraig Quinn at 5.30 a.m.[68] The Irishmen piled into trucks which rumbled off northwards. Many were in buoyant mood, expecting a good period of leave. But before midday the convoy had arrived in the tiny hamlet of La Marañosa, the northernmost section in the Jarama salient. The men were immediately deployed on the higher ground which loomed behind the single street. At the crest, they found their new trenches, extending along the ridge in each direction. Far below them, meandering among olive groves and scrubland, twinkled the river Manzanares. To the left, the hill called the Cerro de los Angeles, geographical centre of the peninsula, could be picked out. On its summit stood the national shrine of the Sacred Heart. It now constituted the main nationalist redoubt in this sector, having been the scene of bloody contests a few months before. On the horizon, some of Madrid's streets and tallest buildings could be clearly discerned.

Despite its unpretentious size, La Marañosa was not an unimportant sector. A kilometre or so to the south-east was a chemical works of some significance; whilst not far to the Irish right was the highly exposed corner of the whole salient, the furthest point reached by the Nationalists in the opening days of Jarama.[69] Though Franco had ruled out offensive action here for the time being, it does not follow that the Irishmen had been moved to a less demanding position. Indeed, occupying the Irish left was a battalion of *requetés*, the fanatically Catholic Navarrese militia, who were regarded as second only to the Legion in terms of effectiveness in battle. Until a few weeks before, the Anglo-Irishman Peter Kemp had been serving with this unit as a second-lieutenant. His battalion held this flank position during the battle of Jarama, and was kept busy in repulsing the republican counter-attacks of 17–19 February.[70]

Kemp corroborates two uncomfortable features of their new sector which were new to the Irish. The first of these was regular attacks by enemy fighter planes, which were able to fly low, strafing along the (more or less) straight lines of trenches. Luckily for the defenders, this technique was still in its infancy, and no serious casualties were incurred.[71] Occasionally, nationalist planes would appear and drive off these pests; at times, too, dogfights in the skies above Madrid could be observed.[72]

Potentially more serious in its consequences was the almost total lack of water supplies – in stark contrast to Ciempozuelos. 'Our chief discomfort [recalls Kemp] was lack of water, for there was no local supply and all our water had to come from Pinto in lorries; there was barely enough to drink, none for washing. The wine, though not scarce, was atrocious.'[73] By now, the Irish had managed to surmount their original distaste for wine, to the extent that many were in no wise embarrassed by reservations of the P. Kemp (BA Cantab) category. Problems were exacerbated by the change in the weather, the cold spring now giving place to a typically sweltering Castilian summer. One of the NCOs' chief preoccupations was the safe delivery of water tanks, in order to maintain both the sobriety and the bodily health of their men. Denis Reynolds recalls the priority attached to protecting this service, and the consternation caused when one delivery was lost during a barrage.[74] Another volunteer got so desperate for a wash that one night he went alone into no man's land and down to the river for a skinny-dip.[75] Yet another was sent out in a detail to search for local water sources in the countryside. They succeeded in finding a well, but elation quickly turned to chagrin and horror on discovering it had been turned into the stinking sepulchre of what appeared to be a whole family from a nearby farmhouse.[76]

After a week at La Marañosa, Pat Hickey wrote home that 'we are getting it pretty easy out here at present it is very quiet'.[77] In contrast, Seamus McKee had the impression that, on the military side, life was more hectic than at Ciempozuelos.[78] If Franco was not entertaining ideas for an advance, the enemy did not take his restraint as representing an armistice. In April, following the opening of the campaign in the Basque country, activity opposite the Irish lines increased. It was now the Republic's turn to launch diversions, in order to harass the Nationalists' conduct of the northern campaign. An infantry assault was made against the La Marañosa sector just before dawn one day in April, but was repulsed with ease. The terrain immediately in front of the defenders' trenches was steeply angled and their line of fire was clear. Moreover, the Irish had the benefit of the assistance not only of the Carlists to their left, but also of the Moors to the right. Once the attack had been broken, the latter pursued the fleeing enemy down the hillside with their traditional war-cry of 'Allah'.[79] To add to enemy distress, their artillery barrage – doubtless because of the poor light afforded to range-finders – fell short, and caused havoc among the attacking lines. One veteran saw enemy soldiers shooting down officers who were attempting to stop the rout. It was a success fully relished in the Irish line after the frustrations of Ciempozuelos.[80]

This incident came to relieve the mounting pressures of boredom, heat, dirt and sickness. By this time, about a third of *Bandera* strength was on sick parade, and over a hundred men actually hospitalised.[81] Various sources pay tribute to the two Irish doctors, who were the most overworked members of the staff. Despite his busy life in the medical section, Sean Roche continued to utilise his Brownie camera for snaps of life in La Marañosa. In particular, he recorded the consolations of religion, which were available in a particularly moving form. The presence of the Carlists meant that Mass was said frequently by their padres at altars carved out of the counter-escarpment of the hillside. A field Mass was evocative for any Catholic Irishman conscious of national history. O'Sullivan (now promoted to major) wrote home that 'it is a glorious sight and carries one back through the pages of Irish history, to our forefathers' fight for the Faith at home and in Penal Days'.[82] One veteran remembers an open-air Mass being said to receive a Protestant comrade (Sergeant Cadell) into the majority confession of the *Bandera*. During the service the young Basque priest officiating was killed by a stray piece of shrapnel.[83]

According to O'Duffy, the chief *requeté* chaplain – a Jesuit – made prodigious efforts to learn English in order to respond to the loyalty and friendship of his Irish parishioners.[84] For their part, the Irish felt a favourable omen in the fact that fate (in their own vocabulary, God) after all intervening vicissitudes, had brought them to fight shoulder to shoulder with the Carlists. It had been through this movement, and with the intention of allying with it, that O'Duffy and his Spanish backers had originally conceived the Irish Brigade. Fraternal regard for the Navarrese soon developed into a wish, expressed by some of the officers, that attempts be made formally to affiliate the Brigade with the Carlist army (and, thus, to leave the Tercio).[85] Many had come to realise that the Foreign Legion was basically a secular – even, in some respects, a pagan – outfit, with ideals that were alien to their culture and little to do with crusade. Doubtless a feeling aided by the experience of 13–14 March, they were no longer conscious of the honour of El Tercio and would prefer to leave it. As it happened, the feeling was mutual amongst the high command of the Legion itself.

5

Crisis and collapse

The home front

Reduced in effective numbers and morale, and with its future more seriously in doubt than even its founder suspected, the XV *Bandera* desperately needed resuscitation. The general picture was not encouraging.[1] Since Málaga there had been no victories, and Guadalajara was an undisguised defeat. There was little sense of being part of a victorious campaign. Indeed, if anything, the reverse feeling obtained – a natural reaction after earlier optimism. Until the nationalist setback of Jarama, it was axiomatic that the Republic was destined to a rapid defeat, and that the Irish Brigade would march into Madrid, sharing the triumph of 'the general cause'. Moreover, hope had long subsisted that help was at hand, and in the most tangible shape – reinforcements. A second batch of volunteers, large enough to constitute a separate *bandera*, was soon to leave Ireland. In the interests of team spirit, officers encouraged men to look forward to the arrival of a fresh unit; and optimism gained some substance of reality through the fact that individuals, and even the occasional small group, turned up from time to time at Salamanca or Cáceres, hoping to join their comrades at the front.[2]

In Dublin, Liam Walsh and the staff of the NCP put huge efforts into launching a 'second wave' of the crusade. Speed was of the essence, since the Free State government, in concert with its associate members of the Non-Intervention Committee, was cohering a strategy aimed (*inter alia*) at stemming the flow of volunteers to Spain. In the face of many difficulties, matters were brought to a satisfactory conclusion at the Irish end. On 6 January 1937, an estimated six hundred volunteers filtered into Passage East, near Waterford.

If the choice of venue was a deliberate double-bluff, it failed to put the authorities off the scent. De Valera was on the lookout for these developments, and hoped to prevent them if such could be managed without too much aggravation and negative publicity. There was a strong Gardai presence, but although parties travelling to the Suir estuary were stopped and questioned, no attempt was made to detain them or turn them back. Meanwhile, O'Duffy was on his way to Ireland in order to assume overall supervision of the expedition. At some point in his journey he was apprised of the renewed collapse of his plans. In a faithful repetition of events at the same site less than three months earlier, once again the troopship allocated by Franco for the transport exercise failed to turn up at Passage East.[3]

The general was later informed that the vessel had been commandeered without warning to help the nationalist navy with the Málaga offensive. On shore, 'it was freely rumoured ... that the ship ... was stopped and turned back by two British destroyers which appeared off the Waterford coast'.[4] Though this was a convenient invention, the British and Free State governments were closely in touch over the affair. In Whitehall, Foreign Office under-secretary Shuckburgh took a cutting from the *Daily Mail* which reported 'several hundred men ... preparing to leave Passage in Co. Waterford to embark for Spain and join General O'Duffy's forces'.[5] A Free State cabinet note of the same date reads: 'I am directed by the Minister for Industy and Commerce to refer to the recent newspaper reports of the embarkation of Irish volunteers for Spain ... and to enclose ... a note respecting the detention of vessels which indicates that the Minister's power in this matter is limited.'[6]

The disappointed party included men who had already failed to gain transport to Spain on (at least) one occasion. Some remained determined to join the ranks of the crusaders, especially those who had been among the first frustrated battalion at Waterford. Others were veterans of the *Dun Aengus*, brave men who – having balked on that occasion at the particularly trying conditions – now sought to fulfil oaths taken to get to Spain by hook or crook. A reporter moved amongst them now, as then, to record impressions:

> Six hundred men drawn from practically every county in Ireland kept vigil all through Wednesday night ... A miniature little army ... of all ages and classes. Some of them were 50 years of age, and many were not yet out of their teens. They represented types of the farming class, the labouring class, the tradesman class. There were clerks and expert craftsmen among them ... The condition of the unfortunate men ... was parlous in the extreme. Ill clad, unkempt, hungry and disillusioned, they presented a sorry sight ... All available shelters were requisitioned but the majority could find no place to lay their heads.[7]

The general's journey home was not entirely wasted. Some ground was recuperated when negotiations to take a group of Dublin men to Spain to act as regimental band for the *Bandera Católica* came to fruition. The Irish Pipe Band organised by St Mary's Parish arrived in Cáceres in late January, some twenty strong.[8] O'Duffy was delighted, since complaints had been made that his men were unable to march to the music played by the Legion's own bands. O'Duffy's persistence was a boost for Irish morale. Moreover, his little triumph may have been all the sweeter since Franco, always sensitive to the slightest demonstration of autonomy, had at first decided that 'there is no necessity for such a band of musicians', ordering that its members would have to serve in the trenches alongside the others.[9] Despite the *generalísimo*'s disapproval, the band was able to perform, to expatriate ethnic satisfaction and amidst considerable local interest, on various occasions, both triumphal (the 'passing-out' parade in Cáceres on the completion of training) and elegiac (the funeral obsequies of those killed in action).

As these events suggest, the home front had not relapsed into quietude in the absence of the warriors themselves. After six months Ireland remained obsessed with the war in Spain. To judge by the number of public events – demonstrations, lectures, special church services – the issue was never far from the popular mind, and was the subject of constant discussion on race-courses and golf-courses, in clubs and pubs. Of course, the newspapers constantly stimulated this appetite. Two or three dailies now had correspondents in Spain. In addition to Gertrude Gaffney – rumoured to be the mistress of the *Independent*'s 'forceful and Catholic' editor, Frank Geary – there was Lionel Fleming, sent to cover the war by the equally forceful but less Catholic *Irish Times* boss, Bertie Smyllie, who told his man, 'I don't give a bugger what your conclusions are, as long as they are honest.' As a result, Fleming filed an admirably objective series of stories and analyses, for which the *Irish Times* suffered the loss of much Catholic advertising custom.[10] Much more to the taste of the 'clerical interest' and the public at large was the attitude of the *Irish Independent*, which continued to print atrocity stories, verbatim reports of pro-Franco speeches, and all the news it could get about the boys on the Madrid front.[11]

If public interest had subsided at all, news of the deaths in action of Tom Hyde and Dan Chute quickly revived it. On 28 February, a Mass was offered for the repose of their souls in a packed Dublin Pro-Cathedral, attended by Patrick Belton, leader of the ICF, and his fellow-TD, P. S. Doyle, who were pictured leaving the church on the front page of the

Independent. The same day, a meeting of 'key officers and men of the Irish Brigade in the Homeland' held under Walsh's chair, resolved to keep up the domestic campaign 'in support of Christ and his Church in Spain'.[12] Later that month, Captain Walsh was pictured packing a large box of shamrock, donated by well-wishers, which it was intended to send to the Madrid front.[13] The blood of martyrs was equally fruitful in other, hitherto less fertile, fields, for on 27 February the *Cork Examiner* made its most committed subscription to date. Under the rubric 'Non-Intervention' its leader stated:

> There cannot be the smallest doubt as to where the sympathies of the overwhelming majority of the Irish people lie in this unhappy Spanish conflict. They all sincerely hope for the sake of European civilization and for the ultimate security of their religion, their families and their homes that General Franco will win … They are willing to do all they can to help what they rightly believe to be the cause of Christianity. There are even thousands of young Irishmen who are eager, if they are afforded the opportunity, to spill their blood in the fight against the minority Government of the Reds. The tragedy of the affair is that for the few brave men we can send, a score will be despatched by the nations that debase the sacred name of democracy by covertly and overtly supporting the camarilla that has unloosed infamies against religion.[14]

Doubtless, part of the *Examiner*'s inspiration was increased activity within the pro-republican lobby. Activists had a reasonably secure base in the North, whence Sean Murray, Communist Party of Ireland (CPI) secretary, had recently retired. The British Labour Party leader in the province, Harry Midgley, also continued to fight the issue, despite furious opposition in his constituency, claiming that 'the Civil War in Spain is being deliberately conducted by Fascists against women and children'.[15] The IRA Congress scored a propaganda coup by bringing over a Basque priest, Fr Laborda, who had some English and a convincing presence. With speeches in Dublin and Belfast, Laborda rightly countered suggestions – tendentiously made by Dr Walter Starkie – that most Basques were suffering under the Red terror and secretly praying for a Franco victory. He revealed to large audiences that his Catholic countrymen were not even clandestine supporters of the 'Christian cause', but patriotic democrats resisting obliteration by a monolithic, militarist 'Spain'. In Belfast, the meeting carried a resolution 'repudiating the Fascist followers of O'Duffy as representing Ireland, North or South'. The *Irish Independent* counter-punched, noting that a crowd of Queen's University students had been ejected from Laborda's meeting for shouting 'Up Franco'.[16] Earlier, the *Independent* had noted equally encouraging news from the other end of the social spectrum:

> Mr Charles McCleneghan (Chairman) and Mr W Trainor (Secretary) have handed their resignations to Derry branch of the National GMWU. They have done so, they state, as a protest against ... the action of the National Exec. in sending a subscription to Spanish Reds. Mr McCleneghan expressed the view that the issue in Spain was not a matter of religion but one of Christianity.[17]

Determined to exploit the sympathy evoked by the self-sacrifice of Hyde and Chute, Walsh (with Geary's collaboration) now launched a new propaganda drive to whip up financial support for the Irish Brigade. Readers of the *Independent* were urged to form local groups of fund-raisers, to send money regularly, and to purchase specially manufactured 'Harp badges' (at 6*d*. each) modelled on those which the warriors themselves wore on their uniforms. A cut-out application form soon appeared for the use of subscribers. Walsh asked readers to wear harp badges in their lapels, since 'whilst it is not possible for all of us to fight in the service of Christ against the forces of the devil in Spain, all of us can show practical proof and appreciation'. The newspaper took to carrying the boldly highlighted exhortation:

> Irishmen and Irishwomen at Home
> Remember the Irishmen in Spain.[18]

But there was another, growing problem affecting precisely those left at home. Hundreds of volunteers' dependants were by now suffering from neglect. No evidence suggests that Walsh was able to alleviate their plight, even with notes raised from seductive harp badges. Amongst those affected was Eamon Horan's family in Tralee. His wife was forced to apply for public assistance, and the humiliation of the Kerry crusader must have been exacerbated by the fact that the application was rejected.[19] A similar case was that of Mrs J. Doyle (Castlecomer), who 'states that she and her three small children are absolutely destitute ... Doyle is an ex-captain in the National Army and is in receipt of a pension of £39.2*s*. 5*d*. p.a. ... But as he has made no arrangements ... no portion can be made available for his wife.'[20] Given the (presumably above-average) economic circumstances of Horan and Doyle, this indicates even worse circumstances among many other families. And given their political standing, the fact that the NCP seems to have been unable to help speaks volumes for the fate of the rest. An example of the latter was Martin Bradley's family in Ballinasloe, Co. Galway, who were evicted from their council cottage by the UDC with seven weeks' rent (£1. 3s. 4d.) outstanding.[21]

Meanwhile, Belton and his allies again attempted to focus pro-Catholic feeling on the defeat of the government, with the aim of obliging de Valera to abandon both non-intervention and recognition of Republican Spain. But the premier's mind was set the other way. In mid-February, in conformity with decisions arrived at by the Non-Intervention Committee, the Free State proposed to introduce a package of legislation – amongst it, measures which would render any attempt to reinforce O'Duffy unequivocally illegal. The situation was replete with ironies: whilst Belton, along with the official opposition, Fine Gael, and various splintered remnants of the Blueshirts, called on the sanction of the One, Holy, Catholic and Apostolic Church, de Valera implicitly summoned up the backing of the British Empire, of which he had once been the hunted and inveterate enemy. His present enemies at home would have roundly approved an estimation of him which later appeared in the Spanish anarchist paper: 'De Valera is no longer the captivating figure of the revolutionary epoch, when at the head of the Sinn Feiners he struggled against London ... Once in power, he converted himself little by little into an absolute dictator.'[22]

The dictator's policy adviser, Joe Walshe, had earlier assured Whitehall that the Free State would adopt any measure decided on by Baldwin's government intended to prevent further transport of volunteer troops. The ostensible objective was to preclude the possibility of a direct confrontation between Irish Blueshirts and English Communists.[23] Shuckburgh drafted a form of words to be used in a public statement by Foreign Secretary, Anthony Eden: 'It would be particularly unfortunate if U.K. Communists found themselves fighting against Irish Catholics.'[24] In fact, what more genuinely worried de Valera (after all, Irish Catholics and British Communists squared up every Saturday night in Glasgow, Liverpool and Manchester) was the possibility that the Irish Civil War might be fought out once again, this time in Madrid, and under the eyes of the world's press – perhaps, worse scenario of all, with the same result.

By the end of 1936, Eden had resolved to comply with the Non-Intervention Committee by enforcing an Act – on the statute-book since 1870 – which forbade British citizens to enlist in the armies of any other warring nation. By interpreting anomalies in the existing bill in a sense specifically relevant to the Spanish War, volunteering was to be made illegal. Whilst this let the British government off the hook of prolonged and divisive legislative procedures, similar relief was not vouchsafed to de Valera. To regard citizens of the Free State as subject to UK law was impossible for the latter, especially as this would directly conflict with his own rapidly maturing plans for radical changes to the Irish Constitution.

Thus the Free State government could not avoid a confrontation with its opponents on the floor of the Dáil. The 'Spanish Civil War (Non-Intervention) Act' was described in a government memorandum as: 'mainly designed to prevent persons from departing from this country … for Spain in order to take part in the fighting there. Previously, our only method of stopping such persons was by refusing them the necessary passport facilities.'[25] In fact, the Act, due to come into force on 25 February, had a more extensive remit, and in practice allowed de Valera to contribute actively to the undermining of the Irish Brigade. The British government was informed that its Irish partner was 'ready to take the necessary measures to prohibit the enlistment, recruitment, departure from or transit through *Saorstát Eireann*' of any volunteers.[26] On 18 February, the Dáil witnessed its most vituperative debate since the struggle over the Anglo-Irish Treaty fifteen years earlier. By the skin of his teeth, and with the support of the Labour Party, de Valera survived the important divisions.[27] Belton contributed a ranting and rambling diatribe lasting two and a half hours. In contrast, de Valera's comportment in the chamber was of the highest quality, both in terms of cool comment and intelligent tactics. Among the latter was the disarming admission that most Irish people were not supporters of the Republic. Indeed, his preamble to the proposed Act included the nice irenic observation that 'no matter what side in the present conflict one's sympathies may lie, and there can be little doubt on which side is the sympathy of the majority of the people of this country …'.[28]

De Valera's attitudes were hardened by a hue and cry over O'Duffy which had recently broken out in the House of Commons. MPs of various left-wing affiliations had got belated wind of the fact that many of the Irish Brigade had transited to Spain via Liverpool, and now put down some awkward questions. On 19 January, Mr Thorne opened the issue by asking Eden why he had not applied the 1870 Act against O'Duffy's men in Liverpool. Two days later, Mr Mander put Eden's understudy, Sir John Simon, under pressure, asking for an explanation 'why action was not taken under section 7 of the Foreign Enlistment Act, 1870, to prevent British ports being used for the departure of General O'Duffy's Irish

Brigade to fight in Spain'. These and other members went on to demand that the Free State be pressed to give assurance that no further Francoist battalions would leave the British Isles. Simon was again cross-examined by Mr W. Roberts early in February, when Sir N. Stewart-Sandeman (whose inspiration may be obvious) exasperatedly intervened to ask 'what action was taken to prevent people from this island [Ireland] going out to help the Reds?'[29] Undeterred, Roberts later cornered Malcom Mac-Donald (Dominions' Secretary), asking:

> is he aware that within the Irish Free State a former officer in the Free State forces recruited a military expedition to fight against the Government of Spain, and that the expedition is now fighting in Spain; and whether he has made representations to the Free State Government that their obligations under International Law, and as signatories to the Covenant of the League of Nations, are inconsistent with allowing such an expedition to be organised or leave for Spain?[30]

All this was bad news for de Valera, and alerted him to the possibility of even greater embarrassment should the Free State be dragged into the widely publicised squabbles between the Soviet Union (on the one hand) and Germany and Italy (on the other) which had become a regular feature of the Non-Intervention Committee. De Valera now had the legal means with which to asphyxiate the O'Duffy Brigade. In fact, so keen was he to encompass its demise that he could not wait for it to suffocate, and instead began to seek a means of stabbing it through the heart – or rather, as veterans often insist, in the back.

Franco's rationale

In early March 1937, Joe Walshe wrote to Leopold Kerney, the Free State Commissioner in Spain:

> Reports are being received in Ireland that the soldiers of the 15th Tercio (Irish Brigade) of the Foreign Legion are to a large extent discontent with their lot. They complain of the bad food, poor clothing and of their treatment generally. They are said to be poor in physique, and with exceptions, bad soldiers. General O'Duffy is said to have visited his men only on two occasions. Could you ascertain whether there is any truth in these reports?[31]

The content of this document suggests that Walshe's source of information lay within the Tercio itself, and may even be traced to its commanding officer, Colonel Juan Yagüe. A ruthless perfectionist, obsessed with the reputation of his regiment and uncompromising in its defence, Yagüe had been uneasy about the Irish from the start. Before the Civil War, foreigners in the Legion had been limited to about 15 per cent, recruited exclusively as individuals and on merit. Enlistment effectively involved the substitution of a legionary's statehood by the Tercio itself, sole object of communal loyalty. During the desperate assault upon Madrid the previous November, the Legion was critically in need of infusions to replace the enormous haemorrhages of its previous campaigns. As a result of a recruiting drive, many foreigners were enlisted; indeed, later in 1937, a company of several hundred French crusaders ('Compagnie Jeanne D'Arc') was integrated as part of a newly formed *bandera*. But to accept the presence of a wholly 'national' *bandera*, whose members remained foreigners, under their own officers, and deployed only on an autonomous basis, was an evil precedent in Yagüe's eyes. To him, the messy compromise which Franco had accepted – doubtless against his own judgement, bowing to the request of important petitioners, including Carlist leaders, General Mola, Juan de la Cierva and various aristocrats and prelates – was anomalous and unworkable.

Yagüe's reservations can be detected early in the existence of the XV *Bandera*. At one point, he complained that the Irish officers were of poor quality, proposing that any arriving with the second *bandera* should carry written accreditation and better references – 'for the honour of our Fatherland'. Though Franco, as its co-founder and ex-commander, was jealous of the reputation of the Legion as well as that of the Fatherland, on this occasion he resisted his subordinate's entreaty: 'Because of the special circumstances obtaining [he replied] it is not at present convenient to oblige the Irish to produce such documentation.'[32]

In Franco's mind, of course, political considerations were paramount. The *generalísimo* had to cope with the problems of intervention as well as those of non-intervention, and it is doubtful which were the more demanding. He realised that the military contribution of Italy and Germany would be crucial to his ultimate victory. Yet at the same time, in terms of his esteem among Spaniards, as well as his external image, and the global impression of the nationalist cause, he was anxious to underplay his foreign debt as much as he dared. Of course, compared with the shares in Franquismo Ltd taken up by Mussolini and Hitler, the portfolio scraped together by General Eoin O'Duffy was unimpressive. As a world power, the NCP, even when allied with the ICF, did not cut much of a dash. It is hardly surprising that O'Duffy was not invited to the diplomatic conclaves, public demonstrations and private celebrations occasionally held in Salamanca or Burgos to mark the epic alliance of 'the saviours of western civilization'.[33]

Although the Irish had been absolved of responsibility for the tragic events of 19 February, it seems likely that the affair did not endear the Brigade to the nationalist high command. Later, during the Ciempozuelos phase, Franco became increasingly aware that the Irish, by nature and disposition, were simply not fitted for the peculiarly brutal struggle in which they found themselves involved. A long series of negative reactions was bound to have been relayed to Salamanca by liaison officers and interpreters: reactions to the fanatical rules of the Legion and the ruthless requirements of training officers; to the executions of Reds in Cáceres; and, above all, to the carnage on display in the streets upon the XV *Bandera*'s arrival in Ciempozuelos. To these, O'Duffy, always keen to protect his men's interests, regularly (and, no doubt, tediously for his hosts) added complaints about material conditions sent up to him by his officers. Yet, as it was, the XV *Bandera* was proving a costly item for the nationalist exchequer. Unlike Franco's other allies, O'Duffy failed to defray any significant proportion of his army's expenses; the Irish were uniformed, equipped, fed and paid entirely by the *Intendencia Mayor* of the nationalist army. Final recognition that there would be no second *bandera* surely did not come as a severe disappointment in Salamanca.

In this context, the military failure of 13 March was almost certainly decisive. It can hardly be over-emphasised that the record of the Irish Brigade on that day, however understandable to modern sensibilities, and arguably justified by conventions prevailing in western military culture both before and after the Second World War, was wholly unacceptable by the standards of the Tercio. The duty of the legionary in action was Spartan: victory or death. As the printed translations of its 'Code', circulated to all Irish officers and NCOs, pointed out, the Legion 'demands a spirit of abnegation and sacrifice which must be pushed to the very limit'.[34] Legionary *banderas* had performed amazing feats of endurance and courage on the battlefield since the opening campaigns of the Civil War, more often than not being the decisive element in nationalist victories. Their average casualty rate in any given action during 1936–39 was in excess of 50 per cent. When, in addition to the futile efforts of one day, the XV *Bandera* refused a direct order to restore matters on the next, the reaction in Yuncos, Yagüe's HQ near Talavera, can only have been one of outrage. The fact that Titulcia itself had never been a serious target was immaterial; the larger military objective, of which the attack was a part, subsumed this detail.[35]

Leaving to one side the sheer 'otherness' of the Tercio's ethic, Franco
and his military aides had some right to feel dissatisfied, even by the standards claimed for the Brigade by its own leaders and supporters, and subscribed by many individual volunteers. On various occasions,
representative claims were made that the Irish had come to Spain in good
earnest, as crusaders who were prepared to die for their cause. O'Duffy
promised as much to Franco in person, and it can hardly be held surprising if the *generalísimo* took him at his word. On the night of 13–14
March, it was the Irish officers – or, at least, a majority of them – who
decided that the supreme sacrifice was not called for on that occasion. As
far as the rank and file were concerned, this was (and for us today, ought
to be) the end of the matter. But we may not easily conclude in precisely
the same sense in the case of the senior staff and, above all, of O'Duffy
himself. These men had unreservedly pledged their military services and
allegiance to the nationalist high command and its war effort. Though 13
March was a thoroughly uncomfortable and frustrating experience for
all concerned, only one man had actually been killed during the action,
and the overall casualty list was hardly of terrifying proportions. All in
all, the perplexity of O'Duffy's Spanish superiors at his behaviour cannot
be cause for surprise on the part of a military historian, however conscious he or she may be of the fact that the relevant analysis is one involving life and death.

On 24 March, soon after the Irish arrived in La Marañosa, Yagüe
paid the village a visit and interviewed liaison staff. As in the case of
Franco's call at Ciempozuelos, O'Duffy himself was absent, and it is
doubtful if more than a few Irish officers knew of the Colonel-in-Chief's
presence. In a report to Franco apparently drafted on the spot, Yagüe proposed the dissolution of the XV *Bandera*.[36] He wrote to Franco severely
criticising the Irish performance in the 'little skirmish' of Titulcia, adding
'we are making ourselves the pawns of a political manoeuvre by this
Operetta General, which is very dangerous for us'.[37]

Yagüe's basic argument was predictable. As he had warned earlier,
the unit was badly led and officered (*'falta total de mandos profesionales'*)
and this had led to disastrous consequences. Some of the supporting
detail, however, seems at first sight somewhat bizarre.

1. Discipline, already very deficient, has been recently relaxed to the
extent that men go into the trenches in drunken states; disobedience is
common, reaching the point that physical violence is offered to officers
by their men.
2. In the administration of the *bandera* there is little morality, such that

the normal meal schedule is thus: breakfast – coffee; lunch – potatoes with meat; dinner – coffee with milk, rice with milk or marmalade. 3. The military efficiency of this unit is completely null. On the whole, I consider that it is a risk to continue the *bandera*, since the security of the front that they occupy is endangered by their presence. The liaison staff should be consulted on the question of which men might be retained in other *banderas* if they so wish; the others should be sent home.[38]

As implied above, the content of Yagüe's report (and some additional points made by senior colleagues) when placed alongside Walshe's memo to Kerney, suggests some collusion between the nationalist authorities and the Free State government in encompassing the end of the Irish Brigade. The comportment of Leopold Kerney is fundamental here. Since the uprising, Kerney had not actually been based in Spain. Circumstances had forced him to settle at Hendaye, leaving a Spanish *chargé d'affaires* in Madrid. This development meant that diplomatic relations between the Free State and the Spanish government were in practice difficult, a situation aggravated by the latter's physical removal to Valencia in November 1936. At first maintaining proper objectivity, Kerney was slowly alienated from the government to which he was legally accredited. Later that year, a republican agent met the Irish envoy in St Jean de Luz, and 'formed the impression that he was a vigorous enemy of our cause'.[39]

In March 1937 – as part of de Valera's design to scupper the O'Duffy Brigade – Kerney was ordered to investigate the question of a number of under-age Brigaders whose repatriation was being demanded by kith and kin. Since this was a military matter, the envoy elected to go not to Burgos but to Salamanca, where he gained audiences with various influential authorities.[40] It would be surprising if, during this visit, Kerney were not provided with material concerning O'Duffy's expedition which might be mutually useful to the parties, both of which now had an interest in bringing about its quietus. It was becoming steadily more apparent to Franco that the XV *Bandera* represented far more trouble than it was worth. Though by now all thought of rapid diplomatic recognition by the Free State had ended, at least Dublin might collaborate (morally and financially) in finding a solution to this common problem. Yet even as late as the first week of April, despite Yagüe's pressure and the nagging conclusions prompted by his own first-hand inspection at Ciempozuelos, there was still no sign of a decision by the *generalísimo*.[41]

Franco was utterly preoccupied by political and military matters of the highest priority. The crucial campaign in the north, initially directed against the Basque Republic in its Vizcayan stronghold, was about to get under way. Simultaneously, the long-simmering issue of competing 'party' influences within the nationalist camp suddenly boiled to the surface, forcing Franco to act. This too – though of a somewhat different order of importance – was an issue to which he had been putting off resolution. It centred in the tensions between Falangists and Carlists, and the pretensions of the former, under their chief, Manuel Hedilla, to an autonomous voice in policy-making. In the second week of April 1937, fears of an attempted Falangist coup precipitated Hedilla's arrest and the promulgation of the Decree of Unification, incorporating all political entities which had joined the improvised nationalist alliance of July 1936 into a single 'movement' under Franco's leadership. The latter was to be the coping-stone of a one-party state – and Franco's personal dictatorship. During these weeks the atmosphere in Salamanca was tense; such were the feelings amongst powerful individuals, the interests at stake, and the secret conspiracies and alliances formed, that no one could be absolutely sure of the outcome.[42]

In the midst of these developments, apparently before he had made up his mind about Yagüe's recommendation – and perhaps before he had even found time for mature consideration of the colonel's report – Franco received a long letter from O'Duffy in which the latter, too, recommended the disbandment and repatriation of the XV *Bandera*.

Wars within wars

Just as the world of the 1930s was violently divided by war and belief; just as Spain was a paradigm of this global division; just as both warring sides in Spain were divided internally amongst themselves; and even as their own compatriots in the ranks of the International Brigades were divided against each other; so, too, had the Irish Catholic Brigade become bitterly riven by internal feuds and mutual misunderstandings.

The origins of these troubles can be traced to the very birth of the Brigade. No fewer than three of O'Duffy's associates from the Blueshirt days seem to have possessed ambitions to rival him as leader of the Catholic crusade. Only one explicitly revealed these plans – Eamon Cronin, who, after ridiculing O'Duffy's proposals, ended up by making a farcical trip to the peninsula on a similar mission. It seems that Thomas Carew of Tipperary and Eamon Horan of Tralee both believed they could do better than their chief.[43] This situation was exacerbated by O'Duffy's reckless offers of high rank in the Brigade to so many personal adherents, loyalists from his dual careers as army Commander-in-Chief and Police Commissioner. These were made in the early, heady days when it seemed that the general would be leading a private army of five thousand or more to Spain. A key example is the so-called 'advance guard' of SS *Alondra*, which arrived in Spain in mid-November, 1936. In a list dictated to Salamanca, Diarmuid O'Sullivan was designated as 'comandante', Carew as 'coronel', and the eight others all as 'capitán'.[44] In several cases, these represented ranks achieved in the Irish army; few of these men attained such distinction in Spain. Carew was given the rank of staff captain with overall responsibility for discipline (*Vigilancia*). James Finnerty was also appointed to the Staff as captain-quartermaster. David Tormey later succeeded as captain and OC of B Company, whilst Sidney Gallagher became second-lieutenant of A Company. Four others were made NCOs; finally, two others remained in the ranks for the duration.[45]

Disappointments often festered into resentment. Even where O'Duffy could blame the Spanish high command – and, as we have seen, Yagüe took a close interest in the issue – this could not wholly remove the canker.[46] Officers who nurtured jealousies against each other sought to strengthen their personal support and popularity among the men, especially amongst local contingents whom they may have led to Spain. Eamon Horan, who had raised the Tralee party, never even achieved NCO ranking. As local leader of the NCP, Horan had been O'Duffy's 'key man' in the south-west, and the general's inability (or reluctance) to reward him commensurately was to have serious consequences for the Brigade.[47] Even at the time, the *Manchester Guardian* correspondent, Frank Jellinek, who was working in the republican zone, picked up rumours – which seemed to have more than the usual degree of credibility – that the Irish Brigade 'were engaged in a small private civil war, the men from Kerry perpetually wrangling with the rest'.[48]

As if this were not enough, O'Sullivan's promotion to OC in place of Dalton (who returned home in early March) was opposed both by Yagüe and by several of the Irish staff. O'Duffy came under sustained pressure from General HQ to concede the appointment of a Spanish commanding officer, along with the integration of the XV *Bandera* as a fully operational Legionary unit – that is to say, an assault force. The events of 13–14 March intensified his discomfiture and decisively weakened his position. Various Spanish supporters of the Brigade – the Duchess of Tetuán (descended from the O'Donnells), air-force chief General Kindelán, and the ex-London ambassador, Marquis Merry del Val, were rounded up to intercede with O'Duffy.[49] The general rejected all these appeals, and stood by his decision to appoint O'Sullivan. Meanwhile, however, the latter's succession was not confirmed by Franco.

Personal dissensions were exacerbated following the emotional events and heated arguments of 13–14 March. Yet providing a discordant descant to all this unease was O'Duffy's own behaviour. Not often to be seen at the front, he led a separate existence, spending much of his time on tourist trips, visiting aristocratic patrons, attending receptions and socialising with his intimates in Salamanca's Grand Hotel. The creation of a pampered, non-combatant few, an entourage whose members had no connections with the old days and the old struggles, was a severe test of the loyalty of the many. The camarilla consisted of Gunning, Meade (Spanish son of a rich émigré Irishman who was the general's official driver) and Arturo O'Ferrall (also of Spanish-Irish descent).[50] The court favourites all held the rank of Staff Captain and lived on the fat of the land, whilst the field officers froze or sweated in the trenches, with little leave, and then only in backwater towns like Talavera. Little wonder that during the confrontation which developed on the night of 13–14 March, most of them were reluctant to lay their lives on the line. Though no detailed account of this 'mutiny' is available, we know that Cahill was its ringleader, and received majority support; and we can be sure that O'Sullivan and Padraig Quinn vigorously backed their long-time chief, along with the professional Tercio officers, Fitzpatrick and Nangle.

During the La Marañosa posting, men in the trenches began to pick up gossip about bad feeling amongst their superiors. The unease that this caused began to act together with their own discomforts, increasing the decline in morale. At the end of March it was revealed to Salamanca that the journalist Gertrude Gaffney had received a series of letters from crusaders' wives asserting lack of communication from their husbands. Apparently, letters home were either heavily censored or simply never posted. The correspondents wished these complaints to be published in the *Irish Independent*, but Gaffney – despite her obvious sympathy for their grievances – had refrained from this step in the interests of 'the cause'. Franco also received a complaint directly from 'the wife of another Irish soldier' that she received no replies to letters sent to the *Bandera*. She asserted that if the *banderistas* knew the state their families were in – having received none of the aid they were promised when their menfolk volunteered – they would clamour for repatriation.[51]

In the first week of April, Legionary Tom Hayes noted 'startling rumours that we were going back to our HQ in Spain, Cáceres, and thence home to Ireland'. At this point – as his mode of expression indicates – Hayes was one of the majority who, though suffering ordinary doses of homesickness, had entertained no concrete desire to abandon their mission. Only a week later, his mood had decisively changed: 'Bandera cracking up – all men are getting very sick & weak, dozens going to hospital each day … All men sticking it out, thin, worn, pale, half gone crazy on conac and having sleepless nights. Things extremely tough. Great rumours about going home.'[52]

Despite his own rapid removal, the movement initiated by Cahill had gathered momentum and now could not be stopped. On 6 April, Captain Cunningham of D Company resigned his commission and requested repatriation. He had been involved, two days earlier, in a serious incident. The report of liaison officers makes deadly reading: 'On the 4th of this month an Irish officer violently reprimanded a cook who was completely drunk. Another Irish officer intervened in favour of the cook, attacking his fellow officer so violently that wounds were suffered by the latter.'[53]

Sean Cunningham – almost certainly the second officer referred to here – was an ex-IRA fighter from Belfast, one of the oldest volunteers, with many close friends among both officers and men. Under pressure, he was persuaded to reconsider his resignation and to take sick leave, but the dam was now bursting.[54] Tom Hayes noted: 'everybody resigning – officers resigned some weeks ago & bandera is becoming smaller and weaker every day'.[55] Half-suppressed jealousies and divisions, rubbed raw by the privations of two months in the trenches, were no longer controllable. In early April, in a contretemps whose circumstances remain obscure, a group of officers confronted O'Duffy with the alternative of disbanding the Brigade or accepting mass resignations.[56] At the same time, apparently bowing to persistent representations from Kerney, Salamanca demanded action over the repatriation of under-age volunteers, despite the general's assurance that the young men named by Dublin were no longer in the firing-line.[57] This was likely to release a flood of applications from other 'minors', the total number of whom (O'Duffy claimed) ran to three figures. With his command disintegrating, O'Duffy was left with no choice. On 9 April he announced his decision to the *generalísimo*:

> I regret to inform Your Excellency that various officers attached to the *Bandera* have been making shameful efforts to foment discontent and lessen the loyalty of the Irish troops, undermining my authority and position as Chief of the Irish force. I am bound to admit that there are

some Englishmen in the Bandera, along with a few corrupted Irish-men, who have been dismissed from their posts because of their mis-conduct. But with pride I can affirm that 99 per cent of the Bandera remain loyal to the Chief who brought them here from Ireland. The men are dressed in rags, we have no clothes to replace these, and never have I seen even beggars so badly attired, yet they remain as loyal as on the day they left Ireland to fight for the faith of their fathers … I am obliged nevertheless, to accept that unfortunately Your Excellency no longer has confidence in the Irish Bandera. We cannot remain here without your full support, neither can we ask other Irishmen to join us on such a basis … Thus no alternative is left but for me to ask Your Excellency to make arrangements in order to return the Bandera to its homeland.[58]

Homeward bound

Franco's path was now clear. As in so many other crises, things had fallen neatly into his lap. But, as perhaps in some of those other cases too, the denouement was not entirely unscripted. It seems probable that Franco had been waiting for O'Duffy to take the plunge. For not only did Franco know what was happening 'on the ground', within the *Bandera*, he also had access to O'Duffy's private thoughts, in the first instance via Gun-ning and, more recently, through a new addition to O'Duffy's staff. The general was delighted with the acquisition of Captain O'Ferrall, recom-mended to him via one of the diplomats and/or aristocratic patrons by whose attention he was constantly flattered. O'Ferrall was a native Irish-man with Spanish family connections. To some extent, he replaced Gun-ning in O'Duffy's favours, soon becoming the general's private secretary. But the new recruit was an undercover agent working for the nationalist secret service. In these moments, it seems likely that he worked on O'Duffy, revealing the extent and details of Salamanca's disaffection, and prodding him towards a resolution which would anticipate and preclude the humiliation of a unilateral decree by the *generalísimo*.[59]

A few days after receiving O'Duffy's letter (though making no refer-ence to it) Franco announced the disbandment of the XV *Bandera*. Writ-ing to General Orgaz and other military authorities he cited 'the present state in which the *Bandera* exists, and the disagreements and other unpleasant events which have taken place in its ranks' as the major reason for his decision.[60] A day later, examining the copy to be sent to O'Duffy, Franco amended the draft in his own hand, in order to sweeten the pill a little. In this version, the lines quoted above were suppressed, and reference was made to 'the enthusiastic response in Spain to the generous Irish support' which the general had represented. But in other places, Franco did not pull his punches. He mentioned in particular Yagüe's central criticism, the *Bandera*'s 'lack of professional officers' and lamented the 'limitation of its military contribution caused by the differing assessment of battle situations between the Irish command and superior authorities' – an unambiguous pointer towards the failed test of 13–14 March.[61]

Meanwhile, news of O'Duffy's capitulation had got back to La Marañosa. Its arrival occasioned the final breakdown of relations between loyalists and 'mutineers' on the one hand, and between the Irish as a whole and the Spanish officers – now seen as informers – on the other. Two weeks earlier, Captain Botana had reported an incident in which he and three colleagues had been fired on from behind, allegedly by an Irish officer.[62] Then, on 10 April:

> Alférez Xavier de Silva was talking to two Irish officers when the commanding officer [O'Sullivan] came up to him. He said that the Bandera was going to be dissolved and that he wished to leave his post and go straight home. The train seemed too slow – he wanted to get back home at once. He asked Alférez Silva 'which is the nearest port to here?' 'Valencia', answered the Alférez. Then [O'Sullivan] said 'I will go to Ireland, and from there to Valencia, because I am sure that they [i.e. the Republic] are in the right'.

On receiving Silva's report, General Uzquiano, Orgaz's chief of staff in Navalcarnero, immediately ordered O'Sullivan's arrest and replacement as OC. The following night, O'Duffy drove to confront Uzquiano, taking O'Sullivan with him. According to the Spaniard, O'Duffy first enquired why Colonel Yagüe considered Ireland as an enemy, and demanded the reason for his subordinate's treatment. Uzquiano (somewhat tactlessly) replied that discipline had collapsed, the officers punched each other publicly and were always drunk. This set the general off into a tantrum, in which he ranted about the poor treatment of his men by the Spanish army. Uzquiano 'listened without comment to this and many other things until he took his leave, and left brusquely'.[63] Two days later, O'Sullivan arrived in Cáceres, reported to the Military Governor, Colonel Martín Pinillos, and was placed under confinement at the *generalísimo*'s pleasure.[64]

In the weeks after Franco's decision to dissolve the XV *Bandera*, various efforts were made in Salamanca to persuade both him and O'Duffy to change their minds, if only to avoid the propaganda setback which the *Bandera*'s collapse would mean for 'the cause'. The Duchess of Tetuán and Fr McCabe met the general and Captain O'Ferrall in a long and bitter meeting. In a remarkable development, the most prominent intellectual of the Irish right – Desmond Fitzgerald, quite an advance on Paddy Belton if the *generalísimo* had only known it – came to Salamanca to plead with Franco to reconsider.[65] All in vain: the Catholic crusade was over.

On 17 April, O'Duffy visited the men at La Marañosa. 'We heard great news from him,' scribbled Tom Hayes: 'He gave a great speech & he told us we were going home to Ireland forthwith.'[66] This proved an exaggeration. True, the *Bandera*'s relief from their trenches was organised with efficiency, and within a week they were in Talavera, base depot of the Tercio. Here the men were required to hand in their weapons and most other equipment, though allowed to hang on to their uniforms (or, rather, the other way about).[67] At some point a plenary meeting of the Brigade was held. Perhaps, after all, looking for a reason to reconsider matters, O'Duffy insisted on a ballot of the whole *Bandera* on the question of repatriation. But things had gone too far, and the 'contra' lobby failed to muster in double figures. The only other business was the setting up of a Veterans' Association and the election of a relevant committee. This was the final display of unity made by the Irish Brigade. For over two weeks their existence was almost forgotten about in Talavera, and they were moved on only when an enemy breakthrough threatened in the nearby Toledo sector, and accommodation was needed for fighting units being brought up in reserve. On 10 May, they at last arrived in Cáceres, where, considering that their commanding officer was being held under arrest somewhere in the town, they were given a surprisingly warm welcome by Pinillos and his population.[68]

More than five weeks of boredom and tense frustration followed. Two factions were now almost openly established in the Brigade. Despite his knowledge of this, the new chief liaison officer, Captain González Camino, was probably wise in applying promptly to Salamanca for O'Sullivan's release.[69] One cause of trouble having been averted, another quickly supervened. The officers had refused to surrender their personal hand-guns in Talavera, and O'Duffy requested Camino to obtain official approval of this. The reason originally cited was a desire to keep the weapons as mementos of the crusade. When this request was denied, O'Duffy asked that at least the officers be allowed to retain their pistols until the date they are leaving Spain. I consider this necessary for the safety of the Irish Officers while here, and am accordingly placing this recommendation on official record, so that responsibility may be properly placed, if any Irish officer should lose his life consequent upon being deprived of his revolver.[70]

Was the general seriously suggesting that his officers, as a corps, were in danger of deadly assault from the good citizens of Cáceres, or was he perhaps obliquely referring to Red guerrillas? One reading of this bizarre document would bear out other evidence, which suggests that officers were fearful of their safety because of threats made by fellow Irishmen. The two 'mutineers' most at risk (it was later alleged) were Cunningham and Horan.[71] In the circumstances, it was just as well that Cáceres was a garrison town, always full of soldiers and not lacking in military police. Despite muttering and plotting, the lid was kept on the boiling pot, and no serious disturbance was reported. On 19 May, after hearing O'Duffy's letter of thanks for the town's promise to preserve and maintain the sepulchres of the dead *banderistas* in perpetuity, the Town Council once again expressed its approbation of the Brigade.[72] They then addressed themselves to the apparently coincidental flood of applications to open new or refurbished licensed premises.[73]

Despite constant harassment of the authorities from O'Duffy's side and from Captain Camino, arrangements for repatriation were slow in the making. Accommodation was in short supply, since new generations of local conscripts were now being housed and trained in the barracks, and many of the Irish had to live in tents. The Spanish summer had arrived with a vengeance, so this was not a serious deprivation. On the other hand, the weather did not relieve the embarrassed feelings of the Irish over the wretched state of their clothing. The German worsted uniforms had long since begun to disintegrate, and few spares were available. Various remarks made by O'Duffy do not seem to have exaggerated the mendicant appearance of his men, though the officer corps was still capable of turning out well (to judge by photographs from this period).[74] Strenuous efforts were made to find civilian clothing, so that the Brigade would make a presentable showing for the return journey. Ordering a supply of 'suits to be made up from trousers and jerseys', Camino complained to Franco of 'the shortage both of tailors and of spare clothing' in Cáceres.[75] In fact, such resources were scarce all over the nationalist zone, most of the textile industry being in enemy hands. Franco was keen to hasten things along, and dispatched his personal orders direct to the commander of the *Intendencia General.* The latter responded with alacrity, and the required gear was on its way to Cáceres only a week after the Irish arrival.[76]

As previous experience may have led all involved to expect, the main problem holding up departure was finding suitable transport. The plan was to send the Irish back the way many had come, via Lisbon. However, the bulk of the Spanish merchant marine was still in republican hands and every available nationalist vessel was engaged in the Basque campaign, now reaching its decisive stages. Not until mid-June was Camino able to report that a suitable ship had been chartered – which O'Duffy claimed was a result of his own personal efforts.[77] On 16 June, the Brigade put on what Frank Thomas – a Welshman who was the Irish Brigade's last 'recruit' – described as 'a riotous evening in the barracks'. The following morning, the men marched to the railway station and entrained for Lisbon.[78]

Four days later, their ferry, the SS *Mozambique* tied up at the North Wall of Dublin Harbour. The reception on the quayside was strangely muted. Customs officials and Gardai insisted on making a thorough search of all baggage, ostensibly with a view to confiscation of weapons. O'Duffy himself was humiliated by having his suitcase opened in public; several officers were relieved of hand-guns they had brought home as souvenirs. Press photographers took shots and a film cameraman recorded the scenes for Gaumont British News as the men formed up to march into town.[79] They did so, not in the four companies of their Legionary organisation, but in two rival groups of men, of almost equal size, for and against their erstwhile leader. Tom Hayes, now ex-D Company, hailed from Tralee, and – apparently only for reasons of local loyalty – joined the group headed by his local boss, Eamon Horan, along with Thomas Carew and other disaffected officers. His last diary entry records the sad event in the barest possible form: 'June 21st, 2 PM set feet on Irish soil. Left Dublin at 9 PM landed in Tralee 3.15 AM. Tuesday. Big reception in Dublin. Split with O'Duffy.'[80]

However, the initial greetings were to some extent misleading. A large and appreciative crowd had been kept away from the quayside on government instructions, as part of the same process by which the returning crusaders were treated as the potential spearhead of some fanciful fascist invasion. But General O'Duffy's composure was soon restored. Once clear of the dock gates – and although the mutineers refused to follow – the loyalist group was applauded all the way to the Mansion House, where an official reception laid on by the Dublin Corporation and Diocese awaited them.[81] Fervent (if, as they were to prove, largely empty) votes of thanks and appreciation were made by bishops and bosses. Meanwhile, the 'contras' had disappeared into dockland pubs, where their leaders were soon busily swelling the expense accounts of various journalists, foremost among them the assiduous representatives of de Valera's *Irish Press*. Thomas Carew was quoted simply as having remarked that 'we are home because the Irish Brigade was badly led', but Eamon Horan was more forthcoming and in the precise terms which his interviewers most appreciated: 'Instead of returning with honour and renown we return humiliated and disgraced. The responsibility rests with General O'Duffy. We were not long in Spain until we were convinced that it was a political campaign'.[82]

Though with great variations, most of the men, whether pro or contra, were accorded a warm homecoming in their local communities. In Galway town, for example, memories of that emotional night the previous December had not wholly faded. The local press reported on a hero's welcome given to two men who had joined the crusade on the spur of the moment by running up the gangplank of the *Dun Aengus*. Messrs Donoghue and McGrath were interviewed, and concurred in their unstinted praise for General O'Duffy – though admitting that the expedition had been poorly clothed and fed.[83] On the latter theme, the newspaper's Dublin correspondent was honest but sympathetic in observation:

> If the war in Spain had been brought to a successful conclusion by the Nationalists, the welcome accorded the return of General O'Duffy and his Brigade could not have been more cordial or spontaneous than it was when they marched through cheering crowds from the North Wall to the Mansion House on Monday. The General looked as if he has been through a period of very great strain ... Many of the men also looked very tired and worn out ... What struck me most was that nearly every man looked as if he had not seen any sunshine for months ... All appeared very glad to be back again.[84]

6

The reckoning

The issues

Did the Irish Brigade fail? If so, what were the reasons? In his account of the 'crusade', General O'Duffy overtly refused to accept failure. On the surface everything he writes is upbeat and bullish. Yet more covertly woven into his memoir, through techniques of denial, exculpation and excuse, is the constant recognition that he had achieved little more than a brave but futile gesture. Even the final sentences of his book cannot disguise this implication: 'We have been criticised, sneered at, slandered, but truth, charity and justice shall prevail, and time will justify our motives. We seek no praise. We did our duty. We went to Spain.'[1]

There are several levels on which assessment of the Irish Brigade should be attempted. In primary place, surely, must come the military reckoning. No crusade can be seen as a success without tangible victories; or (at least) actions where distinction is reflected, be it only in circumstances of heroic resistance or valiant defeat. It must be clear from the material presented above that the XV *Bandera* did not register success on this level.[2] It took part in only three actions. The first occurred in a negative context, which was bound to cancel out in advance any positive aspects which might otherwise be recognised. (Though it must be recorded that the Irish Brigade was left in possession of the field.) The second was a miserably confused episode, in which only the useless deaths of many more men might – when judged by certain benchmarks – have created a positive outcome in terms of reputation. The third was a mismanaged enemy attack in which the Irish, by then in diminished numbers (but aided by experienced units on both flanks) resolutely stood their ground. In the event, of the approximately seven hundred men who were with the *Bandera* at the front, eight (including two Spaniards) were killed and as many again were wounded, two of them seriously, as a consequence of hostile action (making a casualty rate of

3 per cent).[3] Of course, it is valid to ask: how many useless deaths are enough to secure the prestige of a fighting unit? But neither is it perverse to admit that the casualty rate is bound to be some indication of any army's comportment in battle.

War has ever been the most constant and absolute medium of reputations, whether historical or mythic. Neither of the two generic original sources of evidence for the XV *Bandera*, the testimony of its members and the official papers of the Spanish nationalist authorities, supplies sufficient grounds for the attribution of military glory to its name. Amongst the twenty or more written and recorded accounts belonging to the former, only one includes even anecdotal material which (in effect) lays a claim to warrior-hero status; indeed, it is partly for this reason that I regard the source as unreliable.[4] Various tributes are paid to the courage of the stretcher-bearers and ambulance units on 13 March. With this exception, these sources hardly narrate a single deed in which heroism in action, whether individual or collective, can be properly regarded as playing a part.[5] On the other hand, cowardice was not in evidence, even during some prolonged periods of heavy bombardment. Moreover – at least once all were aboard the SS *Urundi* who were going aboard – desertion from the ranks was almost unknown.[6]

As it proved, the reputation of the Irish Brigade was not helped, but rather the reverse, by the campaign of propaganda waged in its support by the *Irish Independent*, as a result of which many people came to believe in a fictional catalogue of battle honours. In early March, for example, having reported Liam Walsh's statement that Major Dalton 'had been slightly wounded during an engagement on the Madrid Front', the paper followed up with the news that the Irish Brigade 'will lead in what will shortly be the final and decisive attack on Madrid. General O'Duffy spends his entire time at the front with the men.'[7] A week later it carried the story that, following the Italian defeat at Guadalajara, the Brigade had been sent to stiffen the nationalist line in that area, the north-east sector of the Madrid front.[8] Later, the Titulcia attack was presented as a tremendous victory in banner headlines:

IRISH BRIGADE WINS MADRID BATTLE

BIG ADVANCE UNDER FIERCE FIRE

REDS ROUTED

The front-page story related Ireland's part in 'the greatest offensive of the war'; 'a magnificent advance of three miles', at which the enemy 'abandoned their trenches when they saw the Irishmen break through'. It conveyed the impression that O'Duffy was personally in the thick of the fighting.[9] The *Independent* was not alone in encouraging readers to consider the Irish Brigade as a major factor in the unfolding of military events in Spain. Early in May, with a front-page item presented as 'Noel Monks sends uncensored truth from Spain', the *Daily Express* headlined the news: 'GERMANS AND IRISH IN THE NEXT ATTACK AGAINST MADRID FRONT'.[10] It was natural for any Irish patriot not committed to the Spanish Republic not only to credit, but to rejoice in such achievements. Perhaps a large majority of Free State citizens were thus later to be exposed to the disillusionment of reality. In the months after the Brigade's homecoming, its leading anti-O'Duffy members tore Frank Geary's false banner of military glory to muddy shreds. Whilst the Catholic patriot in his local snug could soon recover, helping to salve little wounds by bitter jibes, for many veterans the consequences of the *Irish Independent*'s propaganda were to be painful and prolonged.

Yet blame for the negative military reputation of the Brigade cannot be attributed to the men; and little (even) to their leaders. The circumstances in which they found themselves at the front were wholly inimical to success. With hindsight, we can see it would have been far better if O'Duffy and his Spanish backers had stuck to the plan for the Brigade to serve with the Carlists.[11] The proximity of a battalion of *requetés* at La Marañosa served to underline, for the Irish themselves, how unsympathetic they were to the whole ethic of the Legion. O'Duffy (however) was disingenuous to assert that the Brigade was crippled from the start by its limited size – a point intended to shift the blame for failure on to his political enemies at home, above all on to de Valera. In fact, the XV *Bandera* was larger, and not (as he claimed) smaller, than the average Tercio unit in the field.[12] The problem was not that it was too small to contribute, but that O'Duffy refused to place it under direct Spanish command; thus it could not be integrated fully into any nationalist army group; and from this it followed that it could never be employed in any developing, dynamic operations. This logic was implicit from the start, but stood vividly revealed by the events of 13–14 March. On his own terms, however, O'Duffy was right to point out that, unlike the German or Italian forces, with the numbers at his disposal, especially once definitively denied reinforcements, even full operational autonomy would not have allowed a worthwhile contribution. Indeed, the Italian record illustrates that numbers, allied to impressive infrastructure and material resources, do not guarantee a positive outcome in terms of military reputation.[13]

Yet, like Mussolini, if not so blatantly, O'Duffy too nurtured a political agenda. Whilst the charge that a personal political comeback for the general was the main motivation for the Brigade must be rejected, it is difficult to believe that considerations of domestic politics were never in his mind. His original press letter proposing the formation of a brigade is revealing in this connection:

> It is unlikely that any number of men we could send would be of any great assistance from the more physical point of view, but the very fact that a group of Irishmen volunteered their services to help Spain in her hour of peril against the forces of darkness could not fail to have very favourable reactions all over the world.[14]

There is a distinct suggestion here that O'Duffy was not unaware of the propaganda content of his proposal. Whether consciously or not, in one dimension he conceived his Brigade as an instrument calculated to evoke 'favourable reactions' more than to fight and win battles. Its very existence was a vindication of History. It might not be going too far to suggest that the above remarks throw light on O'Duffy's unwillingness to risk major loss of lives of his men in Spain. Perhaps it also provides some explanation of his precipitate haste that autumn of 1936, when it seemed Madrid was about to fall – an event which promised the general a personal political triumph on a world stage, and at an inexpensive cost in terms of blood-sacrifice. Was this a calculated gamble on his part, perhaps instigated by international gamblers of varying distinction, like Juan de la Cierva and Tom Gunning? Whatever the truth here, O'Duffy deserves censure for failing to reconcile his inhibiting fear of losses with the absolute commitment of sacrifice made to 'the general cause' and its leader, General Franco.[15] Somewhere within this contradiction, perhaps, lies the core reason for the military failure of the Irish Brigade.

In many other ways, the Brigade was (literally) its own worst enemy. The anti-heroic assessments disseminated by the 'mutineers' had a permanent influence in another crucial area of the Irish Brigade's reputation. So anxious were the defectors to disassociate themselves from the business, and to scapegoat their ex-leader, that they succeeded in blackening the name of the Brigade as a whole. The anti-O'Duffy press and the parties of the centre-left made immense capital from these tendencies, an investment which to this day returns a (now perhaps rather measly) dividend in terms of national politics. In the years after 1937, the mere existence of such a vehement anti-O'Duffy faction seemed inarguable testimony to the fact that the Brigaders had fought amongst themselves more than they ever fought the enemy. Worse, their fuel in these encounters was not true religion and crusading fervour but the demon drink.

'In Cáceres there was a series of public-house brawls, beating of the "mutineering" members of the brigade and a state of affairs in which the Kerrymen and the Northmen led by *** had to keep their guns at the ready.'[16] An attempt to reconstruct this sordid scenario was made forty years later by Cathal O'Shannon when he directed the Radio Telefís Eireann (RTE) documentary 'Even the Olives are Bleeding'. Filming in Cáceres, O'Shannon pressed Alfonso Bustamente, ex-liaison officer of C Company, on the point of the *Bandera's* drunken reputation, but without success. A local bar-owner cornered by the interviewer – a teenager at the time of the Irish occupation – also failed to rise to the bait. However, one of the Brigade veterans, Matt Doolan, honestly (and, I consider, accurately) conceded that about 20 per cent of his compadres had a drink problem.[17] In Ireland even today, the memory of the Irish Brigade is regularly denigrated by accusations of drunkenness and hooliganism, and execrated for having done so much to confirm negative stereotypes of ethnic behaviour. It must be said that some veteran sources testify to alcohol abuse and occasional violence. It is equally true that most witnesses either routinely ignore, stoutly deny or seek to reduce the significance of such events. The last of these attitudes is both reasonable and realistic.

Drinking certainly helped to undermine morale and to exacerbate personal resentments and unhealthy 'tribal' competition between factions. These evils were rampant during service in the La Marañosa sector. At Ciempozuelos, the palpable proximity of the enemy, which shelled, sniped at and raided the Irish positions constantly, helped to maintain comradely unity among the men. In this period, too, the *Bandera* was still largely undepleted in numbers; there was an excellent supply of water in the town, and only wine was available for off-duty indulgence. Things were very different at La Marañosa. The abject failure of their first attack was a disappointment which began to eat away at morale. Enemy positions could not be observed with the naked eye. The rapidly augmenting sick list put those who remained in the line under the strain of continuous extra duties – long hours in the forward trenches, sentry-go at night, the struggle to maintain communications and supplies. The broiling heat of the exposed plateau, combined with the absence of water sources, had inevitable consequences. From positions immediately to the *Bandera's* left there were visits from pedlars from the Moorish *tabor*, selling brandy and other plundered liquors as well as wine.[18] Little wonder that Tom Hayes noted men around him being 'thin, wan, pale, half gone crazy with conac and having sleepless nights'.[19] There is little doubt – as his liaison officers informed Yagüe – that the collapse of the XV *Bandera* was materially aided by the alcoholic syndrome which this conjuncture inspired. Once the *Bandera* returned to Cáceres, the process of disintegration continued.

One overtly hostile witness, who alleges that drunkenness, fighting (and in-fighting) were ubiquitous from the moment of the volunteers' arrival in Spain must be discounted.[20] At the other extreme, we must also discount O'Duffy's protestations over an issue to which he was personally as well as politically sensitive.[21] Apparently, a far more objective witness was Fr McCabe, rector of the Irish College in Salamanca. In the first week of 1937, the chaplain, Fr Mulrean, told McCabe he was 'worried over the drink problem'. Months later, McCabe encountered General Alfredo Kindelán, commander of the nationalist air force and (because descended from 'Wild Geese') an early supporter of the Irish Brigade. Kindelán complained that 'some of the men had exceeded their measure'.[22] Another intermittent observer, journalist Frank McCullagh, gave an embittered commentary which concentrated on this issue and culminated in the remark that the volunteers were 'drunken savages, blinded by popery and usquebaugh'.[23] But although himself Irish and anti-communist, McCullagh was alienated by O'Duffy's refusal to allow him open access to the front-line positions. On his one visit he had a guarded reception in the officers' mess, later complaining that 'About half a dozen were writing histories of the Brigade and regarded me as a possible rival … They feared I would discover the innumerable intrigues and jealousies by which the Irish unit was split. As a matter of fact, I could easily have discovered enough scandal to fill a volume.'[24]

The reputation of the Irish Brigade remains vulnerable to criticism on the subject of alcohol abuse for two reasons. First, what became ingrained in populist folklore was a contrast between mundane reality and exalted expectations. In the embarrassed national psychology this, and the need to pass off the experience of 'Irish fascism' as a joke – not even an aberration – gives rise to comment which is always anecdotal and humorous, but never innocent. Nevertheless (second) it must be conceded that the theme has a real historical significance because of its contribution to the definitive breakdown of the Brigade's unity and therefore its existence.

Before leaving this contentious issue, it must be emphasised that the record of the Irish Brigade was no different from that of other military units in the context of the Spanish Civil War. It is evident from the memoirs of another participant on Franco's side, the English nurse Priscilla

Scott-Ellis, that even at the front, soldiers in drink would sometimes cut loose from the sanctions of discipline in this respect, risking brutal punishment.[25] The latter was often imposed instantaneously and could include consignment to labour battalions and (not infrequently) execution. In the normal Tercio *bandera*, though members were as fond of the bottle as any, internal discipline was rarely so much as punctured by its effects – a fact which Yagüe's reaction to the Irish situation amply demonstrates.[26] The final argument must be left to a later part of this book, when the experience of the Irish International Brigaders may incline most readers to accept the relevance of the old adage about glass houses and stone-throwing.[27]

Two other factors vitiated the prospects of the Irish Brigade – its politics and its financing. The latter was a worry from the start, and was volubly attested by the dishevelled and physically miserable state in which many of the volunteers returned from Spain. Only the cost of the Brigade's medical supplies was met out of the funds donated by the Catholic population of the Free State during the successful collections held in the autumn of 1936. No information seems to have survived regarding the fund-raising efforts made by Walsh and the NCP. As we have seen, the *Intendencia* (supply division) of the nationalist army provided uniforms (and demob suits), weapons and ammunition, essential food supplies and, above all, pay at the regular privileged rates of the Tercio.[28] In Salamanca, Tom Gunning was widely regarded as both profligate and irresponsible in his use of Brigade funds, whilst (on the other hand) O'Duffy's personal fortune was virtually exhausted in the process. In Dublin, Walsh enlisted the help of the Italian consul, Signor Lodi Fé, who wrote to Count Ciano:

> General O'Duffy told me the last time he was here that he has long since exhausted all his own money for the Irish Brigade. If he still manages to cover the expenses, he owes it entirely to the connivance of his bank, which continues to honour his cheques – on whose orders he does not know ... But I thought it expedient, in order that he should not lose heart, to assure him that for his commitments 'somebody will pay'.[29]

The 'somebody' was Mussolini – or at any rate, the Italian taxpayer. Given that the precipitant crisis of the *Bandera* occurred as an indirect result of Franco's belated attempt to rescue the *Corpo Truppe Voluntaria* (CTV) from disaster at Guadalajara, there was a certain poetic justice in the Italian contribution of £350 which, as a result of the consul's intervention, was made over to defray O'Duffy's expenses.[30] Though a typical gesture on Mussolini's part, both his and O'Duffy's losses on the venture were a drop in the ocean compared with those of General Franco (or, at any rate, his bankers). According to McCullagh, the expedition as a whole cost the nationalist war-chest £170,000.[31] When confronted with figures of these dimensions (perhaps more than £6 million at today's rates) the wonder is that the *generalísimo* delayed his decision to dispense with O'Duffy's services for so long.

Aided and abetted by Liam Walsh at the Dublin end, General O'Duffy constantly asserted that the Brigade had no political connotations. This robust stance was adopted partly in order to fend off accusations (noted above) that the enterprise was a weapon forged to assist his domestic designs. But in addition, with a force which had to present itself as representing all the interests and regions of the island of Ireland, the ideal of unity had to be paramount. The more important it seemed, the more difficult it was to achieve.[32] The Brigade's claim to be a representative cross-section of the Irish people was not without substance. It was least convincing on the confessional front. Only half a dozen non-Catholics joined up; two of these were seconded by the Spanish army, and another converted in the course of his service. Claims that the Brigade served to re-unite the old comrades of the War of Independence, healing and settling the wounds of the Irish Civil War, were perhaps too loudly trumpeted.[33] Though the available data only permit rough estimates, no more than twenty of the volunteers had been IRA anti-Treatyites; but perhaps as many again were Fianna Fáil or even Labour supporters. Another substantial fraction was made up of adherents of W. T. Cosgrave, Cumann na nGaedheal leader and ex-prime minister, now restored as leader of the main opposition party (Fine Gael). This still left a majority within the Brigade who had belonged to the Blueshirts or its derivative organisations in 1933–36. In practice, however, this was not to play a role in fomenting internal dissension; the most inimical influences were the ex-Blueshirt satraps Eamon Horan and Thomas Carew. In the sources, I have found no important indications that volunteers envisaged the Brigade as essentially a Blueshirt organisation.[34]

Men from all parts of Ireland joined the Brigade. Having said this, some regions were clearly underrepresented, most obviously Ulster. From Northern Ireland came some twenty volunteers. Both here and in Co. Donegal, the dominance of the IRA in a zone where its military role was still meaningful, combined with the understandable reluctance of Catholic/republican adult males to abandon their families, severely reduced recruitment. These feelings were much less strong in Cavan and Monaghan, and were (in any case) more than offset by O'Duffy's personal popularity as a local man. As we have seen, the strongest areas of response were in the south-west – above all, in the intensely Catholic Limerick town, along with Kerry, West Cork and Tipperary.[35] During the expedition, interregional suspicions seem to have predominated over company loyalty in the trenches. Some residue of this is detected in the sources, where (for example) more than one veteran comments unfavourably on the Dublin city contingent, whilst the lads from Clonmel (and Tipperary generally) seem also to have inspired little affection among their comrades.[36]

In the final analysis, and even if it did not apply to himself, O'Duffy was surely correct in claiming that 'the little Irish group were the only foreign participants who had no selfish motives'.[37] Neither the Brigade's collective military failure, nor the least attractive of its members' individual human failings, can validly be used to cancel out the idealism of its origins. To quote the general again:

> Our volunteers were not mere adventurers. Over ninety per cent were true crusaders, who left behind them comfortable homes – many left secretly lest anything should arise to prevent them carrying out their resolve. They were not mercenary soldiers. Every man made a real personal sacrifice in going to Spain, and every one returned poorer in the world's goods. Many have been refused their former positions again, and are still unemployed.[38]

The individuals

Thus spake O'Duffy. In so far as they can be recalled and reconstituted, the individual histories of the majority of his men bear out his opinion. The pages of this book have many testaments in its support. We lack space for all the details; to recreate memories, to describe emotions, to retell all the anecdotes – this task must be left for another day and perhaps another writer. But the strong impression remains that at least three-quarters of the volunteers were men of integrity, who (with varying degrees of humility) accepted the contemporary construction of crusaders – men who were prepared to sacrifice their lives, who, in fact, sacrificed material comforts and expected the same of their nearest and dearest and, at the last, were glad of having done so, despite all the failures and the undeserved infamy these brought by association. Some acted from a sense of Irish patriotism, inspired by both the recent and the mythic past. But most felt (as veterans still feel today) that they were Catholics first and Irishmen only second. They nurtured an international (or rather, supranational) idealism as profound, as meaningful and as justified as that displayed by the International Brigades.

The esteem between O'Duffy and his men was clearly mutual. Apart from a minority, who took sides against him more as a token of peer pressure than for any material reason or personal grievance, General O'Duffy remained a figure of admiration. This emotion, it is true, came more from a perception of him as a feudal protector and father figure than as a warrior-hero. Yet it was a feeling shared by many volunteers who never supported him even in the broadest domestic political terms.[39]

Some of these attributes are strong enough even to resist the cynical twist imparted to them by a professional diplomat who met the general during one of the latter's return visits to Dublin.

> O'Duffy is not a man of great intellectual resources; he has neither culture nor much political sense, other than a certain coarse intuition. He is above all a man of action, of great personal courage, disinterested and generous. These qualities in the right circumstances, can make of him a useful and safe tool – therefore it is expedient not to overlook him.[40]

Other views were less mixed. One, more typically military than diplomatic, was that of Peter Kemp. An upper-class Englishman of Irish derivation, Kemp served almost throughout the Spanish War, latterly with the Tercio as a lieutenant. In his judgement, 'The Spaniards were filled with admiration for the bearing and courage of the [Irish] troops. Indeed, the quality of the men was superb. They were truly inspired with the ideal of fighting for their faith ... But they had no chance with the leadership O'Duffy gave them.'[41]

This is not the place for a biography of O'Duffy, nor does this book call for assessment of his overall career.[42] Yet some matters are too closely relevant to the experience of the Irish Brigade to leave on one side. In earlier life and earlier conflicts, he had been a resourceful and courageous leader. Admired by Michael Collins – who had recruited him to the IRA – Eoin O'Duffy had an excellent battle record in the War of Independence, risking his life many times, above all in operations inside Protestant Ulster. Yet even at this stage it was seen that his real gifts were administrative; and these talents he developed during and after the Civil War, in the service of the pro-Treaty cause for which his mentor, Collins, had died. He will be remembered in Irish history, above all, as the Commissioner of Police who, in exceptionally difficult circumstances, did most to forge the Garda Siochana into an effective, unarmed force.

His career in the early 1920s was meteoric; as (at one point simultaneously) Police Commissioner and Army Commander-in-Chief, he wielded power and influence. But in these years, too, he suffered a rapid physical decline, doubtless brought on by a combination of long-term overwork and heavy drinking. As we have seen, his outright identification with the Treatyite side in 1922, and (later) his fanatical anti-communism, made him many enemies of equal commitment, and he lived constantly under the shadow of assassination. During the violent 'Blueshirt Years' (1933–34) he frequently risked death or serious injury at meetings and demonstrations. On one occasion he was, indeed, struck full on the head by a hammer-wielding opponent; perhaps only his hat saving him from a permanently disabling injury. By 1936, he was still only forty-four years old, but looked over sixty.[43]

It is difficult to resist the conclusion that by the time he arrived in Spain, some of O'Duffy's key qualities as a leader of men had critically degenerated. In terms of sheer physical energy it is true that little diminution was in evidence. The general was rarely at rest. But, on the other hand, he was hardly ever at serious work. In Salamanca, out of the ken of his soldiers and field-command, he was rarely to be seen, either in public or private, without a bottle of whisky. In this capacity he was observed by various callers at Salamanca's Grand Hotel, including McCabe, Kemp and McCullagh. The last of these had been prepared for his experience by meeting an earlier guest of O'Duffy's, who pictured:

> a big, benevolent-looking man with a red, clean-shaven face like that of a parish priest. His weak points are bad judgement of men, extreme irascibility, and an absolute incapacity for working with anybody at all … [O'Duffy was] exactly as Phillips described … He treated me to a double peg of Irish to which he sternly refused to add any water.[44]

Not infrequently, the general was incommunicado, at times back in Ireland, at others visiting acquaintances in far-flung cities or country estates – at times he was literally AWOL.[45] This lifestyle did not permit concentration on the job in hand, and much of the evidence in the foregoing pages (borne out by his memoirs) indicates that he never seriously attempted to grasp the details of the context – political, military, social, administrative, legal – in which he found himself. This context was one of truly baroque complexity, and O'Duffy did not understand a word of

Castilian (not to mention Baroque). The effect of all this was to create a total dependence upon his leading subordinates, both in Salamanca and at the front – but especially upon those Irish personnel who claimed command of the Spanish language. Unfortunately – as Sir Percival Phillips noted – the major faculty with which O'Duffy had lost contact was that of judgement of character. Only one of his elite appointments repaid him with both efficiency and loyalty: Diarmuid O'Sullivan. The rest ranged from the weak to the disastrous. Among the former must be placed Patrick Dalton, among the latter Fr Mulrean and Tom Gunning.

The choice of Patrick Dalton as OC did not prove a success. Dalton was an army officer with a good fighting record in 1919–23, but had been 'retired early' (in effect, cashiered) after the mutinous disturbances of the mid-1920s. Subsequently, he had been Blueshirt leader in Dublin during the bitter street battles of 1933–34 with the IRA and Saor Eire. Along with Manuel Capablanca, Dalton must take the credit for moulding the force which impressed both Franco and Yagüe on first inspection. Yet he seems to have made little impression on the ordinary soldier. His decline set in as a result of the events of 19 February, for which he seems to have blamed himself. After little more than two weeks at the front, Dalton developed sciatica and was sent to Lisbon for treatment. He failed to recover and returned to Ireland in due course.[46]

Another official in a highly responsible area was a controversial and divisive personality. The Brigade chaplain, Fr Mulrean, a typical rural priest of this period in Irish history, was physically huge, fanatically puritanical and tactless. He was keen on regular confession, insisting that officers should set an example of eagerness for this sacrament. The disruptive effects were observed by McCabe, who came to Cáceres in January 1937 and stayed for several days, helping his younger colleague with his ministrations. When Mulrean detected any religious coolness or moral backsliding among the officers, he called them publicly to account, demeaning them in the eyes of the men.[47] The officer corps, like any group of adult male Catholics in any decade of modern Ireland, split into those who resisted the cloth and those who knuckled under. This struggle is oddly analogous to that in the International Brigade between political commissars – ideological and puritanical disciplinarians for the most part – and 'secular' field officers.[48] Mulrean's contribution was counterproductive, since his challenge to the officers undermined the very discipline which he sought to impose. At some point he seems to have abandoned his charges altogether and repaired to Salamanca. His effective replacement, Fr Daly, was more popular and successful.[49]

From the moment that O'Duffy agreed to the appointment of Tom Gunning as his personal assistant, he and his men were bought and sold. Gunning was a failed priest and failed journalist, who turned into an arrogant adventurer, out for a good time at others' expense. Heavy drinking, indiscreet and anti-Semitic, he ended up working for the German Ministry of Propaganda before his death in 1940. In the interim, after the disbandment of the Brigade, he added personal defamation to his betrayal of O'Duffy, and (moved by little more than gratuitous spite) intrigued with various nationalist contacts to procure the execution of Frank Ryan, captured leader of the Irish Internationals.[50]

Though this does not wholly absolve O'Duffy from blame, many of the privations imposed on the men in the trenches were needless results of Gunning's incompetence. His liaison with the *Intendencia* was poor or even non-existent. The failure to spot the potential dangers of using German uniforms, and the issue of much inferior equipment (or – in the case of weather-proof materials – none at all) can be ascribed to this cause. Gunning also assumed responsibility for censorship of mail – indicating his links with the Francoist secret service. There were constant difficulties with postal deliveries in both directions. A philatelic historian writes that 'During the six months that the Irish were in Spain I doubt if many letters got through and I know from personal experience that it would appear that very few survived … Perhaps very few letters were written, perhaps many of the volunteers were illiterate.'[51] Gunning seems to have taken a less prominent role after the appointment of O'Ferrall. Both men remained in Spain after the Brigade went home. The latter, at least, seems to have dealt competently with arrangements for the repatriation and its untidy aftermath in Cáceres.

On the question of the Brigade's military comportment, it is (*pace* Kemp) difficult to allocate personal blame. It seems likely that neither O'Duffy nor any of his senior staff ever understood the overall strategic situation in the war, how the Brigade related to it, nor (more importantly) what was expected of the latter by the nationalist high command. This in part arose because they were professionally incapable of this understanding (as Yagüe believed), and in part because none of the liaison staff ever succeeded in conveying it. Despite his own claims, and the protestations of loyalists like O'Sullivan, O'Duffy was not a frequent visitor to the trenches; and one must discount as sheer nostalgia recollections that he knew every man in the Brigade by name.[52] As one witness noted without bitterness (in response to contrary claims), the general did not lead from the front in the 13 March attack, and was not seen to be moving among the companies undergoing heavy bombardment.[53] Then again, for over a century – and even in the Legion – no officer of this rank had been expected to risk his life in such a manner.

The last irony came after General O'Duffy's death, at the age of fifty-two, on 30 November 1944. His old enemy, de Valera, who had been prime minister for over a decade, decreed a state funeral. Almost the whole Fianna Fáil cabinet accompanied the gun-carriage cortège to Glasnevin cemetery, along with the Spanish and German ambassadors and a representative of the Spanish army. But only twenty-one veterans of the XV *Bandera del Tercio* were present to pay their last respects.[54]

Carrying the flag

The XV *Bandera* seems to have flown two flags. One was a company pennant, which imitated the design of the original Tercio banners of the seventeenth century. The other, a standard-flag (*guión*) apparently designed by O'Duffy himself, sported an Irish wolfhound posed against the Irish Tricolour. Corporal Matt Beckett brought one of the former, made by local weavers in Cáceres, back to Westport, and a version of the latter was sent to Ireland by a Spanish veteran of the *Bandera* in the 1950s.[55] In strictly literal terms, neither of these banners was ever waved in earnest again, but metaphorically they have at least fluttered from time to time.

When the Brigade left Cáceres they left behind more than twenty volunteers who were unable to travel. Some half-dozen men were hospitalised with various illnesses (of which some later died).[56] But several men had elected to stay in Spain to fight on, and volunteered (as it were, for a second time) for placement in other Legionary *banderas*. Among them, not surprisingly, were the two professional soldiers, Nangle and Fitzpatrick, along with Peter Lawler; all three were redeployed into various units. Fitzpatrick, however, annoyed the colonel of the V *Bandera* by declaring himself a Freemason – perhaps a reaction against six months spent with his over-zealous Catholic countrymen. Yagüe soon passed this news on to Franco – both men had a horror of Freemasonry that was, if anything, more profound than their distaste for Bolshevism. Fitzpatrick was forthwith 'released' from the Legion on the *generalísimo's* orders.[57]

The Brigade's senior NCO, Staff Sergeant-Major Michael Weymes, was another of those who were determined not to give up the struggle. Two fellow sergeants, Tom Jones and Michael Cadell – the ex-Protestant who had converted to Catholicism at the front – also stayed on in the Legion. With these three to the reserve units of the Tercio in Talavera went at least another six private soldiers. These were Jeremiah McCarthy, James Madden, Daith Higgins, Dennis O'Dea, Andrew O'Toole and Austin O'Reilly; all served in action with different Legionary *banderas*.[58] Another, Peter Kavanagh, requested transfer to the nationalist air force, claiming seven years' service as a mechanic in the air forces of Britain and Ireland.[59]

In this way, until the war ended in April 1939, individual veterans of the Irish Brigade served on all its campaigns in the ranks of Franco's victorious armies. Their fortunes may be regarded – if not infallibly so – as having matched their characters. Madden (aged forty-two) had abandoned a wife and three children in Tipperary to join O'Duffy, whether through zeal for religious freedom or for a less altruistic kind of freedom, I leave the reader to judge. He was allocated to the XIII *Bandera* in June 1937, but the rigorous campaigning demands of the Legion quickly undermined his health. He spent several months in hospital in Salamanca, where an official reported that 'he is 44 years old and his appearance does not seem to suggest that he is fit for the hard service demanded in the Legion'.[60] However, acts of indiscipline had come to Yagüe's attention. The colonel, less pliable over the man than over the mass, refused to recommend his repatriation.[61] But Madden survived the war and successfully applied for repatriation at the cost of the Free State in 1939.[62]

If Madden was amongst the oldest crusaders, Andrew O'Toole was almost certainly the youngest. His misadventures began when he enlisted in the British army, and then deserted from it in 1932 – allegedly aged fourteen! Throughout the period of the XV *Bandera*'s service, his father struggled to obtain his release, but to no avail. In this instance (at least) O'Duffy was right in claiming that the boys had no desire to go home, for O'Toole elected to stay on and was posted to the Madrid front. A year later he is reported in the most dangerous section of the line, the University City salient near the heart of the capital itself, serving with the XII *Bandera*. Later, in Cuesta de la Reina (just south of Ciempozuelos) he apparently again deserted – to the republican army – only to be captured by the Nationalists and sentenced to death. According to his father, he was 'made to dig his own grave, then brought out with other prisoners to be shot [and] left beside dead bodies for hours'.[63] After he had spent a year in prison, the charge of desertion against O'Toole was finally dropped on a technicality.[64]

Whatever the peccadilloes of the martyr, the supreme sacrifice tends to cover multitudes. Sergeant-Major Weymes is a good example. A tough, hard-drinking character from Mullingar, who endeared himself to few subordinates, Weymes had volunteered for the Brigade along with no fewer than three brothers. It seems that in June the latter all summoned up the courage to defy him, and duly went home. Weymes joined another *bandera*, and was killed a month or two later, 'leading his men at Villafranca del Castillo during the fiercely contested Battle of Brunete.'[65] Daith Higgins and Austin O'Reilly were both killed during the last major campaign of the war, the desperate struggle on the Ebro, respectively in September and October 1938.[66] In a sense, therefore, it might be fairly recorded that the Catholic crusaders fought and died in many of the great set-piece battles of the Spanish Civil War.

The six Irishmen killed in action with the XV *Bandera* itself were revered in the memory of many comrades, and of their families; indeed, they still are. But their physical remains were left in Spain, never to be returned and perhaps never to be confidently identified.[67] Only one individual has been granted a memorial in Ireland. Sergeant Gabriel Lee, killed by shellfire during the Titulcia attack, is remembered by a modest plaque on a pew in Dublin's pro-cathedral. No memorial to the Brigade as a whole exists outside Spain. Now and again, small groups of Irish pilgrims turn up in Cáceres to visit the quiet corner of the municipal cemetery where their ancestors were interred in 1937, and to admire the bronze plaque erected in the church of San Domingo before the *Bandera* left for the front.[68] Tom Hyde, nephew and namesake of the first casualty, recalls being brought up (in Midleton, Co. Cork) to look on his martyred uncle as a role model and a species of guardian angel.[69] But, as the years went by, such descendants became either indifferent or (as in this case) even ashamed of any association with Franco's Spain. Ridiculed by their contemporaries for years, veteran *banderistas* were now rejected (at least as such) by their own children. The result was silence.

But they did not disappear into secure anonymity quite as complaisantly as this might suggest. About a month after returning to their homes, more than a hundred Brigade veterans received another call to action from their leader. In July 1937 the loss of the Basque country to the Republic deprived it of much heavy industrial capacity and swung the economic balance decisively in Franco's favour. In particular, Franco's capture of Bilbao, on 19 June, threatened the Republic with the outright loss of the greater part of its merchant marine. Companies with commercial vessels registered in the Basque capital – a large majority of the total – were obliged to transfer their enterprises to the nationalist interest. Desperate to preserve its lifelines with European ports, the Valencia government issued a decree expropriating all Spanish-registered shipping for government use. The action applied to more than seventy vessels, many of which were in British waters or ports, including Derry and Belfast.[70]

The Valencia decree generated controversy and incident in the United Kingdom. In most cases, ships' masters and officers were anxious to obey the owners, whilst their crews were equally determined to ensure obedience to the government decree. The result was a kind of Spanish Civil War in microcosm being fought out on board the vessels, sometimes spilling over to involve British police and port officials, and even the local communities. In various places, pro-Franco elements were organised to go to the aid of the hard-pressed skippers, some of whom were besieged on their own bridges, as if in so many satellite Alcázars. According to Walsh, O'Duffy was contacted (probably by the 'friends of Franco Spain' organised by the Duke of Alba in London) and asked to send men to the North. 'Without hesitation, General O'Duffy despatched upwards of 100 men; nearly all were former members of the Irish Brigade.'[71] Bill Geraghty recalls joining a band of Dublin Brigade veterans led by Captain Hughes, owner of the Midland Hotel. They went off to Derry and were welcomed in various 'safe houses' belonging to Catholic Nationalists.[72] There they awaited the verdict of the Admiralty Court before taking action to secure the ships on behalf of Franco, being prepared (if called upon) to sail them to Spain. Meanwhile, Harry Midgley, MP for the Londonderry Dock constituency and prominent supporter of the Spanish Republic, attempted to organise local action to help the crews.[73] The situation was further complicated by the fact that all this was happening in the midst of the July marching season! As things turned out, the legal hearings took so long to reach resolution that the operation had to be abandoned. The episode had only added a typically frustrating appendix to the story of the Irish Brigade.[74]

The Brigade Association, set up to protect the interests of the veterans and maintain communications, did not survive bitter internal divisions. As we have seen, only some twenty veterans attended O'Duffy's funeral in 1944. Two years after this event, on the tenth anniversary of the Brigade's birth, Seaosam Ó Cuinneaghán, now a solicitor in Enniscorthy (Co. Wexford), attempted to re-establish contact.

> We are all fully cognisant of the many differences – some personal, some perhaps political, but all attributable to the innate weakness of our human nature – that punctuated an otherwise perfect comradeship. Time is, however, still an able physician and in the reminiscences of ten years later, like the good Christian soldiers we are, we can, it is hoped, laugh to scorn what we once felt right to resent.

This was a moving credo, but one doomed to frustration. Doubtless the need for unity and togetherness was keenly felt by many. Ó Cuinneagháin believed the time was ripe: 'Iron Curtains' were thumping down, and surely 'those at home who doubted, discredited, scoffed at our expedition now belatedly see its glorious justification in the tidal wave of communism'.[75] Two years later (1948) when veteran Peter Cleary was ordained priest in Dublin, Padraig Quinn and Ó Cuinneagháin circulated veterans in order to organise a Requiem Mass and a veterans' dinner.[76] Twenty-five years on, these same three men were received in audience by Franco at his Palace of El Pardo near Madrid.[77]

In the intervening period, any plan to re-establish an association was hampered by lack of personal data concerning the ex-comrades. If ever a complete list of members had existed in the NCP offices, it had gone missing. At least a third of the corps had possessed passports in 1936. But these documents were collected by Tom Gunning in Spain, and many were never returned. Gunning was supposed to be making a complete list of names and addresses, though it seems likely he never completed this task. In 1938 he went to Germany, and for a time worked for the Ministry of Propaganda. As Kerney put it, 'two questions present themselves to my mind: did Gunning take these men's passports with him to Germany and might any use be made of them?'[78] Indeed, it was surely not coincidental that around 1942, veteran James Kavanagh received a packet from Germany which proved to contain anti-Semitic material and advice on how to set up a cell of Jew-baiters in Ireland.[79]

By this time, a good many of the veterans had enlisted in the British army. So far from being fascists, with the latently vicious tendencies which Goebbels and his gang assumed they could exploit, the majority of the ex-*banderistas* had an idea of freedom which was not selfish or exclusive. Some responded naturally to the plight of the British people in 1940; others strongly felt (as had their forefathers in 1914) that Catholic peoples like those of Poland and Belgium deserved defending against German barbarism. I do not know whether either of these emotions, or merely his love of soldiering, led ex-Legionary Patrick Hickey to enlist. At any rate, he died in 1944 on the Rhine, fighting in the great war against fascism.[80]

2 Frank Ryan in uniform as staff officer of the XV International Brigade (Photo courtesy of Seán Cronin)

1 Eoin O'Duffy in uniform as Inspector-General of the XV *Bandera del Tercio* (Photo courtesy of Monaghan County Museum)

3   Ciempozuelos, February 1937. A group of Irish Brigaders pose outside a ruined church with its despoiled contents. The collection includes a monstrance (for public display of the consecrated Host), assorted priestly vestments and the *giralda* (weather-vane) from the church tower (Photo courtesy of C. Roche)

4   La Marañosa, April 1937. Irish Brigaders kneel to receive communion at an open-air Mass behind the lines (Photo courtesy of C. Roche)

5   Cáceres, May 1937. The officer corps of the XV *Bandera* not long before departure
     for home (Photo courtesy of C. Roche)

6   Albacete, Summer 1937. Frank Ryan (third from left, back row) with Irish
     members of the British Battalion, including Peter Daly and Paddy O'Daire (on
     each side of Ryan) and Frank Edwards (standing, far right)

The
communist crusade

7

UptheRepublic!

The Irish left in 1936

Ireland's history, ancient and modern, predisposed the nation to involvement in the Spanish Civil War. Yet there were specific reasons for the
emergence of two 'crusades in conflict' in 1936. They can be traced to the
secret report circulated by Police Commissioner O'Duffy in 1931. This
report purported to analyse the menacing strength of the communist
presence in the Free State.[1] Its conclusions were communicated to members of the Catholic hierarchy as well as government officials. O'Duffy's
action was *ultra vires* on a number of counts, and later served to incur the
wrath of the incoming prime minister, Eamon de Valera. More importantly, it made its author the object of personal loathing and contempt.
Along with the Dublin financier and press baron, W. Lombard Murphy,
and the anti-Semitic TD Paddy Belton, Eoin O'Duffy became one of an
unholy trinity of evil reactionaries in the hall of infamy of the Irish left.[2]

O'Duffy's warnings about the Red threat can now be seen as the
opening move in a campaign against organised communism and the
influence of the Soviet Union which was to run in Ireland, with
marathon energy and footsore determination, until the late 1960s. This
feature, once so prominent in the cultural physiology of the nation, has
now vanished. It survives only in the collective unconscious, repressed by
nearly all, willingly forgotten by most, hardly even a matter of curiosity
to the young of the modern Republic. Yet Irish anti-communism
involved – or rather, enveloped – two successive generations with
constant propaganda and agitation, maintained in almost every aspect
of public life. Out of it formed a procrustean prejudice which led
inevitably to endemic persecution of real and alleged communists.
Always unofficially, but nonetheless with a persistence marked by
systematic inhumanity, the people of independent Ireland collaborated
in a process by which communists became second-class citizens, victims

of a social and civil apartheid which was accompanied by constant public vituperation.

Profound fears of the communist programme, and of the growing power of the USSR, enabled opponents in Great Britain to contain the growth of revolutionary communism even in the socially desperate 1930s. In Ireland, such fears were both inspired and intensified by horror of applied atheism. The victory of the party in the ex-Tsarist lands had been followed by an apparently successful onslaught against Orthodoxy and Catholicism alike. Given the increasingly secular culture of northern European politics, this was not a primary theme of discontent, though often it provided a useful optional string to the fiddle of reactionary propaganda. For citizens of the Free State, in contrast, religion was, overwhelmingly, the main item.

In 1932, General O'Duffy, appointed by the bishops as its organiser, sought to mobilise opinion around the Dublin Eucharistic Congress, a massive popular celebration of Ireland's religious commitment. The event might be seen on one level as celebrating the final triumph of Catholic Ireland over its traditional enemy, the English Protestant oppressor. But, at the same time, the energy and motivation which had made this victory possible must not be allowed to dissipate. Thus it was convenient to exploit the occasion to turn Ireland's militant Catholic nationalism – a carapace under which a huge majority of citizens united – to face the new adversary of international communism.[3] It was not to be foreseen, in 1932, that what was regarded as an indecisive and merely tactical defeat of Cosgrave's party at the general election of that year, would precipitate its rapid disintegration; even less that these events marked the beginning of the long-term domination of Irish politics by de Valera and the Fianna Fáil. O'Duffy and his advisers perhaps saw anti-communism as a way of forwarding the general policy of the opposition Cumann na nGhaedheal, which wished quietly to continue its long-established strategy of rebuilding relations with Great Britain. 'Live and let live with the old enemy: but long live the new!' might have been the slogan of leaders of the mainstream opposition in this regard.

This is not to argue that O'Duffy was merely playing politics. His fear of communism was all too authentic, a mental phobia, amounting almost to a personality disorder. From the information provided by his subordinates – the intelligence system patented by his mentor Collins and developed by his colleague O'Higgins – O'Duffy was aware that the actual level of communist activity in Ireland was well-nigh imperceptible. Even during the Spanish War, when recruitment in Great Britain reached record levels, the total card-carrying membership of the CPI almost certainly did not attain three figures, and it had no profile to speak of outside metropolitan Dublin.[4] For O'Duffy, nevertheless, the significance of this group was out of all proportion to its actual size. To him it was like a cancer which unless successfully attacked would grow inexorably, to threaten every cherished value of Irish life. In the interests of balance it is worth stating that these values, for many, including O'Duffy himself, included a normative democratic politics. But it was already too late for merely prophylactic action. To minds like O'Duffy's, the presence of even one pro-active communist in the Free State was a harbinger of doom. In this context, the mundane act of deception represented by the report was transcended by the metaphysical imperatives of its production and circulation.

However, O'Duffy's removal from the post of Commissioner, and de Valera's dismissive attitude to his report, meant that little or no official action was taken against the existence of Bolshevik elements in Dublin. De Valera himself was temperamentally against the legal proscription of extreme elements and took every reasonable action to avoid it. A little earlier, a left-wing organisation, Saor Eire, had attempted to forge an alliance between urban-based communists and rural-oriented radical republican groups. The latter were splintering from the IRA and formed just one strand of the general realignment which took place in Irish politics during the watershed years of 1929–34. Saor Eire was banned by Cosgrave's government in 1931 – on O'Duffy's initiative – and was later succeeded by the Irish Worker's League. By 1934, reaction to the mushroom growth of the Blueshirts had led to the formation of a dedicated Irish Communist Party and of the Republican Congress movement. The latter, organised by Peadar O'Donnell, Frank Ryan and George Gilmore, gained the limited support of radical and socialist elements of the IRA (itself, for similar reasons, enjoying a revival). As always, deciding political affiliation was a matter of personalities and priorities. The two or three hundred IRA men who split to join the Republican Congress were admirers of the record, and believers in the potential, of the latter's leaders. The critical change was that the Congress placed social reform, and acquiring an international social-democratic profile, ahead of 'single issue' nationalism – that is, the struggle against the Treaty and the existence of Northern Ireland.[5]

Meanwhile, the CPI, led by Sean Murray, came into existence. This was a result of events in 1933, when a mounting atmosphere of alarm had spilled over into violence in the streets of Dublin. Sustained clerical agitation, culminating in a week-long Jesuit 'mission' in the pro-cathedral, precipitated a 'spontaneous' attack on the offices of the Workers' League. The headquarters were destroyed by fire and its occupants severely manhandled.[6] The so-called 'siege of Connolly House' was a formative event for two Dubliners who later volunteered for the International Brigades. Bob Doyle was an unemployed sixteen-year-old, an orphan who had been produced as a firm Catholic by the infallibly rigorous methods of the Christian Brothers. Doyle was present in Dublin's pro-cathedral to hear a Jesuit preacher whipping up his audience with an anti-Bolshevik diatribe worthy of his order's most celebrated contemporary product, Dr Josef Goebbels. The sermon culminated with the memorable peroration: 'even here in the Holy City of Dublin these vile creatures are in our midst'. The indignant Doyle joined the thousands-strong mob which marched from the church to Connolly House in Strand Street, where he took part in the destruction of the premises. Shortly afterwards, however, he met Kit Conway (see below) and underwent a (blasphemous) species of Pauline conversion. Conway, who became Doyle's role-model, induced him to join the IRA, and later the CPI. He spent much of 1933–35 as a communist street-soldier, 'living in the worst slums in Dublin' and engaging in regular punch-ups with the Blueshirts. Too young to volunteer for Spain in 1936, he later achieved his ambition to join the International Brigade – and a chance to avenge the death of Kit Conway – early in 1938.[7] Joe Monks, like Doyle, remained a practising Catholic for some time after his political epiphany. Some years older than Doyle, he had joined Saor Eire in 1930. From a republican family, he was acquainted with Frank Ryan, worked for the IRA newspaper (*An Phoblacht*), and had connections with Connolly House. The events of March 1933 – he later recalled the mob's destruction of James Connolly's library, which had been installed in Strand Street – made Monks decide to leave not only the Church but also Ireland itself. He emigrated to London, and later joined with Ryan's group of volunteers *en route* for Spain.[8]

Though they tried to avoid clashing with each other in public debate, the two new parties were fundamentally divided on some issues. The Congress distrusted the political influence of the Catholic clergy, but manifested no objection to Catholicism as such, nor to religious belief and practice in general. In addition, the Congress leaders, despite a distaste for capitalism, were profoundly committed to democracy. In neither case, of course, did communists make such distinctions. One object, however, inspired in the two groups an identical loathing: General Eoin O'Duffy. The reasons for these feelings in Sean Murray and his executive have already been explained. For men like Peadar O'Donnell of the Republican Congress, O'Duffy was a long-established antagonist. Irish Republicans blamed him (perhaps unfairly) for the extreme 'reprisals' policy adopted against the anti-Treaty 'insurgents' in the south-western command during the Civil War – most notably, the infamous atrocity of Ballyseedy (Co. Kerry). Thereafter, as Chief of Police, it had fallen to O'Duffy to act as the main instrument of government vigilance during the years when the IRA was an illegal organisation.[9]

The violent struggles of 1933–34 were carried on by the left against what were seen not simply as reactionary but, increasingly, as fascist elements. There were two separate political commands, inspired by the geographical and socio-economic complexions of their respective support. In the countryside, the battle against the big farmers and farming-based businesses was led by the IRA and the Congress; in Dublin, that against the banks, the transport companies and the slum-landlords, by the CPI. The enemy in both cases, and frequently the object of actual assault, was the Blueshirts. In the quayside and dockland slums closely adjacent to Dublin's town centre, street battles were an almost daily affair. By 1936, however, some of the heat had gone out of this situation. Fianna Fáil's decisive triumph at the February 1933 general election – which enabled it to rule alone – and also at local ballots the following year, was followed by the beginning of the government's compromise settlement with London over the 'economic war' in 1935. On the other side, the faltering of the Blueshirt high command over the Dublin march in August 1933, and the subsequent history of crippling divisions amongst the Blueshirt–Fine Gael opposition, all served to defuse the almost apocalyptic atmosphere.[10]

The call to arms: action or reaction?

The outbreak of civil war in Spain quickly fanned the embers back into life. Indeed, the two men most heavily involved seemed almost to have read each other's minds on the ideal response to the issue which – in a matter of weeks rather than months – came to dominate Irish politics. In a remarkable speech in Dublin, Sean Murray, in every sense except the literally verbatim, raised the issue of physical support for the Republic:

> O'Duffy and Lombard Murphy and other kindred spirits are calling for Irishmen to go and join [Franco's] army of ruffians ... They are backed by the two fascist powers, Germany and Italy ... British imperialism too, is playing a treacherous dirty part in this business ... Are we in Ire-

land to stand aside [and] allow this crime against the people of Spain …? [We] have nothing but contempt for the treason to republicanism of de Valera and his newspaper who are also behind the criminal fascist gang in Spain … The Spanish workers are giving their lives in defence of liberty in every country. I ask every Irish man and woman to answer the question. What are you doing? … We demand that a united front of Labour and Republicanism be formed in this country in support of the Spanish people.[11]

It is claimed that Murray's appeal was made on the very day that O'Duffy's call for Catholic crusaders was printed in the *Irish Independent*. Even if true, it does not alter the fact that its whole dynamic derives directly from the latter event. It may be suspected that the CPI did not need the call from Paris or Moscow – nor even a prompt from Harry Pollitt in London – in order to mobilise itself for action in Spain. To this extent, Murray and his men anticipated the initiative to be launched some weeks later by the French communist leadership, which is accepted by most authorities as the germinal action of the International Brigades.[12] Nothing could more effectively emphasise the distinctive nature of Ireland's involvement in the Spanish Civil War. The personal involvement of O'Duffy ('if only two men go to Spain, I will be one of them') represented a special challenge which the left found irresistible.[13] Given the need to oppose the team of evil forces lined up in Murray's speech, Spain offered opportunities for the formation of an Irish 'popular front', enabling the CPI to develop the Comintern's programme of 'no enemies on the left' – with at least one eye on the next general election. Above all, the yoking together of international fascism and British imperialism in the Spanish context provided a platform for the CPI to collaborate with the IRA Congress. It was hoped to encourage fraternisation by the mainstream IRA and the Labour parties in both the Free State and the North.

In 1933, a Cardiff-Irishman, Pat Murphy, had visited Dublin as a delegate from the National Union of Seamen to the Annual Congress of its Free State counterpart. During the meeting, certain statements from the platform were greeted with scorn from the floor: 'there was always an element [Murphy recalled] that would yell out "we don't want any communism here".'[14] The story illustrates the dilemma of Irish labour organisations. The Labour Party – which had tasted power when it formed part of the coalition government in 1932–33 – had achieved a firmly 'respectable' and constitutional profile. Both the party and its trade-union associates were wholly dependent on the support of working-class Catholics (transport and building workers, agricultural labourers, domestic servants) for their existence. The very idea of any challenge to clerical opinion – especially on the profound emotional issues generated by Spain – was (as it were) anathema. The Labour Party held out no hand of fraternal assistance, far less an arm of protection, to the communists during the period when it was exposed to the vicious effects of popular hostility. On the contrary, union officials, especially in the rural towns, were heard to echo the anti-Red rhetoric of political rivals. Labour and trades representatives on local councils condemned the 'communist atrocities' in Spain, and voted for the so-called Clonmel Resolution.[15] Irish trade unions with a British affiliation were in a dilemma over the pro-republican line being followed by their executive brothers across the water. They risked mass defections unless they officially refused to join in pro-republican activity.[16]

Things were even worse in the North. The leader of the Northern Ireland Labour Party, Harry Midgley, committed himself to the Spanish struggle. Midgley simply failed to understand how any of his economically and socially downtrodden constituents could sympathise with the fascists in Spain. Mobilised by their clergy, Ulster Catholics almost to a person withdrew their support for the Labour Party, and Midgley's political career was ruined.[17]

Paradoxically, it was the bourgeoisie that rallied to the workers' cause in Spain. As the policy of non-intervention was taking shape in September, separate 'Spanish Aid' committees were formed in Dublin and Belfast – as in most major cities of Britain. These were pro-Republican and interventionist, but in a scrupulously non-military way, dedicated to raising funds for, and organising the dispatch of, food and clothing, along with medical equipment and personnel. Nevertheless, in the Free State, Labour and the unions held aloof. In Catholic circles, even this carefully modulated response of the liberal-minded was seen as provocative. Despite the fact that the Dublin committee was staffed by middle-class public figures of pacifist inclinations and innocent of any association even with the Labour Party, its vicarious sympathy for the 'murderous Reds' brought widespread condemnation in press and pulpit.[18]

Fighters, writers … and workers

As the IRA Congress and the CPI began to exchange views about organising an Irish contingent to go to Spain, they did so in an atmosphere of increasing popular condemnation – and, indeed, hatred. In mid-September, Frank Ryan, the Congress movement's gifted publicist, still believed that 'the Spanish trenches are right here in Ireland'. Not long afterwards, he found himself embroiled in a public argument over Spain with Cardinal MacRory, which apparently had the effect of changing his mind. Of the other Congress leaders, at first neither O'Donnell (who had been in Catalonia when the war began) nor Gilmore (who subsequently visited the anti-Franco Basque Republic) were convinced of the need for an Irish volunteer contribution. But then the CPI executive went ahead, appointing an organising officer, the popular ex-IRA veteran Bill Gannon. Subsequently, agreement was reached and the two parties proceeded to collect particulars of volunteers, who were to be ready to leave in November.[19]

Many problems had to be overcome, not least the overt hostility to be found inside their own communities (especially among women). By the time enough volunteers had been recruited to make an expedition worthwhile – at least in propaganda terms – it was common knowledge in Ireland that they would be joining an army organised from Moscow by the Communist International. The situation presented exactly the picture of doubled-dyed treachery which the priests had always striven to implant in the minds of the faithful. Irish Reds, prevented by the virtuous majority from doing so in their own country, were going to Spain to join in the slaughter of clergy. In coping with such feelings, the role of the Republican Congress was paramount. Frank Ryan could draw on a residual bank of (Irish) republican sympathy in Dublin, a war-chest for finance, a news-sheet (somewhat tenuous), and a reliable secret communications system (the latter, as we shall shortly see, was important).[20]

One hurdle that had to be jumped will already be familiar. As with their Catholic rivals, volunteers of the left who wished to exit the country via legitimate channels needed a passport. Few possessed a specimen of this bourgeois luxury item, which therefore had to be obtained from the Ministry of External Affairs. By the time applications were made, in accordance with non-intervention agreements, Spain had been struck off the list of countries to which passports extended normal protection (and, theoretically, access). This failed to inhibit dedicated volunteers. In early October, two applications in particular attracted the attention of the authorities. The Garda Special Branch chief reported that James Cummins and Christopher Conway of Dublin had applied for passports:

Both Conway and Cummins are active members of the Communist Party of Ireland and Conway is also associated with the Republican Congress Group. From information received in this Branch it would appear that both recently volunteered for service in Spain and it would appear that the object of these men in applying for passports is to make their way to Spain via France. It was learned through a friendly source in the Communist Organisation that this was the intention of these men.[21]

Cummins had pleaded a desire to visit France to pay respects at the grave of his brother, who had been killed fighting with the British Expeditionary Force for 'gallant little Belgium' in the Great War. His obliging referee – none other than his parish priest, Fr Joseph Nolan of St Catherine's church – described Cummins as a 'very respectable young man'.[22] Not receiving a reply for some weeks, Cummins wrote to the Minister (de Valera himself) to complain:

> Please use your good office to hasten the forwarding of [the passport] as the slowness of the officials concerned has almost spoiled the travel as owing to the lateness of the season & delay the journey will be anything but pleasant. It will be a sad disappointment if I have to postpone it after saving up for such a long time.[23]

The other applicant, Christopher ('Kit') Conway was a veteran IRA warrior, having fought in both the wars of 1918–23. An irreconcilable 'insurgent', he was jailed by the Free State government and after release opted for exile in the United States. Returning in the early 1930s, he worked as a builder's labourer in Dublin, and was one of the CPI's most effective proselytisers. Left-wing legend records that when he heard of the chance to volunteer for Spain he announced to his fellow workers that: 'Sooner than Franco should win, I would leave my body in Spain to manure the fields'.[24] Conway's application for a passport represented a bitterly subversive joke. He claimed he wished to visit the Marian shrine of Lourdes, then as now a regular destination of pilgrimage by large numbers of Irish Catholics.[25] The pious pilgrim and the parish priest's protégé were seeking to join an armed struggle, other partisans of which were at that very moment creating fresh shrines of martyred priests and nuns. Such scenes were taking place, in some cases, less than fifty miles from Lourdes, just across the frontier in the villages of northern Aragon. On these grounds, if no other, de Valera must have been tempted to reject Conway's application. He may have been an ex-comrade-in-arms of this diehard revolutionary; but, after all, he had seriously considered the religious vocation for himself. In the event, Conway's bluff – if such it was – was called, and both requests for passports were granted.[26]

Some enthusiasts were so moved by the plight of Republican Spain that they did not wait to be organised. Tommy Patten of Achill Island (Co. Mayo) was the first martyr of the cause. He was killed during the fighting at Boadilla del Monte, on the western outskirts of Madrid, in December 1936. Patten was a teenager from the tiny community of Dooega, one of a family of fourteen children. He emigrated to London, got a job in the Guinness factory, and involved himself in IRA work. He went to Spain, apparently of his own volition and under his own steam, in October, well before the main contingent left Ireland.[27] Bill Scott, a Dublin bricklayer and CPI member, was in Barcelona hoping to compete in the Workers' Olympics when the Civil War broke out. With a dozen comrades he joined the pioneer British pro-republican unit, the Tom Mann 'Centuria', formed by the Cambridge graduate Lorrimer Birch. After three months' fighting, most of the survivors were incorporated into the Thaelmann Battalion. Not long after the first International Brigade (the XI) arrived at Madrid on 8 November – the moment when the world expected the fall of the capital to Franco – Scott was encountered by the young Esmond Romilly, who remembered him affectionately in one of the most celebrated memoirs of the war: 'Like most of the quiet kind of Irishmen, Bill Scott had a very nice personality and a way of saying humorous things in an aggrieved kind of manner which made them funnier ... Everyone liked Bill. They elected him political responsible [i.e. Commissar].'[28]

These two – along with Charlie Donnelly – make an ideally representative trio of pro-republican volunteers. Scott, a labourer from the capital city; Patten, a farmer's boy from the remote reaches of Ireland's Gaeltacht; Donnelly, an intellectual and poet from the North. In fact the substantial majority – 66 per cent – of the (approximately) two hundred Irishmen who fought for the Spanish Republic were working-class men from the slums of Belfast and Dublin, along with other substantial urban centres like Cork and Waterford.[29] Such men had suffered, and watched their loved ones suffer, through years of depression. They belonged to communities which were among the poorest in Europe. They had fought in strikes and in the streets, and felt a visceral hatred of the bosses. About sixty Dubliners, many of them unemployed, along with some twenty-five Belfast men, went to join the International Brigades.

In contrast, only about a quarter hailed from rural backgrounds. Co. Donegal, which sent only one man to Spain with O'Duffy, contributed no fewer than seven of the Internationals – perhaps due to IRA influence in that embattled frontier zone. Indeed, the majority of recruits had at some point in their lives been IRA activists; many did not feel it necessary to resign from this organisation upon joining the CPI.[30] These fighters, men like Kit Conway, hard-bitten veterans of their own civil war, survivors of punitive jail sentences and fugitive politics, were violently alienated from the authority of both Church and State.

In terms of political affiliation, a decisive majority of the group which now prepared to leave Dublin were either ex-Congressites or regular IRA members rather than avowed communists, since, despite Conway's presence, it was Frank Ryan who acted as official leader (and spokesman) of the Dublin contingent. Probably by design rather than accident, Ryan's own group (about forty-strong) left on Friday 11 December, aboard one of the few Liverpool ferry sailings not patronised by the O'Duffy Brigade. The departure of a total of eighty volunteers (other groups left from Belfast and Rosslare) 'to fight on the side of the government forces' was widely reported in the press that weekend, alongside (or integrated with) the columns which told the more dramatic story of the SS *Urundi* in Galway Bay. Despite the now open nature of the expedition, and the government's growing commitment to the rules of non-intervention, no attempt was made to hinder any of these departures. It was noted in the Ministry of External Affairs 'that the total of Irish men fighting for the government, with these 80 men, will now amount to 200'.[31] This was perhaps inaccurate at the time, but represented a strangely accurate prophecy of the final head-count of Irish Internationals.

At the quayside, Frank Ryan made a carefully prepared statement to the press in which motivation for the commitment was clearly set out. It represented, he said:

> a demonstration of the sympathy of revolutionary Ireland with the Spanish people in their fight against international Fascism. It is also a reply to the intervention of Irish Fascism in the war against the Spanish republic which, if unchallenged would remain a disgrace on our people. We want to show that there is a close bond between the democracies of Ireland and Spain. Our fight is the fight of the Spanish people, as it is of all peoples who are the victims of tyranny.[32]

Ryan's words were an honest and concise description of policy, and one which accurately reflected the views of most of his men. But only the last two sentences might be seen as 'official' in the sense that they encapsulated the 'popular front' line, laid down by the Comintern. They were words which, even as Ryan uttered them, were being reiterated in every language and medium all over the northern hemisphere, in public meetings assembled in the halls of 'bourgeois democracies' or in back rooms among secret cells of the persecuted. In contrast, the reference to 'revolution' in Ryan's opening sentence was seriously awry from the communist angle. In Moscow's vocabulary, there was no 'revolution' in Spain, and certainly no volunteer was going to Spain in order to advance such a phenomenon. Lastly, Ryan's reference to O'Duffy was (in my view) the key to everything else.

But before the collectivity, the individuality. Since both reason and the historical experience of modern politics suggest that the cause of all can never be precisely the cause of each, what moved these men to offer their lives to defend a distant, foreign community? Some indication of an answer is implicit in the socio-economic circumstances of most volunteers. Nevertheless, in general this is a more difficult question than in the case of the 'Catholic crusaders', not only because personal motivation was more varied in a political-ideological sense, but also because so little of the veteran Internationals' testimony has survived independently of wartime censorship and the meticulously selective conservation policy exercised by the Communist Party and the International Brigade Association.

In general terms, it may be assumed that, in contrast to their rivals in the other camp, the average Irish International was a 'modern' man, in whom the twentieth century had developed a complex persona, a mature affective subject. It was intensely paradoxical given that, once integrated into the Brigades, they were required by an ideological practice far more 'anti-modern' in this respect than the Catholic Church, to suppress or even abandon their selfish instincts in favour of the abstract will of the party. Their cause was a single, communist crusade.

Both Bob Doyle and Joe Monks have left on record their conviction that the struggle in Spain was identical to the struggle against economic exploitation at home. (To this, the former, but not the latter, added religious exploitation.) Doyle hoped that 'every bullet I fired would be a bullet against the Dublin landlords and capitalists'.[33] Tommy Patten, in an existential inversion of this sentiment, bade farewell to his brother with the words: 'the bullet that will get me won't get a Spanish worker' – a claim which echoes Dickens's Sidney Carton or the hero of Sartre's *Roads to Freedom* (who was actually based on a veteran of the Spanish Civil War).[34] Eugene Downing, a Dublin print worker, joined the CPI at the age of twenty-one, at a time 'when you had to be interested in politics whether you liked it or not'. The anti-communist atmosphere even in the worst slum districts was frightening, and everything had to be done 'hugger-mugger' when he left for Spain in 1938.[35] Many other comrades in the International Brigade were motivated not only by class consciousness, but also by (Irish) republican sympathies, usually representing loyalty to kith-and-kin experience, and often marked by specific resentments and inarticulate vendettas, which excited a hatred of the Irish 'establishment' and an instinctive empathy with Spanish republicanism. One such was Peter O'Connor of Waterford, who does not seem to have been a communist in 1936, when he 'answered Frank Ryan's call' to go to Spain.[36] For many like O'Connor, the Spanish Civil War offered (amongst other things) a chance to reverse the decision of the war of 1922–23, to vindicate a cause which had then been tragically overthrown by traitors who were – as he saw things – little less than agents of British imperialism.

But, as always in consideration of the Spanish Civil War, it is the writers who achieve completeness of experience, who become the inevitable heroes of the populist imagination. Charlie Donnelly was the Irish equivalent of England's John Cornford – the Byronic martyr at once unique and utterly characteristic of his type. A young research student at University College, Dublin (UCD) at work on a thesis about James Connolly, socialist martyr of the 1916 Easter Rising, Donnelly was also the author of a handful of superb lyric poems. He never lived to develop this talent or to write about the communist crusade, dying as a member of the XV International Brigade at the battle of Jarama in February 1937.[37]

A less well-known example was Thomas O'Brien, who finally joined the Internationals in the spring of 1938 after struggling with his conscience for many months. O'Brien was a working-class Dubliner who was striving to make a reputation as a writer and playwright in left-wing circles. He helped to set up the New Theatre Group, which adopted Brechtian methods of missionary work amongst Dublin's culturally deprived. Like so many of his generation, he saw his role as that of writer rather than fighter. His encounter with political issues led him into the CPI and, simultaneously (to adapt Auden on Yeats) 'hurt him into poetry'. By the nature of writing and acting, O'Brien inevitably moved into the circle of middle-class intellectuals. In his mix of motives, aesthetic ambition was linked to a residual fear of betrayal of his social origins. In Spain this tension could be positively discharged. His feelings were here akin to those of so many others – he could find in fighting the experience and material necessary for writing and, at the same time, justify the process to his own conscience by defending both his class community and his principles in arms.[38]

Two leaders of the Republican Congress contingent can also, if more loosely, be classified as intellectuals. Frank Ryan, as well as being a veteran of the War of Independence, was a Gaelic scholar and UCD graduate. Until the crisis of the mid-1920s and the 'defection' of de Valera, he was a golden boy of Sinn Fein, being groomed as a future leader. His frustration and confusion in the face of what he viewed as the opportunist success of Fianna Fáil, led to a commitment to socialism – though, as a convinced Catholic, he could go no further than that. Unlike many of his comrades, Ryan lacked personal experience of social deprivation and economic oppression, an experience which often seems to have been necessary, inside the individual pysche, to allow politics to vanquish faith. On the contrary, it was no paradox that it should have been Cardinal MacRory's intervention which provoked him into accepting the leadership of the Irish Internationals. For Ryan, it was in one sense a religious action; a personal demonstration that the true moral conscience of Catholics should lead them to the defence of a beleaguered democratic republic in a modern crusade. Skilled editor of *An Phoblacht* and a sought-after freelance journalist, Ryan had a honed analytical mind and a finger on the pulse of Irish politics.[39]

Ryan's friend, Frank Edwards, was Republican Congress leader in Waterford, and also drew on an *echt*-republican family background. A brother had been 'shot whilst trying to escape' by the Free State army as part of the reprisal policy during the Civil War. Along with Peter O'Connor, Edwards contested the influence of Paddy Dalton and the Blueshirts in his home town. In 1935, on the instance of the Bishop of Waterford, Edwards was summarily sacked from his teaching job in a local Christian Brothers' school.[40] A subsequent campaign failed to get him reinstated, but may have had something to do with the fact that more Waterford men went to fight in Spain for the Republic than for the Franco side.

Another unique feature of the Free State's involvement in the Spanish Civil War is that Irish issues – perhaps better characterised as 'Irish' – helped to inspire dozens of men whose connections with the old country were sometimes tenuous, to support the Spanish Republic. Perhaps the most notable was Sam Wild, an orphan brought up in the back lanes of Salford, who is remembered as one of the most fanatical officers

of the British Battalion, and its only genuinely working-class commander. Wild was reared by an equally fanatical aunt, who indoctrinated him
with Catholicism and Irish nationalism in equal measure. Interviewed in
old age about his motives for going to Spain, he responded to the question: 'How strict was your Catholic upbringing?'

> The priest in our parish, Father Oates, came from the same village in
> Ireland as my aunt and my mother, with the result that he thought he
> had some paternal interest in me ... Every time he saw me he gave me
> a crack with his stick. I was compelled to go to confession and com-
> munion ... My aunt was a militant sort of Irisher, a Sinn Feiner, and
> she instilled in me a profound feeling for the cause of Ireland. Even as
> a kid of ten or eleven years of age, I used to make my way down to
> Stevenson Square and listen to the Irish Home Rulers speak ... I got
> more Irish than English ... a typical Irishman, against everything.[41]

Another 'exile', Bernard Collins, born in London of Irish nationalist
parents, vividly remembered his famous namesake Michael holding
political meetings in his home in the early 1920s. His father told him,
'whatever you do, support the Russians'. Already involved in radical politics, in 1937 he met a certain Fitzgerald, Irish, communist and 'a bit of a
student', who had been wounded at Brunete, and told him of the superb
revolutionary training he had from the Russians in Spain. Collins
promptly marched himself around to King Street to volunteer.[42]

Max Goldberg, from Merthyr Tydfil, half Irish and half Jewish,
refused to volunteer out of respect for his mother's feelings (she had
brought him up a strong Catholic). But he joined the Communist Party
during the Spanish Civil War, and later recalled his main motivation with
voluble brevity: 'I was for Ireland.'[43] Similar feelings moved a Canadian
volunteer with no Irish connections, Bill Williamson, who joined the
Mackenzie-Papineau Battalion in 1938. He was inspired in part by rip-
ping yarns of Irish republican heroism with which he had been regaled
as a youngster by a Fenian friend of his parents.[44] Thus it seems that for
people all over the British empire who identified with the oppressed, 'Ireland' and 1916 had become a symbolic talisman of freedom which somehow melded, in 1936, into 'Spain'. Finally, another Canadian, John Paddy
McElligot – born in Ireland, he had seen his father shot by the British in
1918, and subsequently fought in an IRA flying column. Yet despite these
experiences, and in contrast to the other examples in this paragraph,
McElligot's reasons for going to Spain were not political idealism nor
even revenge, but a desire for violent adventure and an inability to settle,

both aggravated by the poverty and unemployment he found every-where. This case, too, was by no means unique.[45]

For all this, whether in Irish or in universal terms, the main and most immediate motive, a goad which stirred the flanks and the ranks to action, was the need to respond to the 'fascist challenge'. The collective political denomination of all International Brigaders was, after all, '*antifascista*'. Within the Free State, this had a meaning which was present only weakly (if at all) in any other country. Not only had Ireland recruited a total of 48,000 men to the Blueshirts – per head of population more than any other nation – but the paramilitary formations, and unmistakably fascist policy ideas, had been patronised by the main (democratic) opposition party. Above all, General Eoin O'Duffy, the head of the 'Irish Brigade' for Spain, had also been, until recently, the acknowledged leader and/or spokesman of all these movements. Little wonder that left-inspired texts on the question return again and again to the issue of O'Duffy's intervention – if, at times, only with the intention of playing down its importance.

We have noted the fixture of this point in the minds of Sean Murray and Frank Ryan. References, all of them voluble, range from the super-ficially trivial to the obsessive. Eugene Downing remembers to this day that a tip in the *Daily Worker* for a horse running in the Grand National on the day he left London was 'Blue Shirt'.[46] When Joe Monks arrived at Figueras, the main reception station for volunteers near the Pyrenees frontier, he was greeted by a Spanish officer:

> We Irish thought him a comic because he reminded us of General O'Duffy, Ireland's would-be Fuhrer, who was the leader of some six-hundred Irishmen then at Cáceres in the region of Extremadura. O'Duffy was taking orders from General Franco. The fortress com mandant was attired in a blue shirt, black belt and breeches with a Sam Brown belt to complete the attire of the Irish Fascist.[47]

Monks had crossed the Pyrenees with Frank Ryan in a party which included thirteen Irishmen. These men were highly conscious of Ire-land's history, a significant territory which they wanted to contest with O'Duffy. Whereas Yeats had inspired the latter to call up the shades of the O'Neills and O'Donnells, the Irish left in reply enlisted O'Donovan Rossa and James Connolly. But both sides laid claim to the heritage of the 'Wild Geese'. At the time in Spain, and years afterwards, Paddy O'Daire – Don-egal man as he was – was anxious to don the plaid of the great exile warrior septs, and was mortified at the thought that it might be seen by anyone as more fitting to the O'Duffyites.[48] Ryan was suspicious that such attitudes betrayed 'adventurism', an unreal romanticism, amongst the volunteers. But he, too, reacted when he heard about a newspaper story: 'Is the Irish Press comparing the Wild Geese to O'Duffy's hirelings? The Wild Geese were honest-minded men who went out to fight against their country's enemy … To compare O'Duffy's dupes with them is an insult to national tradition.'[49]

But these were only variations on the main theme. When a friend wrote to him to criticise his foolhardy valour at the battle of Jarama, Ryan retorted from his hospital bed:

> What did I come out here for? To be another O'Duffy, directing his men from the rear? … Which reminds me – why must the *Post* and other papers talk of his 'bloodfeud' between O'Duffy and I [*sic*]? We would be out here if there never was an O'Duffy. We smashed his attempts to set up a dictatorship in Ireland … We came here to fight Fascism; it's just an accident for us that O'Duffy happened to be here fighting for it.[50]

All the same, in *The Book of the XV Brigade*, the English-language version of which he edited during 1937, Ryan recorded that '[The Irish] came primarily to fight International Fascism. They had an added incentive in that O'Duffy, traitor ex-General, had induced a body of Irishmen to help the Fascist Generals of Spain.'[51] A feature on 'Irish Volunteers in Spain' printed in the International Brigade's newspaper, *Volunteer for Liberty*, developed Ryan's phrases further: 'They had added incentive in that a careerist ex-General discredited in Ireland, had introduced a body of Irishmen to go to fight for the traitor generals "in defence of Christianity". Irish honour thus besmirched they would redeem, Irish sympathy thus misrepresented they would express aright.'[52]

As the battle of Jarama was still raging, Ryan's namesake Desmond addressed an open letter to the O'Duffy Brigaders which gave voice – if only in a propaganda context – to the feeling that a call from Irish soul to Irish soul could be heard across no man's land: 'Why do you go to fight by the side of the upholders of a land system as crushing and as terrible as that which your own grandfathers fought against in the days of the Land League? The answer is easy: cynical politicians and thoughtless bigots have misled you.'[53]

8

In the ranks of
the Comintern army

The International Brigades

During the Spanish Civil War some 45,000 foreigners enlisted in the International Brigades to fight on the Republican side. This display of commitment was an authentic reflection of the emotions of many millions all over the world. In crude essence, it was a phenomenon unique in modern times: it has not been repeated, for example, in potentially analogous cases, such as those of Vietnam, Nicaragua or Bosnia. As Tom Buchanan has argued, the volunteers – and perhaps the 'aid Spain' movement as a whole – reflected the culture of a generation which believed in personal intervention in politics as a living principle.[1] Until the 1960s the notion remained prevalent that an individual could help change the world by direct action. The element of romantic choice was still residual, surviving as it did mostly through the influence of literature and film, to leaven the utilitarian dough of modern industrial democracy.

Yet this truly international movement, essentially as altruistic as any in history, was controlled in all accidentals by the Soviet Communist Party, acting via the Third International (or Comintern). The existence, constitution, and even military comportment of the International Brigades thus depended on decisions taken in the Kremlin. Of course, even without the intervention of the Soviet machine, thousands of lone volunteers might still have fought for the Republic in militia units, or in the Popular Army (*Ejército Popular*) which was developed to replace the militias in the course of 1937. But the majority would never have been able actually to realise this commitment were it not for the worldwide organisation and resources of the Comintern. Stalin made the flesh of physical resistance from the word of outrage and protest.[2]

Irish volunteers for military service with the Republic thus became soldiers in what one historian has called a 'Comintern Army'.[3] As such, their history is broadly similar to that of any of the thirty-odd other elements which derived from identifiable 'national' backgrounds. To this extent, any specific analysis will be generally valid for the whole force, and especially for the British Battalion and the Fifteenth (XV) International Brigade of which it formed part. In any case, most aspects of army life and battle experience have similar characteristics in any war. Inevitably, therefore, the background realities of the Brigades encroach upon attempts to deal with the special experiences of Irishmen. In a very real sense this was the mission of the organisation. At least since the eighteenth century, to homogenise – in this context an ideally dualistic term – has been the task of military administration. But there was a key difference here, which intensified the situation. This army, made up from politically variable individuals, understood itself to need uniformity in politics as a precondition of military effectiveness. It was a political army in the image of Trotsky's Red Army, which defined itself and its objectives in ideological as well as military terms, in which the political commissar was as important as the field commander, and to which political education was as important as martial training.[4] Indeed, the International Brigades demanded uniformity in everything – except, perhaps, uniforms. On the whole, despite the element of romantic individualism in the motivation of many members, this was achieved. Personal and national identities were submerged to the extent that ethnocentric analysis is problematic. Despite this, the Irish experience retains some unmistakable contours. Explanation courts the dangers of national stereotyping, yet the record indicates that the Irish intruded on the history of the International Brigades quite as much as they were themselves intruded upon by the general imperatives treated above.

Even by December 1936, arrangements by which the initial Irish contingent reached Spain were already operating smoothly, both within Great Britain and on the continent. Groups which set out from Dublin, Belfast and Rosslare reached London, where they were vetted by Communist Party of Great Britain (CPGB) officials and joined by several dozen exiles, among them Joe Monks and Charlie Donnelly.[5] They were then transferred to Paris via boat-trains from Victoria. It had not yet become illegal for men to leave Britain to enlist in Spain. Even so, parties were occasionally picked up by police or customs and sent back to London. Thus volunteers were ordered to travel in discrete (and, hopefully, discreet) groups of two or three, speaking only when spoken to by representatives of bourgeois authority. According to one account, Frank Ryan's party disdained to behave in this anti-social manner. On one crossing, around forty of them occupied the bar, giving out a stirring repertoire of 'rebel' songs, and impressing upon fellow passengers their strong distaste for fascism and Franco.[6]

Once in Paris – paradoxical as this may seem – order was reimposed. The French capital may have been the *locus classicus* of individual transgression, but it was also the historical site of revolution and the headquarters of the Comintern. The organisation of global 'agitprop' was based there, and was supported by the sophisticated infrastructure of what was (since 1933) the largest Communist Party outside the USSR.[7] From this point, the Irish experience of the journey merges with that of other volunteers recruited in northern and western Europe, and North America. They became, literally as well as metaphorically, fellow travellers. From Paris, by various modes of transport, men were filtered down to the Spanish border in Roussillon. They crossed the Pyrenees – in theory, at least, patrolled by armed gendarmes – in parties of a dozen or so, using routes known to local guides and under the cover of night. Parties collected again at the Catalan town of Figueras, in a seventeenth-century fortress which boasted ample barracks, squares and custom-designed (if hardly well-appointed) underground billets.

Frank Ryan crossed the frontier in a party of thirteen Irishmen on or about 14 December. He reached Albacete, HQ of the International Brigades, a few days later.[8] Like Cáceres, Albacete is capital of the province which bears its name. Forming part of the wider region of New Castile, the latter occupies nearly 15,000 square kilometres in centre south-east Spain. The town lies about seventy kilometres south of the main road between Valencia – whence the government of Republican Spain had now been transferred – and Madrid. Before the war, Albacete had some 25,000 inhabitants. It was a typical rural town, lying on an extensive plateau, boasting two small-scale (largely domestic) industries – for both of which, however, it was renowned: knife-making and the manufacture of saffron. Men from Belfast and Dublin regarded Albacete as a backwater. Even today it remains isolated and insular; that it will be the last provincial capital to be listed in tourist brochures as 'unspoilt' seems a fairly safe prediction. In 1936, its modest centre, comprising a main square with gothic cathedral, provincial and municipal buildings retaining a faded eighteenth-century grandeur, a bullring and military barracks, was surrounded by streets of miserable single-storey dwellings. But Albacete was well chosen for its purpose, particularly in the logistical dimension. It was on main railway lines, and had – in Spanish terms – good road communications to most of the front-line zones to north, west and south. Before the arrival of the Irish and British, it had already provided a womb for two earlier regiments, and was to remain the head-quarters of the International Brigades until the summer of 1938, not long before the force was disbanded.

Ryan and his compatriots collected in Albacete in the week before Christmas, at exactly the same time as the Irish Brigade were assembling in Cáceres. The General Staff (*Estado Mayor*) of the Brigades had been in existence for three months, and three Brigades – the XI, XII and XIV, mainly of French-, Italian- and German-speaking volunteers – were in action on the Madrid front. Several others were in the process of forma-tion, including a predominantly English-speaking Brigade. The latter was now designated XV, and its British battalion was allocated the village of Madrigueras, thirty kilometres north of Albacete, as its training centre. Not long after his arrival, Ryan wrote to an American friend: 'We arrived here the 16th of December, 550 strong of which 350 are from Ire-land, 50 being from Belfast, 60 Liverpool Irish, and as you know New York, Philadelphia and Boston are well represented. The Irish lads who enlisted at the beginning are being transferred to the Irish battalion.'[9] Ryan's correspondent, Gerald O'Reilly, was a key figure in Clann na Gael, the Irish society in the USA through which support for the IRA was mobilised. His letter, with its hugely exaggerated figures for Irish partic-ipation, was inspired by the need for propaganda, encouraging commit-ment (both financial donations and further recruits) in North America, and to stake a claim for a specifically Irish allegiance of volunteers arriv-ing from that potentially unlimited source. The statement that an Irish battalion was being formed was also premature. Issues raised by these preoccupations were soon to assume a critical prominence. But Ryan's claims had a certain 'objective truth'. The arrival of the Irish contingent had increased the complement of anglophone recruits, from around two hundred to more than three hundred men. For the high command in Albacete, the Irish contribution advanced the point – political priority as well as military necessity – at which a 'British' battalion could be dis-patched to the front.[10] The problem was that the cause of saving Madrid and the Republic could not wait for these tidily organic agglomerations to evolve into fully fledged battle units. Franco's failure to capture the capital by direct thrust in November had not been due to the arrival of the International Brigades alone. But the fact remained that the battle-field performance of the latter was in a different class from that of most existing loyalist outfits, and this could not be ignored, either by the Defence Committee under General Miaja in Madrid, or by Largo Caballero, prime minister and minister of war, in Valencia.

In the early weeks of 1937 pressure on Madrid abated little, for Franco was merely changing tack to suit his resources. In a series of offensives the metropolis had been cut off from the north and west. The enemy attempted to construct a position from which it could sweep the Sierra de Guadarrama clear of its defenders, removing a natural shield which was Madrid's main barrier to invasion. In addition to the fully formed International Brigades already in position, scratch units were formed from the pool of men in Albacete, with the aim of stiffening resistance or leading counter-attacks at selected points. Early in the new year Franco had to admit that the northern thrust too had failed in its main objective. He was obliged to reconsider his strategy – though Madrid remained the priority target. His army of Africa had fought from Seville to the gates of Madrid, losing over 40 per cent of its sixteen thousand effectives in the process. During ten weeks of fighting in the approaches to, and in the built-up suburbs of, Madrid, the casualty rate in Franco's elite units of Legionaries and Moors reached over 70 per cent. He had fewer than ten thousand experienced men at his disposal on the main front of operations, most of whom had enjoyed no sustained rest since August. He was desperately short of supplies and munitions, and his lines of communication were vulnerable. A respite was inevitable. This relief period – though precarious – offered the chance that a British battalion, quantitatively worthy of the name, might complete the final stages of formation.[11]

The Defence Junta was certainly aware of some of the salient facts concerning the weaknesses of its antagonist. But although now commanding a defensive force which was at least four times the enemy's total, the Republic too was desperately short of experienced and disciplined infantry units. Inside this dilemma, another was interrogatively curled. The interruption to the nationalist onslaught offered the Republic its first opportunity to launch a major counter-offensive. One school of thought demanded that the International Brigades be allowed time to prepare for their indispensable role in this campaign. But others clamoured for the right to call upon them whenever military necessity demanded. In either case, the Brigades were at a premium, made up (in the imaginations of their political masters) of battle-hardened veterans of the First World War. The smooth evolution of the XV Brigade was continually disrupted by emergency demands for assistance. No sooner had the main Irish party arrived, for example, than those among them who actually did have battle experience found themselves drafted into what were little more than *ad hoc* units, dispatched to plug gaps in a front line which now curved across the middle of Spain, roughly from north to south but extending erratically for thousands of kilometres.

Encounters with the enemy

Their first action came about as a result of an enemy thrust in Córdoba province, to the south of Albacete. General Queipo de Llano, nationalist commander in Andalusia, mounted an operation to relieve a besieged rebel outpost situated deep in the government zone. This enclave had formed around the monastery of Santa María de la Cabeza, built on an outcrop of the Sierra Morena, due north of the town of Andújar.[12] During the war's early weeks, more than a thousand pro-rebel refugees from nearby towns gathered in this ancient shrine. The government's myriad priorities precluded operations against them, thus enabling defenders to lay in supplies of weaponry, munitions and food. Queipo came under pressure from the religious lobby and from Franco to save the heroic defenders of Santa María. In the last week of December an attack developed along the line of the main road from Córdoba city towards Andújar – and thus, by distant implication, towards Valencia. Though probably aware of the limited significance of the enemy move, the Valencia government could not be certain it did not represent (or adumbrate) a major offensive. Immediate resistance was required. In a great rush, the XIV Brigade (mainly francophone) was dispatched to Andalusia, but – weakened by the casualties of recent months – it needed strengthening. A company (called No. 1) of the emergent British battalion was one of the units formed and seconded for this purpose. More than forty Irishmen were members, including nine of the thirteen who had crossed the Pyrenees with Ryan.

The company was commanded by Captain George Nathan, a British army veteran, who led a total of a hundred men, incorporated into the 'Marseillaise' Battalion of the XIV Brigade.[13] Joe Monks had enjoyed the benefit of four days' training at Madrigueras when Nathan appealed for volunteers. After stepping forward, Monks heard (to his consternation) that Kit Conway, and not Frank Ryan, had been selected to lead the Irish section of the company.[14] Piling into railway wagons on Christmas Eve, the unit set off for Andújar. On arrival, the men were able to enjoy a Christmas dinner of sorts, whilst waiting for orders. On 26 December they advanced towards the village of Lopera, a few kilometres west of Andújar. By this time, the enemy had already taken an arc of villages to the north and south of the road, establishing a bridgehead of which

Lopera – taken on Christmas Day itself – formed the apex. The British company unknowingly bore down upon the strongest point of the enemy's line. Although they reached a good position overlooking the village, the company was harassed from the air, and such heavy casualties were incurred that assaulting the enemy lines became an untenable proposition. Nathan had no alternative but to pull back. Among the Irish alone, eight men had been killed – including the seventeen-year-old Dubliner, Tommy Woods – whilst several others were wounded. Joe Monks himself was in the latter category. He recalled:

> I got a bullet [which] came down my rifle and right through [my chest] and out my back. I was very shocked, it was like a kick from a mule, terrifying with all the blood spurting out. Old Nathan came along, shook hands with me, helped me back and wished me luck. I'll always have the greatest respect for him. If he hadn't have been there I might have run away: instead I succeeded in sticking with him and having confidence in him.[15]

A vivid account of the Lopera action was published in the Republican Congress newspaper from the pen of Donal O'Reilly, who fought alongside Monks:

> The company forms and moves to the attack. A V-shaped movement with the Irish advancing on the left flank. Kit Conway is fair bursting to get to grips, but first we must lend two of our best gunners – May and Conroy – to the French Battalion. We move through the olive grove with the zing-zung of the bullets playing a tune. Occasionally a snick as a bullet clips off a cluster of leaves. Out from the friendly trees, down a short valley crossing a stream, then up, up, among the hills …
> We move to the crest. The fire is terrific. The language is terrific. Joe Monks is hit. Prendergast's and Dinny Coady's guns are shot to pieces. Bits of guns fly and we think we're all hit.[16]

The Córdoba counter-offensive is alleged to have been the manoeuvre which inspired a republican communiqué to claim that: 'today the advance of our troops continued without loss of territory'. As things turned out, this statement was appropriate. The nationalist advance now stuck, not just for the time being but for the rest of the war, at the lines it occupied before the arrival of the XIV Brigade on the battlefield. Nevertheless, the latter's commander, Major-General Delasalle, was court-martialled on charges of cowardice and treason. His execution by firing squad on 2 January added a final casualty to the tragedy of Lopera.

For its part, Nathan's company was acknowledged to have done a good job – so much so, that it was now transferred along with the rest of the XIV Brigade (around 10 January), direct from Andalusia to the Madrid front, to cope with another emergency. Here, Kit Conway, Frank Edwards and around twenty other Irishmen were involved in further bitter fighting during a counter-attack on Las Rozas, to the west of the city. In this engagement, 'Dinny' Coady, a popular character in both Dublin and Spain, was killed, and Edwards injured. The latter soon recovered enough to send an account of the experience to the CPI paper, *The Worker:*

> We were lying in position on a ridge. Dinny Coady lay near me and another Irishman, Pat Murphy, between us. A shell landed between Coady and Murphy. I immediately felt a sharp pain in my side. Murphy screamed. I glanced towards him. He was enveloped in a cloud of smoke and dust. But I could see his face … he was ghastly pale. I got up and walked down to a ravine where our Company Headquarters section was posted, and told them to send up a stretcher at once. I thought Murphy had been badly hit. Then I got a Red Cross man to rip my clothes off. I had a deep wound under my armpit and a slight scratch on my leg.[17]

Behind the lines at Madrigueras, Frank Edwards's compatriots were meanwhile embroiled in a very different struggle, but one which was also – metaphorically at least – likely to leave permanent wounds. As No. 1 Company was leaving for Andalusia, a crisis began to fester within the British Battalion. Relations between Irish volunteers and the English officers of the battalion deteriorated. The whole affair is difficult to describe, in the sense of reconstructing a firm and detailed narrative. There is a host of references to relevant events, but nearly all differ in detail and/or emphasis, and all are also fragmentary. Precise dates of the main incidents are impossible to establish, and a logical sequence of events is very elusive.

It is necessary to isolate the essential elements of the quarrel. A number of the Irish contingent were set upon forming a nationally exclusive unit. Indeed, even a dedicated communist like Bill Scott, pioneer Irish volunteer, rejected the idea of serving in a 'British battalion'. One of Scott's English comrades in the XII Brigade recalled that 'we were grouped into nationalities. Bill and I comprised the British section … Bill's insistence that he was not British caused a little confusion. He was pacified only by being assured that the arbitrary grouping was very temporary and entailed no loss of Irish independence.'[18]

Most Irishmen in Madrigueras resented the command of English officers who were ex-professionals, with matching attitudes (and even accents). It was not easy for IRA veterans dedicated to struggle against the English oppressor, in a war which – to their minds – was by no means over, to accept a subordinate relationship to such men. This would probably have been the case even had the personalities concerned been gifted in the arts of tact and diplomacy. In fact, the commanders of the British Battalion, Wintringham and McCartney – not to mention their superiors, André Marty (Chief Commissar, based in Albacete) and Lieutenant-Colonel Gal (military commander of the XV Brigade) – signally lacked these qualities. The situation was exacerbated when Captain Nathan – who, ironically, as well as being an excellent soldier, actually did possess such qualities – was discovered to have an outrageously relevant past.

Whilst Nathan was absent in Andalusia, it emerged that in an earlier phase of his military career, during the 'Irish War of Independence', he had been an officer in the unit of British irregulars known as the Black-and-Tans. This was the most hated force in the history of British military presence in Ireland, and prominent in Fenian folklore. It was alleged that Nathan had been involved in various operations of a distinctly shady nature. Many years later it was established that he had indeed been a key member of a hit-squad directed by Dublin Castle, and was personally responsible for the murder of two prominent Limerick Sinn Feiners in 1920.[19] The man who first led the Irish into battle thus proved to be as hateful an agent of English imperialism as any imagination could have invented. *Prima facie*, at least, Nathan appeared to the men in Madrigueras as hardly a lesser enemy of the Irish republican cause than General O'Duffy himself. Accordingly, rumours about the English officers became food at the tables and drink in the bars where the Irishmen gathered in Madrigueras and Albacete. Frank Ryan was disturbed enough by them to issue a New Year message intended to defuse the situation, addressed 'To all Irish Comrades':

> An Irish unit of the International Brigades is being formed … This unit will be part of the English-speaking Battalion which is to be formed. Irish, English, Scots and Welsh comrades will fight side by side against the common enemy – Fascism. It must also be made clear that in the International Brigades … there are no national differences … If we stress the fact that we are Irish it is merely to show the world that the majority of the Irish people repudiate Fascist O'Duffy and his mercenaries who are helping Franco and his Moors. It should be unnecessary, too, to point out that as we came out voluntarily, men of different parties & men of no party, so may we go back when the fight is over.

There is no compulsion on any of us to form any new party or belong to any party … For the sake of the people of Spain & the success of the fight against Fascism – and in the name of the folks at home whom we must never disgrace, I ask for complete unity & the fullest concentration in this, the decisive fight for the liberty of the human race.[20]

Ryan was in an awkward position. It was obvious that the Communist Party was – for good or ill, but irremediably – in the driving seat of the whole operation. Like many others, particularly among the intelligentsia, Ryan accepted that only obedience to the party line was likely to produce the unity and discipline needed to succeed in the military struggle against fascism. On the other hand, as an IRA veteran and a student of history, he knew that the element which was least likely to encourage such unity was intra-ethnic suspicion. The Communist Party had already identified Ryan as an expert journalist whose main contribution was more likely to come via the management of propaganda than on the battlefield itself. Ryan was a useful type of non-communist, 'popular front' anti-fascist (with important North American connections) who could help to buttress the non-revolutionary image of the republican cause abroad, whilst at the same time boosting morale both at the war fronts and on the home front. More immediately, Ryan was the only man with the authority to maintain Irish loyalty on the ground. For all these reasons, he was not to be promiscuously exposed to the enemy: he was more use to the Comintern as a troubleshooter than as a shooter.

Yet Ryan could not simply annihilate his own national feelings, and was evidently under pressure from fellow countrymen to push the case for a 'national' unit. At this stage, he was hopeful that many more Irishmen would arrive in Spain, whether from the old country or the New World. Such a development might enable the formation of an Irish battlefield unit large enough to be vouchsafed the elements of meaningful (if limited) autonomy currently enjoyed by (say) the German and Italian battalions. Thus, Ryan's expression of confidence in the rapid formation of an 'Irish unit', with its own officers and billets, was a sincere one. However, the authorities were now seeking recourse in another formula for unity, in addition to the political logic of anti-fascism. This proposed a commonality based on linguistic principles. The assumption that organising battalions according to major language affiliations would be efficacious, for purposes of military action and vertical communications, was an understandable one, and seems to have proved generally valid. For example, the principle seems to have held good for the Franco-Belge Battalion which formed part of the XV Brigade. The Irish problem, however, resisted, and was perhaps even exacerbated by, the language they shared with their ex-oppressors.[21]

Crisis and split at Madrigueras

All three general studies of the British–Irish involvement in the International Brigades may be regarded as 'official'. They are the work of communist authors, published under the auspices of the party. The earliest of them is William Rust's contemporary account, which refers in passing to the fact that 'the Irish (volunteers) divided themselves between the British and American battalions' – as if he were describing a routine phenomenon of nature, like the behaviour of micro-organisms.[22] O'Riordan offers no details of the affair, merely explaining the sharing between two battalions as being occasioned by losses of personnel during the actions of Lopera and Las Rozas, which for no very obvious reason 'affected its ability to continue as a single unit'.[23]

According to another 'official' account, the crisis arose from the fact that 'many of the Irish volunteers had been in armed struggle against the British government and tended to be hostile to anything British … The main argument advanced by those who wished to leave the British battalion was the wrongs done to the Irish by the British in the past.'

Alexander implies that Ryan was sympathetic to this faction, but that Charlie Donnelly, Peter O'Connor and the Power brothers – the last four all Waterford men – spoke against it. This group maintained that class solidarity was more important than historical enmities, and that no stretch of the imagination could make non-Irish comrades into agents of British imperialism. However, when the Brigade's assistant commissar, Dave Springhall, called a meeting to resolve the issue, the vote went twenty-six to eleven in favour of joining the Lincoln Battalion. In the event (Alexander adds), the minority was obliged to follow the majority, and all concerned left to join the Americans at Villanueva de la Jara.[24]

These three versions also imply that the split between the Irish and the rest of the British battalion was definitive by the New Year. However, this cannot have been the case, since the first groups of American volunteers did not arrive in Albacete until the second week of January and the creation of a Lincoln Brigade postdates this event.[25] As already stated, there are confusing variations over chronology and detail in the recollections of veterans. Yet the evidence suggests that smouldering discontent over the attitudes of Wintringham and McCartney, and about George Nathan's past, burst into flame only when a copy of the London *Daily*

Worker reached Madrigueras, some time after the middle of January. Frank Ryan had obtained the blessing of the authorities – and of Nathan himself – for a recognised 'Irish section' within No. 1 Company before it left for Andalusia. The *Daily Worker* contained a report of the heroic actions of the British at Lopera, but without mentioning any Irishman or Irish unit.[26] Irishmen at Madrigueras were not pleased. Around this time, the Lincolns were allocated billets at Villanueva de la Jara, twelve kilometres north of Madrigueras. Thus all the pieces were in place for a serious breakdown of the much-prized unity of the British Battalion.

Despite having demonstrated impressive leadership qualities, Nathan was required to appear before the Irish 'section' in order to explain his past. This ritual could not have taken place without the support of Marty and the political commissariat. It represented a trial more than an investigative hearing, and illustrates the authorities' recognition of the importance of unity and morale. Nathan did not deny his misdemeanours during the 'Tan War', defending himself on the grounds that he had been an officer acting under orders in wartime. He claimed to have volunteered for Spain as a Jew, but also because fascism was the common enemy of mankind, Jew or Gentile. Though there was considerable sympathy for him, and no formal decision was recorded, it was clear that most Irishmen could no more serve under Nathan than under Wintringham or McCartney. It seems likely that a resolution meeting the case was taken on this occasion.[27] Nathan was removed from his command and 'kicked upstairs' to a job with 'Brigade' (i.e. Staff). He was succeeded by Kit Conway as Commander of No. 1 Company. Not surprisingly, Nathan felt in need of protection and applied (unsuccessfully) to join the Communist Party.[28]

A further complication was that Nathan had originally been elected as captain of the whole battalion by the men, soon after the first arrivals settled in at Madrigueras in November 1936.[29] This was an index of his popularity, and his subsequent ordeal caused some resentment among the non-Irish contingent. Moreover, Nathan's appointment as commanding offifer (later overturned in favour of Wintringham) must have occurred against Marty's wishes, but before the chief commissar had imposed full control. Elections of this kind were an evil precedent for the communist leadership. Not only did they threaten the apparatus of politically guaranteed loyalty to that leadership, but they also smacked of anarchist procedures, which were ideological anathema. Marty may have been exploiting the Nathan issue for two, equally desirable, purposes: first, in order to show the battalion who was in charge; and, second, to divide and rule the troublesome Irish. It therefore seems likely that Marty was the source of the original tip-off about Nathan to the Irish, and that he deliberately arranged for Ryan to remain absent in Madrid whilst his plans matured.

Several non-Irish veterans of the British Battalion who were in Madrigueras at the time testify that the split, when it came, was neither amicable nor peaceful. According to one, 'all the Irish got into trouble with our officers … They didn't like the British. Though they joined us to fight the Fascists, they had a strong antipathy to us.'[30] One British volunteer was asked by Irish mates to join their company shortly after his arrival in late January, 1937: 'They told me there had been a certain amount of trouble … [They] set about electing their own officers … The commandant then threatened to turn machine-guns on the Irish billet … but the Irish showed fight.'[31] 'Trouble' – that is to say, violence – is present in several other accounts. At Madrigueras, writes one:

> a feud developed between the Irish unit and the platoon occupying the neighbouring billet … One night the platoon in question was given the police detail and arrested practically the whole of the Irish detachment, which led to mutiny. The Irish refused to turn out on parade and demanded they should be transferred to the American battalion.[32]

Fred Copeman, later to be commander of the British Battalion, recalled that 'the Irishmen drank like fish … They wouldn't take orders from McCartney. Finally they and the English got drunk and there was a punch-up.' The following day, according to Copeman's story, Ryan told him 'we're out – we're going with the Yanks'.[33]

An American source has the Irish boasting of 'how they had forced the British officers to accede to their transfer by surrounding H.Q. with a ring of machine guns'. Another implies that as 'seasoned fighters' they were more than welcome to the Lincoln's ranks.[34] But, according to his widow, Robert Merriman, the Lincoln's commanding officer, believed that 'the Yanks' wanted nothing to do with the Irish. Indeed, somewhat to the contrary, it was the idea of being lumped with the latter ('a bunch of drunks who spent most of their time fighting amongst themselves') which determined the Americans to form their own battalion in the first place.[35]

The American volunteer William Herrick described in more detail what happened at Villanueva. One day the battalion commissar announced that 'a group of thirty Irish volunteers are joining our battalion'. When they arrived:

> the Irish were a ragged, impoverished-looking crew. Most were from Dublin, and many had fought with the Irish Republican Army against

British rule. Some had served with the British Colonial army in Asia and Africa … They were expert gunsmiths and boasted knowledge of any gun made … They had been training with the English but one day a new Irish war for independence broke out. The English comrades had treated them like colonials, they said, and it became too much to take. One morning the English awoke to find their barracks completely surrounded by Irish volunteers for liberty, armed with guns, knives and cobblestones. A hasty truce was reached before André Marty shot them all … The Americans did not know whether to believe this story.[36]

A temporary and partial resolution to the crisis was reported home by Peter Kerrigan, batallion commissar:

> In accord with wishes of the Brigade H.Q. in dealing with national groups we reported to the Irish section in our Battalion (not the lot who came out with Ryan) & they utilised the opportunity to discuss whether they would prefer to go with the American Battalion … All the comrades who had any connection with I.R.A or I.R.C. or T.U. movement elected to stay but they were in a minority of 11 against 23. They have now gone today to the Americans & we are frankly glad. We know it can be bad publicity both in Ireland & England but they were an awful lot of drunken Irish exiles from Sghuar Adala, petty criminals – hooligan types. So all had to go & again I will say we are glad.[37]

This steady build-up of 'domestic' tension was all the more dramatic and dangerous since a battle against the almost-forgotten enemy was – literally – just over the horizon. By coincidence, opposed sets of high commands were both working on plans for a major offensive in the valley of the Jarama river, south of Madrid.[38] The Republicans wanted their attack to get under way before Franco could replace his manpower losses, and whilst they also – thanks to the USSR – held the initiative in terms of aircraft and tanks. In an atmosphere of suspicion and dissent within the high command, Generals Rojo and Pozas began to assemble the regiments for the first assault wave in the villages of the Jarama region in late January.

Meanwhile, the surviving Irishmen of No. 1 Company, led by Kit Conway, returned to Madrigueras. From this point, the roles of Conway and Ryan in the development of the crisis are the subject of much confusion. According to Kerrigan, a further crisis developed after orders had been received to join the main army on the Jarama. He alleged that the British Battalion was actually on its way to the front, and had reached the town of Chinchón on Burns night (24 January). Here, a party was organised to celebrate the occasion:

It was a great success, but Frank Ryan got up near the end and made a short speech. The essence was the request that the Irish should be transferred to the Lincolns ... This was devastating on the eve of going into action. Marty blew his top [and ordered Ryan's arrest] ... It took the combined efforts of myself, Wintringham and Springhall to finally succeed in getting Ryan released.[39]

There is an obvious verisimilitude between the accounts thus far cited of this crucial affair. Essentially, they are versions of the same story, a fact paradoxically emphasised by their trivial inconsistencies. If they agree about anything, it is that Frank Ryan assumed the leadership of the breakaway faction, or at least acted as the spokesman for the dissident majority once their (democratic) decision had been made. Though not implausible in itself, the claim is sharply discordant with Ryan's earlier statements and his later actions. However, a different perspective emerges from Seán Cronin's biography of Frank Ryan. Cronin reveals that Ryan did not return to Madrigueras with No. 1 Company, but stayed on in Madrid to discharge a Brigade commission. Whilst he and Conway were away, Terry Flanagan had taken over leadership of the Irish section. It was Flanagan who failed to prevent the flare-up of feeling recalled by many witnesses. Later that year, explaining the affair to his New York contact from the censorship-free zone of Paris, Ryan did not mince his words:

The representatives of the British CP wrecked the Irish Unit. While one Irish Section was on the Córdoba Front, and I was 'loaned' to the 12th Brigade in Madrid, for a week which became a month, there was another Irish Section accumulating with Scots, English and Welsh at the Base. I had a Dubliner named Terry Flanagan in charge ... Flanagan was framed as a 'suspect' by Wilfrid McCartney, Battalion commander ... and ex-Black and Tan. The Irish section was shifted off to the Americans. When I came back (end of January) I was told a pack of lies by McCartney ... To the International Brigade authorities I pointed out that Ireland's nearest enemy is British Imperialism, that therefore Ireland's nearest ally must be the British working-class and that therefore the Irish and British must be side by side ... I was able to convict the British of having made a grave political error ... Unfortunately owing to the military situation I could not follow up the matter. The USA lads were on a war-footing and the Irish Unit was indispensable to them ... Someday I'll tell you the whole sordid story of the political density of some so-called British revolutionaries ... The tragedy is that the English sent out the worst officer-type. [But] the leaders of the CP of Great Britain understand our position.[40]

Like others who were not privy to the conclaves of the highest eche-
lons of Comintern leadership, Ryan had only an imperfect idea of the
subtle political calculations on which Communist Party policy in Spain
was based. Nonetheless, and despite all the circumstantial complications,
there seems little reason to doubt his basic loyalty to the policy itself. Thus
his explanation must be considered seriously. But Ryan also made mis-
takes, or at least assumed too much. He evidently believed that he enjoyed
official recognition as commander of the 'Irish Unit' from the General
Staff in Albacete. If this was the case, it was unwise of him to accept separation from his men at all, let alone to have remained absent for nearly a
month. But in fact he should have realised that, as a non-communist, he
lacked the trust of the leadership, and that the status of any 'Irish Unit' was
by no means clear. Notably, it was the CPI member Conway, and not
Ryan, who had been chosen to lead the 'Irish section' in Andalusia.

An attempt must now be made to summarise the events and meaning of the Madrigueras 'split'. The probable sequence of events can be
reconstructed – though still with some elements of conjecture – as follows. Conway led forty-five men with him (under Nathan) to Andújar on
24 December, leaving just fewer than forty to remain in training at
Madrigueras. Ryan left for Madrid some time after 3 January, having
been seconded to the XII Brigade for liaison duty. Whilst there, he met
No. 1 Company (which was still attached to the XIV Brigade) and was
apparently with it in action at Las Rozas for a short spell.[41] In his absence,
the confrontations with McCartney and Nathan took place in
Madrigueras. On 19 January, the Irish were transferred to the Lincolns in
Villanueva, a decision which could only have been Marty's.

Subsequently, however, new Irish arrivals – at this point coming in
at an average rate of two or more per day – were required to stay with the
British. But these recruits inevitably picked up the story about their compatriots in Villanueva. Maybe Flanagan agitated for the new men to join
the old, or perhaps simply pursued his enquiries into the matter too vigorously. When Conway returned to Madrigueras with around twenty
other Irishmen, they learned about the split and its causes, about Flanagan's arrest, and about the offending material in (or, rather, absent from)
the *Daily Worker*.[42] This sufficed – especially since No. 1 Company's Irish
veterans were the actual subjects of grievance in the last case – to fracture
Conway's loyalty to the party line. At this point, a further bizarre complication demands consideration. Whilst in Spain, 'Kit' Conway had
adopted the *nom-de-guerre* of 'Ryan'.[43] It was (therefore) Conway, and not
Frank Ryan, who made the sensational Burns night protest, defying

Marty in public and to his face. Such an act would normally have led to severe retribution. But Conway's heroism, proven quality of leadership and Communist Party membership gave him an unassailable status, and his men were evidently prepared to go to any lengths to protect him. When Ryan returned at the end of January, he managed to bring 'Ryan' back into line.

Thus a major political crisis damaged – even deformed – the British Battalion, and the whole of the XV Brigade, in the very process of its gestation. The opinions of the Irish – though by no means unanimously held – represented a challenge to communist control on several levels. In terms of numbers, they represented about 10 per cent of the total enlisted in the two English-speaking battalions – roughly a hundred out of a thousand by the end of January 1937. So few of them were trustworthy party members that finding a native political commissariat, the key to internal control, was impossible. Yet it was among the Irish, more than any other national group, that such influence was necessary. The inclinations of too many Irish volunteers lay towards an exclusively national, but also democratic, collectivity. They did not fail to grasp the relations between political and military desiderata; life in the IRA had familiarised them with these subtleties. Yet the exigencies of struggle against the British army, coupled in many cases with a religious-cultural resistance to communism as a doctrine, gave them an anti-authority and even (in terms of discipline) an anti-military character.[44]

But more was at stake in this affair than perhaps even Ryan realised. The war effort of the Republic, under communist guidance, was based on developing a new army, founded on military discipline and professional efficiency. Thus Irish resistance to a British-supervised homogenisation was bound to assume an anti-party dimension. Although they differed from the main objects of communist suspicion, the Partido Socialista de Unificación Marxista (POUM) and anarchist militias (which they knew little or nothing about), in effect the Irish played a similarly maverick role. Because this recalcitrant knot of dissent actually existed within the central bulwark of the Comintern programme in Spain – the force on which rested not only the hopes of the Republic, but also the larger Soviet project for international resistance to the Axis powers – it was seen as all the more dangerous. In the calculations of the Brigade staff, and thus of the tiny cadre of Stalin's executive agents in Madrid and Valencia, the Irish Unit was a potential Fifth Column. This explains why the political commissariat Springhall (Brigade) and Kerrigan (Battalion) went to such lengths to appease the Irish discontent with the officer corps; why

Frank Ryan was seconded for so long to Madrid; and Marty's willingness to split the Irish into two camps, a stratagem which might divide them against each other, or at any rate serve to dilute the damage that might be incurred in a battle situation.

The nightmare of Jarama

Franco's offensive in the southern sector of the Madrid front, commanded overall by General Orgaz, was originally scheduled for 27 January, but was held up for technical and weather reasons. Meanwhile, the republican high command had initially fixed its own offensive for 5 February – but this intention, too, was vitiated by failures of preparation. Had things gone to plan, the XV Brigade would have been part of the second wave of the offensive across the Jarama. These plans filtered down in the form of vague rumours, but nonetheless the atmosphere of expectation was considerable. When orders to move at last arrived, however, they came in response to the nationalist attack which began on the evening of 5 February. The enemy's first objective was to cut the Madrid–Valencia road at Vaciamadrid. Ciempozuelos, taken by the southern column under García Escámez in the opening hours of the operation, was designed as the fulcrum of a twenty-kilometre sweep to the north-east, an advance which would take the spearhead column (Barrón) across the plateau of La Marañosa, and down on to the bridge across the Manzanares. The latter advance met with considerable success, and had almost reached its objective when stopped by the XII International Brigade on 9 February. Two days later, the central column (Asensio) took the village of San Martín de la Vega, situated in the centre of a vast rural emptiness which was now to be turned into a charnel-house of death and terror.

As they headed by rail and then road for the town of Chinchón, the three battalions of the XV Brigade had little idea of how things were developing on the battlefield. No officer below *Estado Mayor* level seems to have known whether they were about to participate in an offensive or defensive action. All concerned were unfamiliar with the terrain in which they were to fight, and could only guess at the whereabouts of an enemy which was operating with all its usual speed and ferocity. Until the moment they caught sight of their adversary, many of the men, and even some of the field officers, seem to have been under the impression that they were moving into breakthrough space left by advancing republican troops, ready to back up their offensive. In fact, the previous seven days had seen a dreadful massacre and rout of republican forward units, who (understandably) had neglected all except the most basic defensive precautions. Between 7 and 12 February shattered remnants of these regiments straggled back across the Jarama and fled northwards to Madrid.[45]

In the early morning of 12 February, on a crossroads a few kilometres west of the village of Morata de Tajuña, three battalions (some 1,600 men) of XV Brigade jumped from their lorries and assumed battle formation. Though other units were being rapidly deployed southwards from Madrid, on that day this was the only republican fighting force in the whole southern sector of the battlefield. Blissfully unknown to the poor bloody infantry, to their left, as they faced the enemy, was a hole in the line at least five kilometres wide, stretching all the way down to Titulcia, key to the Tajuña valley.[46] What was worse, as it ground to a halt in the north, the point of the nationalist attack was switched to the centre, and Asensio was reinforced. His task was to break through to Morata, from which point the whole offensive could swing north, behind the new republican lines. Whilst a third battalion (the so-called 'Dimitrov') was kept in reserve, the Franco-Belge and British Battalions began to advance directly towards the cutting edge of the enemy advance, across high land lying each side of a dusty country road running east–west from Morata to San Martín.

Here was the crucible of the whole battle. Asensio's column of Legionary *banderas* and Moroccan *tabors* had to cross the Jarama river via the bridge which lay on the San Martín–Morata road – and did so early on 12 February. Advance units quickly deployed to their right and occupied a high ridge (Pingarrón – the big pimple) which is the dominant physical feature of the area. Some fifty feet below this promontory, looking eastwards to Morata for some five kilometres, stretches an irregular plateau of clay soil, with conical hills, shallow depressions and narrow, snaking passages carved in the interstices by rivulets (*barrancos*): all these features being randomly distributed. Even today, the occasional olive grove and scattered patches of scrub are the sole vegetation. Not far beyond, the green Tajuña valley provides a wide highway to Morata, beyond that to Arganda, and thence to Alcalá de Henares, Orgaz's ultimate objective almost due east of Madrid. Though the attack on Pingarrón heights pulled Asensio's initial drive a few kilometres to the south, once in occupation of them, his field officers were able to discern that the valley, and thus the whole republican defensive system, was open to an enfilading movement from the south. By this time, however, his men had made contact with the XV Brigade, and could not be pulled back and redirected without risking an enemy breakthrough on their flank. Asensio was committed to continue his frontal attack on Morata. And only the XV Brigade stood in Franco's path.[47]

The story of the three days of close-quarter combat which ensued has been told and retold over sixty years and in every appropriate medium – journalism, memoirs, interviews, history, poetry, fiction and filmed documentary.[48] Stripped of myth, drained of sentiment and cleansed of propaganda, it remains an unsurpassed record of heroism mixed with disaster, but above all of tragedy. The British Battalion (the 16th) totalled about five hundred men, organised in four companies, No. 2 being the machine-gun unit. No. 1, under Conway – a hundred men including about forty Irish – was on the right of the advance, nearest the road. It was thus the first to engage the enemy, a platoon of Moorish regulars coming up the steep, broken slope from the river-bridge. On one flank, the Moors drove the Francophone battalion back in disorder almost on impact. They occupied a hill to the right of Conway's men. The British withdrew to the only fighting position available, along a discontinuous ridge which ran across the slope. The Moors were able to open a gap, approximately as wide as the range of the machine-gun which they quickly installed in their new position, whilst their adversary had to deploy on two sides. From the first moment of fire, the 16th Battalion's rate of casualty was appalling.

On the face of things, and certainly in detail on the ground, Asensio had overwhelming advantages. His troops belonged to an elite corps whose ethos stipulated the fanatical and reckless surge of attack.[49] They were experienced not only in the general techniques of infantry offensive, but specifically in fighting in the type of terrain encountered on the Jarama plateaux. They knew how to exploit every fold of the ground, every patch of scrub or clump of olives, all the different phases of daylight and dark. Not least, they were experts in rifle combat and enjoyed a high average standard of marksmanship.[50] Having been frustrated only once during six months of campaign (in attacking the densely defended streets of Madrid), their confidence was high. The contrast on the other side was striking. Most of Gal's XV Brigade had no previous experience of battle and less than a month's military training. His battalions were completely unsure of their ground, and both for this reason and by the fact that three or four languages were in use, suffered from poor and insecure communications.

Jim Prendergast, a Dublin supporter of the Republican Congress and a veteran of the company's earlier battles, was amongst Conway's riflemen. He later sent two detailed reports of the 12 February action to the party's paper, the *Irish Democrat*. His account is vivid, yet remarkably free of party and personal rhetoric. In the early morning light, as the men prepared to advance from the road on to the plateau, Frank Ryan returned from the Brigade field HQ to brief them:

> He told us of the position in the line and that the Fascists were expected to launch a powerful attack under cover of nightfall to finally capture the road. Our Brigade would move in to smash this attempt at all costs. [Waiting for the order to move] I spread my blanket under a tree and lay down ... Dan Boyle, a Belfast lad, gave me an English cigarette ... Dan was in fine form though he had just read his obituary in a misinformed paper. It was a happy group under our tree. Dan, Ted Bourne and Dick O'Neill. And before long three of us would be wounded and one killed ... Dan, handing the last of his fags around, did say his generosity was based on the possibility of not finishing them later perhaps.

Once the enemy was encountered and the broken ridge mentioned above was occupied, Conway's men commenced firing whilst two other companies fell in to their left.

> They were advancing on our left ... Men were being hit pretty fast. A young English chap fell over close by ... Sean Goff tumbled over, his hand to his head ... Kit danced furiously from position to position. 'Don't waste your fire boys', he kept shouting. We took up new positions. I saw Paddy Duff moving back, hit in the leg. Shells were exploding on our left ... My rifle was burning hot. Kit ... handed me a note. It was from Frank Ryan's H.Q. We must hold on to our positions at all costs ... Kit told me to convey instructions to the section to our left to move to the ridge covering our left flank. I looked through his binoculars and saw the Moors creeping up on our left. We were in great danger of being cut off. I sped away to the left ... I found the section leaders and gave my message. What's left of the others are in the white house on the ridge, I was told. I moved to the white house and shouted. No reply. I went into the yard. They were there all right, but they were all dead. [Prendergast returned to his own company.] Somebody called my name. It was young Paddy Smith. Blood was pouring from his head and his arm ... 'At the rate the boys are being hit we'll never hold out', said a first aid man ... Kit was standing on top of the hill. He was using a rifle now and after every shot turned towards the men issuing instructions ... Suddenly he shouted, his rifle spun out of his hand and he fell back ... I rushed up the hill. Kit was lying across his blankets, somebody dressing him. 'He was hit in the groin' one of the boys whispered ... He opened his eyes and spoke, his voice broken with agony. 'Boys, don't leave me for the Fascists.'[51]

Prendergast's account highlights some significant aspects of the battalion's position, and its behaviour under the most testing conditions imaginable. It was fortunate, at least for the Brigade as a whole, that some fifty veterans of Lopera and Las Rozas were among the men of No. 1 Company who bore the main brunt of the fighting. Indeed, the experience of Lopera seems to have been sharply relevant. Prendergast conveys the difficulties of keeping men together, and the anxious search for a suitable defensive position, once it became clear that the battalion was advancing not merely towards, but virtually into the midst of, an attacking enemy. Not long afterwards it became clear that the forward position represented a ridge too far: the line became untenable, subjected to artillery fire whilst the Moors trickled forward in the *barrancos* between the hills. A higher ridge about 500 yards to the rear (the rim of the main plateau) was occupied by the machine-gun company. Although their heavy Maxims were useless, since the wrong ammunition belts had been issued, this unit was able to provide sufficient covering rifle fire to enable an orderly retreat. By the time the enemy realised that the front positions were vacant, and began a general advance, the appropriate belts had been brought up for the machine-guns, which were now brought to bear with emphatic effect. The enemy, in its turn, was forced to withdraw.

The British Battalion had stopped Franco's best troops in a day's work which counts among the most impressive achievements of modern warfare. The regulars and Legionary *banderas* had never before been held up so effectively in open countryside, and the quality of the opposition came as a genuine surprise to them.[52] The British inflicted heavy casualties on units that were already depleted of veterans, and for whom – though Orgaz did have limited reserves of new, untried conscript regiments – replacement was simply impossible. Indeed, one important caveat must be stressed here. Despite a mythic belief to the contrary in English-language sources, and frequently reproduced in connection with this action, during the battle of Jarama in general, and the whole five-month 'battle for Madrid' of which it formed part, at no stage were the defenders in an inferior position in numerical or technical terms. But although the British Battalion was neither significantly outnumbered nor outgunned by the forces actually facing it, its achievement was nonetheless an epic one. The assertion may be ultimately incapable of proof, but this writer is confident that its conduct – especially on 12 February – represents the greatest single contribution to the victory of Jarama, and thus to the survival of Madrid.[53]

On the other hand, the fate of Prendergast's 'happy group' of four men – three disabling injuries (including one to himself) and one fatal-ity – is a sobering reflection of the price paid for the victory. Only 25 per cent effectives of No. 1 Company, and about 33 per cent of the others, were still in the line at the end of the day. Kit Conway, after two days of suffering, died on 14 February, almost certainly unaware of the magni-tude of his achievement. As for Dan Boyle, the rumours of his death proved to be only slightly exaggerated; Jim Prendergast and his other mates were not called upon to repay his cigarettes.[54]

Though Prendergast's and other accounts suggest a good working relationship between Ryan and Conway, it is evident that the former was a staff and not a field officer; that is to say, one of a senior team which supervised and co-ordinated operations from rear positions. In thus dis-posing, the Albacete authorities were stressing his skills as organiser and troubleshooter, in both of which he had proved his value to them. Yet Ryan, too, was destined to make a heroic intervention in the battle of Jarama. On 13 February, the defensive line occupied by the battalion was undermined. The setback was precipitated by a withdrawal of the two other battalions, under severe pressure to the north of the Morata road. In consequence, Bert Overton, whose company had been transferred to replace Conway's on the extreme right, withdrew his men without orders. In turn, this exposed the battalion's machine-gun positions, which were soon surrounded, with most of the gun-crews being cap-tured. The following day (14 February), bereft of this fundamental ele-ment of defence, the battalion was overwhelmed by a new attack, and forced back to the Madrid–Chinchón road in disorder.

Luckily, the enemy was this time more cautious in pursuit. Perhaps reduced strength and cumulative exhaustion held it back; though, in addition, Asensio was now feeling the weight of republican reinforce-ments which had arrived on the southern flank the day before. At any rate, the whole XV Brigade was allowed time in which to regroup. This process was certainly aided by the survivors of the other two battalions, and of sixty fresh Britishers who had been acting as guard for Brigade HQ. But Gal himself, along with Ryan and the Scots-Irishman Jock Cun-ningham, took an inspiring part in proceedings to restore morale. Led by the two latter men, at the head of some 140 of the British Battalion, 'the great rally' began – a determined march along the road back towards the enemy. In the gathering dusk, their adversary now fell back, probably under the impression – underlined by the constant chorusing of 'The Internationale' – that fresh units had arrived in this sector too. Before nightfall, the positions held that morning had been reoccupied.[55]

On the next day (15 February) there were further sharp exchanges. Ryan reported:

> I got a slight flesh-wound in the arm from a bullet which went through the head of a man beside me. It made me – even gentle me! – fighting mad ... Half an hour later a tank shell burst beside me and I got a wallop in the left leg that knocked me down ... There was no blood. It must have been a stone thrown by the shell. I limped for a few minutes, then I felt OK ... Shortly after ... I got a bullet through the left arm. It's a clean wound, high up, and will be OK in a few weeks.[56]

Probing attacks on the XV Brigade line continued for a few days longer, but Franco had decided on a general consolidation. Broadly speaking, the positions retaken on 14 February were to form part of the final line of entrenchment which persisted until the end of the war.

Though the two succeeding days, briefly described above, had been somewhat less successful than the glorious twelfth, by their end the over-all situation had swung in favour of the Republic. The crucial factor was the Nationalists' lack of assault troops, which had by now dwindled to their lowest point in the war – fewer than five thousand men on the whole Jarama front. It was this which precluded Asensio from ordering his *banderas* to outflank the British and advance along the Tajuña valley on 12 February. The republican air force, led by Soviet fighters and pilots, gained control of the skies above Jarama during the second week of the battle. Moreover, the deployment of more than fifty Soviet tanks brought about a definitive stiffening of the republican line of defence – but this was some five kilometres to the north of XV Brigades' positions, in front of Arganda. More significant was that in the course of 12–13 February, the 1st Republican Army Brigade, the core of which comprised units of the celebrated 'fifth regiment', commanded by Enrique Líster, reached the main danger point and moved into position on the left of the British. With other units on their way, a certain defence in depth had now been achieved here as elsewhere on the republican line.[57]

The Lincolns at Pingarrón

On 15 February, republican defences were completely reorganised. Miaja, head of the Defence Junta, replaced Pozas in overall command; Gal became Divisional Commander (B) in the Centre, based at Morata, whilst Líster was given command of C Division and the whole southern sector, with his HQ in Chinchón. The intention was to move, at last, on to the offensive, in order to exploit the frustration, exhaustion and depletion of the nationalist army. In theory, it is difficult to fault the idea for a classic counter-attack. Miaja and his adjutant, Rojo, rightly sensed that the enemy offensive had run out of steam. In terms of morale and propaganda, the Republic desperately needed a 'real' triumph, as distinct from the defensive victories won at Madrid and Jarama. In practice, however, suitable conditions were simply not in place. At any rate, the decision was to mean that the carnage of the Jarama valley was still only half complete.

The XV Brigade now found itself digging in at the southern extreme of General Gal's command, at the point where it joined hands with that of Líster. The latter had been given the honour of opening the counter-offensive, which stood no chance of success without the preliminary capture of Pingarrón heights. After two days' rest, and diversionary attacks in the northern sector, Líster's 1st Division – the best Spanish troops available – stormed on to Pingarrón on the night of 18/19 February. But the opposing *banderas*, though at first driven off the top, refused to admit defeat and returned to the attack at first light. Five days and nights of ferocious, unremitting combat ensued. The 'big pimple' was soaked in the blood of hundreds of infantrymen from a dozen countries. On 23 February alone, the flat-topped summit, about the area of two football pitches, changed hands no fewer than four times.[58] Now it was Líster – like Asensio before him – who was suddenly short of crack troops. Before this day was over, he was forced to call for assistance from Gal, and Gal's replacement as Brigade commander, Copic. They responded by giving the Lincoln Battalion the order to attack.[59]

The Americans were selected because (at least on paper) they were prepared for action, and because their comrades in the other three battalions had already 'done their bit'. The new battalion, four hundred strong, left Villanueva on 15 February and moved by stages to take over the positions previously held by the British. In this first week they saw little action beyond the digging of trenches. In the ranks led by Captain Merriman was an 'Irish Company', which mixed the forty men who had left the British in mid-January with about the same number of Irish-American expatriates. Most of the latter, including its joint commanders, Paul Burns and the three Flaherty brothers, were Bostonians; but nearly all of these men were second- or older-generation Americans who had lost meaningful contact with the old country. Jason Gurney, who came to know them well, asserts that they 'had no real interest in Ireland as such. Some of them were not Irish in any way but simply enjoyed the general atmosphere of the company.'[60]

The affair of 23 February was a strictly diversionary attack intended to relieve pressure on Líster's men, not far to the south. Indeed, a few days earlier, a nationalist *bandera* had made a similar move in the opposite direction, intended to relieve the pressure on Captain Zamalloa, defender of Pingarrón. The Lincolns were ordered to advance into the same square mile of the battlefield and to storm the same ridge on which Conway and his men had fought and died on 12 February. The Bostonian journalist Paul Burns recorded his impressions of the day (in which he was later to be wounded):

> In one of those interludes beneath an olive tree I looked around – on my left was Charlie Donnelly ... to the right of the Irish section, the American section dug in and fired ... Donnelly joined me under an olive tree. We fired until our rifles burned our hands with scarcely a word beyond the 'Hi, Charlie how's it going?' and the reply, 'Pretty good. How's the rest of the boys?'[61]

This small wedge of land – known as La Jara, the arrow – therefore represents a corner of a foreign field which is forever Ireland. Moreover, the action fought by the Lincolns on that day was uncannily similar to the earlier episode, and men like Eamon McCrotty, Dave Levy and Bill Henry fell in circumstances similar to those in which Kit Conway, Bob Hilliard and Dan Boyle had lost their lives. As it proved, however, the day's work carried out by the Lincolns was to much less positive effect, for on the same day Líster's men lost their grip upon Pingarrón heights.

Conscious of the many tempting weaknesses in the enemy's rear, the Madrid Junta was still unwilling to abandon the chance of a breakthrough. On 27 February the order arrived for another assault on Pingarrón. In his memoirs, Líster passes over his failure in this final mad spasm of death; but as a loyal communist he could not resist his superiors' demands.[62] The Lincolns were called in for the final wave of the onslaught. Despite promises, neither artillery nor tank support was in evidence. Merriman protested the lunacy of his orders, and for some time resisted them.[63] Perhaps someone then reminded him of the fate of Colonel Delasalle. At any rate, the battalion finally went 'over the top' in a useless attempt to scale a densely fortified position, during which Charlie Donnelly and a hundred others fell. The American battalion was reduced to the same condition as its British comrades. With this last repulse, the Junta reluctantly called off its offensive, and the battle of Jarama came to an end.

9

Struggle for identity, struggle for victory

The Connolly Column

After the prolonged slaughter of Jarama, little more than fifty of the original eighty Irishmen were alive. Moreover, about half of this number were in hospital recovering from wounds which, in many cases, were serious enough to spell eventual repatriation. However, in the ten-week period between the arrival of pioneer groups and the end of their first great battle, dozens more Irish volunteers had turned up at Albacete. Such was the nature of the Republic's February emergency that even some of these were immediately sent into action. In any case, by the time their commanders accepted a stalemate on the Jarama front, between forty and fifty Irish members of the XV Brigade (in a muster of perhaps 750) were fit enough to help occupy the lines which faced the enemy in front of Morata de Tajuña. For most of them, an extended phase of trench warfare was now to provide their daily environment.[1]

Naturally, this was, at first, seen as blessed relief from the nightmare of imminent oblivion and the even worse agony of some unimaginably horrible injury. Minds as well as bodies were mangled by the trauma of Jarama, but this was a universal, not merely an Irish, problem amongst its volunteer survivors. More particularly for the Irish contingent, the breathing and thinking space which suddenly supervened in the spring of 1937 allowed other problems – political and collective – to reassert priority.

The issue of national collectivity remained outstanding and, as such, a source of irritation. The rule that all fresh volunteers arriving from the Free State should join the British Battalion was strictly adhered to once the original split had been allowed. This policy left a band of around fifteen survivors of Pingarrón somewhat isolated in the ranks of the Lincolns. They represented a seemingly recalcitrant minority, obstinately divorced from a growing majority in the British Battalion. André Marty and his new British assistant Will Paynter were anxious that these men should return to the British ranks.[2] Speaking apropos of his Irish comrades, veteran Jim Brewer recalled that 'it was Bill Paynter who quashed any idea that we should be in national groups'. Another remembered that 'after a couple of months they [the Irish Lincolns] realised how silly they'd been and came back and joined the British'.[3]

What pressures were exerted on them, whether by their 'orthodox' compatriots or by the Albacete authorities, can only be surmised. It seems that when Frank Ryan returned to Spain after several months' home leave (in early June) he collaborated with Paynter in the task of encouraging reunification. In fact, however, these efforts met with little success; there is no reliable evidence even of one individual electing to rejoin the British.[4] Indeed, once scattered details are pieced together, it seems certain that neither Paynter nor Ryan achieved the eventual reintegration of the Irish in one fighting unit – but, rather, Franco. The battle of Brunete in July 1937 finished the process which that of Jarama had begun, leaving hardly any battle-fit Irish survivors among the Lincolns.

In the meantime, however, the persistent physical division of the contingent saw the old question once again steadily gaining in prominence: how could the distinctiveness of the Irish be maintained without disrupting the community and purpose of the whole? Some radical hardliners among the Irish contingent were hoping to tackle this problem in seeking to use the title 'James Connolly' for an exclusive Irish section. Behind the trenches of the Jarama front, various events were organised to celebrate Irish identity. The anniversary of the Easter Rising was marked by a large international gathering and concert on 29 March. On 12 May a day of celebration was held to honour the memory of James Connolly, on the anniversary of his execution. Once again, representatives of many other nations attended – including Britain – to demonstrate solidarity in what was a welcome opportunity to strengthen a common bond of hatred of British imperialism.[5] An American observer was deeply impressed:

> Kelley [*sic*] … was the first to step out to speak. When he spoke of our recent dead … he did so loudly but solemnly. But when he spoke of James Connolly … he spoke buoyantly and with eloquence in a beautiful Irish brogue … He paid tribute to the Lincoln Battalion for naming one of its companies the James Connolly … He likened the struggle of the Irish to that of the Spanish people who were accomplishing today what the Irish find still as unfinished business in their war against the forces of darkness and colonialism.[6]

A resolution to this effect was passed under the aegis of 'We of the James Connolly Unit of the International Brigade'.[7] Around the same time, Kelly (from Ballinasloe, Co. Galway) wrote a propaganda letter to the *Aberdare Leader* – a South Wales local weekly sympathetic to the Republic – signing himself as a member of the 'James Connolly Unit, Irish Section, Albacete'.[8]

But what was 'The James Connolly Unit'? The main source of information on the existence of an Irish unit with this denomination is the writings of the O'Riordans: the Cork city veteran, Michael, and his son and collaborator, Manus. Their treatment is inconsistent and frequently misleading.[9] Certainly, the internal organisation of the International Brigades is not an easy thing to describe schematically. So many changes were attempted or imposed in so short a period that misunderstandings are easy and apparent inconsistencies abound. Confusion on the present issue arises mainly from the absence of contemporary references, originating inside or outside the notional Irish group, to a 'James Connolly' unit or column. Frank Ryan never used the term in any extant writing, despite the fact that he was evidently sympathetic to the principle of a (non-autonomous) Irish unit and deeply respected the memory of James Connolly as a Catholic socialist and hero of the Easter Rebellion.[10]

Though appropriate in many ways, the title posed problems for the communist authorities. In Mick Kelly's version, despite its ideological soundness, it contained sentiments which might well be resented by some British comrades. For this reason, it was never allowed to spread outside the Lincoln Battalion, within which (as Tisa's account illustrates) no negative reaction was likely.[11] Just as Irishmen had fought and died with two different battalions at Jarama, so this division persisted for some time after the battle was over. This situation probably reflected more the growth of effective Brigade discipline than the personal inclinations of those concerned. But it meant that, although individual routine experiences may not have been in dramatic contrast, the two groups occupied discrete sections of the line, and were able to communicate face to face only on special occasions or during periods of leave.

From Jarama to Brunete

Never again were the International Brigades to register such an unequivocal military success as that represented by their role in the defence of Madrid (November 1936 to March 1937). More particularly – though through no fault of their own – the British were not destined to emulate their brilliant action during the battle of Jarama. These desperate encounters had been crucial to the immediate survival of the Republic. Failure at the University City, or at Jarama, or at Guadalajara, would have meant the capture of Madrid, with dramatic consequences both for the course of the war and for its meaning to subsequent generations. These battles gave the Republic a substantial opportunity to win – or at any rate to achieve a stalemate, which would in practice have led to victory by 1945 at the latest. For the remaining eighteen months of their sojourn in Spain, the Brigades were at times to be involved in fighting of comparable intensity, but not of equal significance. The two celebrated occasions were both republican offensives – Brunete and the Ebro – neither of which, even had it succeeded, could have substantially altered the final outcome of the war.

For the XV Brigade, the period of three months in the trenches of the Jarama front was a test of a different kind from that of battle. These circumstances allowed time for many to reappraise their feelings, and even critically to re-examine their commitment to the cause. The process was sharpened, in many cases precipitated, by the ordeal men had suffered in the hell of Jarama. These individual agonies easily connected with the collective grievances which develop in almost any army in any war. The relative absence of the enemy allowed complaints about conditions to rise to the surface: inadequate food, clothing, equipment and supply of news from home; lack of leave, tobacco, drink and sex. Though efforts were made in Albacete to deal with all these categories, fundamental doubts, fears and rumours persisted in affecting morale. As a result, military discipline on the one hand and political education on the other were rapidly strengthened, and their increasing demands were soon noticed among the rank and file.[12]

Approximately two kilometres directly behind the section of line occupied by the British and Lincoln Battalions lay the village of Morata de Tajuña. With only 3,500 inhabitants at the outbreak of war, it was a smaller and poorer *pueblo* than Ciempozuelos. Unlike the latter, it had not been the scene of fighting, and though within range of enemy artillery, was not a serious strategic target. Its population had been evacuated (or fled of their own volition), but the bars and *fondas* (dosshouses) had later been re-opened for army use. Just behind a central plaza stood the burned-out church. Today, in front of the crudely restored building, the curious traveller can read the names of townspeople who died for God and Spain at the hands of the Reds. Among these 'martyrs' are two members of the MacCrohon family, descended from Irish soldiers who came to Spain in the seventeenth century. Two hundred years later this family had become the local *caciques* – landowners and founders of the local building society.[13]

Even had they become aware of them, the Irish Internationals would hardly have appreciated the business achievements of their predecessors. In any case, it seems the delights of the town were basically off-limits, and almost no mention of it is made in recollections left by Brigaders. Jason Gurney, who managed to sip the occasional glass of *anis* in Morata (a famous brand of the liqueur is made in nearby Chinchón) described the place as 'not very exciting', but he appreciated the lazy atmosphere of a township 'where the war seemed a thousand miles away'.[14] The main problem as far as access was concerned was that the town was a base for Líster's communist 5th Regiment, whose officers and men naturally took priority.

Boredom and resentment were often alleviated. From time to time, new recruits arrived in the line having completed their training in Madrigueras, whilst (also at recurrent but random intervals) comrades wounded in the winter fighting returned to the line from hospital. As well as improving morale, this gradually allowed less onerous tours of duty and even the odd spot of leave in Madrid or Albacete. Entertainments were arranged – unique occasions such as the 'James Connolly' day, and more routine diversions like soccer matches. But the enemy had by no means gone away. Careless physical movement, even when made behind trenches or emplacements, was often severely punished by snipers, and night-time reconnaissance forays (by both sides) were a regular occurrence. In mid-March came the sudden spate of nationalist attacks, which included the XV *Bandera* action near Titulcia, sustained for three or four days all along the Jarama front. During this scare, the Madrid Defence Junta, coping as it was with the main event – the battle raging around Guadalajara – probably remained confident that what was happening further south was a diversionary tactic. However, the lower ranks – as also in the case of the attacking enemy – had no such awareness. This was the moment when the International Brigade Irishmen and the *Bandera Irlandesa* came closest to a direct confrontation. But the moment passed, and normal service was resumed.[15]

During the spring of 1937 the Irish were divided not amongst two, but into three different sections of the XV Brigade. The third unit was the new 20th Battalion, formed in order to undertake action in Andalusia. Those enlisted in this corps seem to have been either keen new recruits with previous military experience, or dedicated veterans who had been wounded and now returned from convalescence eager to get back at the enemy. Around this time republican strategists like Vicente Rojo were developing ideas of guerrilla warfare and systematic sabotage behind the nationalist lines. It is possible that the 20th Battalion, now seconded as part of a new regular army brigade (the 86th), began as a support unit for such experiments.[16] At any rate, at least five Irishmen left Albacete in mid-March as members of this 'task force'. Their ostensible mission was the defence of the town of Almadén, with its strategically important mercury mines.

Almadén is situated in the foothills of the Sierra Morena, the northernmost reaches of Andalusia, on the borders of New Castile and Extremadura. The English-speaking company in the new battalion was commanded by Lieutenant Robert Traill, a young Cambridge graduate who had been training as a Comintern agent in the Lenin School in Moscow when the war broke out. Traill – whose family probably originated in Co. Antrim – arrived on board a Soviet supply ship and spent several months in the Republic's Officer Training School in Valencia.[17] According to Monks, the preparation was worth while, for Traill proved a competent and dedicated field commander who, despite (or perhaps because of) his youth, was an example to his men, especially those, like Paddy O'Daire and Peter Daly, who also aspired to leadership. For nearly four months, Traill's men fought a series of engagements in an obscure military zone, a huge amorphous patch of no man's land on an axis from Pozoblanco to Chimorra, operating in terrain so remote and rebarbative that neither side was able to maintain coherent lines.

In the event, the nationalist attempt to break through to Almadén was frustrated, and the precious mines – so coveted by Franco's ally, the Third Reich – remained in republican hands until shortly before the end of the war. Late in June, the 86th Brigade was broken up, and the men of 20th Battalion were returned to Albacete. The human losses sustained in this campaign seem to have been normal by the standards already set. Only nineteen of the company's original ninety-two men returned to base unscathed – 'we came back in one lorry', as Joe Monks recalled. But at least this time, there was only one Irish casualty: Peter Daly, who had again (as at Jarama) been badly wounded in the leg.[18]

Meanwhile, in early June, the XV Brigade at Jarama was relieved and retired to rest quarters behind the lines at Mondéjar in the Tajuña Valley. The respite was made possible by the steady expansion and maturation of the regular republican army – the *Ejército Popular*. This force had been largely generated in the time and space provided by the resolute services of the International Brigades during the prolonged winter crisis (a fact which no Spanish source has ever acknowledged). Indeed, the structure and organisation of the new army were in many ways modelled on the Brigades, along with the communist 5th Regiment. Its maturation meant that the period of relaxation enjoyed in the early summer climate and pleasant surroundings near the river Tajuña was as short as it was idyllic. Before the end of the month, signs increased that something new and big was on the horizon; it was the first full-scale and authentic republican offensive.[19]

The battle of Brunete was planned mostly as a result of Communist Party initiative. Its underlying logic seemed unimpeachable. The Nationalists were fully taken up with their campaign in the north. Following the expensive capture of Vizcaya and the fall of Bilbao (mid-June), further bitter resistance in the Asturian and Cantabrian mountains was to persist well into the autumn. This meant that Franco had few reserves to spare in the centre; and it was of some significance that both the Italian and German units were also mostly committed to the northern struggle. In contrast, the republican position seemed promising. Not only were Soviet supplies of (often excellent) equipment reaching a peak, and recruitment levels of International Brigade volunteers higher than ever, but also the training and equipping of the new mass conscript army were well advanced. Finally, in the wake of the terror-bombing of Guernica, an atrocity which gained worldwide attention, sympathy for the Republic was rapidly gaining ground even among the ruling classes in the three great democracies.

The Republic's generals aimed to launch an overwhelming attack on the northen salient of the nationalist lines to the west of Madrid, a position which in macrocosm represented a massive 'bulge'. Successful penetration of this protuberance would threaten most of Franco's Army of the Centre (about one-third of his entire forces) with isolation and the risk of annihilation. Though few in Valencia expected to produce the latter, they were aware that even moderate success could lead to enemy panic, large-scale retreats and the break-up of his front. Above all, in terms of home morale and foreign opinion, it would represent the final relief of the siege of Madrid, an indispensable symbol of the triumph of 'No Pasarán' and the opening of a new phase of the war. In the first days of July, the XV Brigade left its base camps in Albacete province, whence they had been recalled for final briefing and training exercises. They were ferried by fleets of Soviet trucks around the eastern fringes of the capital, following minor roads and roundabout routes towards the Guadarrama mountains. In the foothills overlooking enemy positions to the south, the big gun batteries were being assembled, and infantry regiments, supported by Soviet armoured units, were massing in readiness.

When the offensive opened on 6 July, the XV Brigade was in the centre of the attack, following up Líster's main thrust towards the town of Brunete itself. At least 1,500 men, distributed in three English-speaking battalions (a new US/Canadian unit, called the 'Washington', had been formed), were soon involved in vicious fighting around the village of Villanueva de la Cañada. Like all their other fortified positions, Villanueva was defended with fanatical determination by small numbers of the enemy. In this phase of the battle, and a few days later on the so-called 'Mosquito Crest' – a term redolent of the broiling temperatures in which the battle took place – seven Irishmen were killed, including Mick Kelly and the Salford-Irish communist, George Browne.[20] On 12 July, with the general offensive grinding to a halt, Frank Edwards recorded in his diary: 'I feel very lonely now as I am the only Irishman [among the Lincolns] left in the line.' During fifteen days and nights of unrelenting battle, his prose understandably began to acquire New Testament resonances:

> Got the heaviest aerial and artillery bombardment yet received during the war. One piece of shrapnel missed my head by inches ... Marching all night through soft sand at the end my feet are raw, no socks. We went into battle immediately ... Nearly collapsed with heat and exhaustion. We are still holding out. Both feet had to be bandaged by First Aid Men ... We are retreating slowly. The heat is terrific. We are parched with thirst, we are now 12 hours without a drink. Some of our Spanish comrades have collapsed with the heat.[21]

At Brunete, the flexible fighting qualities of the nationalist rank and file, coupled with the initiative of their (young and ambitious) field commanders, enabled them to contain a massive enemy attack, by which they were outclassed in terms of equipment and outnumbered on the ground by around ten to one. In contrast, the republican command structure proved incompetent at every level. Field communications and logistical infrastructures were generally chaotic. It was only with enormous effort and huge losses that the nationalist counter-offensive was finally held at the end of the month. The net gain to the Republic – in exchange for some twenty thousand casualties – was a chunk of land about six kilometres square.[22] Yet the conduct of the XV Brigade had again been superb, and their so-expensive prize, Villanueva, was the only major enemy position which remained in republican hands.[23]

A long retreat

In the grim aftermath of Brunete, with the British Battalion reduced to a total complement of less than three figures, Frank Ryan again attempted to put an end to the physical separation of the men for whom he was (at least in his own eyes) still responsible. Now based in Albacete, and engaged full time in publicity and propaganda work, Ryan prevailed upon André Marty to allow the repatriation of Edwards, O'Connor and Prendergast (along with Joe Monks, who had not been involved at Brunete). The demand flew in the face of Brigade policy, and Ryan's success in making it illustrates the extent of his influence among the republican elite. At the same time, Marty recognised that this concession might help to heal a running sore. The official explanation was that the men concerned were needed on the 'home front' to counter clericalist campaigning against the Spanish Republic in the Free State. There was little doubt that all four had earned honourable retirement. Although their exit from the scene still failed to bring about the final integration of the surviving Irish, it seems that, as far as Albacete was concerned, the case was no longer a special problem.[24]

Like all other 'national' groups, the British had small numbers of volunteers who served outside Battalion ranks. Some fought by choice with non-English-speaking units. Others were members of the Brigade anti-tank battery. Others still belonged to (theoretically) non-combatant support groups operating on a Brigade-wide basis. These were many and varied: they comprised (*inter alia*) the Command Staff (*Estado Mayor*), guard corps at field headquarters and base camp (Albacete), communications, transport, kitchens and several sections of the medical services.[25] In these circumstances, the handful of grizzled and scarred Irish veterans who stubbornly refused to abandon the Lincolns ceased to represent an alternative focus of emotional or political loyalty for the others, the majority who were now integrated into the 16th Battalion. It was not perhaps a coincidence that Peter Daly, who had returned after a spell in hospital and a longer period of officer training, was now promoted to captain and appointed to command the British Battalion. As if this were not enough reward and incentive for the Irish effort, Daly's close friend and *compadre* of two campaigns, Paddy O'Daire, became his adjutant.[26]

After a short vacation in the Tajuña Valley in August, the XV Brigade moved out once more towards the front line. For the first time, they were going to operate outside Castile. Their new battle-zone was in Aragon; to be more precise, the wide and fertile valley south-east of Zaragoza,

watered by the middle reaches of the great river Ebro.[27] The city of
Zaragoza – capital of Aragon – had been held by the Nationalists since
the start of hostilities, whilst republican lines ran through various
strong-points to its north and east. As is well known from George
Orwell's *Homage to Catalonia*, this front had been relatively quiescent
since the invasion of eastern Aragon by Catalan (mostly anarchist) militias a year earlier. The extensive village-studded area which the militias
had occupied was a strongly Catholic rural community, and if only for
this reason, would otherwise have fallen to the rebels.

By the same token, however, the violent revolution carried through
by the CNT led to seething grievances among the majority of Aragon's
population. Political instability within the region was at first exacerbated
by the strong reimposition of government control which followed the
overthrow of the dissident ('revolutionary') organisations and their militia power in the early summer of 1937. Essentially, however, the
Aragonese peasantry welcomed the end of anarchist rule and the consequent reversal of land collectivisation. Many praised Stalin and the Spanish Communist Party for this equivocal salvation. Meanwhile the militias
were forcibly disbanded and regiments of the new Popular Army took
over the front lines. This was all the more necessary since the nationalist
campaign in north-western Spain was reaching its final stages. Santander
fell in mid-August, leaving only the Asturias region still to be overcome.
Soon, Franco would be finally rid of his second front, and free to turn his
attention to the east. As well as having an underlying political motive,
therefore, this probably represented the last chance the Republic was
likely to have of capturing Zaragoza, with its large working-class population which enjoyed a reputation for radical action. Be all these as they
may, it was, arguably, a good plan for the Republic to get in the first blow
– if only on the age-old principle that attack is the best form of defence.

The primary phase of the new offensive, under the overall command
of General Pozas, was intended to develop along both sides of the river,
and aimed at Fuentes del Ebro, a village about twenty kilometres from
the capital. On 24 August around eighty thousand troops, supported by
considerable matching accessories, advanced from a curved front
extending for some 150 degrees around Zaragoza. The XV Brigade,
having travelled to Valencia by truck, and then by train northwards into
the Pyrenees foothills, were immediately pitched into action against the
initial objective, the town of Quinto. The next day, in his first action as
commanding officer, Daly was shot in the stomach. O'Daire succeeded to
command on the spot, and on the following day completed the capture

of Quinto by taking Purburrel Hill, a strongly fortified outpost over-looking and commanding the village.[28]

Since the main attack on Fuentes had ground to a halt, the XV Brigade was diverted to another target – the town of Belchite. This settlement of nearly four thousand inhabitants, the scene of two ferocious pitched battles of house-to-house fighting (the second during its recapture in 1938), was utterly dismantled in the process, and was later selected by the Francoist regime to remain in its ruined state as a silent but voluble monument of the Civil War. However, the British Battalion never managed to arrive at Belchite itself. Whilst the Lincoln and Dimitrov Battalions were fighting their way into the town, O'Daire's men – against a collective will, strongly expressed – were diverted six miles to the north in order to hold at bay an enemy relief force, descending from Zaragoza. Behind them, the nationalist garrison of Belchite held out against determined onslaughts for day after day. Bob Doyle of Dublin, a member of the machine-gun company, recalled episodes in the week's fighting which ensued:

> The lads in the anti-tank squad were firing and singing 'hold the fort for we are coming'. Since I got no orders, I then retreated with my squad back to the olive groves. We had to abandon our wounded ... We sent out a patrol for the wounded, and we heard the jubilations of the Moors, and some reported the shootings of prisoners.[29]

As Doyle's words suggest, the main counter-attack on the British section (near the *pueblo* of Mediana) was led by the Moroccan *tabores* of Colonel Sáenz de Buruaga, their old adversary from the Jarama battle. Once again, he was stopped; but once again the ranks of the British effectives dipped below the century mark as a result of his ministrations.

Belchite at last capitulated on 6 September. On the same day, Peter Daly died of his wound in hospital at Benacasim. Frank Ryan, who was not far away at field HQ, sent a snap and a short obituary to his American contact, suggesting that Daly had been the sartorial opposite of the famously neat Captain Nathan: 'You couldn't make him look respectable, with his hat always cocked sideways, and if he put on a new tunic in the morning it would be a rag by evening.'[30] Two more Irish volunteers had died in Belchite's streets with the Lincolns. The first was expatriate Dubliner Charlie Regan – 'a fighting Irishman with a burning hatred for Fascism' – as his section leader later described him; and, on the last day of resistance, Jim Woulfe of Limerick was killed by an enemy grenade.[31]

The XV Brigade had registered what must be regarded as a victory.

But, on this occasion, it was gained by overwhelming force and locally superior equipment, and marred by acts of brutal vengeance against brave enemies. Following it, the whole Brigade was held for a spell in reserve, whilst the main focus of the Aragon campaign shifted far to the north. By this time, O'Daire, now to be groomed for even higher command, had been sent off for further staff training. His place as OC was taken by the experienced Harold Fry. After a lull of four weeks, reinforced by the new Canadian ('Mackenzie-Papineau') Battalion, the Brigade returned to action. It was ordered forward in support of what was arguably the first armoured 'blitzkrieg' attack in history – an attempted breakthrough near Fuentes. The new commander-in-chief, Casado, seems to have believed an unexpected triumph was within his grasp, and poured every available unit into the advance. Enrique Líster, whose exhausted division was also sucked in, referred to it as 'the most stupid operation of the entire war'.[32] Fry was killed outright in this operation, along with a dozen others of his battalion. The Ulsterman, Joe Murray, and the London Irishman and CPGB member, John Tierney, also lost their lives during the Aragon offensive.[33] As what was to be a hard winter closed in – more quickly in the Pyrenees foothills than in many other parts of Spain – the battle for Zaragoza petered out into stalemate. The British were at last pulled out of the line and returned for another period of recuperation to their Tajuña valley billets.

The period of relative success enjoyed by the republican cause – if thus we can describe the limited, even Pyrrhic, 'victories' of Jarama, Brunete and Aragon – was now over. The next major campaign, that of Teruel, though initially successful, was punished by a determined enemy counter-attack. After a campaign fought in atrocious conditions, the Republic was faced with an overwhelming disaster, which represented the military turning-point of the war. Not long afterwards, the nationalist forces reached the Mediterranean, thereby cutting the republican zone into two.[34] Thereafter, with only one temporary setback, they were able to concentrate on mopping up the 'Catalan pocket'.

By this time the International Brigades as a whole made up only 20,000 men of an army now nearing 750,000 in strength; moreover, with many more being locally conscripted, considerably less than 50 per cent of the former were non-Spaniards. For example, on the eve of the Teruel campaign, the English-speaking element of the 57th ('British') Battalion was 149 out of a total muster of 450. Nevertheless, the Internationals' contribution was still regarded as fundamental by the Republic's high command – particularly when it came to operations of a daring and des-

perate kind.[35] At first, partly in order to demonstrate Spanish self-suffi-
ciency, they were kept out of the Teruel campaign, only to be called into
the fray once the enemy counter-attack opened – on the last day of 1937.[36]
In more than four weeks' continuous operations, involved at first in
mountain fighting in Siberian conditions, and then in vain attempts to
blunt the point of the main nationalist thrust, the British Battalion (now
commanded by Bill Alexander) lost 15 per cent of its effectives. Two
weeks later the survivors were assigned to an audacious mission to
destroy enemy communications at Atalaya and Pedregosa. The Brigade
was not withdrawn until just before the final loss of Teruel, when the
campaign was effectively at an end. With more than fifty men of the
British contingent dead, wounded or recovering in hospital from the
effects of exhaustion and exposure in sub-zero temperatures, the battalion had sustained losses of over one-third, and was again reduced to a
muster of fewer than a hundred men.[37]

Taking advantage of the massive devastation of his opponents'
resources, and widespread demoralisation inside the republican zone,
Franco soon opened a new offensive. His objective was nothing less than
the capture of Valencia. Not surprisingly, the republican high command
soon committed the International Brigades to the defence of Aragon.
Here they were to suffer their greatest disaster. Soon after the attack
began, the XV Brigade was pushed out of Belchite. For the first time in
the war, on the orders of General Rojo – 'arguably the best tactician in the
Spanish army' – all the International Brigades were assembled as a single
division around the focal point of republican defences, the town of
Caspe.[38] This time, however, nothing could halt Franco's advance. Hit by
four separate enemy thrusts, the lines disintegrated. An atmosphere of
confusion was punctuated only by outright panic; desertion and treachery were only momentarily halted by summary executions.

The retreat became a rout. On the last day of March, the XV Brigade
found itself outflanked and surrounded west of Gandesa. For many
units, it was every man for himself. Near the village of Calaceite, some 140
members of the British, Canadian and American Battalions were surrounded and captured – luckily for them, by armoured units of the Italian Black Arrows. Frank Ryan was the senior officer amongst the
prisoners, whilst Bob Doyle and several other Irishmen were amongst
those he led into a prolonged and arduous captivity.[39]

But the loss of Ryan and so many comrades did not bring to a close
the commitment of radical Ireland to the cause of Republican Spain.
Indeed, it is astounding that even this blow did not end the capacity for

renewal of the International Brigades. In Ireland, as elsewhere, men who had been uncertain or lukewarm – above all, those for whom the Spanish War, and the sacrifices of others, had precipitated a political journey towards communism – now stepped forward. Some were undoubtedly inspired by the circumstances of Frank Ryan himself, especially since a multi-partisan publicity campaign quickly got under way in the Free State to urge his release.[40] Among the hundreds of new volunteers who came to Spain in the spring or early summer of 1938, to join a cause which in general opinion was already lost, were Michael O'Riordan (Cork), Michael Lehane (Kerry), and Thomas O'Brien and Alec Digges (both Dublin). They were soon to go into action in the last republican offensive, the attack across the Ebro, in the last week of July 1938. As early as 10 April, the numbers of British Brigaders, swollen by many who now voluntarily abandoned 'cushier' jobs in the rear, was 140 and had reached 200 by the time the offensive began.[41] Though significantly reduced from the 600 who had gone into battle at Jarama eighteen months earlier, considering the consistent recent losses these figures are a testament to the collective resilience of Communist Party organisation as well as the personal commitment of many individuals.

The Ebro operation was intended to take the pressure off Valencia, but also, by joining hands once more with their southern armies, to press a substantial pocket of Francoist troops against the sea. The objective assigned to the XV Brigade was the town of Gandesa, and the main scene of action the Sierra del Caballs which lies to its south and east. The 57th Battalion command had now fallen to the honorary (Manchester) 'Irishman', Sam Wild, veteran of virtually every major engagement since Jarama, who in a politically transparent gesture, entrusted a Catalan flag to one of the Irish contingent.[42]

For mile after intoxicating mile, the men retraced in the *élan* of victorious advance the same terrain over which they had been beaten into humiliating flight by their enemy a few months earlier. But before Gandesa, the peak which was to become legendary as 'Hill 481' (correctly, Puig de Aliga) dominated the skyline. As it happened, the enemy had decided to make Gandesa the rallying point of their retrenchment; and Puig de Aliga, about two kilometres outside the town, was 'the authentic key point' of this tactic.[43] On the third day of the battle, the Internationals were once again faced with elite Legionary and Moroccan units which had been rushed to the point of greatest danger, and the whole republican advance in this sector stalled. On 27 July, just before the battalion could reach its objective, the hill was occupied by none other than the VI

Bandera of the Foreign Legion – the same unit which had denied the XV Brigade possession of the heights of Pingarrón during the battle of Jarama. As one account puts it, 'the losses of both defenders and attackers during these days were impressive'. Sadly for the Internationals, they were not able to reverse the decision of their previous encounter with the indomitable Tercio.[44]

Despite weeks of assault training, the British stood little chance of conquering the densely fortified and steeply sided outpost by dint of unaided infantry rushes. Yet, from the start, it was obvious that the river barrier, and strong enemy air presence, would preclude the deployment of the artillery batteries which were indispensable to fighting in such terrain. After a week – and several bloody attempts to storm the position – they gave up the attempt. Around them blazed the contest for the Sierra de Pandols, which raged on for more than two months, through August, September and into October. Twice more, after short rests on the banks of the river, battalions of XV Brigade were sent back into this inferno to hold a hill or to reinforce a ridge.

By mid-September the Republicans had been forced back almost to their starting positions. The British Battalion mounted its last action, which successfully prevented an enemy tank breakthrough. It was, fittingly, one of the bravest and most intense they ever fought. Lieutenant Johnny Power, the last of the three Waterford brothers, had rejoined the British from the Lincolns after the loss of Belchite. During the Ebro battle he became the last leader of No. 1 Company, as Kit Conway had been the first. On 23 September, Power's company was cut off and surrounded but he 'managed to fight his way out with a handful of men'.[45] Power, one of the original eighty, had survived; but behind him he left three Dubliners – Jack Nalty (another pioneer), George Green and Liam McGregor.

The seismic aftershocks of battle went on until November, but by then the Republic had agreed to demobilise the Internationals. Fifty-eight members of the English-speaking battalions remained on their feet; another hundred or so regained the use of them in time to march down the Diagonal at the farewell parade in Barcelona on 15 November. Of the Irish contingent, some fifteen men were present to savour this historic – indeed legendary – occasion.

10

Faces of defeat

Political mores and human morale

Service in the combat units of the International Brigades was demanding beyond any normal level of toleration, in every aspect, and for almost every waking moment, of individual existence. The usual circumstances of battle were atrocious, even by the standards of the First World War. Living conditions were lower than those which had prevailed on the western front; for example both rest periods and leave were shorter and less frequent. There were some compensations. Once the logistical infrastructure behind the republican lines was sorted out (spring–summer 1937) the quality of small arms, ammunition and a variety of heavier weaponry – largely but not exclusively Soviet – was generally satisfactory. Food was basic and unappetising, though reliable in supply and rarely fatal. But the volunteers for liberty did not march on their stomachs. Uniforms were supplied irregularly and were rarely appropriate to the climatic and/or topographical demands of a particular campaign. Above all – a virtually unanimous complaint – the provision of footwear was appalling. The regulation-issue *alpargatas* (rope-soled sandals of primitive manufacture) may have been suited to the task of leading sheep to pasture but they quickly fell apart during forced marches or sustained operations away from depots. Especially if the terrain was hard going, shoes and socks were lost with depressing frequency and painful results. Whilst the myth that the British Battalion fought without guns may be laid to rest, there were certainly times when they fought without shoes.

Of course the hardships described above were felt in common by all volunteers. Moreover, the physical privations they imposed represented a continual test of resolution, but they were unlikely to be decisive in undermining the morale of men used to the ruthless test of battle itself. A less generalised reaction, however, can be observed in the area of moral commitment. In this less material and more intangible zone, a clear difference can be felt between Irishmen and others; or, at any rate, between Irishmen and others from the British Isles. This difference can only be described as cultural.

The negative reaction of Irishmen to the rules of uniformity imposed by membership of the International Brigades can be refined into two kinds: socio-political and religious. The majority of Irishmen in Spain – a feeling hardly unknown in the ranks of the O'Duffy Brigade – found discipline irksome. Most just grumbled, even where they had no concrete disagreements of principle or policy, simply because regulation offended their sense of propriety. However, a substantial minority of men who went to Spain in the earlier period (CPI members as well as IRA) were nearer the Spanish anarchists, or to the revolutionary POUM, in their personal beliefs, than they were to the Partido Comunista de España. This represented a correspondence, not a conscious empathy – most volunteers had little idea of what these heretic movements stood for. But any tendency to transgression against the Moscow line was potentially dangerous to both parties concerned. Whether or not individuals consciously conformed to a 'natural rebel' stereotype already long established in Irish folklore, this is exactly how, in practice, many volunteers actually behaved. They displayed the kind of political cussedness often proudly proclaimed to be peculiarly Spanish. I refer to a compulsive tendency which was anti-authority, not just anti-authoritarianism. The Irish 'mutiny' of January 1937 was the earliest to occur in the ranks, and remained one of only two mass protests ever to take place off the battlefield.[1] It was evidently the cause of considerable foreboding in Albacete and Valencia, but the problem was defused by sensible concession. The virus of 'nationalism' was isolated and, accordingly, attenuated. Nonetheless, the urge towards nonconformity had a powerful relationship with that to express a national identity.

We cannot judge which element of this explosive mixture played the leading role in the decision to leave the British Battalion and join the Lincolns. At any rate, the move challenged even Frank Ryan's authority, and was taken by a majority of more than two to one of those present and voting. The existing presence of many Irish-Americans in the ranks of the Lincoln Battalion (a group which included a handful of IRA expatriates) was one incentive. But it was also believed – as it proved, rightly – that both political and military discipline would be less rigorous here than in the British Battalion. However, even this spirit of tolerance had its limits. One Irishman who had enlisted in the USA was Pat Reade, described as 'veteran of World War I, the Irish Republican Army and the

Wobblies. Brave to the point of recklessness ... a die-hard anarchist and an outspoken anti-Communist.' The long-serving political commissar of the 17th (Lincoln) Battalion, Steve Nelson, felt that Reade's inspirational courage outweighed his occasional anti-party outburst. When, in a more repressive atmosphere, Nelson was replaced by Dave Doran, Reade was rapidly ejected from the battalion and the Brigades.[2]

As the war wore on, the supply of spontaneous recruits coming forward for the Internationals consistently diminished. This problem was aggravated by Comintern policy. Adverse publicity about the behaviour of adventurers and criminals who had escaped to Spain – not wholly the invention of the capitalist press – led to an increasingly rigorous political vetting of volunteers. From the summer of 1937, men were first interviewed by local agents, again in London, and (often) for a third time in Paris, before being passed for Spain. Unfortunately, a high degree of party loyalty did not guarantee a comensurate level of resolution in combat. Joseph Lowry was a member of the CPGB who clearly did not measure up to the situation and was 'sent to Albacete for repatriation' shortly after the battle of Brunete.[3] Thomas O'Brien was a dedicated CPI member, who only decided to volunteer when he could no longer bear his inward agonising. He arrived in Spain in mid-April 1938, but was soon in hospital with a fever. He crossed the river Ebro with his comrades on 25 July, but within a few days he left the line, for a reason which even his biographer cannot identify. O'Brien spent one day in hospital, and was subsequently relieved combat duty. Only two letters home survive, and neither mentions a reason for his absence from the front – despite persistent enquiries from home. A photograph taken in Barcelona and dated '8 August 1938', not long after he was under fire, shows no sign of a wound. In one letter he states he is 'acting clerk for the XV Brigade at this depository ... I remain unfit for front-line service ... There are hundreds of auxiliary service chaps hanging about Spain doing absolutely nothing.'[4]

Further pressure on the ranks came because the usual reaction to military failure in Albacete was to increase the powers of the commissars and the degree of 'political consciousness'. In practice, this meant continuous propaganda activity in the ranks. Following the defeat of the dissident communist parties in Barcelona (May 1937), such elements of persuasion were stepped up. Later, in the wake of Teruel, as the military fortunes of the Republic steadily worsened, the fear of treachery in the army increased. The International Brigades were (wrongly) felt to be prone to political infiltration by subversives. In the calm interlude before the Ebro offensive (April–July 1938), the level of indoctrination reached saturation point and seemed to take priority over military training. Those who could not or would not respond felt trapped 'between the bullet and the lie', as an American veteran later encapsulated it. Beginning in September 1937, a series of decrees incorporated the Brigades into the Popular Army. Foreigners and Spaniards were now subject to identical regulations. One consequence was that repatriation of Brigaders on grounds of outstanding service or compassion was discontinued. A majority of foreign Brigaders felt that, as volunteers, they were morally entitled to a different code in such matters.

Despite occasional casual references by witnesses, there is no evidence to suggest that individual acts of lawless violence or felony were more likely to be committed by Irishmen. Though drunkenness was endemic, lists of inmates of both town and provincial jails at Albacete, to which military offenders were consigned, do not reveal excessive numbers of Irish names.[5] Yet the attractions of alcohol locked leaders and led into a vicious circle, for drinking was often a reaction to rigorous discipline. At times, the moral approach was adopted in an attempt to break the spell. In May 1937, a rather smug American volunteer reported:

> With only a handful of exceptions we have excellent self-discipline …
> An example of one of the exceptions … is a sailor of Irish descent, a
> 'tough guy' who got drunk last night and wanted to beat up the battalion and the town … After a bloody struggle with the guards … with
> swollen lips and eyes and his clothes bespattered with blood he was
> placed under the scornful eyes of the whole battalion and shamed to a
> condition lower than a dog's … His conscience must wrack him with
> indescribable tortures.[6]

During a lull in the Aragon fighting in March 1938, the duty officer punished a group of three Irish members of the British Battalion with two days' jankers and a fine of half their month's pay for 'being absent twenty-four hours without permission; and going to the town of Híjar and getting drunk there'.[7]

Though desertions were continuous during the battle of Jarama and the period of trench life which followed, the numbers of Irishmen involved were no higher than the average. Most unsuccessful deserters ended up in Camp Lucas, set in isolated countryside outside Albacete, ostensibly for 're-education'. A young Scot, John Angus, managed to save many British delinquents from this severe and punitive regime, in the autumn of 1937, by persuading them to re-enlist *en bloc*.[8] Some, however, were recalcitrant and expiated their sins in other ways. Eugene McParland, for example, served three months in a Spanish labour battalion for an unspecified offence, and then worked as an ambulance driver, before being repatriated in August 1938.[9]

At least two Irishmen were successful in escaping from the Brigades and from Spain. Patrick Keenan left the scene of the action either just before or (more likely) during the first days of British engagement at Jarama. He got to Valencia and contacted the British consul, claiming to have answered an advertisement in an Irish newspaper recruiting workers for the Spanish Railways. The consul, helped by an American reporter needing a story, smuggled him on board a British warship, HMS *Brazen*, which was headed for Marseilles. Arriving at the Irish embassy in Paris, Keenan changed his plea, admitting he had joined the Internationals, but asserting that in Albacete 'the authorities suspected that some of the [Irish] volunteers were associated in some way with the Blueshirt movement', and he found himself suspected of sabotage.[10]

There were cases of Internationals whose sense of direction was less reliable. One incident involved the half-Irish Peter Kemp and took place in Aragon in the lull before the Ebro offensive. A deserter from Belfast was picked up by a patrol from Kemp's *bandera*. Though not completely convinced by the Irishman's story that he was a sailor, shanghai'd into republican ranks after a drunken spree in Valencia, Kemp knew that unless he intervened the man's life would be forfeit. His strenuous attempts to obtain conventional treatment for his prisoner foundered on the determination of his commanding officer, Colonel Peñarredonda, who loathed all foreign intervention. Apparently moved by a desire to hurt Kemp himself as much as the victim, Peñarredonda ordered that the man be shot. Kemp was ordered to supervise the shooting.[11]

The case of the mad Irishman

The worst instance of insubordination amongst the Irish contingent ended with an identical ritual. In early 1938, Maurice Ryan – like his famous namesake, he hailed from the Limerick area – was a member of the machine-gun company in the British Battalion. He claimed to have come to Spain from the French Riviera, where he had been a successful gigolo. In one sense, it seems, the International Brigades offered him a holiday. His main motive in volunteering (or so his story went) was to find and kill his own brother, who was serving with the O'Duffy Brigade. He certainly proved to have fratricidal instincts.

Ryan was 'a bull of a man, a huge fellow [and] a tremendous drinker'.[12] More than once he was drunk whilst in action, and on one occasion was hit by a sniper's bullet after consuming a bottle of wine. Yet his subversive wit and physical bravado brought him considerable popularity. Moreover, in some respects, Ryan exhibited a commendably professional attitude. He was corporal (*cabo*) in charge of one of the three weapon sections in the company. Just before the Ebro battle he contributed an article to the International Brigade magazine on 'The Heavy Machine Gun', which made some salutary points:

> The gun is usually worked from a gunpit built especially in the trenches, and it is then when it is employed at its best advantage ... The gun must be able to control all sections of the front at a moment's notice ... It is essential that the whole team work in perfect harmony.[13]

When Commissar Kerrigan visited Ryan's company a few days before the Ebro crossing, he reported that 'they were in good spirits. Same trouble here as elsewhere ... a certain amount affected by the Repat[riation] issue. Still, I dont think the position is bad.'[14] Rarely can a prediction have been more awry, nor 'perfect harmony' more horribly untuned. A few days into the battle, during the initial stages of the assault on Hill 481, Ryan suddenly opened up with his gun on his own comrades, who were attempting, under heavy defensive fire, to climb the steep terrain in front of his position. John Dunlop takes up the story:

> Just inches above my head there was a long burst of machine-gun fire but it was coming in the wrong direction. I looked back and I could see one of our own machine-guns actually firing on us. That more or less ended our attack. I told Sam Wild and it turned out that we'd been fired on by a gun under the command of the Irishman Maurice Ryan. He was flailing drunk. I don't know how many of our blokes had been hit and wounded by this man but he was overpowered and arrested ... If he'd been sent on down the line to Barcelona, lawyers there would have appeared for him and he would have got off. He came back to the battalion with orders for him to be executed by his own comrades. I was told some time later that Sam Wild, the battalion commander and George Fletcher, second in command, took Ryan for a walk and told him to go ahead and then they shot him in the back of the head. Apparently George Fletcher was in tears over that because he was very fond of this bloke.[15]

Hurried consultations among the Brigade's field officers in effect constituted a drumhead court-martial. Not only was there apprehension about the unsatisfactory outcome of a formal trial, but it was felt that adopting such a course would mean that the necessary example for the men would be diffused and wasted. On the other hand, since the battle raged on, the latter could not be assembled, nor could even a firing squad be spared from among the men on Hill 481. Thus, Sam Wild and his adjutant volunteered to carry out the grim duty. On or about 5 August, they took Ryan for what was known in Spanish as a '*paseo*': a walk in the woods of the Sierra de Pandols, from which only the two officers returned.

Strenuous attempts were mounted by the authorities to 'explain' the Ryan incident. The line taken was that he was a fascist *agent provocateur*, who coldly decided to wreak the worst damage he could when about to be uncovered. His previous behaviour helped many to believe this story. 'Although extremely amusing, I regarded him myself as an agent for the other side', as one later rationalised matters.[16] The version recollected by the Welsh volunteer Jim Brewer, who took over Ryan's gun after the incident, illustrates the differences of emphasis in memories affected by official 'explanation':

> George Fletcher was the machine-gun company commander then, and there was an Irishman, number one sergeant on this gun. He was a bit of an odd character and George had taken a dislike to him and didn't trust him very much. We were engaged in a battle one afternoon and this chap was deliberately, I think, trying to sabotage his gun … This chap subsequently was shot, he was one of the few people who was actually shot there for an offence.[17]

Ryan, indeed, may have been a fascist saboteur. It seems at least plausible that he escaped the vigilance of Comintern vetting procedures by travelling to Barcelona from France under his own steam. One volunteer thought he was 'bloody mad'; another felt that his execution was (in part) the result of the fact that Irish officers 'were very stern with their own fellows because they were expected to be … the personification of knight-errantry, superior to the rest of us'.[18] Perhaps the most extraordinary account has never been published. The Mancunian Bob Clark, whose memoirs in general rarely recall any personal or place names, was deeply impressed by Ryan (whom he calls 'Paddy'):

> Altogether an amazing character, and very fond of declaiming his aristocratic lineage. Most of the lads believed him as he was very well educated and spoke three or four languages fluently. He was very popular but too fond of the booze … If any man had the makings of an excel-

lent officer, he had. His humour was irresistible and when he was sober he was a very likeable chap ... for a while he was a model soldier and about the best machine-gunner in the whole Fifteenth Brigade ... [He was] destined to be executed by men of his own company on the Ebro front [but] even after his execution nobody could really hate his memory.[19]

Issues of religion and race

In William Herrick's novel ¡*Hermanos!*, the Yanks training in Villanueva de la Jara are urged to moderate their irreligious conduct in order to demonstrate solidarity with the Irishmen who are about to join them. The political commissar warns his men: 'they're probably Catholics and will be easily offended by the careless anti-Catholic remarks that comrades make. So watch your tongues.' As a policy reminder, he adds: 'We're not anti-Catholic at this time.' It was not only tongues which have – in a manner of speaking – to be watched by the semi-fictional Lincolns. Conforming to their leader's exhortation, they stop utilising the leaves of prayer-books – in plentiful supply, since they are billeted in a convent – as a convenient item in personal hygienic care. It proves to be a wise precaution. When the Irish arrive, they 'all wore holy medals under their shirts, and made the sign of the cross before embarking on maneuvers'.[20]

Though a good illustration of the high-school culture nurtured by the new 'brothers' of the ex-sisterly house, Herrick's anecdote is perhaps too fundamental in its particulars. But the commissar was certainly right on one point. By early 1937 the republican government had regained control of civic affairs – at any rate outside Catalonia and Aragon. It adopted official toleration of religion, and the tendency to violent persecution of the clergy was dampened down. The Communist Party supported this; they were keenly aware that Catholicism was still the spiritual affiliation of most Spaniards. Comintern agents in Spain would not have seen the point of Stalin's (later) rhetorical question: 'How many divisions has the Pope?'

Yet toleration was both grudging and ineffective. The government accepted the fact that Rome itself was irretrievably enlisted in the ranks of its enemies. Apart from the sanctions of sovereignty (regaining control of the streets from the *enrageés*) and the dictates of common humanity, a motive for toleration was to influence lay Catholic and broadly liberal opinion in the world at large. Here, the Republic hoped for tangible diplomatic returns. In practice, however, little could be convincingly restored. Churches and other religious buildings which were not destroyed, or not in use for military purposes, remained closed, usually boarded up and daubed with the meaningful legend 'National Monument'. Most surviving clerics remained in confinement (prison or house-arrest). In the circumstances, the authorities were bound to regard them as actual but dormant – as distinct from merely potential – agents of the nationalist cause. Some were nevertheless released, on strict conditions forbidding display of the cloth or public performance of their office. A few were allowed to attend field hospitals and minister (strictly upon request) to the dying, whilst many nuns served as nurses.[21]

Joe Monks gives vivid illustrations of the irredeemably religious character of both Irish and native Republicans. Out on patrol one dark Andalusian night, Monks and Frank Conroy heard someone muttering on the silent sierra. To their amazement they found fellow volunteer, Seamus McBroin:

> an exile from Erin who had spent his working life in the north of England … He was the oldest man in the company … We listened to him recite the Requiem in Latin. 'You are Irish … God bless you both'. We were speechless. He told us that he was praying in advance for the souls of the boys that were soon to die. We cleared off and left him, feeling as we did that we had encountered a banshee.[22]

Monks himself sustained a serious wound shortly afterwards. In hospital in Orihuela, he met some Spanish students who 'made it clear to me that they were not Anti-God but as they say in Spanish "antifascista y anti-cura". Most of them proclaim themselves Catholics and expect to be able to practise their religion when the war is over … Even the nuns in the hospital showed no malice towards us.'[23]

Whatever their personal feelings or official policy, Brigade commanders could not ignore certain religious givens, such as observation of the Christian calendar. For example, in December 1937, on the Teruel front, Robert Merriman ordered that 'tomorrow, the 25th, shall be considered a feast-day'.[24] Meanwhile, strictly clandestine access to Mass and other Catholic sacraments had been made available to a select few – men regarded as politically trustworthy or indispensable, despite the presence of this aberration in their personalities. Frank Ryan seems to have attended Sunday Mass on a regular basis when working in Madrid, and conversed with the officiating priest – of course, a republican supporter. He was aware that such stories provided good propaganda for domestic consumption in the Free State, and were equally useful for dissemination amongst Irish Catholics in the USA.[25]

The only outspoken pro-republican priest in Ireland was Fr Michael Flanagan, an ex-President of Sinn Fein and one-time confidant of de Valera. As a result of his support for the IRA, Flanagan had been suspended from his ministry by the Catholic hierarchy. To the government's embarrassment, this troublesome priest now stumped the country condemning Franco – 'that true Christian knight' as he was pictured by most Catholic sources – as a monster, and the Spanish bishops as agents of oppression. In 1938 Flanagan was invited by the republican government to Barcelona, in order to investigate the extent of religious freedom. After satisfying himself on the point, the priest told William Forrest of the *News Chronicle*, who had been in the loyalist zone throughout the war, that there were

> greater facilities here to celebrate Mass than in any other country he had visited ... The Government which controls all transport had even sent a car to his hotel to take him to the Chapel ... Catholic opinion has unfortunately been influenced ... by the lies that have been spread about nuns and priests in Republican Spain.[26]

As far as the priest – if not the reporter – was concerned, we must in charity assume this was a case of '*sancta simplicitas*'. However, finance minister Sean McEntee now complained to de Valera that the priest's 'utterances were becoming more and more imprudent ... he is directly employed by the State and should impose a discreet restraint upon himself whatever his own personal views may be.' Ironically, whether or not true in December, Fr Flanagan's statements about the free exercise of the faith were shortly to be justified – though hardly in the manner he may have hoped. Barcelona fell to the Nationalists only a few weeks after he had left.[27]

Though not loaded up with miraculous medals and rosaries, on the whole the Irish contingent in the XV Brigade publicly respected their cradle religion even where privately they did not practise it.[28] And – as Herrick's story rightly implies – the behaviour, official and otherwise, of less respectful comrades could cause grievance. When the Irish first arrived in Albacete, commissar Dave Springhall 'asked about the reactions to the wrecked churches and the replies suggested that none of the Irish, particularly the non-believers, liked to look upon a desecrated church. Indeed one youth had been seen to physically close his eyes to such scenes.'[29] Springhall, and doubtless other colleagues, were evidently briefed in advance on the aggravation that such scenes might cause to men from a Catholic background. Indeed, stories about the fascists using churches as fortresses, or told of priests firing from church towers upon innocent women and children, are so ubiquitous in the extant evidence that it seems they were deliberately disseminated, acting to immunise tender consciences.[30] It is no accident that after the passage quoted above, Monks goes on to record being told that the local fascists made their 'last stand' in the church. But, he revealingly adds, 'we heard too that there were pueblos where the local Republicans did not harm the priest or the Church; but lorry loads of incendiaries from the bigger towns came and burned the churches'.[31]

An Irish ex-army officer, Charles McGuinness, was on the march to the Madrid front when he allegedly witnessed his International Brigade comrades take part in a 'rare orgy of blasphemy' in a church which provided their billet. He promptly deserted rather than 'fight in a cause for which I had lost all sympathy'. The Irish legation in Paris reported McGuinness's arrival there in destitute circumstances, and his request for financial help in order to return to the Free State.[32] Less dramatic but more credible were the experiences of the Lurgan volunteer, Jim Haughey. Haughey and a companion (it is claimed) had been wrongly imprisoned for desertion in Barcelona 'in a jail where conditions were horrific'.[33] Like other malingerers – real and alleged – they were brought back to the battalion during the prolonged preparation period before the battle of the Ebro, a period when the Brigades were being bombarded with a programme of indoctrination more saturating than an enemy artillery barrage. This provoked a pathetic reaction. A fellow Irishman recalled 'Haughey's naive Catholic faith in asking prior to the Ebro offensive whether or not the IBs might have a priest to minister to them at the front'.[34]

The contrary tendency is also present. A handful of Irishmen in the throes of political reaction against the Catholic Church were capable of strong anti-clerical feelings. There were also those party loyalists who made the transition from Catholicism to communism with a simple exchange of accidentals. Bob Doyle, for example, came to look on the commissar as he once had the priest. Even Chief Commissar André Marty – 'the butcher of Albacete' to most – impressed him as being 'a very fatherly-looking figure'.[35] That the authorities behind the International Brigades should display an equivocal attitude towards Catholicism is understandable. Evidence of a similar degree of equivocation over racial considerations is perhaps more surprising. The difficulty was caused by the presence of North African troops in the ranks of the enemy – so-called 'mercenaries' who were at once the most effective in battle and the most inclined to atrocity against soldiers and civilians alike. Even before the volunteers experienced the latter on the battlefield, racial prejudice towards them was evident in the propaganda statements of many on the left. In one of the first Irish pronouncements on the Civil War, Sean Murray, founder and secretary of the CPI, referred to Franco as being 'at the head of a Mohammedan army of coloured Moroccans and the cut-throats of every nation under the sun', adding rhetorically, 'are we in Ireland to stand aside? … if we did we would be traitors to the best traditions of our race.'[36] Fr Flanagan, reaching for the worst insult in the republican litany – though seemingly apt in this case – referred to the Moors and Legionaries as 'The Black and Tans' of Spain.[37] The poet 'Sommhairle Macalasteir' made several similarly contemptuous references to Franco's Muslim troops.[38]

In contrast, the Alabama poet Langston Hughes, visiting his soul-mates amongst the Lincolns, empathised with the North Africans as slave-soldiers, whose actions were explained by white colonialist exploitation and command.[39] Another black American in Spain, Salaria Kee, volunteered for a republican nursing unit 'because I was a Catholic … I always wanted to help the nuns as a nurse in this kind of work. I assumed there would be nuns helping the poor in the Spanish Civil War, on the side of those who were defending democracy.'[40] Initially rejected on racial grounds, Salaria persisted and eventually went to Spain with the Red Cross. There she tended a wounded Irishman, Patrick O'Reilly, and fell in love with him. Although she obtained written permission from her brother at home, the republican authorities at first refused to allow them to marry, and only relented on the intervention of the US ambassador.[41]

Defeat, humiliation, resistance

Capture and imprisonment by the enemy began for some volunteers on the second day of the battalion's Jarama action. Two Irishmen were reported amongst the thirty-odd members of the machine-gun company, commanded by Harold Fry, who were captured by Moroccans. The survivors were released, following consistent pressure by the British government, in late April 1937.[42] Over the period April–October 1938, during various actions in Aragon and Catalonia, at least another four Irish Brigaders fell into nationalist hands and survived.[43] By far the most serious incident happened around Gandesa during the chaotic retreats of late March 1938. Hundreds of Brigaders were rounded up by flying columns of the advancing enemy. Among some 140 soldiers of the 57th Battalion taken prisoner in the vicinity of Calaceite, at least 13 were Irish.[44] Others were cut off from the main body and simply disappeared – like Andrew Delaney, who had only arrived in Spain a few weeks earlier, and who was either killed in action or shot upon capture. In the prevailing circumstances the effective distinction between such fatal encounters must have been a fine one.[45]

All these prisoners were transferred from various points in north-central Spain to the camp at San Pedro de Cárdena, a secularised seventeenth-century monastery, about seven kilometres outside Burgos, the nationalist capital.[46] The story of their experiences is told in many a published memoir, synthesised in the official history of the British Battalion.[47] The regime in this '*campo de concentración*' – as San Pedro was officially known – was hard and often punitive. However, conditions slowly improved, and virtually all prisoners survived the ordeal. In the course of 1938–39 they were released in batches as exchanges were arranged; the Republic agreed to release captured members of the Italian CTV, along with various Spanish nationalist officers in their custody.[48]

Exaggerated rumours circulated among the British and Irish prisoners about the exchange rates negotiated in these various deals. For example, it was good for morale (as well as representing a culturally familiar anti-Italian ritual) to assert that one *brigadista* was worth ten members of Mussolini's army. One individual prisoner, often mentioned as the potential champion in terms of his exchange value, also made a vital contribution to the well-being of all the prisoners. The conduct of Frank Ryan, from the moment of his capture, was both clever and courageous.[49] Ryan, expert in matters of internal morale and external propaganda, was aware of the crucial significance of his own comportment. Holding the rank of major, he was the senior officer among all the English-speaking prisoners. Having earlier helped to negotiate the acceptance of the need for the military salute among recalcitrant Brigaders (a delicate matter, especially with his fellow countrymen), immediately on capture he fastened on to the psychological importance of refusing to give the fascist salute, or to utter pro-Franco slogans, even when threatened with physical attack. He deliberately made his experience in these matters the epitome for all. His leadership inspired a spirit of resistance. His example helped other leaders – that is to say, the party activists – to preserve discipline among the men and to communicate an *esprit de corps*. Ironically, perhaps, his status as a sincere Catholic, knowledgeable about the ethics of his religion, also enabled him to ameliorate the use of enforced religious observance as a punitive weapon by the authorities. Consequently, in some respects, and despite Jarama, Brunete and the Ebro, the battle just outside Burgos was the finest hour of the International Brigades.

The Ryan case: heroism and propaganda

During his two years as a prisoner of Franco, Frank Ryan achieved international fame. This stemmed from the fact that the Nationalists themselves identified him as a prize from whom much valuable propaganda could be derived. Having one of its senior staff officers in their power gave them an opportunity to destroy the reputation of the International Brigades, especially in the English-speaking world. The Francoists were anxious to portray the International Brigades not as idealistic heroes of democracy but as cynical opportunists and gangsters. They strenuously sought to identify Ryan with alleged war crimes. The charges against him were reported in the *New York Times*:

> When the Republicans captured and held Brunete for a short time last summer he is alleged to have commanded firing squads of Internationals that executed Nationalist prisoners without giving them any sort of trial and to have shot down with his own pistol a number of Nationalists who were surrounded and offered to surrender.[50]

One nationalist official confirmed to Kerney that Ryan was accused of having 'commanded firing squads and to have executed prisoners with his own hands'. But, at the end of 1938, Kerney complained to Burgos that his government was still 'in the dark as to the nature of the special circumstances and of the crimes in question'.[51] No evidence linking him to such crimes could be produced by Ryan's prosecutors. In the meantime, however, the Francoist case was buttressed by a windfall bonus in another part of the orchard.

The news that Ryan had been captured reached the ears of Tom Gunning in Salamanca. This worthy, who nurtured political and personal resentments against the Republican Irish leader, made it his business to obtain Ryan's execution. Approaching the Francoist administration, Gunning, in his own words, 'asked for Ryan's death with tears in his eyes'.[52] He deposed to them that Ryan had been one of the chief IRA gunmen in the 1920s, and had more recently been responsible for the murder of a retired British naval officer. Gunning told the pro-Burgos

American reporter, Carney, that 'he was very much in favour of Ryan being shot, but recommended that failing that, he should be handed over to the British – a fate which it is supposed Ryan would resent more than shooting'.[53] This was meat and drink for the Burgos authorities. They could portray Ryan as a ruthless killer wanted by British justice who, hardly surprisingly, had carried out vicious crimes against the Spanish people; ideal proof that the International Brigades were essentially the scourings of the west's criminal classes. The outlook for Ryan was grim. Apparently, he had already been condemned to death, by a drumhead court-martial held in Alcañiz or Zaragoza, before he reached San Pedro. In May 1938, he was taken from the concentration camp to a jail in Burgos itself, in order to stand trial again for his life. Never informed of charges nor given any chance to defend himself, he was condemned to death for a second time. For much of June he was held in the death cell in Burgos.

As happened very few times during an uninterrupted forty-year career in the relevant capacity, Franco hesitated to sign the death warrant. The whole Ryan affair backfired on the Nationalists. Quite contrary to expectations, a British diplomat, Sir Robert Hodgson, visited San Pedro and met Ryan. Whitehall then responded positively to the latter's demand for official complaints about nationalist treatment of POWs. In Ireland, a popular campaign for Ryan's release grew in influence. A committee was formed which included representatives of all the pro-government parties in the Free State. There were newspaper articles, speeches and demonstrations. The pro-Francoist lobby was stymied, for – even within the empire of lies spawned by the Spanish War – no one could allege that Ryan was a Red or a priest-killer. Indeed, the Papal Nuncio in Ireland wrote on his behalf to the Duke of Alba, Franco's representative in London. De Valera had already committed himself to saving Ryan's life.[54] He went so far as to intimate to Burgos that his execution would seriously delay any Free State decision to recognise Franco's government.[55] As if this degree of ecumenicism were not enough, General O'Duffy joined in the campaign. Almost as though publicly atoning for Gunning's execrable behaviour, he took Ryan's sister to tea in a Dublin hotel, and wrote to General Franco. It was perhaps O'Duffy's most effective intervention with the *generalísimo*, who replied that 'if the representations made on Frank Ryan's behalf are found to be correct, you may rest assured the sentence will not be carried out'.[56]

Thus, Frank Ryan became an object of admiration in many parts of the world. Not only had he won the propaganda battle with Franco but also, through it, he secured considerable attention for the plight of his fellow prisoners in San Pedro. Not surprisingly, he was the last of all Franco's English-speaking prisoners to be released. Though Franco had stepped back from the death sentence, he had not altered the verdict of the court nor pardoned the prisoner. Ryan's sentence was merely commuted to thirty years' imprisonment. Late in 1938, Kerney was informed that an exchange deal involving Ryan could not be contemplated since 'it is not a question of a prisoner of war but of a criminal who has committed the most repugnant crimes'.[57] When the Spanish Civil War came to an end on 1 April 1939 – exactly a year after his capture – Ryan remained behind bars.

Epilogue: The
peace of history

The established interpretation of Ireland's military intervention in the Spanish Civil War has altered only circumstantially since 1939. Broadly summated, it holds that the contribution of the International Brigaders was both honourable and valuable, whilst that of the XV *Bandera* was neither. This orthodoxy is mediated to us via constant demonstration. Whilst (with the few exceptions noted above) the O'Duffy Brigade has never been publicly memorialised or monumentalised, no great length of time passes without some ritual celebration of the Connolly Column. All this, of course, fits comfortably into the overarching consensus of enlightened opinion (expressed in whatever medium) about the Spanish Civil War as a whole.

But after sixty years, it seems that historians are beginning to look at the events of 1936–39 as scholars, rather than as propangandists and memorialists of the republican cause. This – the defence and celebration of 'the Last Great Cause' – is intended not to discover, illuminate and explain, but to inspire and articulate present political commitment. The new generation is beginning to privilege investigation over assumption, balance before emotion, candour against commitment. The process is still perhaps more aspiration than actual achievement.[1] But it is, nonetheless, a proper aspiration. For me, the story of Ireland and the Spanish Civil War is deeply representative of this intense historiographical (and, in wider terms, intellectual) problematic. Of the crusades which were in conflict in Spain, paradoxically it was that of the agnostic left which is still seen as true and that of the religious right which is perceived as false. To suggest otherwise is to risk being suspect to the silent majority, or even accused by their self-appointed spokespersons, of being 'objectively fascist'. But whatever benedictions and whatever plagues attach to our memory of these crusaders must descend equally on both (and all) of their houses.

Vituperation of the XV *Bandera* was (of course) ubiquitous in contemporary sources sympathetic to the Republic. But here, and in much subsequent commentary, the line of approach was rarely to condemn every aspect and every member of the enterprise, *tout court.* More often than not, the rank and file were portrayed as mere dupes of O'Duffy. In his turn, O'Duffy was presented as a crude political opportunist, attempting to play a tough away fixture in a competition several leagues above his capacity.[2] The fact that Franco was allied to Germany and Italy fitted neatly with another technique, allowing the unparalleled moral guilt of Nazism and the Holocaust to stick by association to all those who fought for the nationalist cause. In contrast, the Irish International Brigaders and their leaders – including ruthless operatives of Stalin – were permitted to benefit by their association with the democratic aspirations of the Spanish people, an infallible agency which, by virtue of the Republic's defeat, conveniently inhabits the ontological realms of utopianism.

The reputation of the Catholic Brigade lost out in every dimension. Little acknowledgement was ever forthcoming from Francoist Spain. From the start any feelings of gratitude or solidarity were suffocated by an ineradicable embarrassment, to which the military ineffectiveness of the enterprise, the circumstances of its collapse and wider propaganda considerations all contributed.[3] The frequently encountered view that the Irish Brigade was present in Spain mainly in order to provide Franco with a propaganda feature illustrating his wide popularity in the outside world is wholly unsustainable. Some such notion may have been present in the plans of men like Juan de la Cierva and Luis Bolín at the outset, but it quickly evaporated. Subsequently, as we have seen, Salamanca took care to elide any public refererence to the Irish presence. When the first history of the war appeared in Spain, twenty years later, it made no mention of the Irish contribution.[4]

A selection from modern (including recent) comment will present the state of the case. The doyen of British scholars of Spain's modern history, for example, is dismissive. Like many others, his comments are aimed more at the leader than his followers, though it's not difficult to detect a stereotyping sneer:

> [On Franco's side] the only organized – if that is the word – contingent was General O'Duffy's Irish Brigade. Whatever fighting qualities it may have had were ruined by its commander's political ambitions and his propensity for hard liquor; the Brigade was shipped home having had little opportunity to fight in the Crusade.[5]

Another British author, who devotes dozens of pages to the International Brigades, dismisses the Irish Brigade with the remark that 'their contribution can be ignored'.[6] A recent textbook on the Europe of 1919–39, which has enjoyed wide distribution in student circles on both sides of the Atlantic, uses similar means in order to reinforce the required impression:

> The [international] brigades … left 10,000 dead; testament both to their bravery and to the poor quality of many of the officers … The Nationalists were unable to attract anything like the same number of volunteers. 'General' O'Duffy led his Irish contingent of 'blue shirts' with such whiskey-sodden incompetence that he was probably an asset to the Republic.[7]

Despite overwhelming contemporary support from the literary-artistic world for the republican cause, a light which guided so much subsequent history, literary historians have been less inclined to culturally indiscriminate comment than historians proper. Most surprisingly thoughtful is the Irish-Spaniard, Ian Gibson – a lifetime advocate of Spain's Second Republic:

> O'Duffy founded the Irish fascist party and when the Spanish civil war broke out wanted to aid Franco 'to win the battle against Marxism'. He and his men … arrived in Spain with great fervour: they felt profoundly Catholic, fraternal friends of an authentic Christian Spain threatened by the Moscow-directed red hordes. But their intervention was not successful. One day – I seem to recall because of the misty conditions prevailing – they opened fire on some other nationalist troops, causing casualties. The adventure did not endear them to Franco, and shortly afterwards the Irish blue shirts returned to their green island, not without having gained a great reputation in Salamanca for their love of potatoes and nostalgia for the rich butter of their land.[8]

Indeed, despite the malodorous deposit left by the returning Brigaders in the popular Irish imagination, not all observers were condemnatory even in intellectual circles. In an acute contemporary analysis, Mair Mitchell compiled a judgement which established the basic integrity of the Brigade yet also conveyed the rich contradictions of the Irish intervention with an intriguing use of irony:

> To materialists it seems incredible that anyone could seriously fight for anything but the things of this world. Such materialists believed anything of the members of the Irish Brigade rather than that they were actually ready to die for religion. There may have been exceptions but

it is almost certain that the majority believed that the faith they cherished was imperilled. [Yet these] courageous volunteers were formed to help those in Spain who, popularly called 'patriots', had brought over Moors to kill Spaniards and who had allowed Mallorca to pass under Italian influence. And Irishmen fighting for the Catholic faith had as their allies on the Cáceres front, Germans, whose Nazi leaders had persecuted Catholicism in Germany. Such Irishmen were supporting a Catholic crusade championed by army officers many of whom were Masons ... Most [of the Irish International Brigaders] were good Catholics, and they were found fighting with, or for, men who thought little of church-burning [and] had prohibited in Barcelona the celebration of Christmas.[9]

Yet the actual textual evidence left by Ireland's literary heritage is much less sceptical – indeed, near-unanimous in its witness against the Catholic Brigade and in favour of the 'Connolly Column'. Several considerations are working together here. In modern Ireland, literary culture has had greater and more direct political impact (both in terms of meaning and influence) than in the UK. It goes without saying that the Irish contribution to literature – I use the term in the privileged, prestructuralist sense – is incalculable. It is a culture intimately bound up with problems of ideology and modernism.[10] For a people still emerging from the dual hegemony of religious belief and linguistic ethnocentrism, the spiritual importance of this culture stands at a cultural premium. There is a more relevant point still. Ireland's self-image as a freedom-loving, internationalist and generous people is hardly consistent with the embarrassing episode in its past which O'Duffy's doings represent. The writers of the 1930s have a role in the here-and-now – helping to elide the fascist element in Ireland's history.[11]

From this perspective it is unfortunate that W. B. Yeats's passing flirtation with O'Duffy and the Blueshirts left a permanent memorial in verse.[12] Yeats's apostasy makes the martyrdom of his potential successor, Charlie Donnelly, of supreme significance. Donnelly abandoned his destiny as the first scholarly biographer of James Connolly in order to die in the ranks of the 'Connolly Column'. However, despite Donnelly's personal commitment to socialism, his lyrics, few in number, fail to convey the explicit propaganda of 'No Pasarán' – the essential message of anti-fascism and anti-imperialism. It was left to other writers to consecrate the images and put across the necessary messages.

> Who would think the Spanish war
> Flared like new tenure of a star,

The way our rhymes and writings are?
That Hilliard spilled his boxer's blood
Through Albacete's snow and mud
And smiled to comrade death, Salud.
That Charlie Donnelly, small, frail,
And flushed with youth, was rendered pale –

...

... Dublin boys have striven, and are
Knit to that alien soil, where war
Burns like the inception of a star.[13]

The intention here was to emulate Yeats's achievement in myth-making epic by writing out the names of martyrs in verse. The same technique was deliberately revived – and then just as deliberately flogged to death – fifty years later, in a ballad that has had at least as much influence around the world as Yeats's celebrated 'Easter 1916':

Vive le quinte brigada
No paseran the pledge that made them fight
'Adelante' was the cry around the hillsides
Let us all remember them tonight.

Bob Hilliard was a Church of Ireland pastor
From Killarney across the Pyrenees he came
From Derry came a brave young Christian Brother
Side by side they fought and died in Spain.

Tommy Woods aged 17 died in Cordoba
With Na Fianna he learned to hold a gun
From Dublin to the Villa Del Rio
Where he fought and died beneath the blazing sun.

This song is a tribute to Frank Ryan
Kit Conway and Dinny Coady too
Peter Daly, Charlie Regan, and Hugh Bonner
So many died, I can but name a few.

Danny Boyle, Blazer Brown, and Charlie Donnelly
Liam Tumilson and Jim Brady from the Falls
Jack Nalty, Tommy Patton and Frank Conroy
Jim Foley, Tony Fox and Dick O'Neill.[14]

Also less subtle than Blanaid Salkeld, but as effective in its way as Christy Moore, was the satirical verse of 'Somhairle Macalastair', a writer who excelled in vilification of the enemy. He employed a challengingly assertive language, referring directly to the immediate Irish past, and pointing up a connection between the events of 1922 and 1936 which made immediate and vibrant sense to his readers.

> O'Duffy's dupes are killing as their Fascist masters bid.
> Gas bombs are falling on the Mothers of Madrid.
> (The birds at Ballyseedy picked flesh from off the stones
> And Spanish suns at Badajoz are bleaching baby bones.)
> …
> O'Duffy calls his 'godly band' and leads them to the fray.
> (They murdered Liam Mellowes upon Our Lady's Day.)
> …
> They cant of Salamanca, our Irish Pharisees;
> 'Tis the flag of black reaction they flaunt upon the breeze.
> They hope to lure out Irish youth to learn their murder trade
> And bring them back to Ireland as a Fascist shock Brigade.
> …
> O'Duffy crowned Dictator 'midst the rolling of the drums
> And the fools that listened to him are rotting in the Slums![15]

As a quick retrospective glance will show, vivid contemporary images like these, perhaps combined with Rex Warner's side-thrust against 'the drunken general and the Christian millionaire', exert their influence on historians' constructions of the past even today.[16] After all, it was in response to the famous questionnaire circulated in 1937 by the Left Book Club ('Writers Take Sides on the Spanish Civil War') that Samuel Beckett entered his response of 'UptheRepublic'.[17]

Against the negative spiritual sanction of poetry, music and drama, the reputation of the XV *Bandera* is helpless. Yet, ironically, O'Duffy sailed to Spain – as Moore's ballad makes inaccurately explicit – with all but the official blessing of the Catholic Church, then the absolute arbiter of spiritual sanction. A few weeks after the Irish Brigade left Spain, the Spanish hierarchy issued an official justification of their pro-nationalist stance:

> The Church, despite her pacific spirit … could not remain indifferent … The one side was attempting to suppress God, whose work must be accomplished by the Church … and the Church herself was suffering immense harm as to persons, possessions and rights, such as perhaps no institution has ever suffered in history.[18]

The supreme irony, the most bitter betrayal, was the subsequent failure of the Church to offer any recognition of the effort made by its crusaders. No doubt, in the privacy of the confessional, many a veteran was con-

soled for the neighbourhood scorn which was worse and more prolonged than anything he suffered in Spain; perhaps the priest sometimes
went further and remonstrated in person with the loudest amongst the
scorners. But in public neither they nor their episcopal superiors ever
praised the Irish Brigade's contribution to the defence of the Church. To
use what seems in the circumstances an appropriate metaphor, they
washed their hands of the whole affair; no blood was upon their conscience. At Glasnevin in December 1944, not a single member of the Irish
hierarchy, the clerics who had been his deeply venerated mentors, was
present at O'Duffy's graveside alongside de Valera, his political enemy.[19]
The International Brigade magazine had prophesied on their enemies'
return to Ireland: 'Perhaps by now, O'Duffy's dupes, sadder and wiser
men, realise that the Irish Catholic Hierarchy ... betrayed them as it has
betrayed the Irish people's struggle so often in the past.'[20]

Charlie Donnelly's best-known poem consists of the grim aphorism
he is reported to have uttered shortly before his death on the slopes of
Pingarrón: 'even the olives are bleeding'. Forty years on this inspired
encapsulation of the Spanish Civil War formed the title of a television
documentary broadcast by RTE. Veterans of the Irish Brigade, and the
International Brigade were asked whether they would have fought and
killed each other in Spain had such an outcome been demanded by the
circumstances. All replied in the affirmative – though it was also notable
that each, in his own way, expressed reservations.[21] The first of these facts
is hardly surprising. After all, in 1936 Ireland's Civil War, in some ways
hardly less brutal and uncompromising than that of Spain, was fresh and
bitter in their memories, even where they had not participated in the
killing.

The virulent attacks on O'Duffy and his men made in much of the
work of myth-making communicators emphasises the point that the
presence of the Irish Brigade in Spain provided the crucial motivation
for the IRA Congress presence, and that the battles over Ballyseedy still
demanded to be refought – not only in 1936, but in 1996. Many Irishmen
who joined the International Brigades were looking for a chance to
refight the Irish Civil War. Indeed, the possibility of direct encounter was
used on both sides as a rallying cry in battle and in between as a tonic for
jaded morale. Frank Ryan reported that 'down in Andalusia, someone
spread the story that O'Duffy's men were opposite us. When the order to
go over the top came, you should have seen our lads charge. "Up the
Republic" ... rang out all along the line.'[22] Keen was the ambition in many
hearts to settle accounts for the defeat of 1923, and for every bitter feeling

the word 'Ballyseedy' evoked. The longer this went unfulfilled, the more discontent grew, to the extent that the frustration made a contribution to problems of morale among the Irish Internationals on the Jarama front.[23]

As it happened, the XV *Bandera* and the XV Brigade were stationed in relatively close proximity during the extensive period of vigilant trench warfare which followed the stand-off in the Jarama Valley. For the whole of March 1937, they occupied positions situated no more than ten kilometres apart; some outposts, or foraging groups, were at times considerably closer. A vague subsequent awareness of this coincidence may have been at work in O'Duffy's assertion that he heard the voices of Cockney International Brigaders manning the armoured train at Ciempozuelos.[24] As the Irish entered Ciempozuelos, the storm-centre of the battle had already moved several miles to the north-east. All the same, if Generals Gal and Líster had succeeded in counter-attacks – of which Donnelly was one victim – O'Duffy's trenches would have been directly athwart the breakthrough, and in the path of the advancing XV International Brigade. Perhaps thankfully, the Irish volunteers were spared this ultimate test of their commitment. Naturally, however, there was constant speculation in Ciempozuelos on the prospects of meeting the Irish Reds bayonet to bayonet. In the same spirit as the rumour spread abroad 'down in Andalusia', when the XV *Bandera* attacked across the valley on 13 March, it was passed around the ranks that an Irish contingent was among the defenders of their objective, the village of Titulcia.[25]

On the other side, John Dunlop later heard the story that 'when the Americans were at Jarama, some of O'Duffy's boys had arrived and they hoisted an Irish ham up, inviting the lads to come across for a slice … of course the Irish ham was shot to pieces in no time at all'.[26] Ivan O'Reilly (D Company, XV *Bandera*) remembered an occasion when, reconnoitring at night, his ears picked up the brogue in the faint voices of an enemy party evidently engaged in a similar mission not far away in the dark of no man's land.[27] He may have been mistaken, but his experience has the character of allegorical truth. Certainly, until June 1937, the Lincoln Battalion was stationed only a few kilometres across the valley from the northernmost position occupied by the XV *Bandera*. The American-Irishman, Marty Hourihan, was in command and the Irish company was neighbour (on their left) to the Spaniards of the 11th (Líster) Brigade, whose sector in turn stretched down to Titulcia.[28] Despite these close shaves, there is no evidence that Irishmen ever fired on each other in Spain.

References on both sides to the dreadful weather conditions which dominated the month of March 1937 are redolent of a shared experience. Indeed, it is the mundane, even trivial, privations of trench life which seem to provide an elemental language of understanding, even empathy – if hardly one of reconciliation. As with all wars, but notably so with modern trench warfare, the battle against the enemy represented by oppressive conditions and intrusive military discipline tends to create an irenic spirit among the ordinary ranks, who observe each other across no man's land. International Brigader Joe Monks refers sympathetically to stories about the O'Duffyites' tribulations: 'they were in threadbare uniforms and were very cold and they used to actually dig up some of the shallow graves where dead were buried to get the coats off them.'[29] Months of trench life could erode commitment, even the fierce commitment of 1930s Irishmen, turning men against their own masters. In the struggle for survival, loyalties could become atavistic, reverting to the tribal or the personal. On both sides, this tendency was exacerbated by ineradicable political divisions amongst the leadership. In terms of continuity, at least, men came to hate the officers, or other units, more than the absent and insubstantial enemy.

One consolation was usually available to both sides. Wine was cheap, easy to preserve, and often powerful to those unused to it. William Herrick, in his novel about the Lincoln Battalion, writes about the aftermath of its first day of combat at Jarama. Volunteers gather to act as a burial party. 'Joe Garms laughed … "When it comes to buryin' the Irish is always front'n cenner. There'll be extra vino rations".'[30] Stereotyping apart, the Irish International Brigaders frequently had better excuse than the Irish Brigade for resort to the bottle. Not only were their 'chances of death' from enemy action considerably higher at any given moment of their service, but they traversed far more ground, and in many places of their campaign there were simply no supplies of clean water. At Ciempozuelos, at least, there was an excellent fountain of reliable water, though positions at La Marañosa were less well provided.

It lies beyond debate that, as things worked out, the Irish Internationals were called upon to suffer more than their rivals during the war itself. Their fighting record is outstanding by any standards; they had dimensionally more casualties; dozens of survivors were both physically and mentally scarred by the Spanish experience in ways which lessened the quality of the lives remaining to them. In addition, they had to endure the fact of defeat, both in detail and in general; the latter representing what they could only see as the unjust overthrow of all their hopes. Of course, many were consoled by the lasting comfort of a justified sacrifice, the recurrent thought that they had not sought to avoid the call of conscience nor flinched from the enemy's fire. When the world of 1945 contemplated the moral and material cost of fascism, their stand in 1936–39 assumed a transcendental meaning for the politically conscious. Those who lived to see the restoration of democracy in Spain following Franco's death in 1975, this time one which was both reformist and genuinely pluralistic, must have felt enormous satisfaction. In all these convictions, the ex-*Brigadistas* were permanently supported by a warm glow of political approbation, scholarly appreciation and public commemoration.

Yet in all essentials – as opposed to accidentals – there is no qualitative difference between the experiences of both sides. As commentators as different as Manus O'Riordan and Frank Ryan have admitted, the vast majority of their enemies were not fascists. As Paddy O'Daire came within a short distance of recognising, the men of the Irish Brigade were overwhelmingly motivated by a cause which was no less genuinely felt and no less morally valid than that of the Internationals. Though few of them laid down their lives, and fewer still were physically crippled, veterans were subsequently obliged to endure a lifetime of public contempt, a feeling often reflected even in the family circle itself. Few felt much sense of personal fulfilment – far less triumphalism – in the military victory of the Nationalists. True, many were content to think that the practice of their Faith had been preserved in Spain. But even in a period where the crimes of applied communism were beginning to assume a more prominent role in public perception, little or none of their implications was carried over to the credibility account of the ex-*Banderistas.* The communist crusaders were established as 'premature antifascists'; but nobody ever hailed the Catholic crusaders as 'premature anti-Stalinists'.

Ultimately, the historian can only seek to explain, and hope that explanation will enable understanding. Some horrors of the past may defy explanation; they must be subject to judgement based on empirical evidence and ethical standards. The nationalist cause in Spain was not inherently evil nor was that of the Republic inherently good. The records of their comportment must now be examined with equal and parallel rigour. This will never be enough to enable complete reconciliation – though it seems to me that many survivors are not personally averse to being reconciled. After all, the Spaniards themselves have managed this immensely difficult process in all its major essentials.

Notes

Archival references

Archival references use sequences of three figures from larger to smaller unit (for example, for the Spanish repositories legajo/carpeta/folleto), where all are present. If two are sequential, they appear thus (leg./carp. or carp./fol.); if only one is present, it is given the relevant prefix.

Prologue

1   A feeling encountered even at the time. Charlie Donnelly gave as his reason for joining the International Brigades that: 'the disgrace, the stain upon Ireland caused by O'Duffy must be wiped out'; quoted in Manus O'Riordan, 'Irish and Jewish Volunteers in the Spanish Antifascist War', typescript of lecture (1987) in IBA Archive, Box A-14 D/3, p. 12.
2   This treatment – predictably prevalent in reactions to a recent book about the Blueshirts – can be further spiced up (to taste) by rib-tickling innuendos about O'Duffy's alleged homosexuality; see, for example, A. Cronin's review of M. Cronin's *The Blueshirts and Irish Politics, Sunday Independent,* 7 Dec. 1997.
3   Mayle, *Fine Gael, 1923–1987.* The only surprising fact in this catalogue is that O'Duffy's image is not airbrushed out of the photograph cited.
4   For relevant apologias, see my 'Battleground of Reputations', pp. 108–10 and 130–2.
5   Interview (with Jim Fahy) broadcast on RTE Radio, 1988.
6   Interview transcript, quoted in Johnson *et al., Spanish Civil War Collection,* p. 37. (Murphy joined the CPGB in 1942). On the hypothetical battlefield encounter of the rival groups, see below p. 210.
7   Keegan, *The Face of Battle,* p. 58.
8   De la Cierva, *Brigadas Internacionales,* p. 271. ('The history of the unknown Irish *bandera* is still to be written … whatever their frustrations, this enthusiastic force wanted not to dig trenches but to be among the vanguard of attack'.) Their rivals receive an identical amount of space in the – also recent – communist equivalent, Alvarez *et al., Brigadas Internacionales,* p. 153. This speaks of 'a veritable bouquet of heroes', but ignores the non-communist Ryan.

Notes

Chapter 1

1   *Irish Independent*, 10 Aug. 1936. The nuns' story was a typically tendentious offering. It implied that the corpses resulted from recent atrocities; in fact the display was of distinterred nuns who had died from natural causes.

2   Ibid.

3   Walsh, 'General O'Duffy', p. 209.

4   The *Independent* kept up a barrage of pro-Brigade propaganda. Its reporter, Gertrude Gaffney, later enjoyed exclusive access to the Brigade's fortunes for publication in Ireland. On the financing of the Brigade, see below, pp. 112–13.

5   These included Juan de la Cierva, inventor of the autogiro, who had offices in London; Alonso Merry del Val, ex-ambassador to Great Britain, now a leading member of the Falange; and Luis Bolín, future head of Franco's intelligence service. See Thomas, *Spanish Civil War*, p. 159ff.

6   Unless otherwise noted, the following details are based on Bowyer Bell, 'Ireland and the Spanish Civil War', and two accounts by Keogh: *Ireland and Europe*, esp. pp. 65–78, and 'An Eye Witness to History'.

7   The Carlist faction had been involved in the conspiracy from the beginning, and – paradoxically, given its parochial profile – had taken the lead in international organisation. Ramírez was inspired by a romantic notion of joining two small but 'historic' Catholic nations against the new international (communist) infidel. The Irish crusaders were to serve with the Carlist militia (*requetés*), guardians of the fanatically Catholic traditions of the kingdom of Navarre. Mola – whose base was in the Navarrese capital, Pamplona – had failed to attract support from Berlin or Rome. At this early stage, the rising was seeking to recruit assistance from outside Spain.

8   Walsh, 'General O'Duffy', pp. 205–6.

9   Quoted in O'Duffy, *Crusade*, p. 12. MacRory's letter was dated 5 Aug.; the date of Ramírez's letter to O'Duffy (12 Aug.) suggests formal ratification of a 'gentleman's agreement' already reached (probably via telephone). The London plotters were making other, similar, initiatives. Tony Hyde read an appeal in the British press for the formation of a volunteer nationalist brigade. Juan de la Cierva was under observation by the Special Branch; see reports on his movements (collated by the Comintern agent in the Foreign Office, Donald MacLean), PRO FO 371/W11988 – 12773 – 12847/9549/41.

10 *Irish Independent*, 15 and 19 Aug. 1936.

11 *Cork Examiner*, 28 and 29 Aug. 1936.

12 *Irish Independent*, 15 Aug. 1936.

13 *Cork Examiner*, 15 Aug. 1936. Keogh asserts that 'the call to form an Irish brigade … had been made independently of O'Duffy by Colonel Carew *on 18 August*'; *Ireland and Europe*, p. 70 (my emphasis). But the resolution was passed on 14 Aug., and was 'warmly approving of the lead given by General O'Duffy'; *Irish Independent*, 15 Aug. 1936. The general had not stated specific intentions to organise or lead a brigade in person. He claimed his commitment was dependent upon the response and he would not formally accept the charge unless sufficient volunteers were forthcoming; see *Crusade*, p. 15, corroborated by speech reported in the *Cork Examiner*, 31 Aug. 1936. By this time Carew had clarified his position, stating that offers received by him would be forwarded to the NCP in Dublin.

14 More information on the 'domestic' context will become available with the comple-

tion of the Ph.D. thesis on Ireland and the Spanish war in preparation by Mr F. McGarry of Trinity College, Dublin.

15   *Cork Examiner*, 13 Aug. 1936.

16   Ibid., 31 Aug. 1936. Though second only to the *Independent* in coverage of the anti-clerical outrages, the *Examiner* remained sceptical over the 'crusade' because of the embarrassment that O'Duffy now represented to Fine Gael. In contrast, the day following O'Duffy's letter, the *Independent* began its pro-brigade campaign with a lead story about Pope Pius XI's outrage at the persecution of the Spanish Church: see issue of 11 Aug. 1936.

17   In response to the Spanish ambassador's complaints, de Valera even offered to try and ameliorate the 'extreme' stance of the pro-clerical lobby; see Aguilar's telegrams to Madrid, 5, 14 and 20 Aug. 1936, AMAE, A.Ba. R-153/15 and R-415/44.

18   Foreign Ministry, Madrid, to Aguilar, 23 Aug. 1936, ibid., R-415/44 ('*puede informar que ofrecimiento mediación no podría encontrar éstas circunstancias ambiente propicio*').

19   Aguilar to Foreign Ministry, Madrid, 1 Aug. and 8 Sept. 1936, ibid. R-153/15. The ambassador was at heart pro-insurgent, and had stayed at his post in order to help members of his family, who were caught in the loyalist zone, to reach safety.

20   It is unlikely that this trip was connected with the Brigade project. The general prided himself on being a man of his word, and was anxious to discharge commitments entered into before the Ramírez initiative. (Cf., however, Bowyer Bell, 'Ireland', p. 248.) On the other hand, his punctiliousness on this occasion indicates weaknesses of judgement which were to grow in importance; a certain readiness to abandon his post when invited to take off and have a good time, and an inability to establish priorities.

21   *Cork Examiner*, 21 Aug. 1936.

22   See, for example, ibid., 18 Aug. (Leitrim); 27 Aug. 1936 (Offaly); and cf. Bowyer Bell, 'Ireland' pp. 245–6.

23   *Irish Independent*, 21 Sept. 1936, as quoted in Keogh, 'Eye Witness', p. 449. The text is not fully coherent, a condition attributable to the Cardinal's patently reluctant self-censorship. The careful concern of the bishops over public statements can be observed in an Appendix, 'A Record of Pulpit-Propaganda', which O'Riordan compiled in an attempt to illustrate precisely the reverse; *Connolly Column*, pp. 211–16.

24   De Blacam, *For God and Spain*, p. 29. The work was much recommended from the pulpit and in the Catholic press generally. Not surprisingly, it enjoyed wide circulation. Despite the text's equivocation on the point, Brigade veterans interviewed by me referred to it as part of the meld of influences on their decisions to enlist.

25   *The Universe* (Irish edition), 18 Sept. 1936. On 'the hero of Benburb', see pp. 30 and 219, n. 34.

26   P. Smith, interview.

27   *The Universe*, 25 Sept. 1936. See Stradling, *The Spanish Monarchy*, for information on the origins of the 'Wild Geese'.

28   Quoted in *Tuam Herald*, 5 Sept. 1936. Franciscans and Jesuits had adopted similar stances in the seventeenth century, when Irish soldiers had left for Spain to fight for the 'Catholic Cause'. See Stradling, *The Spanish Monarchy*.

29   *Cork Examiner*, 28 Aug. 1936.

30   Quotations in this paragraph are from ibid., 22 and 24 Aug. 1936. Though the Aragonese capital was indeed held by the Nationalists, Cronin's mention of Saragossa as the Brigade's specific destination seems to have been made in error for 'Salamanca'.

31   This method of collecting for causes approved by the Church is still prevalent in Ire-

land. O'Duffy had inspired sympathy for a mass fund-raising campaign by claiming that 'the workers of Russia had collected £486,000 to aid their Spanish Comrades in their nefarious work'; *Irish Independent*, 10 Aug. 1936.

32   *Cork Examiner*, 29 and 31 Aug. 1936. This meeting was also the subject of a rare (London) *Times* report about O'Duffy on 31 Aug.

33   Later that month, a press advertisement drew attention to a special fund for medical and other necessities for the Brigade – but it was already too late; *Cork Examiner*, 29 Aug. 1936.

34   For more detailed analysis of the Free State government's handling of the volunteer issue, see, see, pp. 14–17, 84–91.

35   *Cork Examiner*, 25 Aug. 1936.

36   S. Walshe to French Resident Minister, 18 Aug. 1936, INA, Dept of Taoiseach file S-9177.

37   Press release of 25 Aug. 1936, ibid.

38   C. A. Macguidhir to government, 9 Oct. 1936, ibid. However, various manuscript notes indicate that other officials (or ministers) were not entirely disposed to accept this ruling. By the time they received this report, they were aware that recruitment was under way for the Republic too; see pp. 132ff.

39   Mr Roberts to Dominions Office, 29 Oct. 1936, PRO, FO 371 20579/W12958/9549/41. Later that day the same official added the gloss that 'if a similar warning [against allowing enlistment] was considered appropriate in any of His Majesty's colonies or protectorates, this wd be issued by the authorities of the territory in question'; ibid.

40   As a further complication, the Hague Convention stipulated that 'the responsibility of a neutral power is not engaged by the fact of persons crossing the frontier separately to offer their services to one of the belligerents'. Thus, individuals holding passports could not be prevented from travelling. However, it also stated that 'corps of combatants can not be formed nor recruiting agencies opened on the territory of a neutral power to assist the belligerents'. Both the NCP and various Comintern agencies infringed this provision. See Pike, *Conjecture*, p. 73ff.

41   Memo. by Walshe, 11 Nov. 1936, INA, DFA 227/87.

42   This item was reported by *El Adelanto de Salamanca*, the newspaper closest to the status of official organ, under the front-page headline, 'Ireland will shortly recognise the government of General Franco'; 28 Nov. 1936. (The nationalist government had already been recognised by Italy and Germany.)

43   Despite having powerful rivals, Franco held the stronger cards. He had absolute command of the army of Africa, by far the most effective fighting force, and fruitful contacts with sources of external assistance, including Portugal, Germany and Italy. See Preston, *Franco*, esp. chap. 7.

44   Letter (of 12 Aug. 1936) quoted in O'Duffy, *Crusade*, pp. 12–13.

45   Ibid., p. 15.

46   Quoted in Moloney, *Westminster*, p. 64.

47   Report dated 25 Sept. 1936, forwarded by Home Office to Foreign Office; PRO, FO 371/20579/W12847/9549/41. In view of later developments (see below, p. 118) I suspect that, far from being reliable, Gunning was 'planted' with O'Duffy by Luis Bolín, in order to act as informer.

48   O'Duffy gives a telescoped account of this peregrination in *Crusade*, pp. 16–18 and 23–4.

49   Del Burgo, *Conspiración*, pp. 249–50.

50   *Connacht Tribune*, 3 Oct. 1936 (report syndicated from British United Press).

51   For Cabanellas, see Cortada, *Dictionary*, p. 99; for Mola, ibid., pp. 340–1.

52   O'Duffy, *Crusade*, p. 18.

53   Preston, *Franco*, esp. pp. 180–6.

54   *Connacht Tribune*, 3 Oct. 1936 (received via an *Irish Independent* reporter in St Juan de Luz, France – thus certainly an official nationalist press release). Cf. O'Duffy, who has the news given him by one of Mola's aides: 'General Franco gladly accepts Ireland's offer of a volunteer brigade'; *Crusade*, p. 23.

55   The general arrived in Dublin on 3 Oct. Franco's attitude to the Brigade at this stage is uncertain. Despite his preoccupations, he was not likely to rubber-stamp a decision of this kind. He was a strong admirer of the *requetés* and probably had few apprehensions about a force intended to serve on the northern front – relatively unimportant at this stage of the war. Even if some reservations were expressed, Mola would have been able to call on some of his credit for supporting Franco over the leadership.

56   On the Waterford *débâcle*, see below, pp. 31–2.

57   The accounts given by O'Duffy himself of his two meetings with Franco constitute the only extant record; *Crusade*, pp. 65–7, 70 and 85–7.

58   Ibid., p. 68. The main point of this meeting was to determine the use of £32,000 collected by the ICF; see *El Adelanto de Salamanca*, 10 Nov. 1936 (which contains the unique reference to O'Duffy to be found in the main nationalist newspaper).

59   Ibid., pp. 65 and 70. De la Cierva held honorary rank in the Tercio, and was virtually a minister without portfolio in the Franco cabinet. However, a few weeks later he was killed when his plane crashed after taking off from England on another pro-Franco mission. *El Adelanto de Salamanca*, 11 Dec. 1936, gave considerable space to the event, mourning his death as that of a national hero.

60   O'Duffy, *Crusade*, pp. 85–7. This is the only extant record of the agreement and some clauses may be regarded as *ex post facto* elaborations. O'Duffy's direct subordination to Franco was in respect only of the overall well-being of the Brigade, not in terms of military command, and especially not of command in the field. The latter would of course be held by the commanding officer of any army group(s) in which the Irish were to serve. It was also important that Juan Yagüe held the post of Inspector General of the Tercio as a whole.

61   For further analysis of the relationship between the Irish Brigade and the Legion, see below, pp. 48–52, 82–3, 91ff.

Chapter 2

1   Geraghty interview; Kavanagh reminiscences.

2   Keogh, 'Eye Witness', p. 453, apparently citing O'Duffy, *Crusade*. NCP records contained statistics and other data concerning recruitment. O'Duffy is known to have kept records in his Blackrock home, but they seem to have disappeared without trace following his death in 1944: Walsh, 'General O'Duffy', p. 226.

3   Cronin, *The Blueshirts*, pp. 113–18.

4   On the change in Cronin's attitude, see below pp. 41–2.

5   *Cork Examiner*, 24 Aug. 1936. He stated that nearly half these offers were from Northern Ireland and other parts of Great Britain. It was reported that eighty letters per day were coming in, and that the project 'has attracted considerable support both here in

Ireland and in England'; ibid., 19 Aug. 1936.

6   Ibid., 20 Aug. 1936. This statement was inspired by the need not to lose supporters to the newly born ICF and its anti-Semitic leader, Belton. It was issued in O'Duffy's absence by Liam Walsh – himself an anti-Semite.

7   *Irish Independent*, 13 Aug. 1936 (it is possible that the paper's editor did not detect the faint note of irony in this exhortation).

8   Both letters in *Cork Examiner*, 19 Aug. 1936.

9   T. Dalton, interview.

10   *Cork Examiner*, 25 and 27 Aug. 1936.

11   Ibid., 28 Aug. 1936. O'Duffy claimed that the final total of applications reached 6,000 – still well short of the 20,000 originally proposed; see *Crusade*, pp. 13–14.

12   There can be little doubt that some individual members of military units sent to Spain by the Soviets, Nazis and Fascists were authentic volunteers. But only in the case of Ireland is it demonstrably true that all who went – and, moreover, from both sides – did so voluntarily.

13   Ibid., p. 56.

14   INA Dept. of Taoiseach, file S-9197.

15   Smith, interview.

16   Quinn to Dunphy, 22 Sept. 1936, INA S-9197.

17   Same to J. Doyle, 23 Oct. 1936, ibid.

18   P. Dunphy to Doyle, 4 Nov. 1936, ibid.

19   Dunphy to Doyle, 7 Nov. 1936, ibid.

20   See Appendix A, pp. 253–64.

21   It is instructive to recall that the CPGB, backed by the Comintern, managed to raise the comparatively modest total of 2,000 volunteers for the International Brigades in a period stretching over twenty-two months (Oct. 1936–Aug. 1938).

22   Sisters Emanuel and Alphonsus, recalling a visit of Irish Brigaders to the convent of Bom Suceso, Lisbon, in Dec. 1936; 'Even the Olives are Bleeding'.

23   What follows on the motivation of the volunteers is based on extant material relevant to the following veterans: P. Dalton, W. Geraghty, T. Hyde, J. Kavanagh, D. Reynolds, P. McBride, P. Smith, M. Becket, P. Hickey, J. McCarthy, S. Cunningham, M. Fennell, W. McCormack, F. Fitzgerald, M. Doolan, P. Quinn and G. Timlin.

24   *Irish Press*, 11 Nov. 1936. The Board reinstated O'Connell in his job by a majority of one vote, but by then his passport had come through, and he left for Spain via Liverpool later that month.

25   Letter to author from D. O'Reilly (son), 6 Mar. 1995. (Mr O'Reilly snr died in Rochdale in 1976.)

26   Reynolds, interview.

27   Evidence of daughter, Ann Dolan, given to L. Ó Laoi, Nov. 1997.

28   *Irish Independent*, 26 Oct. 1936.

29   Ibid., 18 Aug. 1936. Not all this reportage was completely divorced from reality, if only in the sense that it often contained (broadly) accurate predictions of impending developments.

30   Evidence of Michael Reynolds (son), Moylough.

31   See programme advertisement for the Mall Cinema, Tuam (Co. Galway) in the *Tuam Herald*, 13 Sept. 1936.

32   'The Minstrel Boy', by Thomas Moore, printed in Lyons, *Land of the Poets*, p. 29.

33   *Cork Examiner*, 1 Aug. 1936, article by L. Nunan-MacSwiney. The siege of the famous

Alcázar kept this theme in the news – and in the thoughts of many Catholics – for the whole summer.

34   Ibid., 22 Aug. 1936, 'The Irish in Spain – Famous Exiles who Rose to Prominence – Soldiers and Statesmen in Spanish Service', by J. O'Farrell Rowe. The piece is decorated with a portrait of the hero of the battle of Benburb (1646), Owen Roe O'Neill.

35   'Ireland and Spain – Old Memories', reprinted from *The Irish World* in the *Tuam Herald*, 19 Sept. 1936.

36   Aldgate, *Cinema and History*, esp. p. 113ff.

37   *Tuam Herald*, 10 Oct. 1936.

38   Quoted in Keogh, *Ireland and Europe*, p. 84.

39   For the Oughterard contingent, see *Connaught Tribune*, 17 Oct. 1936. For P. Hickey, evidence of Mrs A. Byrne (daughter), Sept. 1995; J. Kavanagh and others were allocated to a previously unknown 'partner' whilst waiting for transport to Galway in the Belvedere Hotel.

40   *Irish Independent*, 17 Mar. 1937. The casualties were Messrs MacSweeney and Horan of Mitchell Street. A third Tralee man, Tom Foley, also died as a result of this action.

41   O'Duffy, *Crusade*, pp. 58–9.

42   Groups as far away as Sligo town were standing by for the Passage East sailing (see O'Duffy's letter cited in note 43). This puts a query against the claim that 6,000 volunteers were registered – for, if true, sufficient numbers for a first voyage should have been provided by the counties of the southern seaboard alone.

43   Quoted from a 'sample' letter to Mr Gallagher of Sligo, O'Duffy, *Crusade*, p. 62.

44   This and the next paragraph are broadly based on O'Duffy's account in ibid., pp. 61–4.

45   The names of the four cruise ships were chosen for their initial letter as well as genus. Thus *Alondra* (skylark), *Avoceta* (avocet), *Aguila* (eagle) and *Ardeola* (heron).

46   O'Duffy, *Crusade*, p. 92.

47   Ennis, 'Catholic Moors', pp. 39–43.

48   E. Morgan to L. La Roux, 4 Jan. 1937, in the possession of Mr B. Boles, Cahir, Co. Tipperary, to whom I am much indebted for providing a copy. Morgan's lack of sympathy was typical of British Catholic intellectuals. His addressee was a Breton Nationalist, exiled in the Free State, who wrote biographies of several leaders of the Easter Rebellion.

49   *Irish Press*, 12 Nov. 1936.

50   Despite this, de Valera's personal attitude was surely equivocal, in that he cannot have been entirely displeased at the prospect of the unruly O'Duffy and large numbers of followers leaving Ireland, perhaps destined for a glorious martyrdom.

51   Since his book, *Crusade in Spain*, was published before the Spanish War ended, and whilst legislation inspired by non-intervention was still in force, O'Duffy refrained from recording information which might have exposed himself and others to prosecution.

52   See Manning, *Blueshirts*, pp. 101 and 149.

53   *Tuam Herald*, 22 Aug.; *Connaught Tribune*, 29 Aug. 1936.

54   Bowyer Bell, 'Ireland', pp. 250–1.

55   There were other, more complex factors which helped to make up O'Duffy's mind. Lack of space precludes elaboration of this story; I hope to publish the relevant material elsewhere.

56   O'Duffy, *Crusade*, pp. 91–5. De la Cierva wanted the general to accompany him to Amsterdam, perhaps in order to assuage doubts over the financing of the expedition.

But O'Duffy decided to go on to Salamanca to prepare the reception of his main party. De la Cierva's plane crashed, killing all on board. See ibid., p. 157.

57   O'Duffy's account is in ibid., pp. 98–102 (but its author was not present). My main additional sources for what follows, cross-referenced to the present footnote in abbreviated form, are: Geraghty and Reynolds interviews; Kavanagh reminiscences; contemporary reports in the *Irish Press* (14 Dec. 1936), *Clare Champion* and *Mayo News* (both 19 Dec. 1936); 'Fighting for Franco' (evidence of W. McCormack) by D. Ryan; *Limerick Christmas Gazette*, 1995; Hayes, Diary; 'Memories of War in the Olive Groves' (evidence of M. Fennell) by T. Coleman; *Irish Times*, 30 Apr. 1987; Lindsay, *Memories*, pp. 53–6; and McKee, *I was a Franco Soldier*, pp. 7–11. McKee was either planted (by the IRA or the CPI) from the beginning, or was later persuaded to put his name to this bitterly hostile report of the expedition.

58   McBride, interview.

59   McCormack, see n. 57.

60   Opinions of various private interlocutors in Galway, 1990–95.

61   *Mayo News* (see n. 57). Other parties reached Galway too late to board the tender – which, in any case, was crowded to the gunnels, with some passengers hanging on to deck ropes for grim death; see Coleman (n. 57).

62   No roster survives, and available estimates (too many to cite here) range from four to seven hundred. O'Duffy himself gives 'close on five hundred', a figure confirmed by my independent estimates. It includes fifty-odd men who failed to board the *Urundi*, and is collated with the figures for the four Liverpool–Lisbon contingents and that of 663 given for the first complete muster in Cáceres; see below, p. 45.

63   Lindsay (see n. 57).

64   These were K. Geoghan, M. Donoghue and J. McGrath; *Irish Press* (n. 57). The quotation in the previous sentence is from Patrick Lindsay, who later became an eminent lawyer and Fine Gael TD. However, his reaction stands in contrast to that of the three men just named. Lindsay claims that whilst he waited to board the tender, his classics professor, Fr T. Fahy, persuaded him to pull out. Lindsay had been offered a commission 'which I foolishly and recklessly accepted'. Fahy asserted that 'none of them will fight: they will probably die of dysentry [*sic*]. They will never make any showing'; see n. 57. This smacks of *ex-post-facto* exculpation; perhaps its author was one of those who could not face the transfer operation in Galway Bay (see below). O'Duffy confirms that Fr Fahy was present at the embarkation; *Crusade*, p. 99.

65   *Connaught Tribune* (see n. 57). The *Dun Aengus* was as solidly constructed as the ancient stone fortress on Aran Mór after which it was named. Shortly after this voyage, it was caught in another vicious storm, during which some local passengers knelt to pray for their lives. Yet the skipper managed to go to the aid of a cargo ship in distress off the Aran Islands; see ibid., 26 Dec. 1936.

66   Kavanagh (n. 57) alleges that the men had to perform this exercise whilst carrying their bags, partially disabling one arm.

67   Among them was Bill Geraghty's pal, Danny Farrell. The *Irish Press* reporter, doubtless present as a result of a government tip-off, interviewed some of the defectors and filed a story about their 'protest at ill-treatment'. However, several later managed to rejoin the Brigade by other means. The *Urundi* belonged to the German East Africa Liner Company. When questioned in his Hamburg office, the firm's manager admitted his ship had 'disappeared', but denied it was carrying Irishmen to Spain. Lloyds of London confirmed that the ship had left Hamburg on 8 Dec.; see *Connaught Tribune*,

26 Dec. 1936.

68   *Irish Press*, 20 Nov. 1936. See also the syndicated story in the *South Wales Echo*, 21 Nov., noting that 'although for the most part members of General O'Duffy's Blueshirts, the party wore mufti'.

69   O'Duffy, *Crusade*, p. 92.

70   Ibid., pp. 96–7.

71   See Pike, *Conjecture*, pp. 60–1.

72   Details of 'the Lisbon experience' given here represent a digest of material derived from all four relevant expeditions; see esp. O'Duffy, *Crusade*, p. 93; Ó Cuinneagháin, *Saga*, p. 6; 'Even the Olives'.

73   The homily was printed in leaflet form and distributed for the men to keep in private missals: 'To the Irish Brigade fighting in Spain'. (P. Smith copy, private possession, Loughrea.)

74   Ó Cuinneagháin, *Saga*, p. 8. A different impression was given by veteran W. McGrath, who claimed he was sent to 'flush out' some Brigaders from a Lisbon brothel, where he found the prostitutes sporting rosaries around their necks – items donated to the crusaders by a convent in Cork; Boles interview.

75   Franco to O'Duffy, 2 Jan. 1937, AGM, CGG 151/3/1. One reason for the inattention paid to the operation in Britain was that it coincided exactly with the period of the abdication crisis, which began late in November 1936 and drove everything else off the front pages for over a fortnight.

76   See McCarthy, 'Adventures'.

77   See Keogh, 'Eye Witness', p. 475, and sources there cited.

Chapter 3

1   For these precedents, see Stradling, *Spanish Monarchy*, passim. The Brigade was about to retrace the footsteps of an Irish Tercio to the province of Extremadura, where it had served in the army of King Philip IV fighting the Portuguese in the 1650s.

2   The seminarists – on holiday when the war started – were later repatriated; INA, DFA, 210/81; *Connaught Tribune*, 24 Sept. 1936. Fr McCabe was thus at a loose end, and was soon sucked into the life of the Brigade. O'Duffy was not present in Salamanca and makes only passing reference to the reception; *Crusade*, p. 102. A news blackout of matters sensitive to the Non-Intervention Committee was in operation; the local daily, *El Adelanto de Salamanca*, made no mention of the Irishmen's visit.

3   Reynolds, interview.

4   'Dark Rosaleen', by James Clarence Mangan, printed in Lyons, *Land of the Poets*, p. 26.

5   Lawler's story was related to P. Kemp and is quoted here from the latter's book, *Mine Were of Trouble*, p. 87. See also D. Ryan 'Fighting for Franco', *Limerick Christmas Gazette*, 1995. This is based on the recollections of veteran Bill McCormack, who recalls 'we were wined and dined, we had a great time; it was like Hollywood'.

6   The following two paragraphs are based on McCullagh, *In Franco's Spain*, p. 218ff. The author was a retired army officer who had published best-selling studies of revolutions in Russia and Mexico. His account is fragmentary because reporters were not permitted to file news stories on foreign military presence. In both zones files were subject to audit without warning, and offending matter could lead to confiscation, and even to expulsion from Spain.

Notes

7   M. Beckett's Portuguese visa, stamped on 17 Dec., fixes the *Ardeola*'s date of arrival in Lisbon: Beckett Collection, Westport.

8   This figure was later reported to W. Tierney by veteran S. Cunningham; see 'Irish Writers', p. 37.

9   Carr, *Chances of Death*, pp. 112–13. The diarist was daughter of one of Britain's richest men, Lord Howard de Walden. The present writer's standards are less demanding, but when he stayed there in 1995, the Hotel Álvarez was seedy and run down.

10 For a modern guide to city and province, see Scheller and Navareño, *Cáceres*. In the 1930s, the town had a population of some 18,000 and its province *c.*400,000; figures projected from the *Pequeño Larrousse* for 1916, pp. 1097–8.

11 García, *Estructura agraria*, passim.

12 For Cáceres during the Civil War, I rely on the recent work of J. Chávez Palacios. See his recent studies, *Represión en Cáceres* and *Huídos y Maquis*.

13 For the fall of Badajoz and subsequent atrocities see Thomas, *Spanish Civil War*, p. 373ff.

14 The *generalísimo* moved his HQ to Salamanca early in October 1936.

15 AGM, CGG, Sección Justicia 145/2 and 3, Jan. 1937. See also ibid., 33/15.

16 'Información Burgos', 31 Jan. 1937, ibid., Sección Ejército del Centro, 1/7/2. The suspicion arises that if such a warning was necessary then the cause of security was already hopelessly lost.

17 Chávez Palacios, *Huídos y Maquis*, pp. 36–80, incorporates detail concerning these operations.

18 See the documents in AGM, CGG, leg. 147. An army officer accused of spying was sent to Cáceres for '*juicio sumario*' in late Sept. 1936 (carp. 9); meanwhile, a group of Civil Guards who had ostensibly 'escaped' from the republican zone were being rigorously interrogated (carps. 2–7).

19 Canales had received the death sentence earlier, but Franco had not confirmed it. See Veiga, *Fusilamiento en Navidad*, passim, and Chávez, *La represión*, pp. 271–3. Today a square in the town is dedicated to his memory.

20 See the advertisement in *El Adelanto de Salamanca*, 3 Oct. 1936; '¡Españoles, Extranjeros, al Tercio!'.

21 See pp. 95–6.

22 *Cork Examiner*, 21 Aug. 1936. The story ranges from ignorance (much of 'northern Spain' was still in government hands) to pure invention (the pirate flag).

23 G. Gaffney, 'With the Irish Brigade in Cáceres', *Irish Independent*, 1 Mar. 1937.

24 English translations of Tercio regulations drawn up for Irish use, now in the Military Archives, Cathal Brugha Barracks, Dublin; quoted by permission of the archivist, Commandant P. Young.

25 For independent evidence on these matters, see Kemp, *Mine Were of Trouble*, esp. pp. 110–17; and Stradling, *Brother Against Brother*, passim.

26 See O'Duffy, *Crusade*, pp. 105–7, whose details on the Tercio as a whole are unreliable. During 1936, anything over 500 men came to be regarded as optimum fighting strength for a *bandera*; see sources cited in Stradling, *Brother Against Brother*. Each company of the XV *Bandera* had a Spanish liaison officer. O'Duffy was correct to claim that his men were the first non-Spanish unit to be integrated with the Tercio. He himself accepted the rank of General de Brigada (Brigadier) which, though lower than that he had attained in the Irish army, was technically superior to that of most of Franco's outstanding field commanders, not excluding Yagüe.

27   I include here, along with Captain William Meade, Spanish-born son of an Irish immigrant, two career officers of the Legion – Nangle and Fitzpatrick – who were involuntarily transferred from the V *Bandera*. They were of Irish Protestant landowning stock, and further disadvantaged in their enforced company by English public-school accents; see the contrasting accounts in O'Duffy, *Crusade*, p. 148 and Kemp, *Mine Were of Trouble*, pp. 108–10.

28   O'Duffy, *Crusade*, p. 105.

29   Alfonso Bustamante, ex-liaison officer B Company, interviewed in 'Even the Olives'.

30   Veteran private soldiers P. Smith and D. Reynolds (interviews) and J. Kavanagh (reminiscences) paid tribute to the training, and even McKee was impressed; see *I was a Franco Soldier*, p. 17, which asserts mendaciously that the training officers were German. W. Geraghty (interview) had experience in the Irish Reserve Force, and found the training only indifferently useful. Some information here is derived from a later interview with Mr Geraghty (held on 2 Dec. 1995).

31   For partial reconstruction of company membership and command, see Appendix C.

32   Ó Cuinneagháin, *Saga*, p. 9; see also M. Beckett, 'Irish Brigade'.

33   These developments show that Franco was able to equip his assault troops with standard German small arms in time for the battle of Jarama. At much the same point, however, the International Brigades were receiving issue of new Soviet rifles.

34   W. McGrath's story that the *Bandera*'s uniforms were German SS issue can be discounted; Boles, interview.

35   'With the Irish Brigade in Cáceres', *Irish Independent*, 1 Mar. 1937.

36   The Irish Tercios in seventeenth-century Flanders had marched under a white and green flag of similar design, but featuring an Irish harp in an upper quarter. The company pennants were commissioned from local weavers by the town council of Cáceres at a cost of 38 pesetas, 50 centimos each; AHM Cáceres, Libros de Actas, 3 Feb. 1937, ff. 43v–4 and 27 Mar. 1937, ff. 62v–3.

37   'Spirit of the Irish Brigade', *Irish Independent*, 2 Mar. 1937.

38   P. Hickey to Mother, 1 Feb. 1937.

39   As its name suggests, the parish was founded by Dominicans, but later passed into Franciscan hands. It was appropriate for the Irish crusaders to worship with Franciscans, as most of their seventeenth-century predecessors had been ministered to by Franciscan chaplains.

40   Routine Order No. 14, 29 Dec. 1936; Beckett Collection, Westport.

41   It is possible that local worshippers were banned from San Domingo as a precautionary measure. In any case, the *Bandera* would certainly have filled the church for the relevant Sunday Mass.

42   See Cronin, 'Blueshirts, Sports and Socials', pp. 43–7.

43   Quoted in Ryan, 'Fighting for Franco'.

44   P. Hickey to parents, 6 Mar. 1937.

45   Various other military units were stationed in Cáceres, and the presence of officially tolerated brothels cannot be ruled out. McKee's credibility runs out when he goes on to describe a fist-fight between Irish and Moors, both parties drunk on white wine; see *I Was a Franco Soldier*, pp. 18 and 21. (Moorish troops were zealous muslims and would not have taken wine of any colour. In any case, their involvement in such an incident would have been punishable by death.)

46   O'Duffy states that two pesetas per day were docked (*Crusade*, p. 109), but from other

sources it seems that weekends, when most men ate outside their messes, were not counted.

47 Like their opposite numbers among the Internationals, the Irish Brigade relied on tobacco supplies reaching them from home, finding the local cigarettes a desperate last resort. Alfonso Bustamente recalled enjoying 'Sweet Afton' when interviewed by Cathal O'Shannon in 'Even the Olives'.

48 Surviving veterans vehemently assert that the use of alcohol was strictly controlled and never caused serious trouble. For further consideration of the issue, see pp. 110–12.

49 McKee, *I Was a Franco Soldier*, p. 16.

50 Quoted in Ryan, 'Fighting for Franco'.

51 D. Reynolds was another member of this detail, led by Sergeant Baldwin, an ex-Christian Brother. Smith saw shootings of (as opposed to by) several Civil Guards, whom he was told had fought for the Republic.

52 Difficulties were caused by red-tape arising from Non-Intervention regulations. In an attempt to circumvent this, the *Bandera* was allowed to use Irish stamps on homeward correspondence, which was not franked in Spain; information of Sñr Antonio Rubio, Municipal Archive, Cáceres. See also below, p. 118.

53 Naughton and Watterson, *Irish Olympians*, esp. pp. 9–10, 27, 31–2. In San Francisco, the ex-parson Bob Hilliard, later of the British Battalion, International Brigade, had won a boxing medal under O'Duffy's leadership.

54 *Poems of Thomas Davis*. See O'Duffy, *Crusade*, p. 115.

55 See theatre tickets and fly-sheets, Beckett Collection, Westport. Serving soldiers (especially legionaries) were given concessionary rates in cinemas, restaurants and shops.

56 O'Duffy, *Crusade*, pp. 115–16.

57 Ibid., passim. Other reports were relayed to the *Independent* by a 'Special Representative'. This was probably Gunning, who had once been on its reporting staff; they incorporated verbatim extracts from O'Duffy's speeches; see issues of 15 Jan., 10 and 11 Feb. 1937.

58 T. Hyde's commonplace-book (in private possession). Another example of the species is in the possession of the Dalton family in Waterford.

Chapter 4

1 Málaga duly fell to the Nationalists on 9 February.

2 O'Duffy, *Crusade*, pp. 123–4, and Hayes, Diary, both date the inspection as 6 February; Ó Cuinneagháin gives 5 February in *Saga*, p. 6. Though Preston overlooks the Cáceres interlude, he gives the date of Franco's journey as 7 February; *Franco*, p. 217.

3 The Jarama battle zone covered 200 square kilometres of open countryside south-east of Madrid, which the Irish entered near the start of the last phase. For details, see Thomas, *Spanish Civil War*, pp. 588–96, and Aznar, *Historia* II, pp. 68–84. Like most accounts, these erroneously give the opening date as 6 Feb. An account from the International Brigades' point of view is given on pp. 162–70.

4 Fennell, 'Spain 1936–37', pp. 12–13. See also similar accounts by Ó Cuinneaghán, *Saga*, p. 11, and Beckett, 'Irish Brigade', p. 6. Given guerrilla activity in the region and the coincidence of the air attack on Plasencia, Fennell's version is plausible. At this stage

of the Jarama battle, the Republicans were anxious to disrupt enemy supply lines.

5 O'Duffy, *Crusade*, pp. 133–7. This places the scene of the bomb-damaged track at Navalmoral, not Plasencia. But O'Duffy seems to have reached Valdemoro by car. His odyssey on the night of 18–19 February involved round trips of sixty-five (Valdemoro–Navalcarnero) and eighty kilometres (Valdemoro–Toledo) respectively, in a battle zone, the latter involving two drives across the face of the enemy line.

6 *Voz del Combatiente*, 7 Feb. 1937.

7 Gárate Córdoba, *Partes*, I, p. 100.

8 *El Adelanto de Salamanca*, 11 Feb. 1937. The next day the war columnist added: 'on Saturday when we took Ciempozuelos, we began to cart away hundreds of wounded, along with lorries full of bodies.' In the first official military study of the war, Aznar also noted the 'teams of soldiers specially assigned to the task of burying numerous bodies of the 18th International Brigade [*sic*] which had been destroyed in the Ciempozuelos sector'; *Historia*, II, p. 74.

9 See ibid., pp. 80–1.

10 Gárate Córdoba, *Partes*, I, p. 106. See also republican *partes* for the same period, ibid., II, esp. p. 212, and Aznar, *Historia*, II, p. 106. These attacks are described by Peter Kemp, who was serving with the Carlist defenders; see *Mine Were of Trouble*, pp. 73–81. They were not (however) carried out by Internationals. Nationalist sources constantly exaggerate the foreign element in the loyalist army (and, of course, vice versa). Several secondary sources repeat Aznar's erroneous assertion that the defenders of Ciempozuelos were a non-existent '18th International Brigade'; *Historia*, II, pp. 71 and 74.

11 *Voz del Combatiente*, 16 and 18 Feb. 1937.

12 The following account is based on: O'Duffy, *Crusade*, pp. 137–40; Ó Cuinneagháin, *Saga*, pp. 14–15; Hyde, Geraghty, Smith and Reynolds, interviews; Kavanagh, reminiscences; McCarthy, 'Adventures'; Beckett, 'Irish Brigade', p. 6; Fennell, 'Spain, 1936–37', pp. 14–15; and Ennis, 'Catholic Moors' p. 41.

13 McCarthy writes that they followed the main Toledo road due south then turned east along another surfaced road towards Ciempozuelos. But most other accounts indicate that the route lay across country. McCarthy may be correct, since the marchers were followed not only by an ambulance but also a lorry carrying the heavy machine-guns, ammunition and other equipment; see letter from L. McCloskey, 25 Feb. 1937, printed in *Drogheda Independent*, 17 Apr. 1937.

14 Gárate Córdoba, *Mil dias de fuego*, pp. 189–90.

15 Private information states that a Spanish historian has seen the Tribunal's report, but my search among the files of the *Sección de Justicia* and cognate divisions of the AGM drew a blank. The only reference is a report of the funerals in Cáceres of the victims of 'the incident at Ciempozuelos', 21 Feb. 1937; AGM, CGG 30/80.

16 O'Duffy claims that the opposing commander and his adjutant were killed; *Crusade*, p. 139. It is not implied that the Canary Islanders were poor soldiers. The unit was not, in fact, disbanded. Falangist troops were normally despised by the Legion, but this unit, encountered by one British Legionary on the Madrid front later that year, was praised as an exception to the rule; see Stradling, *Brother Against Brother*, p. 60.

17 Ennis states that the skirmish began at 8.30 a.m., thus the *Bandera* left Valdemoro no later than 8.00 a.m., three hours before the time specified to O'Duffy; 'Catholic Moors', p. 40. Hayes, Diary, estimates that 'we had been travelling about a half-hour'.

18 *El Adelanto de Salamanca*, 25 Feb. 1937. This was the only report of Irish action to reach these pages, and the existence of an Irish unit (as such) is carefully occluded.

19 T. Hyde's commonplace-book.

20 Fennell, 'Spain, 1936–37', p. 18.

21 Quoted in O'Duffy, *Crusade*, pp. 143–4. This material is apparently selected from a fuller account which is no longer extant. O'Duffy himself was not present at this point; when he caught up with his men he learned about the action fought earlier in the day, and promptly left Ciempozuelos again in order to report and investigate.

22 See above, p. 62. O'Duffy rationalised the grim aftermath of slaughter by asserting that the town's capture had taken place 'only a few days before'; *Crusade*, p. 143.

23 Reynolds interview. Several other witnesses supply information on this point – but none corroborates O'Duffy's claim that the *Bandera* got on with burying the carcasses as soon as they could.

24 For the fortifications of both sides in this sector of the front, see Montero Barrado, *Paisajes*, esp. pp. 99–109. I inspected these emplacements on 7 May 1995. The lie of the land across from the railway station (a saddle-back between two conical hills) allowed the defenders to dig a communications trench from which they could spread out to both sides along the front line. Co. Cavan-born Dennis Reynolds claimed that farmers from the wetlands of central Ireland were able to pass on skills in trench-digging even to Great War veterans; interview.

25 This is deduced from the series of snaps taken by Séan Roche, mostly dating from the early days in Ciempozuelos. The commercial role of the Moors is commented upon by both Frank Thomas and Peter Kemp in their published accounts of life in the army of Africa.

26 See below, pp. 168–70.

27 See, for example, J. J. Ganose, 'El tren blindado. Su relación con otras armas y servicios en la guerra', *Voz del Combatiente*, 17 Mar. 1937. This celebrated the successful use of the weapon during the battle of Guadalajara – which also gave rise to a number included in the song-book of the International Brigade.

28 Ó Cuinneagháin, *War*, pp. 22–3; O'Duffy, *Crusade*, p. 146.

29 Ó Cuinneagháin, *War*, p. 6; Fennell, 'Spain 1936–37', p. 19.

30 *Voz del Combatiente*, 6 Mar. 1937. In fact Ireland was experiencing rather more than a downpour; much of the Free State was affected by storms and blizzards which took their toll in lives and lasted until Easter.

31 See O'Duffy, *Crusade*, pp. 147–8. To these privations must be added other normal accompaniments of trench life (for example, lice) and unhygienically prepared food (for example, diarrhoea).

32 Thomas, *Spanish Civil War* (1965 edn) pp. 490–1. The 88s represented one of Nazi Germany's major hardware prototypes, and made an invaluable contribution at Jarama. The German request probably stemmed from an impression gained when the VI *Bandera* acted as guards during a short rest period; see Stradling, *Brother Against Brother*, p. 98. The Irish found the Germans cold and aloof – though enjoying their coffee. Note that the armoured and artillery sections of the German expeditionary force were not part of the notorious 'Condor Legion'.

33 One veteran, however, testifies to Mulrean's presence among the men on the day of the attack on Titulcia; Geraghty, interview.

34 See Routine Orders of 14, 15 and 23 Mar. 1937, Beckett Collection, Westport.

35 P. Hickey letter, 6 Mar. 1937.

36 *Irish Independent*, 29 Mar. 1937.

37 L. McCloskey letter, 1 Mar.; *Drogheda Independent*, 17 Apr. 1937.

38   See O'Duffy, *Crusade*, p. 150 (and most of the written accounts and interviews cited above, n. 12). This phenomenon is also to be observed on the other side; here, frequent coincidence of phraseology and anecdote in the letters of British International Brigaders is evidence of political commissars' intervention.

39   Azaña, *La Velada*, p. 88.

40   Ó Cuinneagháin, *War*, pp. 9–10. For amplification of these incidents, see Stradling, 'The Propaganda of the Deed' and 'History and the Triumph of Art' in Stradling *et al.* (eds), *Conflict and Coexistence*, pp. 132–58.

41   Deduced from material in Casas de la Vega, *El Terror*, p. 309ff. As elsewhere, a roll of honour of victims, in nationalist discourse martyrs 'fallen for God and Spain', can be found on the church wall. In this case there are 121 names, including 40 clerics. Thirty-three murdered staff of the psychiatric hospital, members of the Order of St John, were later beatified; *L'Osservatore Romano*, weekly edn, 28 Oct. 1992.

42   Foss and Geraghty, *Spanish Arena*, pp. 300–1. This has a foreword by Franco's London representative, the Duke of Alba, and includes an account of 'The Communist Programme for the attack on England'. At least one of these writers may have been Irish, but they make no reference to O'Duffy and his men. Thirty years later, Luis Bolín was still careful to practise what he preached. Though he personally helped to organise the Irish Brigade, his own memoirs managed to overlook its existence, even in a detailed breakdown of the make-up of Franco's armies; Bolín, *Vital Years*, pp. 349–54.

43   Thomas, *Spanish Civil War*, p. 412. (I have been unable to trace Fitzpatrick's manuscript cited by Lord Thomas.)

44   Letter from 'An Irish Brigader', *Irish Independent*, 16 Mar. 1937. Two events in particular were variously witnessed. Two of the veterans interviewed by me in 1994 claimed to have seen the bodies of nuns in the convent at Valdemoro, where they spent the night of 18 February – an incident also referred to in several written accounts. (W. Geraghty insisted upon its veracity in a later interview held in December 1995.) The most common story, corroborated in detail by O'Duffy and Ó Cuinneaghán in addition to the sources just cited, concerns the torture and murder of a Ciempozuelos doctor on his own surgical table.

45   The name of the town square in 1975 is noted from 'Even the Olives', made in that year. Sunday, 7 May 1995 was Mother's Day, which in Spain is combined with a major feast-day of the BVM.

46   A recent account of the battle suggests that Franco reneged on his promises of support and deliberately left Roatta and his army to stew in their own juice; see Preston, *Franco*, pp. 229–33.

47   An exception is M. Fennell, who remarks that 'as an offensive action this was doomed to failure long before it started. It was fundamentally a diversion'; 'Spain, 1936–37', p. 26.

48   Lister's regiment occupied the sector on the left of the XV International Brigade; see below, pp. 173ff. A month after the Irish attack, they were still in residence; see air surveillance report on 'Unidades Identificadas' on the southern Madrid front, 15 Apr. 1937, AGM Ejército del Centro, 1/13/12. For troglodyte machine-gunners, see Montero Barrado, *Paisajes*, pp. 88 and 92.

49   Cf. remarks of an Irishman in the Lincoln Battalion, occupying diagonally opposite trenches, about six kilometres to the north: 'On March 13th a great rainstorm blew up. It was blowing a gale with such force that one could not stand. It was the worst weather I have ever experienced'; O'Connor, *Soldier*, p. 18.

Notes

50 Quoted in Graham, *Battle of Jarama*, p. 51.

51 This supposition is made because the nationalist aviation, which would normally have been in action against the guns, was completely immobilised by weather conditions; Kindelán, *Cuadernos*, p. 70.

52 F. Fitzgerald to G. O'Shaughnessy, Mar. 1995 (letter in private possession).

53 Reynolds, interview.

54 Fitzgerald to O'Shaughnessy (see n. 52).

55 Fennell, 'Spain, 1936–37', p. 26.

56 Ó Cuinneagháin, *War*, p. 20.

57 Smith, interview; Ó Cuinneagháin, *War*, pp. 20–1; O'Duffy, *Crusade*, pp. 156–7; and cf. the more fanciful account of Fitzgerald (see n. 52). Fennell was in the mining party, and was later told that the train had been destroyed. But he dates the incident to a point before 13 Mar.; 'Spain, 1936–37', p. 25.

58 Gárate Córdoba, *Partes*, II, p. 241.

59 Routine Orders of XV *Bandera* for 14, 15 and 23 Mar. (signed O'Sullivan), Beckett Collection, Westport.

60 O'Duffy, *Crusade*, pp. 161–3. But surely the Irish HQ had the use of a field telephone? Such an instrument would be of limited use to O'Duffy, who spoke no Spanish. On the other hand, the Duke of Algeciras had direct access to Franco's offices in Salamanca.

61 Ó Cuinneagháin, *War*, p. 21. A soldier in another nationalist unit later heard the rumour that 'an officer of the vanguard [of the Irish attack] protested to a Spanish leader, telling him that they had come to defend the Catholic religion, not to be cannon fodder'. The context here strongly suggests Thomas Cahill was the officer in question; Gárate Córdoba, *Mil días de fuego*, p. 211.

62 McKee, *I Was a Franco Soldier*, p. 27.

63 Parte issued by F. Martín Moreno to *Adelanto de Salamanca*, 14 Mar. 1937; see also, Gárate Córdoba, *Partes*, I, p. 118.

64 See below, pp. 93–4 for the role of this crisis in the process of disbandment of the Irish Brigade.

65 Tisa, *Recalling the Good Fight*, pp. 57–8. See also Ryan, *Book of the XV Brigade*, p. 83.

66 Based mainly on Ó Cuinneagháin, *War*, p. 25; but see also, O'Duffy, *Crusade*, p. 163, and McKee, *I Was a Franco Soldier*, p. 28.

67 P. Hickey to Mother, 20 [? 25] Mar. 1937.

68 P. Quinn to M. Fennell, Mar. 1976 (letter in private possession).

69 On the factory's capture, British Ambassador Chilton had described it (12 Feb. 1937) as 'the only important chemical factory in Spain'; PRO, FO 371 21284/W3191/1/41.

70 Kemp, *Mine Were of Trouble*, pp. 68–81.

71 Beckett, 'Irish Brigade', p. 7.

72 Geraghty interview, 2 Dec. 1995.

73 Kemp, *Mine Were of Trouble*, p. 70.

74 Reynolds, interview.

75 Geraghty, interview.

76 Smith, interview.

77 P. Hickey to Mother, 31 Mar. 1937.

78 McKee, *I Was a Franco Soldier*, p. 28.

79 Fennell, 'Spain, 1936–37', p. 27; Ó Cuinneagháin, *Saga*, p. 23.

80 Reynolds, interview. See also, O'Duffy, *Crusade*, pp. 176–8.

81 Hayes, Diary.
82 Quoted in O'Duffy, *Crusade*, p. 178.
83 Reynolds, interview.
84 O'Duffy, *Crusade*, pp. 179–80.
85 Ibid., p. 181.

Chapter 5

1 *Times* correspondent W. Steer returned from the nationalist zone and was inter-viewed by the British Foreign Office around this time. In his opinion the war was a stalemate, and he 'suggested that the ultimate solution for Spain will be the same as for Ireland'; PRO, FO 371 21824/W2902/1/41.
2 See, for example, Yagüe to Franco and reply, 3 Apr. 1937, AGM, CGG Org. 156/19. In March, two Post Office workers abandoned their jobs and left for Spain. The question of whether it was politic to fill their posts was important enough to be scheduled for cabinet discussion; Draft Executive Council agendum, 2 Mar. 1937, INA, Dept of Taoiseach, file S-9657.
3 O'Duffy, *Crusade*, pp. 103–4 and 123.
4 See below, n. 5.
5 PRO, FO 371 20590/W18970/9549/41.
6 J. Leydon to Transport Secretary, 7 Jan. 1937, INA, Dept of Taoiseach file S-9704.
7 *Waterford Weekly Star*, 8 Jan. 1937. Among the frustrated crusaders on this occasion were thirty men from Limerick (information of D. Ryan).
8 St Mary's was the Catholic pro-cathedral in Dublin, near an extended district of council flats. Its male parishioners were active in street warfare against the IRA-socialist left, members of the so-called 'Animal Gang'. A flavour thereof is conveyed in the band's title: 'St Mary's Anti-Communist Pipe Band'; see O'Riordan, *Connolly Column*, p. 107. The only other member of the 'Second Irish *Bandera*' to arrive in Spain was its chaplain, Fr Daly of Enniskillen; see O'Duffy, *Crusade*, p. 169. (The Irish Brigade was often referred to as the '*Bandera Católica*' in nationalist documents even after incorporation in the Tercio.)
9 M. Capablanca (*Bandera* Training Officer) to Franco n.d.; Franco to Capablanca, 19 Jan. 1937, AGM, CGG 60/78/1.
10 Oram, *Newspaper Book*, p. 187. Unlike Gaffney, the *Irish Times* and *Irish Press* reporters were not permitted access to the XV *Bandera*.
11 See, for example, almost every issue for Mar. 1937, including exclusive photographs of the *Bandera* in training, prominent attention to Pope Pius XI's condemnations of communism, pro-nationalist speeches by Belton, several academics, and a whole team of Jesuits. Geary also ran an opportunist correspondence page, in which, by giving selective space to agnostic and even pro-republican voices, he stimulated rich returns from the outraged faithful.
12 *Irish Independent*, 1 Mar. 1937.
13 Ibid., 5 Mar. 1937.
14 *Cork Examiner*, 27 Feb. 1937.
15 *Irish Independent*, 24 Feb. 1937.
16 Ibid., 25 Mar. 1937. For Starkie's articles see ibid., 22 and 23 Mar. The intervention of the troublesome Basque undoubtedly explains the sudden spate of Jesuit speeches in

Notes

this month. Such heavyweights were difficult even for the *Irish Press* to ignore – see, for example, the full coverage given to Fr F. Woodlock's Mansion House diatribe against 'Agents of the Comintern', 23 Mar. 1937.

17 Ibid., 1 Mar. 1937.

18 Ibid., 12 and 16 Mar. 1937. Meanwhile, various local councils had passed votes of sympathy with the relatives of the men killed in action; see, for example, ibid., 2 Mar. 1937.

19 Ibid., 13 Mar. 1937.

20 Walshe to Kerney, 23 Mar. 1937, INA, DFA letter-book 'B'. On Doyle, see p. 26.

21 *Connaught Tribune*, 27 Feb. 1937.

22 *Solidaridad Obrera* (Madrid), 29 Aug. 1938.

23 Note by Shuckburgh, 3 Dec. 1937, PRO, FO 371 20587/W17160/9549/41.

24 'Proposed Issue of Public Statement …', 14 Dec. 1937, ibid., 20589.

25 Undated Memo headed '(Estimates) Non-Intervention in Spain', INA, DFA 227/87.

26 Executive Council minutes of 2 Feb. 1937 (item 2), ibid. Dept of Taoiseach S-9177.

27 Keogh, *Ireland and Europe*, pp. 83–5; Bowyer Bell, 'Ireland', pp. 253–4. Coogan (*Long Fellow*) unaccountably overlooks this masterly performance by the chief, which contributed so greatly to the growth of his reputation and 'image' as a statesman.

28 INA, DFA 227/87. In this draft, de Valera has corrected (? Walshe's) words 'no doubt' to 'little doubt' and deleted the word 'vast' which had originally amplified 'majority'.

29 Hansard, 319 HC DEB 5s, cols 31, 323–34, 733–4, 1405–6 and 1757.

30 Ibid., 320 HC DEB 5s, 233–4.

31 Walshe to Kerney, 6 Mar. 1937 (marked 'secret'); draft entered in INA, DFA, letter-book 'B'.

32 Yagüe to Franco and reply, 17 Jan. 1937, AGM, CGG Org. 156/20/1.

33 In *Crusade*, O'Duffy describes ceremonies and receptions laid on by various local, relatively minor dignatories of Church and state; but this cannot disguise the fact that he was never to be seen (as it were) on High Table.

34 See copies in the Irish Military Archive, Cathal Brugha Barracks, Dublin.

35 For detailed comment and citation of sources on the Foreign Legion's role in the Spanish War, see Stradling, *Brother Against Brother*. See also above, pp. 48–50.

36 'El Tercio – Inspección … La Maranosa 24 de Marzo de 1937, El Coronel Primer Jefe, Juan Yagüe', AGM, CGG Org. 156/20/14. (The document is copied in various versions in this and other *legajos*.)

37 Yagüe to Franco, 29 Mar. 1937, ibid., 23/1–4. It is noteworthy that at this stage Yagüe hoped for the redistribution of the men: 'if the rank and file themselves wish to join other *banderas*, it would be a good reinforcement, since they are good soldiers.'

38 As n. 36. The reasons for Yagüe's moral objection to the Brigade's diet seem obscure. When compared with that described by Frank Thomas (serving in the VI *Bandera*) and that obtaining in the British International Brigade, there seems no significant disparity or peculiarity. For example, potatoes were not an unfamiliar constituent in the local diet. Perhaps Yagüe was reacting to forthright Irish opinions about Spanish (and army) food, openly shared by O'Duffy and passed on by liaison.

39 Report of Francisco Ayala, Valencia 7 June 1937, MAE, A. Ren. R-1069/10.

40 Keogh, *Ireland and Europe*, pp. 85–90. Pressure on Salamanca to repatriate a handful of named 'minors' began even before the Non-Intervention Act became law. The chief liaison officer reported to Franco's aide-de-camp O'Duffy's admission that 'more than 100' of his volunteers were below the age of majority; Camino to Martín

Notes

Moreno, 25 Feb. 1937, AGM, CGG Org. 156/21/5.

41 See Franco's order to Yagüe of 3 Apr. that fresh volunteers arriving at Cáceres should form a 'reserve company' and trained ready to replace losses to the XV *Bandera*; ibid., 19.

42 The most detailed account is in Preston, *Franco*, p. 255ff. Hedilla made a bid for the support of Colonel Yagüe, amongst others, but there is no reason to believe that Franco doubted the loyalty of the latter; ibid., p. 260. The decree of unification was issued on 19 April and the arrest of Hedilla took place a week later.

43 See pp. 8–9.

44 'Irlandeses – Infantería', Nov. 1936, AGM, CGG Org. 154/50. A subscript note adds that 'within the next five or six days, between 700 and 2,000 men will be arriving'.

45 See Appendix C, pp. 265–6. Carew's post may have been reckoned (by Gunning) to limit the possibilities of his ingratiating himself with the rank and file.

46 The number of posts available was further reduced by the secondment from existing *banderas* – no doubt on Yagüe's insistence – of two professional Legionary officers, Nangle and Fitzpatrick.

47 Disquiet among Kerrymen was not helped by the fact that four of the six men killed in action were from the town of Tralee. However, Tom Hayes states that Horan was hospitalised for virtually the whole time the Brigade was at the front: Diary.

48 Jellinek, *Civil War in Spain*, p. 532.

49 Reported by McCabe, who himself was later sucked into behind-the-scenes negotiations; Journal.

50 Most of these staff officers were fluent Spanish speakers who had been conveniently 'found' for O'Duffy by the nationalist authorities.

51 Note dated 29 Mar. 1937, AGM, CGG Org. 156/23/4. Miss Gaffney was described as 'an editor of the *Irish Independent* who recently made a trip to Spain with which she was very satisfied'. (Her normal job was editor of that paper's 'Woman's Page'.) There seems little doubt that all this information was made available to Franco via some official Free State agency.

52 Hayes, Diary.

53 Collated report by Uzquiano to Salamanca, 12 Apr. 1937, AGM, CGG Org. 156/23/6.

54 Though Cunningham soon returned from hospital, he did not withdraw his resignation, which was later accepted and recorded; Routine Order no. 170, 29 May 1937 (signed O'Sullivan), Beckett Collection. The delay explains Cunningham's presence on the 'team photograph' taken in Cáceres some time in May.

55 Hayes, Diary.

56 Here I have made an extrapolation from O'Duffy's press release to the *Irish Independent* printed on 1 May 1937: 'About the middle of April, I received requests from upwards of 300 officers, NCOs and men to make arrangements for their return to Ireland.'

57 A. Sagroniz to M. Moreno, 25 Mar. 1937, AGM, CGG Org. 156/21/13.

58 O'Duffy to Franco, 9 Apr. 1937, ibid., 19/4-7. The attempt to blame Spaniards and Englishmen (by the latter he presumably intended Nangle and Fitzpatrick) – both types imposed on him by Yagüe – for the collapse of the Brigade, was not repeated in the general's memoirs.

59 See Kerney to Dublin, 29 Feb. 1940, INA, DFA 244/43. It may be deduced that O'Ferrall dictated the terms and tone – if not the actual words – of O'Duffy's letter to Franco.

231

60 Franco to Orgaz, 13 Apr. 1937 (asking him to pass on the decision to Colonel Yagüe); AGM, CGG Org. 156/23/8.

61 Franco to O'Duffy, 14 Apr. 1937 (draft corrected in holograph), ibid., fol. 13.

62 F. Franco to Moreno, 29 Mar. 1937, AGM, CGG Org 156/22/4. Frank Thomas, who later met Irish Legionaries in Cáceres, strongly conveys their feeling that the interpreters were nothing more than spies, to be hated rather than trusted; see Stradling, *Brother Against Brother*, p. 124.

63 Uzquiano to Yagüe and Orgaz, 12 Apr. 1937, AGM, CGG Org. 156/23/6. Silva was liaison officer in A Company, which O'Sullivan had commanded before his promotion. Though the latter was suffering from stress which had reached the point of explosion, it seems likely that the Spaniard's mention of Valencia (the republican capital) was almost calculated to precipitate a 'treasonable' outburst.

64 See ibid., carp. 26, cables and memos, 11–22 Apr. 1937, passim. O'Sullivan claimed to be acting on Yagüe's orders. Pinillos could not understand him and telephoned Yagüe, who refused to explain on the phone but insisted that O'Sullivan was not allowed to leave. Thoroughly perplexed, Pinillos got on to Franco. In his turn, the *generalísimo* cabled Yagüe; the latter's reply referred guardedly to Uzquiano's report. On 19 April, Franco still had not seen a copy of this document – and one did not reach him for another three days. Thus the O'Sullivan incident was not instrumental in Franco's final determination of the issue. Imperfect communications between the protagonists over this tiny farce may have been conditioned by the much greater farce in Salamanca, described above pp. 95–6.

65 Letter from D. Keogh to Fr A. McCabe, 10 Feb. 1979, McCabe Papers.

66 Hayes, Diary.

67 Yagüe to O'Duffy, 30 Apr. 1937, AGM, CGG Org. 156/22/2.

68 Hayes, Diary; O'Duffy, *Crusade*, pp. 238–41; on the Toledo battle and the Irish arrival in Cáceres, see Stradling, *Brother Against Brother*, pp. 108–18. No source gives details of where and how the ballot was conducted, but several have its result as 654 for and 9 against. A more plausible explanation for it than that suggested in the text was O'Duffy's need for palatable propaganda reasons for withdrawal – in this case, an overwhelming democratic decision.

69 Camino to Franco, 13 May 1937, AGM, CGG Org. 156/22/11. This reports Irish disquiet over O'Sullivan's continued imprisonment. Without waiting for the *generalísimo*'s reply, Camino ordered O'Sullivan's release the next day, and applied to Salamanca for endorsement – which he received by return cable; ibid., fols. 5 and 14.

70 O'Duffy to Camino (n.d. but May 1937) ibid., fol. 6.

71 See *Irish Press* interviews with returning members, cited by Keogh, 'Eye Witness', p. 487.

72 AHM, Libros de Actos (21 Oct. 1936–7 July 1937), Meeting of 19 May 1937, fol. 78.

73 Ibid., fols. 72–80, passim. Sñr Antonio Rubio, Municipal Archivist, told me that his father fondly remembered the Irish soldiers and their good reputation among the Cacereños – despite 'their legendary fondness for strong drink'. However, J. Kavanagh recalled that 'in Cáceres there was a lot of Irish very drunk and caused a lot of trouble and we became more or less unpopular'; reminiscences. The issue of excessive drinking is addressed directly below, pp. 109–12.

74 See J. Roche's photograph of the officer corps taken in May 1937. In his letter to Franco (above n. 58) and in the expostulations made in Uzquiano's office (above, n. 63) the general described his men as existing 'in wretched rags which make them seem like

Notes

beggars'. He now asked for 320 suits and 270 pairs of shoes to be provided as soon as possible; holograph list of 9 May 1937, AGM, CGG Org. 156/22/12.

75 'Cuenta para S.E. sobre repatriación ...', 12 May 1937, ibid., fol. 11.
76 Intendente General to Franco, 17 May 1937, ibid., fol. 16.
77 Franco to Yagüe, 14 June 1937, ibid., fol. 17; O'Duffy, *Crusade*, pp. 241–2.
78 Thomas, a corporal in the VI *Bandera*, was sent to hospital in Cáceres with wounds received in the battle near Toledo. Here he was 'adopted' by the Irish inmates, who later contrived (with O'Duffy's approval) to smuggle him out of Spain – disguised as an Irishman; see Stradling, *Brother Against Brother*, esp. pp. 117–24.
79 An extract from the newsreel (*British Movietone News*, vol. 9, no. 420A) is used in 'Even the Olives'. See also Cunningham, *British Writers*, p. 289. It seems likely that Franco, irked over the Irish officers' refusal to hand in their pistols (weapons which, as Camino pointed out, were in short supply) had alerted de Valera with the relevant information; Camino to Franco, 13 May 1937 (above, n. 69).
80 Hayes, Diary.
81 O'Duffy, *Crusade*, pp. 243–9 on the homeward journey and arrival.
82 O'Riordan, *Connolly Column*, pp. 100 and 215; Keogh, 'Eye Witness', pp. 486–7, and press material utilised therein.
83 *Connacht Tribune*, 26 June 1937. Michael Donoghue was still in uniform and carried a bust of General Franco.
84 Ibid.

Chapter 6

1 O'Duffy, *Crusade*, p. 249. The assessment which follows has been impeded by lack of evidence about the feelings and actions of the Brigade's officer corps. There is a void between O'Duffy's memoirs and those of his nearest-ranking subordinate, Sergeant J. Cunningham (next come corporals Beckett and Fitzgerald; all other witnesses were private Legionaries). Detailed accounts were compiled by Captain N. Fitzpatrick and Lieutenant G. Timlin. Diligent search has failed to reveal any trace of the former source, whilst published extracts from the latter suggest that the complete artefact would not shed a different light on crucial issues; see Kilfeather, 'Spanish Inferno'.
2 The military record of the XV *Bandera* is examined at various points above, both in narrative detail and with the deployment of some broader analysis; see pp. 63–6 and 74–80.
3 This reckoning does not include about a dozen men who died of illness.
4 F. Fitzgerald (A Company), as represented in D. O'Shaughnessy 'Spanish Civil War Revelations', *Limerick Leader*, 10 June 1995; see also three letters of Fitzgerald, to D. Ryan et al., Mar. 1995 (in private possession). And also above, p. 76.
5 For mention (as it were in dispatches) of medics Leo McCloskey, Joe Bergin and Sean Roche for their comportment on 13 Mar., see O'Duffy, *Crusade*, p. 157. A case in point here is James McCarthy, who compiled his 'Adventures with the Irish Brigade' in 1967. McCarthy was a strong Catholic who acted as *enlace* (runner) for A Company, which was that nearest to the enemy in all three actions specified above. His narrative reveals how little the individual soldier apprehended of the battle: but also (perhaps) how little there was to apprehend – since no source retails stories of derring-do they may have heard afterwards. At the risk of accusations of national stereotyping, it needs

saying that the remarkable absence of vainglory in the extant accounts of veterans is, in itself, an impressive body of evidence.

6   Tom Hayes alleges (without giving a date) that a group of four soldiers made a break for the Portuguese border. Two were captured, but two others – both American-Irish – got away and later took ship for Mexico. The fate of the former couple is unknown; Hayes, Diary.

7   *Irish Independent*, 9 and 10 Mar. 1937.

8   Ibid., 18 Mar. 1937. This was relayed from a *Daily Telegraph* correspondent, who added that the Irish 'have fought best for the patriots' (sc. the Nationalists).

9   Ibid., 25 Mar. 1937.

10   *Daily Express*, 5 Apr. 1937. The story was not intended to flatter Irish sensibilities, but, on the contrary, to characterise Ireland as an interventionist nuisance in the same league as Germany, and thus to embarrass the Free State (Germany and Catholic Ireland being, of course, just two of Lord Beaverbrook's pet hates).

11   See above, p. 50. Notably enough, O'Duffy claims to have rescinded his earlier decision not to fight against the Basques, whom (he came to consider) were the dupes of Soviet agents and 'no more entitled to partition from Spain than six counties of Ulster are to partition from Ireland'; see *Crusade*, pp. 195–9.

12   Ibid., p. 237.

13   On the same day as the Irish advance towards Titulcia, Mussolini exhorted his troops 'to smash the Internationals, which would be an invaluable success, especially politically'. Unknown to Il Duce, his army had already been routed at Guadalajara by a force including the Italian ('Garibaldi') Battalion, an event which guaranteed the miserable military reputation before history of the (otherwise by no means ineffective) CTV; *La Agresión Italiana – Documentos* (Valencia, 1937), p. 277.

14   *Irish Independent*, 10 Aug. 1936.

15   For additional material and comment relevant to this issue, see above, passim. In practice, the exigencies of non-intervention made it impossible for the *Bandera* to evoke 'favourable reactions all over the world'.

16   *Irish Press*, quoted by Keogh, 'Eye Witness', p. 487. The asterisks almost certainly stand for Captain S. Cunningham. Returning veterans immediately came under pressure from reporters on the point of drinking; see, for example, *Connaught Tribune*, 26 June 1937.

17   The sound-track included noises-off of breaking windows and shouts, intended to convey an impression of violent misbehaviour among the peaceful citizens of Cáceres. O'Shannon also refers to 'an unpublished memoir' (unknown to the present writer) describing 'the inevitable pay-day scenes which took place by those who had taken more than their fair share of vino and were all out for trouble'; 'Even the Olives' – printed synopsis of programme.

18   Spanish liaison officers should (perhaps) have prevented or more closely supervised this traffick. But such commerce was the acknowledged privilege of Moroccan troops, who also provided important sources of tobacco, an absolutely indispensable military material.

19   Hayes, Diary.

20   McKee, *I Was a Franco Soldier*, passim. Inspired and published by a propaganda source, this includes obviously fictional embellishments, such as frequent brawls between the Irish and the Moors. The only other account of this nature is also suspect. It comes from ex-Sergeant W. McGrath, reminiscing in old age with a friend, Mr

B. Boles of Cahir (Tipperary), via whom it reached me; Boles, interview.

21   The general's comments are transparently casuistic: for example, 'I am proud to say that I did not observe one member of the Brigade under the influence of drink at any time'; *Crusade*, p. 112. This can only be true if he never looked in the mirror whilst brushing his teeth at night. In one place, he recognises that 'if an Irish soldier did take too much to drink … I could appreciate the reason', but then quickly resorts to the 'rotten apples' explanation ('a few doubtful characters', p. 160).

22   McCabe, Journal. Both opinions are reported indirectly. It seems that McCabe had no personal evidence to adduce. He felt that Mulrean himself was a greater danger to the Brigade than the bottle; see below, p.117. McCabe turned against O'Duffy, but earlier he was impressed by both leader and men, sharing their motivation and approving of their enthusiasm. Watching the *Bandera* on parade 'was an inspiring sight, linking up the present with the historic past …'; he was also impressed by Padraig Quinn and Tom Hyde in Cáceres; McCabe's sermon before the men left for the front, exhorting them to discipline, struggle and sacrifice, was recalled later by McCarthy; 'Adventures', p. 6.

23   McCullagh, *In Franco's Spain*, p. 218. In contrast, he also recorded that during the visit to Ciempozuelos noted below (n. 24) he went for Mass in the convent chapel on a weekday morning, to find that the place was crammed to the walls with 300 Irishmen in full battle-dress, most of whom took communion; ibid., p. 296.

24   Ibid., p. 245, see also pp. 263–4. McCullagh was given a guided tour of the Ciempozuelos trenches by Captain Cunningham; ibid., pp. 297–300 and Ó Cuinneaghán, *War*, p. 25.

25   Carr, *Chances of Death*, for example, pp. 49–51.

26   Stradling, *Brother Against Brother*, pp. 106–7.

27   See below, pp. 157, 174–5 and 189.

28   A rough calculation based on the rates of pay in the Legion advertised in *Adelanto de Salamanca* (3 Oct. 1936) suggests that the total wages bill for the Brigade ran to 620,000 pesetas, or approximately £25,000 by 1937 rates.

29   Lodi Fé to Ciano, 29 Jan. 1937, quoted in Keogh, 'Eye Witness', p. 476. (Keogh quotes from the Italian Foreign Ministry Archives in the original. I am grateful to Anna Hearder for translating this and the other Italian extracts used in this source.)

30   Ibid., pp. 477–8. These pages include a list of the general's expenses to the end of Jan. 1937, totalling £685.

31   McCullagh, *In Franco's Spain*, p. 306. If the figure given above (n. 28) is doubled (the usual rate) for the cost of rations and uniforms, the total still falls some way short of McCullagh's.

32   The most insistent denials of 'politics in the Brigade' came in April 1937, and undoubtedly reflected Franco's banning of politics in the nationalist zone and the forced unification of all contributing parties (see above, p. 96); see O'Duffy, *Crusade*, pp. 116–17.

33   See, for example, G. Gaffney's report, 'Spirit of the Irish Brigade', *Irish Independent*, 2 Mar. 1937.

34   See, for example, letter home by J. O'Cunningham (later 'Seosamh Ó Cuinneaghán'): 'The fact that most of this Brigade have Blue Shirt tendencies in no way affects my position as an Irish Republican', 17 Jan. 1937 (in private possession). The writer, like his namesake, the OC of D Company, was from Belfast.

35   See above, pp. 26–7.

36   See, for example, Beckett, 'Irish Brigade', p. 9.

37 O'Duffy, *Crusade*, p. 233.

38 Ibid., p. 248.

39 A conclusion based on the sum testimony of all the veteran witnesses utilised in this study. Of course there are exceptions. For example, in his later years Ivan O'Reilly expressed contempt for the general, though this arose from retrospective reaction, not contemporary experience; letter from Dave O'Reilly (son), 1995.

40 Lodi Fé to Ciano, 29 Jan. 1937, quoted (in Italian) by Keogh, 'Eye Witness', p. 478.

41 Kemp, *Mine Were of Trouble*, pp. 87–8. This assessment was based on information and opinions provided by three veteran officers of the XV *Bandera* whom the author met at various points later in the war; N. Fitzpatrick, G. Nangle and P. Lawler.

42 A biography is in preparation by Patrick Long of Monaghan County Museum. For a pen-picture, see his article in *The Northern Standard*, marking the centenary of O'Duffy's birth, Oct. 1992.

43 See, for example, the striking degeneration in appearance between photographs taken as Chief of Police in 1924 and at an NCP function ten years later; Stradling, 'Franco's Irish Volunteers', pp. 42 and 44. According to Liam Walsh, he smoked between seventy and eighty cigarettes a day, but 'notwithstanding the base accusations of some … he drank in moderation … he preferred Irish whiskey'; 'General O'Duffy', pp. 226–7.

44 McCullagh, *In Franco's Spain*, p. 150. Despite his later quarrel with the general and accusations of 'vanity … incompetence and temper', the writer also acknowledged 'his indefatigability', adding that 'to describe the difficulties he overcame would take a whole chapter'; ibid., p. 264. Cf. Kemp, *Mine Were of Trouble*, p. 86.

45 See, for example, typed message 'Para el Teniente Coronel Barroso', Salamanca 27 Mar. 1937: 'From Seville they report that General O'Duffy left at four o'clock this afternoon for an unknown destination'. A handwritten secretarial reply orders, 'Carry on searching … the *Generalísimo* wishes to see him urgently'; AGM, CGG Org. 156/1/2.

46 O'Duffy, *Crusade*, p. 119. Matt Beckett, a reticent witness who, as quartermaster-corporal, listened to many comments, claimed many years later that 'Dalton was a liability at the front'; 'Irish Brigade', p. 8. Joe Cunningham, also a quartermaster NCO, implied that Dalton and Smyth left for other than strictly medical reasons; *War*, p. 21. Dalton seems to have accepted that his order to advance in attack formation had drawn the fire of the Canary Islanders on 19 Feb. a confession made to his own brother and to Tony, brother of Tom Hyde (who was killed in the encounter) before his death in 1956; Dalton and Hyde, interviews. It seems possible that the Judicial Tribunal had criticised this error. See above, pp. 64–6.

47 McCabe Journal. Before the *Bandera* left for the front, McCabe observed 'it's quite obvious that the Irish Brigade isn't going well and the Chaplain is partly to blame'.

48 See below, p. 186ff.

49 Assessment based on statements of various veterans, including Leo McCloskey, Joe Cunningham and Paddy Smith.

50 See below, p. 199.

51 Shelley, *Guide*, p. 4. This fails to consider the effects of the later 'going to ground' of XV *Bandera* veterans. Complaints about the mail service were relayed to G. Gaffney when she visited Ciempozuelos before going home; Reynolds, interview.

52 He was in Ciempozuelos for perhaps four short spells in all, and made a similar number of visits to La Marañosa. It was some days after the 13 Mar. action (and certainly later than 17 Mar. when he was absent again) that he distributed to all ranks the shamrock contributed to the *Irish Independent*'s appeal; see above, p. 87.

53 Ó Cuinneaghán, *War*, p. 21.

54 *Irish Independent*, 4 Dec. 1944. In mitigation it must be said that long-distance travel was prohibitively expensive and difficult in Ireland during 'The Emergency', and that many veterans were serving in the British armed forces.

55 The pennant is part of the exhibition stand in Clew Bay Heritage Centre, Westport. It displays the crossed serrated clubs of the Tercio, red on a green background, but not the crusaders' motto, 'In Hoc Signo, Vinces', recalled by some witnesses. See also McKee, *I Was a Franco Soldier*, p. 17, and *Sunday Independent*, 1 May 1955.

56 For example, Legionary Eugene McDermot died in Salamanca on 2 July 1937, whilst Thomas Doyle was gravely ill in the same hospital; Military Governor to Franco, 27 July 1937, AGM, CGG Org. 156/21/8.

57 Yagüe to Franco, 3 Aug. and endorsement of 9 Aug. 1937, ibid., fol. 20. Lawler, too, was apparently released from his obligation after he contracted an illness in Cáceres; ibid., fol. 21.

58 See lists of personnel, July/Aug. 1937, ibid., carp. 22 passim. However, Higgins, O'Toole, O'Reilly and O'Dea do not figure in these. Mulrean (who also stayed on) later told Kerney that 'about 16' of the Irish Brigade re-enlisted; Kerney to Walshe, 22 July 1940, INA, DFA 244/22. If the non-combatant staff officers (i.e. Gunning, O'Ferrall and Meade) are counted with the persons named in the text, Mulrean's estimate seems exact.

59 Report by Camino, 8 May 1937, AGM, CGG Org. 156/22/10.

60 Memo of Nationalist FO, 9 Mar. 1938, MAE, A.Bu. R-1059/300/6.

61 Espinosa de los Monteros to Yagüe, 6 Apr. and reply 29 Apr. 1938; ibid., fols. 8–9.

62 Kerney to Walshe, 24 May 1939, INA, DFA 210/55. Dennis O'Dea also served throughout the war, and was repatriated, having been discharged from the Legion in Tetuán, Morocco, in 1940; ibid., fol. 143.

63 Walshe to Kerney, 2 Nov. 1937, ibid., letter-book B; Kerney to Walshe, 29 Aug. 1938, ibid., 241/12; T. O'Toole to S. McEntee, 26 June 1939, ibid., 210/60.

64 Memos of Nationalist FO, 11 Apr. and 6 June 1939, MAE, A.Bu. R-1059/300. A further file on the case exists at ibid., R-1784/13. The British army arrested O'Toole when he disembarked in the UK, but shortly afterwards released him (doubtless to cover their embarrassment at having recruited him in the first place) and he returned home in July 1939. See also O'Duffy, *Crusade*, p. 237.

65 Ennis, 'Catholic Moors', p. 43.

66 Memo from Kerney to Nationalist FO, 4 Sept. 1939, MAE, A.Bu. R-1059/297; Martín Moreno to Jordana, 16 Nov. 1938, ibid., 298. O'Reilly was a member of the *Primera Bandera*, that is, the original core of the Legion founded by General Millán Astray in 1920, loaded with prestige and battle honours.

67 In May 1995, Sñr Antonio Rubios, Municipal Archivist of Cáceres, informed me that, although the cemetery headstones were still in place, the remains had been taken to the sepulchre at the Valle de los Caídos, and re-interred alongside other fallen of the '*cruzada*'. These catacombs are accessible only to family of the deceased, who must go to considerable trouble to obtain permission. However, Mr Leslie Ó Laoi, nephew of Gabriel Lee, pursued enquiries on this matter through the Irish embassy in Spain. The latter was subsequently assured by Spanish government sources that Don Antonio's belief is without foundation.

68 Evidence of the Sacristan of San Domingo, May 1995.

69 Mr Hyde was interviewed by the author in Dublin on 21 Sept. 1994. Many accounts

testify that Lieutenant Hyde was, indeed, the exact opposite of Sergeant-Major Weymes.

70 For more background information, see Stradling, *Cardiff*, pp. 59–65.

71 Walsh, 'General O'Duffy', p. 211.

72 Geraghty, interview.

73 Walker, *Politics of Frustration*, p. 98. One of the skippers was a pro-Republican and received shelter in the MP's home until the end of the war in 1939.

74 Decisions eventually went in favour of the Republic and it is doubtful that O'Duffy would have challenged this verdict. In any case, Valencia had no effective means of taking possession of the ships – the SS *Atalaya* and the SS *Covetas* – and (as in Cardiff) they and their cargoes were impounded to be set off against the debts of the Republic in the UK; see PRO, FO 371/21403/97 and 113.

75 Circular letter by Ó Cuinneaghán (n.d. but 1948), McCloskey collection (private possession).

76 Invitation and programme (signed by Ó Cuinneaghán, Quinn et al.), 26 Aug. 1948, ibid.

77 *The Nationalist and Leinster Times*, 4 Aug. 1972, and a contemporary cutting from *El Alcázar*, both with photographs (in private possession). The honoured visitors were described by the Spanish correspondent, in the conventional discourse of the Francoist movement, as '*antiguos combatientes de la Cruzada de Liberación*'. It is interesting that present at this same audience was 'Don Adolfo Suárez González, director general de Radiodifusión y Televisión'.

78 Mulrean stated that the passports were later returned, but it seems that the latter took this to be mere surmise; Kerney to Walshe, 22 July 1940, INA, DFA 244/143. Ó Cuinneaghán's passport was returned by Walsh in July 1937; accompanying letter with 'Irish Brigade Association' letter-head (private possession).

79 Kavanagh, reminiscences.

80 Interview with Mrs A. Byrne (daughter), Dublin, 1995. Other private correspondents have recalled comrades encountered during the Second World War who had been members of the Irish Brigade in Spain; for example, letter from Mr T. Geraghty, 1995. See also Mr Geraghty's letter to the editor of the *Irish Times*, 6 Dec. 1994.

Chapter 7

1 Some of O'Duffy's material found its way into James Hogan's influential book, *Could Ireland Become Communist? The Facts in Full*, which appeared in 1935 (printed Dublin, no publisher given). De Valera later assured the Dáil that the numbers of Bolsheviks actually identified by Special Branch reports gave no grounds for O'Duffy's alarmist conclusion: Coogan, *Long Fellow*, p. 475. This did not prevent the government from continuing to invigilate the situation. In 1937, Sean MacEntee ordered another 'secret investigation' into the levels of communist activity in the Saorstát: UCD Archive, Box P67/528.

2 Michael O'Riordan, *Connolly Column*, pp. 23–45, and Manus O'Riordan, 'Communism in Dublin in the 1930s: the struggle against fascism', in Klaus, *Strong Words*, pp. 215–39. Compiled respectively by father and son, these contain accounts of the background political context in which the present chapter is set.

3 Cronin, *Frank Ryan*, p. 51.

4   O'Riordan, 'Communism'. The CPI does not seem to have kept systematic written records, but some files may have perished in the burning of Connolly House in 1933.

5   Cronin, *Frank Ryan*, pp. 50–62.

6   O'Riordan, 'Communism', pp. 220–1, gives a detailed account of the siege – which certainly seems both symbolic and prophetic of the fate of Irish communism.

7   Doyle, interview; *An Phoblacht*, 11 Sept. 1986.

8   Monks, interview.

9   The Ballyseedy incident is the source of more tall tales than any event in the folklore of the southern Irish 'troubles'. For a dispassionate account see Younger, *Ireland's Civil War*, p. 501.

10   For details of important events which can only be referred to *en passant*, see Manning, *Blueshirts*, passim, and Cronin, *Blueshirts and Irish Politics*, passim.

11   O'Riordan, *Connolly Column*, p. 32.

12   See, for example, Cortada, *Dictionary*, p. 267.

13   *Cork Examiner*, 8 sept. 1936.

14   'Memories of the Seamen's Struggles' ms. (1971), NMLH CP/IND/KLUG/11/01.

15   O'Riordan, *Connolly Column*, pp. 41 and 97–101. This caution paid off since the party nearly doubled popular vote at the 1937 general election.

16   For British labour organisations in relation to Ireland, see T. Buchanan, 'British Trade Union Internationalism and the Spanish Civil War' (unpublished D.Phil. thesis, University of Oxford, 1987), pp. 209–32. I am most grateful to Dr Buchanan for his kindness in sending me a photocopy of this chapter of his thesis.

17   See Walker, *Politics of Frustration*, pp. 85–113. (I am grateful to Dr Tom Buchanan for this reference.)

18   O'Riordan, *Connolly Column*, p. 42.

19   Cronin, *Frank Ryan*, pp. 78–83. Another source states that O'Donnell 'worked closely with Sean Murray ... in organising the volunteers'; McInerney, *Peadar O'Donnell*, p. 171.

20   Klaus, *Strong Words*, p. 15; O'Riordan, *Connolly Column*, p. 55.

21   Officer M. Mansfield to Commissioner, 9 Oct. 1936; INA, DFA file 2/1043. The query reached the Department of External Affairs via that of Justice.

22   Testimonial dated 5 Oct. 1936, ibid.

23   Cummins to Minister for External Affairs, 27 Oct. 1936, ibid.

24   O'Riordan, *Connolly Column*, p. 74.

25   Mansfield to Commissioner (n. 21).

26   J. J. Stearne to S. A. Roche, 13 Oct. 1936, ibid.

27   See Williams, *Memorials*, p. 52; 'Spanish Civil War fighter Recalled on Achill', *Irish Times*, 8 Sept. 1986; and Stradling, 'War of Ideals?'.

28   Romilly, *Boadilla*, p. 44. On Scott, see also O'Riordan, *Connolly Column*, p. 49, and the article by 'C Q' in *Volunteer for Liberty*, 15 Nov. 1937.

29   This and other statistical conclusions drawn in this paragraph are based on the table which appears as Appendix D, p. 266–71. One authority states that 'some four hundred Irishmen, most of them old IRA men' joined the International Brigades, but gives no source; Bowyer Bell, *Secret Army*, p. 134. O'Riordan's book deals only with those who remained ideologically sound – that is, CPI or committed 'popular front' socialists. For this reason, and because of the extra numbers of Irish Internationals revealed by my research in the Spanish Archives, it may be unwise to discount Bowyer Bell's assertion.

30   Bowyer Bell, 'Ireland', p. 265.
31   INA, DFA file 225/10 (14 Dec. 1936).
32   Quoted in Cronin, *Frank Ryan*, p. 84.
33   Doyle and Monks, interviews.
34   Quoted in *Irish Times*, 8 Sept. 1986.
35   E. Downing, interviewed in 'Homage to Heroes', *The Tribune Magazine*, 25 Feb. 1996.
36   'Return to the Valley of Jarama', *Irish Times*, 7 Oct. 1994.
37   On Donnelly, Tierney, 'Irish Writers', pp. 43–5.
38   On O'Brien, Klaus, *Strong Words*, pp. 11–39.
39   Based on Cronin, *Frank Ryan*, pp. 1–75, passim.
40   O'Riordan, *Portrait of an Irish Anti-Fascist*, pp. 1–2.
41   Quoted in Corkhill and Rawnsley, *Road to Spain*, pp. 14–19.
42   B. Collins, interview (North Kensington Local History Project).
43   Francis, *Miners against Fascism*, p. 187.
44   Bill Williamson, interview.
45   See Gerassi, *Premature Antifascists*, pp. 34–6.
46   'Homage to Heroes' (see n. 35).
47   Monks, *With the Reds*, p. 2.
48   For the contest over 'history', see Stradling, 'Battleground of Reputations', pp. 117–20.
49   Ryan, letter dated 5 Feb. 1937 (possibly intended for publication in *An Phoblacht*), printed in Acier, *From Spanish Trenches*, p. 106.
50   Ryan to G. O'Reilly, 17 Feb. 1937, ibid., p. 115.
51   Ryan, *Book of the XV Brigade*, p. 28.
52   'Irish Volunteers in Spain', by 'CQ' (? F. Ryan), *Volunteers for Liberty*, no. 23 (Nov. 1937).
53   Quoted (from *Spanish News*, 26 Feb. 1937) by Mitchell, *Storm over Spain*, pp. 224–5.

Chapter 8

1   In a lecture on 'British Volunteers', given as part of the Nottingham University Conference 'International Involvement in the Spanish Civil War', 15 June 1996. The figure given is that favoured by most recent commentators. Arrivals were unevenly distributed in a chronological sense, and at any given point musters were less than one-quarter this total. Death in action, wounds, illness and desertion continuously reduced the ranks.
2   The idea for the Comintern to capture supply and organisation of volunteers seems to have originated in the executive of the French Communist Party, possibly with Jacques Duclos; see Delperrie de Bayac, *Les Brigades Internationales*, pp. 9–10.
3   Richardson, *Comintern Army*. There is no satisfactory study of the International Brigades as a whole. In addition to sources already cited, my treatment is derived from the following: Castells, *Brigadas Internacionales*; Brome, *International Brigades*; Nesterenko, *International Solidarity*; and Alvarez, *Historia política*. For analysis of the Republican army, of which the Brigades formed part, see Alpert, *Ejército republicano*.
4   Richardson, *Comintern Army*, pp. 90–135.
5   Ryan later claimed that sixty men joined him from Liverpool alone. After Harry Pollitt had spoken in Liverpool in March, he was approached by four women with Irish surnames who enquired after the well-being of menfolk serving in the British Battalion; see letters dated 16 Mar. 1937, NMLH, CP/Ind/Pol/2–6.

Notes

6   Greenhalgh, interview.

7   D. W. Pike, 'France' in Cortada, *Dictionary*, pp. 216–17; Richardson, *Comintern Army*, p. 31ff.

8   Cronin, *Frank Ryan*, p. 85.

9   Printed in Acier, *Spanish Trenches*, p. 110. Cf. M. Levine, who confirms that 'only a few Irishmen' were in Albacete by the end of the year; *From Cheetham to Cordova*, p. 39.

10   Two weeks later, Commissar P. Kerrigan reported 'around 500 or so' at Madrigueras; letter to Pollitt, 4 Jan. 1937, NMLH CP/Ind/Poll/2/6.

11   My treatment of the general military situation during the 'Madrid phase' (Nov. 1936–Mar. 1937) is derived from the following: Colodny, *Struggle for Madrid*; Hills, *Battle for Madrid*; the relevant alphabetical entries in Cortada, *Dictionary*; Thomas, *Spanish Civil War*, p. 467ff; Montero Barrado, *Paisajes*; and Aznar, *Historia*, II, pp. 9–38 and 67–90.

12   Thomas, *Spanish Civil War*, pp. 630–1; Monks, *With the Reds*, p. 9.

13   Alexander, *British Volunteers*, pp. 85–8.

14   Monks, *With the Reds*, p. 8.

15   Ibid., p. 10.

16   Quoted in O'Riordan, *Connolly Column*, pp. 59–60.

17   Quoted in ibid., p. 62. As we have seen (above, p. 133) Pat Murphy, who is recorded by O'Riordan as one of the Connolly Column's Liverpudlians (p. 164), was in fact born of Irish parents in Cardiff.

18   Watson, *Single to Spain*, p. 30.

19   Richard Bennet provided the evidence in a *New Statesman* article, 25 Mar. 1961, reproduced *in extenso* in the *Irish Press*, 29 Mar. 1961. Later, *An Phoblacht* unequivocally stated that Nathan had been 'a member of the Dublin Castle murder gang' (11 Sept. 1986); IBA Archive, Box B8.

20   Photocopy of holograph draft, dated 'Albacete, New Year's Day, 1937', ibid., Box C/8/6.

21   One witness reports that the authorities exercised patience at various provocations, but 'had to crack down when some of the Irish began speaking Gaelic to each other'; Eby, *Between the Bullet*, p. 25.

22   Rust, *Britons in Spain*, p. 37.

23   O'Riordan, *Connolly Column*, p. 67. A similarly cryptic procedure is adopted in the same author's contribution on 'Ireland' to Nesterenko, *Solidarity*, p. 197.

24   Alexander, *British Volunteers*, pp. 68–9. The figure of thirty-seven votes cast dovetails with Monks' figure of forty-three Irish absent with No. 1 Company to give a total of eighty – exactly the number reported to have left Ireland in December; see Monks, *With the Reds*, p. 7.

25   See, for example, Carroll, *Odyssey*, pp. 93–4; Rosenstone, *Crusade of the Left*, pp. 32–3; and Richardson, *Comintern Army*, p. 76. Cf. the 'official' version by Tisa, *Recalling the Good Fight*, pp. 20–4.

26   Anon. ('A British Working Man'), *In Spain*, p. 13; see also Castells, *Brigadas*, p. 158. Rust, one of the *Daily Worker*'s correspondents in Spain, went out of his way to make amends in the first 'official' history, with glowing references to the Irishmen of No. 1 Company and to Conway himself; see *Britons in Spain*, pp. 25–8.

27   I have relied on an account of the 'trial' given by another Jewish volunteer, Maurice Levine; see *From Cheetham to Cordova*, and interview. Levine's source was Jim Prendergast, who with Monks, Edwards and some other veterans of the Córdoba campaign strongly supported their commander's cause. Moreover, none of this company

subsequently elected to join the Lincolns. See Manus O'Riordan, *Portrait*, pp. 3–4; Monks, *With the Reds*, p. 8.

28 Alexander, *British Volunteers*, p. 129. Michael Economides, a Lopera veteran, recalls: 'In the 1st Company Kit Conway was commander. We were on manoeuvres one day when [Conway announced to the Irish] "Comrades we are being blackguarded. They've put the Black and Tans to command us"'; Economides, interview. At Jarama, Nathan acted as chief liaison officer, but was often in the front line. Reinstated in the field, he died at Brunete. McCartney (who may also have been a Black and Tan, but was unpopular for other reasons both with the men and the party) was 'accidentally' shot in the leg by Commissar Springhall and invalided home.

29 Levine, interview.

30 Bloom, interview.

31 Anon., *In Spain*, pp. 13–14. This avowedly hostile source is the equivalent in the Internationals of S. McKee in the XV *Bandera*.

32 Gurney, *Crusade in Spain*, p. 77. See also evidence of D. Renton in MacDougall, *Voices*, pp. 24–5.

33 Copeman, interview. Colourful accounts by such as Gurney and Copeman, who had shuffled off political allegiance, contrast with bland versions supplied by the ever-solid. The former may have exaggerated in order to make a good story. The latter play the affair down with all the sang-froid they can muster. For example, Albert Charlesworth's interview:

[AC] ... there was a little bit of trouble ...

[Q] What sort of trouble?

[AC] Well I don't know, really ... We had too much time on our hands ... plenty of time ... I think that's it ...

34 Eby, *Between the Bullet and the Lie*, p. 26; Tisa, *Recalling the Good Fight*, p. 24.

35 Merriman and Lerude, *American Commander*, pp. 85–6. Accounts of the split in general histories of the Internationals contain some farcical distortions: see, for example, Brome, *International Brigades*, pp. 124–5; Castells, *Brigadas*, pp. 158–9.

36 Herrick, ¡*Hermanos!*, p. 65. Though inserted in a work of 'fiction', the quoted passage represents a documentary recollection. The author (whose real name was Bill Harvey) was present on the occasion he describes, and his account is circumstantially confirmed in Eby, *Between the Bullet and the Lie*, pp. 25–6.

37 Kerrigan to Pollitt, 19 Jan. 1937, IBA Archive, Box C 9/8. Earlier, two London-Irishmen had been sent home in disgrace: one (Black) who had 'developed a strong anti-semitic campaign against Capt. Nathan' and another (Moroney) 'also in Capt Nathan's company ... a very bad element ... associated with a man who is at present in hospital with venereal'; same to same, 10 Jan. 1937, ibid., 9/6.

38 Thomas, *Spanish Civil War*, p. 588.

39 Kerrigan, interview. Several sources refer to this incident. Kerrigan is unique in locating it at Chinchón but Alexander (*British Volunteers*, p. 69) agrees that it took place on Burns night. Cf. Toynbee, *Distant Drum*, p. 130.

40 Quoted in Cronin, *Frank Ryan*, pp. 90–2.

41 'It was getting hot, but Frank Ryan managed to guide us safely to our allotted positions'; quoted from P. Smith's article in *The Irish Democrat*, 9 Oct. 1937, in O'Riordan, *Connolly Column*, p. 67. But could this in reality have been a reference to Conway? (see below, n. 43).

42 Levine (interview) says that a total of forty-five fit survivors of the company returned

'in late January'. His figure is too high; perhaps Conway's return to Madrigueras co-incided with the arrival of a new batch from Ireland. The event was recalled by Welsh volunteer, T. A. R. Hyndman: 'by February with the arrival of a large group of Irishmen, we were almost a complete unit of 400 men'; Toynbee, *Distant Drum*, p. 124.

43   This cryptic subterfuge appears to have been the result of some arrangement between Ryan and his (effective) second-in-command, the significance of which can only be a matter for speculation. See Frank Ryan's letter printed in *The Worker*, 27 Feb. 1937, quoted by O'Riordan, *Connolly Column*, p. 62 and n. 19 on p. 66.

44   Richardson confirms that the political rein was looser in the Lincolns than in other units: 'the Americans were viewed with unrelieved contempt by the Comintern hierarchy of the International Brigades as little more than adolescent dilettantes and were treated accordingly'; *Comintern Army*, p. 77.

45   For the opening phase of the battle, see Thomas, *Spanish Civil War*, pp. 588–90; Colodny, *Struggle*, pp. 110–11; Longo, *Le Brigate Internazionali*, p. 215ff; Líster, *Memorias*, pp. 187–8.

46   Alexander, *British Volunteers*, p. 95.

47   Jason Gurney, who was acting as scout and map-maker to the 16th Battalion, has left the most detailed eye-witness account of the first two days at Jarama. He claims to have realised the enemy's missed opportunity during the battle itself; see *Crusade in Spain*, pp. 110–11. An extra dimension is provided by the text, photographs and maps in Montero Barrado, *Paisajes*, pp. 89–97. My treatment here has also been illuminated by a visit to the site made in May 1995, and by use of the modern *Cartografía Militar de España* maps nos. 582 (Getafe) and 583 (Arganda), printed on scale 1:50.000.

48   Alexander's chapter on Jarama draws on many of these. It provides a broadly accurate and satisfying narrative of the British action; *British Volunteers*, pp. 91–109. O'Riordan includes a chapter devoted to the Irish contribution; *Connolly Column*, pp. 67–76. Though genuinely confused on some points and deliberately misleading on others, this is useful for the selections it prints from contemporary eye-witness descriptions.

49   For the unique extant account by an English-speaking participant on the nationalist side, see Stradling, *Brother Against Brother*. This confirms that the Dimitrov battalion of East European volunteers (the 18th) had to be committed to support the Franco-Belge battalion (15th) during the course of 12 February. Indeed the latter's losses were such that it ceased to exist as a battalion, and survivors were later transferred to the XIV Brigade.

50   Gurney describes the Moroccan approach vividly: 'the effect of those brown, ferocious bundles suddenly appearing out of the ground at one's feet was demoralizing'; *Crusade in Spain*, p. 108.

51   Quoted in Cronin, *Frank Ryan*, pp. 94–5.

52   See Stradling, *Brother Against Brother*, pp. 94–5.

53   See the high praise accorded the British by Robert Colodny, a Lincoln veteran who returned to Spain to research his detailed study in the 1950s: *Struggle*, p. 124. On the other hand, Enrique Líster makes no reference to the role of his comrades of the International Brigades, implying that he, Líster, was mainly responsible for Franco's failure at Jarama; *Memorias*, p. 187ff.

54   Frank Thomas's account amply justifies Kit Conway's fear of being left wounded on the battlefield and at the mercy of the Moors; see Stradling, *Brother Against Brother*, passim. At the same time, one British Brigader stated that in this campaign 'we didn't

take prisoners'; C. Morgan, interview transcript, in Cook, *Apprentices of Freedom*, p. 66.

55 Ryan's description of 'the great rally', taken from his official record (*The Book of the XV Brigade*), is quoted almost verbatim in Cronin, *Frank Ryan*, pp. 95–7.

56 Letter to G. O'Reilly, 5 Mar. 1937, quoted ibid., pp. 97–8.

57 Líster, *Memorias*, p. 192; Gurney, *Crusade in Spain*, p. 115.

58 Líster, *Memorias*, pp. 193–4.

59 An accurate narrative of the Lincoln Battalion's participation at Jarama appears in Rosenstone, *Crusade of the Left*, pp. 35–49. See also Carroll, *Odyssey*, pp. 97–102. The struggle for Pingarrón heights on 18–27 Feb. represents the last phase of the battle; but many accounts of the Jarama engagement are confused about the topography, since the whole of the high ridge which runs down the western rim of the plateau lying between the Jarama and Tajuña rivers is sometimes called the 'Sierra de Pingarrón'.

60 Gurney, *Crusade in Spain*, p. 136.

61 Quoted in Cronin, *Frank Ryan*, p. 98.

62 Líster, *Memorias*, pp. 193–4.

63 Carroll, *Odyssey*, pp. 100–2.

Chapter 9

1 For narrative treatment of this phase, see below, p. 173ff.

2 A communist member of the South Wales Miners' Federation executive, Paynter arrived in Spain early in May; Francis, *Miners Against Fascism*, p. 169ff. He was called in to sort out various political difficulties inside the British Battalion; and one of his tasks was to address the Irish question.

3 Brewer and Jump, interviews.

4 Cronin, *Frank Ryan*, pp. 119 and 264. The Irish Lincolns included (*inter alia*) Mick Kelly, Paddy Roe McLoughlin, Charles Coleman, Peter O'Connor and the three Power brothers.

5 Alexander, *British Volunteers*, p. 163. The fact that such expressions could easily get out of hand and cause resentment among English comrades is illustrated in Thomas, *To Tilt at Windmills*, p. 58.

6 Tisa, *Recalling the Good Fight*, p. 59.

7 Quoted in O'Riordan, *Connolly Column*, pp. 77–8, from the *Irish Democrat*, 12 June 1937. See also O'Connor, *Soldier of Liberty*, pp. 23–4. O'Connor and Kelly were both serving with the Lincolns.

8 *Aberdare Leader*, 29 May 1937.

9 See esp. O'Riordan, *Connolly Column*, pp. 58–60. These pages are part of a chapter with the same title as the book, and contain the densest patch of references to a 'Connolly Column' or 'Unit'. There is no reference between p. 67 and the last on p. 137. Like other Irishmen who arrived in Spain in the period after Brunete, O'Riordan himself was never a member of a putative 'Connolly Column'. See also O'Riordan's contribution to Nesterenko, *Solidarity*, pp. 196–7.

10 Nevertheless, one of Frank Ryan's letters is described by O'Riordan as 'an account of the activities of the "Connolly Column"'; *Connolly Column*, p. 62. Castells goes even further, placing Ryan in charge of a 'Connolly Company'; *Brigadas Internacionales*, p. 127. This is doubtless the origin of a further garbled reference; Zaragoza, *Ejército*

Popular, p. 75. The term is not used by the modern authority; Alexander, *British Volunteers*.

11 Space does not permit detailed review of this issue, which is especially problematic because of the overwhelmingly negative nature of the evidence. To cite only one medium, K. Johnson, IWM Sound Archive, has reviewed more than two hundred hours of the taped interview collection and compiled many transcripts without encountering a single mention of the title; see *Spanish Civil War Collection*. Apart from the O'Riordans, there are only a scattering of references to the denomination 'Connolly', a mere two or three of them contemporary. All the latter refer exclusively to casual usage within the Lincoln Battalion in the period between Jarama and Brunete (i.e. Feb.–July 1937). In 1992, a memorial tablet to the Irish Brigaders killed in Spain was placed outside Liberty House, the Trade Union HQ in Dublin. This artefact has a solemn official standing, and was meant to be invested with unique status in Ireland itself. Yet its inscription makes no reference to a 'Connolly Column'; see Williams, *Memorials*, p. 53. Indeed, the title is not invoked by any memorial to the International Brigades in Ireland – even that of Peter O'Connor's Waterford; see ibid., pp. 56–7. Subsequent application of Connolly's name to the whole Irish contribution to the International Brigades is an *ex post facto* propaganda technique, imparting a spurious ideological-national unity to a heterogeneous experience.

12 See Alexander, *British Volunteers*, pp. 71–83.

13 The standard authority states that the MacCrohon were a branch of the O'Sullivan clan, and mainly occupied the Dingle peninsula. It seems likely that they came to Spain in the retinue of the great Earl O'Sullivan in 1603; MacLysaght, *Surnames*, p. 65.

14 Gurney, *Crusade in Spain*, p. 140. The *pueblo* seems to have reacted to its Civil War experience in a similar way to Ciempozuelos (i.e. by tending the other way politically), for the streets, including the main Plaza del Caudillo, in 1995 still bore the names of nationalist heroes. However, Morata is also the site of the memorial to the dead of the International Brigade set up in 1994; see Williams, *Memorials*, pp. 132–4.

15 For references to the convulsion of the Jarama front on 13–15 March, see below, pp. 209–10 where the question of the proximity of the pro-republican volunteers to their pro-nationalist compatriots is also examined.

16 See above, pp. 47–8. This aspect of the war forms the strategic backcloth to the mission of the hero Robert Jordan in Hemingway's *For Whom the Bell Tolls* (1940) – which can be reliably dated to the spring of 1937.

17 For Traill, see Stradling, *Cardiff*, pp. 122–3.

18 Monks, *With the Reds*, pp. 9–12. The quotation is from the same author's interview. See also O'Riordan, *Connolly Column*, pp. 80–2, and Alexander, *British Volunteers*, pp. 111–16 (with a useful map on pp. 114–15).

19 For the respite at Mondéjar, see Alexander, *British Volunteers*, pp. 108–9.

20 Brown, Political Commissar of the British Battalion, was born in Kilkenny in 1906, but got his political education in the Irish Clubs of Manchester and Salford; see Jenkins, 'Prelude to Better Days', p. 163.

21 Quoted in O'Riordan, *Connolly Column*, pp. 88–9.

22 A significant proportion of the republican dead were panicking refugees, caught and summarily executed by their own side '*pour encourager les autres*': see Thomas, *Spanish Civil War*, pp. 712–15; Cortada, *Dictionary*, pp. 94–7.

23 On 28 July, however, a mutinous situation arose in the British ranks. Forty-two survivors who were still able to fire a rifle refused an order to go back into the line. Luck-

ily, the order was countermanded before the situation came to a head: see Alexander, *British Volunteers*, p. 130.

24   See Cronin, *Frank Ryan*, p. 121, who also prints a photograph of Ryan with thirteen fellow countrymen, taken in Albacete around this time (Aug. 1937). It may be estimated that a total of around forty Irishmen were currently enlisted.

25   It is in these areas where most of the volunteers not identified by O'Riordan but figuring in the official musters from the Salamanca Archive can be found: see Appendix D, p. 266.

26   Alexander, *British Volunteers*, p. 144. The group photograph noted above (n. 24) shows Ryan with his arms round the shoulders of Daly and O'Daire – and was doubtless inspired by celebration of their appointments.

27   The following account of the Aragon offensive of 1937 is based mainly upon Thomas, *Spanish Civil War*, pp. 722–8 (see p. 104); Cortada, *Dictionary*, pp. 32–3 and 81; and the specific 16th Battalion accounts by O'Riordan and Alexander.

28   O'Riordan, *Connolly Column*, pp. 90–1; Alexander, *British Volunteers*, pp. 146–9. The capture of Quinto (and, later, Belchite) was followed by the shooting of large numbers of enemy prisoners, apparently ordered by Colonel Copic, but carried out under the personal direction of the American commander, Maj Merriman. See Carroll, *Odyssey*, pp. 154–9, and Nelson and Hendricks, *Madrid 1937*, p. 204. No evidence exists to connect any Irishmen in the Lincolns, or members of the British Battalion, with these atrocities, though it is difficult to believe they remained ignorant of them. Later, Frank Ryan was to be accused of complicity in these crimes; see below, p. 199.

29   Doyle, interview.

30   Quoted in Cronin, *Frank Ryan*, p. 124.

31   Ryan, *Book of the XV Brigade*, p. 269.

32   Líster, *Memorias*, p. 299. However, Thomas states that Líster himself was responsible for the 'reckless' tank manoeuvre at Fuentes; *Spanish Civil War*, pp. 726–7.

33   His card-index fiche records that Tierney went missing on 17 Sept. – a day when the Battalion was not in action; AHN, PS AR-127. He may have deserted; according to O'Riordan he survived the war; *Connolly Column*, p. 165.

34   Cortada, *Dictionary*, pp. 451–2 and 528–9; Thomas, *Spanish Civil War*, pp. 788–94.

35   The tendency on the republican side to underplay the military contribution of the '*interbrigadistas*' is seen even in the account of a dedicated communist leader like Enrique Líster, who persistently refers to their role as more politically symbolic than militarily effective; see *Memorias*, esp. pp. 375–85.

36   This date is given by Alexander, who was present and in command of the British Battalion; *British Volunteers*, p. 161. However, both Thomas and Proctor state that the Internationals did not become involved until mid-January; *Spanish Civil War*, p. 792, Cortada, *Dictionary*, p. 528. The latter view is confirmed by Martínez Bande, *Batalla de Teruel*, p. 192.

37   Figures in these two paragraphs are derived from three muster-lists of the British Battalion (one incomplete), covering thirty days of the two-month period, 21 Dec. 1937 to 21 Feb. 1938; AHN, PS AR-7. These and other details have been collated with those given in Alexander, *British Volunteers*, pp. 161–8. The Irish dead in this phase of the struggle included David Walshe of Ballina and Sergeant Francis Duffy O'Brien.

38   M. Alpert, 'The Republican Army', in Cortada, *Dictionary*, p. 47.

39   See below, p. 197ff.

40   Cronin, *Frank Ryan*, p. 156ff.

41 Alexander, *British Volunteers*, pp. 199 and 204.

42 O'Riordan, *Connolly Column*, p. 126.

43 Martínez Bande, *Batalla del Ebro*, p. 136; Mezquida, *Batalla del Ebro*, pp. 62–75.

44 Ibid., pp. 151–6. Cf. Thomas, who is more critical of nationalist failures in the early stages of the battle; *Spanish Civil War*, p. 838ff.

45 Alexander, *British Volunteers*, p. 214; see also Dunlop, interview. Power was a communist who had voted against the decision to join the Lincolns in January 1937. However, he then remained loyal to his enforced affiliation until virtually all in his group were dead or repatriated.

Chapter 10

1 The term 'mutiny' is used by Gurney, and by Martínez Bande in his early history of *Las Brigadas Internacionales*, p. 127; Herrick calls it 'another war of Irish Independence'; ¡*Hermanos!*, p. 79.

2 Carroll, *Odyssey*, pp. 165–6. It appears that Reade, like Kit Conway, emigrated to the USA after the Irish Civil War. The Wobblies were the indigenous US anarchist movement. Steve Nelson, though a loyal communist, was of working-class origin. Doran, in contrast, was the son of a wealthy businessman, and knew that the party existed in a sphere which placed it above criticism by the workers. On Reade, see also McKenna, interview.

3 Lowry's index-card describes him as 'British', but his father had a Dublin address; AHN, PS AR-127. No reason for repatriation is given. Michael Lehane's card records him as having been sent home at the same time as Lowry, although no injury or sickness is mentioned (ibid.). O'Riordan lists Lowry as being from Co. Antrim; *Connolly Column*, p. 164.

4 Klaus, *Strong Words*, pp. 22–4. As the author states, 'a minor mystery surrounds O'Brien's own wound'.

5 For example, details of 'Alimentación de Prisioneros' (Dec. 1937–Apr. 1938), AHN, PS MAD-2209, contain only two 'Irish' names: Maurice Henry and James Quinn. Bob Doyle's response to questions inadvertently hints at a spell in Camp Lucas. He says at one point, for example, that the Political Commissars were 'responsible for the care of prisoners ... er ... the er ... volunteers, the Brigaders, in every way'; interview.

6 Quoted in Nelson and Hendricks, *Madrid 1937*, p. 102.

7 'Ordén de la Brigada para el día de Hoy, 7 de Marzo de 1938', AHN, PS AR-120. The offenders were McCormick, McGill and Howey, none of whom figure in O'Riordan's lists. The duty officer was Merriman. Another American evidently unimpressed with the Irish claimed that 'the British Battalion was far more unruly and disruptive than the American ... They drank what they liked, which was everything. Worse than drink, however, were the disruptive international rivalries'; Eby, *Between the Bullet and the Lie*, p. 25.

8 Angus, *With the International Brigade*, pp. 6–8.

9 Card-index, AHN, PS AR-127. McParland's mother had a Cheshire address, but he described himself as 'Irish'. He enlisted at Albacete on 30 July 1937.

10 Paris Embassy to Department of Foreign Affairs, Dublin, 22 Feb. 1937, INA, DFA 210/164. See also Brome, *International Brigades*, p. 229. Both Keenan's stories were false: dozens of the British Battalion abandoned the Jarama Valley in haste on 12–14

Feb. Keenan was lucky in the strength of his legs and his choice of direction. (The other successful deserter was C. McGuinness, see below, p. 196.)

11   Kemp, *Mine Were of Trouble*, pp. 173–5. The identity of this victim is unknown. Peñarredonda's regiment was routed by the International Brigades in the first days of the Ebro battle, during which the colonel's personal incompetence and cowardice were fully exposed; see Thomas, *Spanish Civil War*, p. 840.

12   J. Dunlop, quoted in MacDougall, *Voices*, pp. 145–7. Dunlop's name appears with Ryan's in the 2nd (Machine Gun) Company on several pay-lists of the Battalion for Dec. 1937 to Feb. 1938, AHN, PS AR-7.

13   *Volunteer for Liberty*, issue published on 13 Aug. 1938, p. 5.

14   P. Kerrigan 'to Bill [Paynter] or Springy [D. Springhall]', 15 July 1938, IBA Archive, Box C 23/6.

15   Dunlop, interview.

16   Ibid. Another veteran recalled: 'One bloke was definitely a Fascist who had been planted there as an informer … What happened exactly I'm not too sure but the story became common knowledge. We were making an advance around Gandesa … this "Fascist" … mounted his machine gun and pointed it in the opposite direction – against us. Anyway he forthwith disappeared. Whether he was taken out and shot I don't know'; Williamson, *Toolmaking and Politics*, p. 51.

17   Brewer, SWML interview transcript, pp. 22–3. See also the suggestion of deliberate betrayal in the version given by S. Fullerton in MacDougall, *Voices*, p. 297.

18   Dunlop and Brewer, interviews. (The latter evidently took Sam Wild to be Irish.)

19   Clark, 'No Boots to my Feet', pp. 29 and 42. Neither of the two 'official' accounts gives coverage to the case. Alexander (following Rust) includes Ryan in the Roll of Honour of those killed in battle; *British Volunteers*, p. 274, and cf. Rust, *Britons in Spain*, p. 197. O'Riordan, who was present at Hill 481 from first to last, and thus may have known better, also records him (in two separate places) among the glorious dead; *Connolly Column*, pp. 127 and 163.

20   Herrick, ¡Hermanos!, pp. 64–5.

21   For the religious situation in the republican zone, cf. Abella, *La vida cotidiana*, I, pp. 34–9 with the more sceptical treatment of Díaz-Plaja, *La vida cotidiana*, pp. 141–62.

22   Monks, *With the Reds*, pp. 11–12.

23   J. Monks, report (for F. Ryan), 5 Feb. 1937, quoted in Acier, *Spanish Trenches*, pp. 122–3. See also the remarks of a British Battalion commander who later became a Catholic; Copeman, *Reason in Revolt*, pp. 82 and 99, and in Corkill and Rawnsley, *Road to Spain*, p. 77.

24   See 'Orden de la Brigada para el dia 25-12-37', AHN, PS AR-6.

25   Cronin, *Frank Ryan*, pp. 121–2.

26   From a *Catholic Herald* item (6 Jan. 1939) based on reports in the *News Chronicle* and the *Daily Worker*; see INA, Office of the President, file S-11083.

27   Material on the case was forwarded by J. McElligot (Department of Finance) to M. Moynihan (Office of the Taoiseach). See their exchange of letters in ibid. Flanagan's post was doubtless awarded by de Valera for old time's sake after the priest was suspended. He was editing a government-sponsored County History of Ireland. The Taoiseach asked his minister to interview Fr Flanagan, and to suggest that he devote more time to history and less to politics.

28   A communist with the Lincolns, Mick Kelly, asserted that '75% of our Irish Unit are Roman Catholics'; *Aberdare Leader*, 29 May 1937.

29 Monks, *With the Reds*, p. 4.

30 This, of course, is an exact parallel to the spreading of 'Red atrocity' stories among the XV *Bandera* at Ciempozuelos; see above, pp. 70–4. I do not claim that such an incident never took place but that it did not happen in every *pueblo*. The 'priest in the church tower' story is well-nigh universal and has now been immortalised on the celluloid of Ken Loach's recent film, *Land and Liberty* (1995). Versions are so congruent in detail that they were obviously received by groups of men from one source (speeches by commissars, or perhaps the so-called 'wall newspaper' posted up at the front) rather than having the limited currency and varied morphology which comes from individual transmission.

31 Monks, *With the Reds*, p. 7.

32 O'Duffy, *Crusade*, pp. 31–2; see also INA, DFA file 10/225. O'Duffy calls him 'Captain C. J. McGuinness'. The account is quoted from a written source unidentified by me. It displays a crude racism, and relates certain details of the 'orgy' which are remarkably close to those depicted in a nationalist propaganda newsreel.

33 Dunlop, interview, where he also refers to Haughey as 'a Catholic from Laugharne'.

34 The formulation is that of Manus O'Riordan, in a letter to C. Geiser, 7 Apr. 1993; IBA Archive, Box D-3, file G/1. The source here was E. Downing. Michael O'Riordan states that Haughey was killed on Hill 481, but later includes him in the 'List of Survivors'; *Connolly Column*, pp. 128 and 164. Bob Doyle states that he was in the prison camp of San Pedro at some point in 1938–39; interview.

35 Ibid.

36 O'Riordan, *Connolly Column*, p. 31.

37 Ibid., p. 37.

38 Cunningham, *Spanish Civil War Verse*, pp. 385–8.

39 See *Volunteer for Liberty*, 1 (23), 5 Nov. 1937. This was the official Comintern line, which the republican government (with limited enthusiasm) also tried to promote.

40 Gerassi, *Premature Antifascists*, p. 43.

41 O'Reilly – from Thurles, Co. Tipperary – deserted from the British army and seems to have joined Frank Ryan's group in London in December 1936. He told his father – apparently without irony – that 'I fought against the priests who machine-gunned the poor women and children and would be classified as a red'; letter of 12 Nov. 1938, INA, DFA 210/164. Here the volunteer is called 'John' – but his identity is not in doubt since Officer Quinn of the Dublin Gardai tells his colleague in Thurles that 'in Spain it appears that O'Reilly married an American lady who was a member of the International Red Cross'. In contradiction to her husband, the said lady insisted that 'both Pat and I were very strong Catholics, not communists'; Gerassi, *Premature Antifascists*, p. 197.

42 Martín Moreno to J. A. Sagroniz, Salamanca, 21 Apr. 1937; MAE, A.Bu. R-593. Alexander says that thirty men were captured but an official *parte* claimed thirty-nine British prisoners; *British Volunteers*, p. 183; *El Adelanto de Salamanca*, 14 Feb. 1937. Three were shot, twenty-three were released in April and a further three at later dates. See Ambassador Chilton to Sagroniz, 1 June 1937, conveying Eden's thanks to Franco for release of prisoners; MAE, A.Bu. R-1051/24–110.

43 These four POWs (not present on the earlier lists, see n. 44) appear on a consolidated list of Irish prisoners drawn up in preparation for an exchange deal involving Italians, probably in late 1938; 'Elenco de miliziani de Nazionalita Irlandese … nel campo di

concentratamento di San Pedro', ibid., R-1051/75. The names were James Forcell, Vincent O'Donnell, Tom Heaney and John Lennon.

44   'Relacion nominal ... de los prisioneros extranjeros ingresado en este Campo de Con-centracion', 8 Apr. 1938; AGM, CGG 56. This list has been collated with that referenced above, n. 43.

45   Delaney's fate was eventually enquired after by the Free State government, but Kerney was unable to provide details of the missing man. Burgos stated that no prisoner of that name was in their hands; Kerney to Mamblas, 28 Dec. 1938, MAE, A.Bu. R-833/19 and M. Moreno to Mamblas, 20 Jan. 1939, ibid., R-1051/24–110.

46   See a series of eleven lists, all headed 'Relacion nominal por oficios, nacionalidad y residencia de los prisioneros extranjeros' in AGM, CGG 56 and 58. As their heading suggests, these give details of the age, occupation, city of residence and nationality of a total of 481 men; signed by the camp commandant, Julio Claves Arellano.

47   Alexander, *British Volunteers*, pp. 187–95 and Francis, *Miners against Fascism*, pp. 239–44.

48   It seems possible that the scrupulously proper behaviour of the XV Brigade's Italian captors may have been reinforced by the possibility of exchange negotiations.

49   Cronin, *Frank Ryan*, pp. 134–66. Ryan was usually kept apart from the others, and was often held on other sites away from San Pedro. Cronin's material is drawn on – except where otherwise cited – in this and the following section.

50   Quoted in Cronin, *Frank Ryan*, pp. 146–7; see also pp. 119 and 265. As Cronin surmises, charges may have related to an alleged incident after the capture of Villanueva de la Cañada, during the battle of Brunete. Ryan was not a combatant, but followed up as a member of field HQ. The same applies in the cases of Quinto and Belchite, where similar atrocities took place later that year. These were carried out on the orders of Colonel Copic, Brigade Commander-in-Chief Ryan was present at Copic's field HQ as a member of his *Estado Mayor* (see above, p. 81).

51   This and the previous quotation are taken from Kerney to Mamblas, 24 Dec. 1938; MAE, A.Bu. 833/19.

52   Kerney to Dublin, 24 May 1938, INA, DFA 244/22.

53   Ibid., 2 June 1938. The murdered Briton was Admiral Henry Somerville, living in Co. Cork, who in 1936 was apparently 'punished' for encouraging unemployed Irishmen to join the British Navy; O'Riordan, *Connolly Column*, p. 122.

54   Within a fortnight of Ryan's capture, de Valera telegraphed Kerney that he 'would greatly appreciate a lenient attitude towards Ryan's case. Public opinion here would be greatly incensed if punishment involves Ryan's life'; 14 Apr. 1938, INA, DFA 244/8.

55   See S. Murphy to J. Walshe (London High Commissioner) asking him to seek an interview with the Duke of Alba, 22 Apr. 1938; ibid.

56   From a letter to the *Irish Times*, 14 May 1952, by K. Cahill, quoted in Cronin, *Frank Ryan*, p. 157 (and see also p. 267). See also Obituary of Ryan's sister, Ellie; *Sunday Tribune*, 7 May 1995. Cahill was a veteran of the Irish Brigade who joined the Falange and was himself in Burgos around this time; see Kerney to Dublin, 19 Dec. 1938, INA, DFA 244/22. Unlike Gunning, Cahill was lacking neither in loyalty to O'Duffy nor sympathy for a compatriot.

57   Kerney to Mamblas, 24 Dec. 1938; MAE, A.Bu. 833/19.

Notes

Epilogue

1 See, for example, the closing remarks of the latest English-language textbook, Esenwein and Shubert, *Spain at War*, pp. 272–3. Unfortunately, they are not convincingly borne out in the substance of the work.

2 Cf. 'O'Duffy's Inglorious Dupes', *Volunteer for Liberty*, 1 (2), June 1937, p. 6; with – fifty years on – Manus O'Riordan, 'Irish and Jewish Volunteers in the Spanish Anti-Fascist War' (15 Nov. 1987), IBA Archive, A-14/D-3/6.

3 See, for example, the recent reference (comprising all of ten words) by the Franco apologist, R. de la Cierva, *Historia Esencial*, p. 389. This is slightly improved upon in the same author's even more recent *Brigadas Internacionales*, p. 269.

4 Aznar, *Historia Militar* (1st edn, 1956). Not until 1987 did the first relevant entry occur in a Spanish publication; Rubio Cabeza, *Diccionario* II, p. 579. During the Franco regime (1939–75), foreign contribution to the 'war of liberation' was consistently played down. This was partly a matter of pride and partly an attempt to minimise Franco's links with Hitler and Mussolini; but, more importantly, a response to accusations of abetting an 'alien invasion' of Spain, turning them instead against a Republic backed up by 'the Red Mongol horde' sent by Stalin. See Salas Larrazábal, 'La intervención extranjera y las ayudas exteriores', in *Aproximación*, pp. 131–65.

5 Carr, *Civil War in Spain*, p. 145. Preston, *Spanish Civil War*, (1986 edn), is actually dedicated to the International Brigades. In contrast, H. Thomas, in various editions of his standard account (*The Spanish Civil War*, originally 1961), has been rigorously noncommittal; see 1977 edn, pp. 592, 768 and 979.

6 Beevor, *The Spanish Civil War*, p. 145.

7 Kitchen, *Europe between the Wars*, pp. 250–1. I do not know why this writer appears to cast doubt on O'Duffy's military title. Even more slick and casual is Norman Davies's comment that 'the Irish Brigade of General O'Duffy [were] blatant adventurers'; see Davies, *Europe*, p. 984.

8 Gibson, *Un irlandés en España*, p. 165.

9 Mitchell, *Storm over Spain*, pp. 213–18. Subsequent treatments were based on this original. W. Tierney wrote that '[O'Duffy's] account of the religious fervour of the Brigade cannot be discredited … [he] was treated more roughly by his contemporaries than perhaps he deserved'; 'Irish Writers'. A literary historian compares the *banderistas* with the *brigadistas* thus: 'That [the former] were sincere … concerning the religious mission … and that they were politically more naive than their counterparts on the left, are matters which are entirely sound in spite of what their disparagers have contended'; Ford, *A Poet's War*, p. 149.

10 See Cairns and Richards, *Writing Ireland*.

11 However, the embarrassment is present during this period in more than just the Blueshirt phenomenon; see the Channel Four TV documentary 'A Great Hatred' (written and presented by S. S. Montefiore) broadcast on 15 Oct. 1997.

12 Ellman, *Yeats*, pp. 280–1; W. B. Yeats, *Collected Poems*, pp. 321–4. It should be stressed that Yeats's support for O'Duffy was withdrawn long before the Spanish expedition. Two other writers who resisted the appeal of the Spanish Republic were Oliver St John Gogarty and Frances Stuart (though neither expressed commitment to the other side).

13 From Blanaid Salkeld's poem 'Casualties', printed in Cunningham, *Spanish Civil War Verse*, p. 176.

14   Christy Moore, 'Vive el quinte Brigada' (set to the tune of 'If you Ever Go Across the Sea to Ireland').

15   From 'Ballyseedy Befriends Badajoz', printed in Cunningham, *Spanish Civil War Verse*, pp. 385–6. See also 'Off to Salamanca in the Morning', ibid., p. 387. The 'Macalastair' poems mostly appeared in issues of *The Worker*, a cyclo-styled news-sheet issued by the CPI at irregular intervals in late 1936. For analysis, and revelation of its author's real identity, see Klaus, 'The Authorship'.

16   See R. Warner's poem, 'Arms in Spain', printed in Cunningham, *Spanish Civil War Verse*, p. 387.

17   Cunningham, *British Writers of the Thirties*, p. 419ff.

18   *Joint Letter of the Spanish Bishops to the Bishops of the Whole World Concerning the War in Spain, July 1937* (London, 1938), p. 15.

19   See Whyte, *Church and State in Modern Ireland*, where no hint is given of any link between the Irish Church and the O'Duffy Brigade.

20   'O'Duffy's Inglorious Dupes' (the article is almost certainly by Frank Ryan). However, my impression is that a majority of veterans never formulated, much less articulated, any sense of betrayal by their Church.

21   'Even the Olives'.

22   Ryan to O'Reilly, 11 Feb. 1937, quoted in Acier, *Spanish Trenches*, p. 116.

23   This feeling also contributed to the murderous antipathy which developed between the Internationals as a whole and the Spanish Foreign Legion, of which the Irish Brigade formed part. See Kerney to Walshe, 14 May 1938, INA, DFA 244/8.

24   O'Duffy, *Crusade*, p. 146.

25   Ó Cuinneagháin, *War*, p. 16.

26   Dunlop, interview.

27   Letter to author from D. O'Reilly (son), 1995.

28   See Gurney, *Crusade in Spain*, pp. 136–42, passim.

29   Monks, interview.

30   Herrick, ¡*Hermanos!*, p. 99.

Appendices

APPENDIX A

Partial list of the XV *Bandera*'s Irish members

Name	Rank	Company	Origin/Location	Sources
J. Ahern	cpl	C		11
James Ahern	cpl	B		11
Dan Ahern			Rathkeale, Lk	4, 17
Frederick Ahern		D/A	Clonlong Lk	13, 17
Louis Aherne			Limerick	3, 9
Mick Aldridge				4
? Baldwin			Tipperary	3
A. Bamill	sgt	D		11
Mat Barlow			Longford	10
Johnny Barron			Cashel, Ty	4
J. Baxter	cpl		Dublin	5, 11
Matt Beckett	cpl		Westport, Mo	3, 4, 11
J. Bergin		Medic	Clonmel, Ty	3, 5, 10
James Berry	sgt	B		11
John ? Boland				11
A. Bradley	cpl			11
Martin Bradley	cpl	D	Ballinasloe, Gy	2, 11
B. Brady	cpl		Tullyco, Cn	3, 5, 11
C. Brannigan			Monaghan	3, 5, 11
Henry Brannigan	sgt	D		1, 11
Christopher Bray			Limerick	17
P. Breen		B		11
Ned Brien			Dublin	3
J. J. Broderick	sgt	B	Tralee, Ky	5, 11
B. Brogan	sgt	D	Kildare	9, 11
William Broggy			Limerick	2, 8, 17

Name	Rank	Company	Origin/Location	Sources
Richard Brophy		B		10, 11
? Brown			Carnew, Ww	4
T. Burbage			Longford	4
A. Burke			Dublin	5
M. Burke			Tralee, Ky	18
Michael Burns			Westport, Mo	11
Johnny Butler			Tipperary	6
M. Butler	sgt	D		11
N. Butler	sgt	D		11
Robert Butler	sgt	A	Blackrock, Dn	1, 4, 10, 11
W. Butler			Cashel, Ty	5
T. J. Byrne	sgt	D		11
M. Cadell	sgt	D	England	3, 11, 14
M. Cagney	lt	B	South Mall, Ck	2, 4, 6, 8, 10
Kevin Cahill				2, 7
Thomas Cahill	lt	A	Thurles, Ty	1, 2, 4, 5, 10
Maurice Carbery			Dublin	3
Tom Carew	capt	Staff	Tipperary	1, 3, 10
J. Carey			Westmeath	8
Jeremiah Casey				7, 14
Paddy Casey			Mullagh, Ld	4, 5
Sean Casey			Roscommon	9
F. L. Caslin			Dublin	4
Tom Casserly	sgt		Dublin	2, 4, 6, 9, 10, 11
Anthony Casserly				2
Jack Caughan			Belmullett, Mo	11
C. Caughey	sgt	Staff		11
G. Caughie			Belfast	1
P. Cavanagh	cpl		Ballinrobe, Mo	11, 12, 14
Sean Cavanagh				8
Joe Chambers	cpl		Westport, Mo	11, 12
Lenny Chambers			Westport, Mo	11
Dan Chute			Tralee, Ky	1, 5, 10
J. Clancy	lt	D	Tipperary	4, 8, 6, 10
Sean P. Clarke	sgt		Cootehill Cn/Dublin	2, 4, 11
J. P. Cleary			Limerick	3, 4, 5, 17
John Cleary			Belfast	4
J. Coates			Castle Blaney, Mn	5, 9
Pat Coffey			Limerick	17
M. Collins	cpl		Limerick	5, 11, 17
M. Comerford			Thomastown, Kny	5

Name	Rank	Company	Origin/Location	Sources
P. Comerford			Thomastown, Kny	5
K. J. Condon				11
B. J. Connolly			Longford	1, 10, ?11, ?14
Jack Conroy			The Neale, Mo	12
? Coogan			Galway	3
John Corway			Dublin	3
Bill Coughley			Youghal, Wd	3
Philip Cronin	sgt	Staff		11
Jack Cross			Limerick	2, 5, 10, 17
John Crowe	cpl		Milford, Ce	2, 11
Andrew Crowley	cpl		Kilrush, Ce	1, 2, 11
John Crowley			Clonmel, Ty	5, 7
John L. Crowley			Dunmanway, Ck	5
L. Crowley			?Dublin	2
Sean Crowley	cpl			4
W. D. Crowley			Dundrum, Dn	5
T. B. Crystal	cpl			11
John Cummins			Tullow, Cw	4
Sean Cunningham	capt	D	Belfast	1, 4, 10
Joseph Cunningham	sgt	C	Knockbeg, Cw	1–4, 6, 10, 11
S. Curtin		A		11
Matthew Curtis			Knocklong, Lk	7, 14
W. M. Curtis	cpl			11
M. Cusack	cpl		Castlebar, Mo	11, 12
Patrick Dalton	maj	Staff	Waterford/Dublin	1, 2, 6, 9, 10, 21
C. Daly	rev	Staff	Enniskillen, Fh	2, 6
Pat Daly	cpl			4, 11
? Darcy			Dublin	9
F. Delaney				1
G. Delaney				14
W. H. Delaney	sgt	C	Emly, Ty	11, 16
William Delaney			Ballycumane, Lk	17
J. Dillon	sgt	D	Dublin	9, 11
M. Dineen			Tralee, Ky	18
J. Donnelly				10
Sean Donnelly	cpl		Carlingford, Lh	2, 5 11
Michael Donoghue			Galway	2(2)
Matt Doolan			Cork	11, 15, 22
Bill Doran			The Curragh, Ke	3
J. Doyle			Clonlong, Lk	17
James Doyle			Thomondgate, Lk	17

Name	Rank	Company	Origin/Location	Sources
John Doyle			Ballyneety, Lk	17
Joseph F. Doyle	sgt	C	Castlecomer, Kny	1, 11, 14
Thomas Doyle			Roscrea, Ty	10
? Doyle			Tralee, Ky	18
T. L. Duane	cpl			11
John Duffy			Ballybay, Mn	5, 14
Joseph Duffy				5, 14
T. Duignan	cpl			11
Leo Dunne			Dublin	4
Pat Dunny	sgt	C	Carlow	4, 11
John C. Dunphy	sgt		Carlow	4, 11
P. Dwyer			Clonmel, Ty	10
Victor Ennis				1
James Fahy			Limerick	17
P. Farrelly	cpl			11, 15
L. E. Feeney			Lishmore, Wd	3
Maurice Fennell		C	Rathkeale, Lk	3, 17, 18
Mick Fennessy			Clonmel, Ty	2, 4, 5
M. Flanagan	cpl		Kilkenny	4, 11
James Finnerty	capt	Staff	Wexford	1, 3, 6, 10, 21
A. Fitzgerald			Tralee, Ky	1, 5, 18
Bill Fitzgerald			Limerick	16, 17
Eugene P. Fitzgerald			Dungarvan, Wd	7, 17
Frank B. Fitzgerald			Dungarvan, Wd	16, 17
Sean Fitzgerald			Midleton, Ck	4
Sean N. Fitzgerald			?Cappagh, Wd	5
T. Fitzgerald			Tralee, Ky	18
Noel Fitzpatrick	lt	D		3, 6, 9, 10
Barney Fitzsimmons	sgt	A	Kells, Cw	4, 11
R. Fluskey	cpl			11
William Fogarty			Knocklong, Lk	7, 14
Tom Foley			Tralee, Ky	1, 10, 18
P. Forrelly				2
Patrick Fox			Athenry, Gy	2, 11
Jim Frawley			Limerick	16, 17
M. J. Freeman	dr	Medic	Dublin/London	3, 6, 10
Padraig Furey			Dundrum, Dn	3, 8
? Gaffney			Sligo	15
P. J. Gallagher	lt	A	Sligo	1, 4, 6, 10, 14, 15

Name	Rank	Company	Origin/Location	Sources
Sean Garraghan			Longford	1, 10, 11, 14
Kevin Geoghegan			Galway	2, 11
William Geraghty			Dublin	3
Patrick Gilbert			Limerick	2, 4, 10, 17
? Gilman	cpl			11
J. Graham			Limerick	5, 17
Tom Gunning	capt	Staff	Leitrim	6, 9, 10, 14, 21
M. Halloran			Tralee, Ky	18
Joseph Halpin				3
A. Hamill	sgt	D	Monaghan	5, 8, 11
F. Hamill				5
Peter J. Hand	cpl			1, 15
J. Harte			Newtown Forbes, Ld	5
? Harvey	cpl			11
J. Hayes				14
Thomas Hayes		D	Tralee, Ky	3
M. Healey	cpl			11
Laurence Heaney			Dublin	3
Frank Hempenstall			Dundrum, Dn	3
J. Hendry			Monaghan	5
C. T. Hennessy			Dublin	5
D. Herlihy				2
Patrick Hickey			Dundrum, Dn	3
D. V. Higgins	cpl		Ballyhooly, Ck	5, 11, 14
J. Hill	cpl		Clonmel, Ty	5, 11
Gerald Hobbins	cpl		Tulla, Ce	2, 3, 11
Thomas Hobbins	sgt	B	Tulla, Ce	2, 11
John Hoey	cpl		Dublin	1, 2, 10, 11, 15
Edward Hogan				1
? Holloway			Carrick-on-Suir, Ty	3
? Holohan			Arklow, Ww	4
Bernard Horan			Tralee, Ky	1, 10, 18
Eamon Horan			Tralee, Ky	1, 5, 9, 10
Ned Horan				3
George Hore			Carlow	4
Charles Horgan	lt	C	Mallow, Ck	1, 5, 6, 10, 21
Tom Hudson	sgt	C	Newmarket, Cw	4
J. Hughes	sgt	B	Longford	4, 9, 11
Paddy Hughes	capt	Band	Monaghan	3, 6, 10
Tom Hyde	lt	A	Midleton, Ck	1, 2, 6, 9, 10
T. Jolly		A	Blackrock, Dn	4, 11

Name	Rank	Company	Origin/Location	Sources
Thomas Jones	sgt	D	Belfast	8, 9, 11, 14
Dermot Jordan			Wexford	4
Kevin Judge			Dublin	4
A. Karnell			Thomastown, Kny	3
G. Kavanagh			Cork	5
J. Kavanagh		C	Dublin	2
Tommy Kearney		B	Carrick-on-Suir, Ty	3, 24
? Kearns	dr	Medic	Newbliss, Mn	3
Joe Kelleher			Cork	3
Denis Kelly	lt	C	Dysart, Gy	2, 6, 10, 21
J. Kelly	sgt	D		8, 11
Luke Kelly			Blackrock, Dn	3
M. Kelly			St Mullins, Cw	4
J. Kenny			Cork	5
Michael Kenny			Toomevara, Ty	2
P. J. Kenny			Dublin	5
P. J. Keogh				14
Riden Keogh	cpl			11
Brendan Kielty	sgt		Belfast	2, 4
? Kility	sgt		Tyrone	8
Patrick Killeen	cpl		Whitegate, Ce	1, 2, 11
A. King	cpl			11
Martin Kinsella			Enniscorthy, Wxd	7
T. Kinsella			?Dublin	2
J. Knowles			Dublin	2
W. La Fere			Tullamore, Oy	5
Patrick Lannergan				1
P. Lawler	lt		Kildare	3, 10, 14
J. Lawlor	sgt	D	Carlow	2, 10, 11
W. Leary			?Dublin	2
Gabriel Lee	sgt	A	Dublin	1, 2, 10, 11, 15
Bill Levey	sgt	A	Dublin	3, 4, 11, 15
? Little			Waterford	16
J. Lonergan			Clonmel, Ty	5
P. M. Lonergan		B	Northampton	24
Joe Lydon			Oughterard, Gy	2
Liam Lynch			Oughterard, Gy	8
H. McArdle	cpl		Monaghan	5, 11
T. McArdle			Monaghan	5

Name	Rank	Company	Origin/Location	Sources
Phil McBride		B	Newbliss, Mn	3
Sean McBrien	cpl			11
C. McCabe		B		13
F. McCabe			Ballyconnell, Ck	5
P. McCann			Monaghan	5
J. 'Stan' McCarthy			Ballyvaughan, Ce	2
James McCarthy			Enniskeane, Ck	5, 15
Jeremiah McCarthy			Clonmel, Ty	1, 3, 5
John McCarthy	sgt	B	W Cork	1, 10, 11, 14
P. McCarthy			Enniskeane, Ck	2, 5
T. McCarthy	cpl		Ballydehob, Ck	2, 3, 11
W. McCarthy			Bandon, Ck	5
? McCaughey		C	Belfast	3
Leo McCloskey		Medic	Portmarnock, Dn	3, 4, 8, 10
V. McConnell			?Dublin	2
Bill McCormack [aka T. Keane]			Limerick	17
Eunan McDermott			Ballyshannon, Dl	6, 10, 14
James McEvoy				14
P. McGarry				11
T. McGhee			Tullaveen, Cn	3, 8
C. McGrath			Dublin	4
Gerry McGrath			Ballyleague, Ky	19
John McGrath			Salthill, Gy	2, 10
Thomas McGrath	cpl		Youghal, Ck	2, 10, 11, 18
W. F. McGrath	sgt	B	Cork	3, 5, 11
D. McGuinness			?Dublin	2
F. McGuire			Monaghan	5
John C. McGuire			Dromod, Lm	1, 5
Frank McHale			Swinford, Mo	12
Vincent McHugh			Ennis, Ce	2
Seamus McKee			Dublin	23
James McKenna	cpl		Dublin	4, 11
Joe McKenna			Belfast	4
John F. McKernan			Cootehill, Cn	3
P. MacMahon				1, 6
Tom McManus				1
William McMorran				14
Tom McMullen			Westport, Mo	2, 4, 10, 11, 20
C. McNamara			Dublin	2
Peter McNamara			Limerick	17
Sean MacNamara	sgt	C	Ennis, Ce	2, 11

Name	Rank	Company	Origin/Location	Sources
Thomas McNamara			Limerick	17
James McNiece			Limerick	17
Reg McNulty	cpl		Dublin	6, 11
Thomas McQuinn	cpl		Oughterard, Gy	2
Sean McStewart			Dublin	8
John MacSweeney			Tralee, Ky	1, 2, 10
William McSweeney			Rathbane, Lk	17
John J. Madden				7, 14
T. Maguire	cpl			11
Dan Maher	cpl	B	Clonmel, Ty	5, 11
Sean Maher	cpl	A		11
Chris Mahon			Blackrock, Dn	3
J. Mangan			Blackboy Pike, Lk	17
J. Manning			Toames, Ck	5
A. Marnell			Stoneyford, Kny	5
John Martin	sgt		Drung, Cn	2, 3, 5, 11
R. Matthews	cpl		Carlow	4, 11
J. J. Maughan			Ballina, Mo	12
W. Meade	capt	Staff	Spain	6, 9, 10
Thomas Meaney			Limerick	17
? Meaney			N. Ireland	4, 11
J. Mohan			Monaghan	5
Tony Monaghan	cpl		Dublin	5, 10, 11
? Monteith			Enniskillen, Fh	4
George Mooney			Blackrock, Dn	3
Jim Mooney			Dublin	3
Michael Moore	cpl		Caherconlish, Lk	11, 17
W. Moore			Limerick	5, 17
Jack Moran	cpl	A	Shrule, Mo	3, 4, 10, 11, 15
James Morrisey			Thomastown, Kny	5, 13, 15
Frank Mulcahy	sgt	A	Tralee, Ky	11, 19
John C. Muldoon	sgt		Navan, Mh	1, 10, 11, 14
? Mulligan	cpl			15
Tommy Mullins			Westport, Mo	4
J. Mulrean	rev	Staff	Moate, Wh	5, 6, 21
? Mulvanny				8
Mick Munnelly			Ballina, Mo	11
P. Munnelly			Crossmolina, Mo	12
Edward Murphy	lt	B	Wexford	1, 4, 6, 9, 10
H. Murphy	cpl		Dublin	4, 11
John Murphy	cpl			11, 14
M. W. Murphy			Longford	5

Name	Rank	Company	Origin/Location	Sources
R. Murphy			Dublin	4
Sean B. Murphy	sgt	D	Cork	1, 10, 11, 14
'Spud' Murphy			Ballinasloe, Gy	2
Tom Murphy	cpl		Cashel, Ty	1, 5, 11
James Murray	cpl			11
Gilbert Nangle	lt	C	Derry	9, 10
F. Nevin			Dublin	5
J. Noonan	cpl			11, 15
Billie Norris			Youghal, Ck	3
C. O'Brien			Cashel, Ty	5
John O'Brien			Clonmel, Ty	2, 4, 5
Mick O'Brien			Dublin	11
T. O'Brien			Dublin	5
William O'Brien	sgt			11
? O'Brien			Cork	9
Christie O'Connell			Thurles, Ty	7
M. O'Connell			Bandon, Ck	5
D. O'Connor			Tralee, Ky	19
John O'Connor				7, 14
M. O'Connor			Dublin	2, 10
? O'Connor	sgt		Connemara	8, 10
Denis O'Dea			Tullamore, Oy	7
M. O'Donnell			Tralee, Ky	5, 2
Manus O'Donnell			Tralee, Ky	19
S. O'Donnelly	cpl			14
C. B. O'Donoghue	sgt		Bandon, Ck	5, 11
? O'Dowell				23
Thomas O'Dwyer				1
Arturo O'Farrell	lt	Staff	Meath	7, 14
Cornelius O'Grady			Doon, Lk	17
Michael O'Grady			Blackwater, Lk	17
Christy O'Halloran	cpl		Tralee, Ky	5, 11, 18
P. O'Higgins	dr	Medic	Dublin	3, 6, 21
D. O'Keefe	cpl			11
G. O'Leary			Tralee, Ky	5
'Mick' O'Leary			Rathmore, Ky	18
Dan O'Mahoney			W. Cork	4
K. M. O'Malley				10
Tyrell O'Malley				10
H. O'Neill				10

Name	Rank	Company	Origin/Location	Sources
Ignatius O'Neill	sgt	B	Dublin	4, 9, 11
Michael O'Neill			Kildare	9
Michael O'Neill			Knockraha, Ck	16
Michael O'Regan	cpl			11
Austin O'Reilly				8, 14
Ivan O'Reilly				5
Sean O'Reilly	sgt	B		11
? O'Reilly				11
J. O'Riordan			Tralee, Ky	19
Tom O'Riordan	lt	B	Midleton, Ck	1, 4, 6, 10
M. O'Shea			Clonmel, Ty	5
Christy O'Sullivan			Limerick	16, 17
Dermot O'Sullivan	capt	A	Killarney, Ky	1–3, 6, 9, 10, 21
Rory O'Sullivan			Kenmare, Ky	6, 8
Andrew O'Toole			Dublin	7
Jeremiah O'Toole				8
Martin O'Toole			Ennis, Ce	3
S. Pidgeon			Dublin	4
J. M. Poland	cpl		Bandon, Ck	5, 9
P. Power			Limerick	17
Mark Price				4, 10, 11
Tom Prior			Clare	3
John Quilty			Lisnagry, Lk	17
Padraig Quinn	capt	C	Gowran, Kny	1, 2, 4, 6, 10, 15, 21, 22
Ronnie Quinn			Tuam, Gy	2, 3, 6
J. Regan			Clonmel, Ty	5
Denis J. Reynolds		D	Cootehill, Cn	3
John Riordan		D		11
J. Roche		Medic	Bandon, Ck	3, 5, 10
J. Rodgers			?Dublin	2, 14
Patrick Rowe			Limerick	17
J. Ryan			Cashel, Ty	5
Teddy Ryan			Dundrum, Dn	3
Jim Scullion			Enniskillen, Fh	15
Tom Shaw	sgt	C	Ballinacurra, Ck	3, 11, 20
A. Sheehy	cpl		Garryowen, Lk	4, 11
Andrew Sheehy			Ballyleague, Ky	19

Name	Rank	Company	Origin/Location	Sources
J. J. Sheehy	sgt	C		11, 15
Micky Sheehy			Ballyleague, Ky	19
Paul Sheehy			Garryowen, Lk	17
Tom Shortiss	cpl			1, 11
P. J. Skeehan	cpl		Broadford, Ce	2, 11
James Slattery			Clonmel, Ty	1, 5
John Smith			Tully, Cn	3, 7, 14
Patrick J. Smith		D	Stradone, Cn	3, 5
Thomas F. Smith	capt	B	Ulster	1, 10, 21
Harry Stewart	cpl		Oughterard, Gy	2, 11
G. Sullivan			Tralee, Ky	19
M. Sullivan	sgt	A		11
Jim Sweeney			Tralee, Ky	19
Paddy Tierney			Dublin	3
George Timlin	lt	A	Waterford/Dublin	1, 4, 6, 10, 11
Richard Timoney		D/B	Tralee, Ky	11, 19
Mick Tobin	cpl		Carlow	4, 11
W. Tobin			Cashel, Ty	5
David Tormey	lt	B	Moate, Wh	1, 6, 9, 10, 13
Desmond Traynor			Limerick	17
J. Traynor	cpl			11
J. Treanor			Ballybay, Mn	5
Thomas Troy	sgt	D	Tulla, Ce	1, 2, 10, 11
'Rocky' Tucker			Belfast	3
Dan Tully	cpl			11, 15
Hubert Tully			Ballinasloe, Gy	2, 11
Tom Tully	cpl			11
J. Twomey	sgt	A	Turner's Cross, Ck	4, 11
A. Walker	cpl		Kells, Mh	5, 11
Dan Walsh	cpl		Wexford	4, 11
John Walsh	cpl		Midleton, Ck	10, 11
Nicholas Walsh		B		3
Sean Walsh			Limerick	5, 17
Thomas Walsh			Roscommon	2
Patrick Ward			Belfast	4, 11
Michael Weymes	sgt	Staff	Mullingar	1, 4, 10, 11, 14, 21
P. Weymes			Mullingar	4
? Weymes			Mullingar	4
Christopher Whelan			Limerick	17
Dennis Whelan			Dublin	9, 11

Name	Rank	Company	Origin/Location	Sources
Sean Whittle			Waterford	5
Tony Whittle	cpl		Waterford	5, 11
J. Wolohan			Arklow, Ww	5
Willie Young			Cootehill, Cn	3, 16

Key to Sources
1   Ennis, 'Catholic Moors'
2   Press reports (some in private collection)
3   Private information and tape interviews
4   Ó Cuinneaghán (2 sources)
5   SS *Aguila* passenger list
6   Kilfeather, *Sunday Independent*, 1960
7   Irish National Archives
8   McCullagh, *In Franco's Spain*
9   G. Gaffney, *Irish Independent*, 1937
10 O'Duffy, *Crusade*
11 M. Beckett, Official Lists and 'Irish Brigade' (Westport)
12 *Mayo News*, 19 Dec. 1936
13 McCloskey Collection
14 Spanish Archives
15 McCarthy Ms., NLI
16 L. O Laoi Collection
17 D. Ryan, *Limerick Chronicle* and Collection
18 M. Fennell, 'Spain, 1936–37'
19 T. Hayes, *Diary*
20 Stradling, *Brother Against Brother*
21 Tom Hyde, common-place book
22 'Even the Olives', RTE
23 McKee, *I Was a Franco Soldier*
24 Shelley, *Guide*

APPENDIX B

Spanish officers seconded to XV *Bandera*

Duque de Algeciras, liaison with Franco	10, 21
Marqués de Monasterio, adjutant	4
Cap. Manuel Capablanca, training officer	10, 21
Cap. Juan Botana Rosé, chief staff officer	10, 14, 21
Ten. Mariano Archenderreta, *pagador*	10, 14, 21
Alf. Alfonso Bustamente	21, 23
Ten. Pedro Bove	10, 14, 21
Alf. Piloto Alvaro Matamoros, liaison	10, 21

Alf. Oscar López Fernández, armoury adviser	4, 14
Cap. Camino, chief liaison officer	14
Alf. Antonio Miracles Sanz	14
Alf. José Luis Segimont	14
Sarg. de Intendencia José Izquierdo Soriano	14
Sarg. de Caballería Ricardo Martorell	14
Sarg. interprete Rafael Figueroa Bermejillo	14
Sarg. interprete Duarte Boy-Harvey	14
Sarg. interprete Francisco Larios Carver	14
Sarg. interprete Muchand Sobraj	14
Sarg. interprete Mariano Amodeo Mayoral	14
Leg. Tomás Martín	14
Leg. Ruperto Castellanos Vila	14
Leg. Cesár Silva Vázquez	14, 10
Leg. Luis Marijuán	14

(For source key, see Appendix A)

APPENDIX C

The command and unit structure of the XV *Bandera*

Brigade Inspector-General: E. O'Duffy (General de Brigada)
Brigadier Staff: Capt T. Gunning (Secretary) (then A. O'Ferrall), Lt W. Meade (Interpreter)
GOC: Teniente Coronel P. Dalton (then Capt D. O'Sullivan)
Staff Officers: Capt J. Finnerty (QMS), Capt T. Carew (Intelligence/Vigilancia)
Chief Liaison Officers: Capt Botana (then Capt F. Camino)
Staff Sgts: M. Weymes (HQ Sgt-Major), C. Caughey (Armourer), P. Cronin (QMS)

A Company

CO: Capt D. O'Sullivan (then T. Cahill, P. Quinn)
Lts: T. Hyde (then T. Cahill, G. Timlin), S. Gallagher
Liaison: Lt P. Bove (then Lt Silva)
Sgt-Major: G. Timlin
QMS Sgt: B. Fitzimmons
Sgts: G. Lee, R. Butler, J. Twomey, E. Mulcahy, M. Sullivan, W. Levey (then J. Moran)

B Company

CO: Capt T. F. Smith (then D. Tormey)
Lts: E. Murphy, M. Cagney

Liaison: Alférez A. Bustamente
Sgt-Major: I. O'Neill
QMS Sgt: W. F. McGrath
Sgts: J. Hughes, J. McCarthy, J. J. Broderick, T. Hobbins, S. O'Reilly, J. Barry

C Company

CO: Capt P. Quinn (then G. Nangle, C. Horgan)
Lts: G. Nangle, D. Kelly (then C. Horgan)
Liaison: Lt Falco
Sgt-Major: T. Hudson
QMS Sgt: J. Cunningham
Sgts: S. MacNamara, W. F. Delaney, J. F. Doyle, J. J. Sheehy, P. Dunny (then T. Shaw)

D Company

OC: Capt S. Cunningham (then A/Capt J. Clancy)
Lts: N. Fitzpatrick, J. Clancy
Liaison: ?
Sgt-Major: H. Brannigan
QMS Sgt: S. B. Murphy
Sgts: M. Butler, N. Butler, B. Brogan, T. Jones, A. Bamill, J. Dillon, M. Cadell, J. Kelly, T. J. Byrne, T. Troy (then J. Lawler)

Reserve NCOs: P. McGarry, B. Kielty, C. B. O'Donoghoe, J. Martin, J. C. Muldean, T. Casserley
Reserve officers: Lts O'Riordan, Hughes

APPENDIX D

International Brigaders of Irish origin

Contains only the names of those who are attested in the cited sources as Irish

Name	Born	Place	Other Details	Sources
Robert Armstrong				CT
Archie Bailey	280312	Belfast	labourer	SA
Victor Barr	131116	Belfast	labourer	MO, SA
Paddy Barry		Mayo		MO
William Barry		Dublin	killed 1236	MO, IB
William Beattie		Belfast	killed 0737	MO, NM
James J. Beirne		Cavan		MO

Name	Born	Place	Other Details	Sources
? Black				IB
Kevin Blake	.	Dublin		MO
Henry Bonar		Dublin	killed 1236	MO
Hugh Bonar		Donegal	killed 0237	MO
Ted Bourne				SC
Danny Boyle		Belfast	killed 0237	MO
Phil Boyle		Donegal		MO
Jim Brady		Belfast	killed ?	CM
Peter Brady	230514	Cavan		MO, SA
Michael Brennan		Kilkenny		MO
George Browne		Kilkenny	killed 0737	MO, BA
Liam Burgess		Mallow		MO
Harold Burrows	030416			SA
Joseph Byrne	220413	Dublin	metallurgist	SA
Paddy Byrne	280399	Dublin	sailor	MO, SA
Dennis Coady		Dublin	killed 0137	MO
William Colling	170111	Belfast		SA
Charles Colman		Cork		MO
Frank Conroy		Kildare	killed 1236	MO
Kit Conway		Tipperary	killed 0237	MO, IA
Colum Cox		Dublin		MO
Seamus Cummins		Dublin	wounded 1236	MO, NM
Pat Curley			killed 0237	MO
Peter Daly		Enniscorthy	killed 0837	MO, BA, SA
William Davis		Dublin	killed 0737	MO, NM
G. Deegan			killed 0138	BA
Alec Digges		Dublin		MO, OB
John Dolan			killed 0237	MO
Tom Donavan		Skibereen	killed 0338	MO
Charlie Donnelly		Tyrone	killed 0237	MO, BA
? Donovan				ER
Gerry Doran		Dublin		MO
Sean Dowling		Castlecomer		MO
Eugene Downing		Dublin		MO, GK
Bob Doyle	140216	Dublin	ship's cook	MO, SA, OB
Gerald Doyle		Limerick		LC
Paddy Duff		Dublin		MO
Frank Edwards		Waterford		MO, OB
John Finnegan	180309		Lincolns 0338	SA
Andrew Flanagan		Roscommon		MO
Terry Flanagan		Dublin		MO, OB
Jim Foley		Dublin	killed 1236	MO

Name	Born	Place	Other Details	Sources
James Forcell	040704	Dublin		SA
Tony Fox		Dublin	killed 1236	MO
W. H. Fox		Dublin	killed 0737	MO
Tony Gilbert			captured 0338	IT
P. Glacken		Donegal	killed 0138	MO
Sean Goff		Dublin	wounded 1236	MO, NM
George Gorman		Derry	killed 0738	MO
James Green		Dublin	killed ?	IB
Leo Green		Dublin	killed 1236	MO
James Haughey		Lurgan		MO, IB
T. Hayes		Dublin		MO
Tom Heeney	1920	Galway		MO, SA
Bill Henry		Belfast	killed 0237	MO
James Hillen		Belfast	wounded 1236	MO, NM
Robert Hilliard		Killarney	killed 0237	MO, BA
Dennis Holden		Carlow		MO
John Hunt		Waterford		MO
Hugh Hunter		Belfast		MO
Jack Jones		Wexford	killed 0738	MO
P. Keenan		Dublin		MO, IA
John Kelley		Waterford		MO
Chris Kelly			wounded 0238	SA, IA
J. Kelly		Roscommon	killed 0737	MO
Michael Kelly		Ballinasloe	killed 0737	MO, SC, SA
David Kennedy	300315	Ballycastle		SA
Steve Kenny		Belfast		MO
Thomas Kerr		Belfast	died 0838	MO
Esla Kumpaleyner			'Hirlandais'	SA
J. Larmour		Belfast		MO
William Laughran		Belfast	killed 0737	MO
George Leeson				KJ
Michael Lehane		Kilgarvan		MO, SA
John Lennon	040708	Waterford	cook	MO, SA
Maurice Levitas	010217	Dublin	plumber	MO, SA
Joe Lowry		Antrim		MO, SA
Thomas Lynch		Dublin	killed 0338	MO
John MacAleenan		Down		MO
Alan MacLarnan		Dublin		MO
Eugene MacParland	1915		ambulance	SA
Patsy McAlister				IT
Seamus McBroin				JM
Paddy McDaid		Dublin	killed 0237	MO

Name	Born	Place	Other Details	Sources
Paddy McElligot	1905			JG
Bert McElroy			killed 0237	MO
H. McGrath		Belfast	killed 0938	BA
Pat McGrath		Cork		MO
Liam McGregor		Dublin	killed 0938	MO, SA
Eamon McGrotty		Derry	killed 0237	MO
Charles McGuinness		Dublin		EO, IA
Paddy McIlroy		Dublin		MO
Paddy Roe McLaughlin		Donegal		MO, SC
W. McLaughlin		Belfast	killed 0737	IB
Chris Martin		Cork		MO
Michael May		Dublin	killed 1236	MO
John Meehan		Galway	killed 1236	MO
Ewart Milne		Dublin	medic	SP
Joe Monks		Dublin		MO, NM
Brendan Moroney		Ennis		CC
? Moroney				IB
Michael Mulligan		Belfast		KW
Thomas Murphy	1903		promoted lt 1937	SA
Ben Murray		Belfast	killed 0338	MO, SA
Joe Murray		Antrim	killed 0837	MO
Jack Nalty		Dublin	killed 0938	MO
Michael Nolan		Dublin	killed 1236	MO
John O'Beirne	230899	Portumna	labourer	SA
Francis D. O'Brien		Dundalk	killed 0138	MO, SA
Thomas T. O'Brien			killed 0237	MO
Tom O'Brien		Dublin		MO
Brian O'Callaghan				DT
Peter O'Connor		Waterford		MO, SA
Paddy O'Daire		Donegal		MO, SA
Hugh O'Donnell	1899	Donegal	stoker	MO, SA
Vincent O'Donnell	190404	Dun Laoghaire		MO, SA
J. O'Driscoll		Cork		MO
Liam O'Hanlon	041113	Belfast	labourer	MO, SA
Dick O'Neill		Belfast	killed 0237	MO, IB
James F. O'Regan		Cork		MO
Donal O'Reilly		Dublin		MO
Patrick (John) O'Reilly				IA, JG
Michael O'Riordan		Cork		MO, OB
John O'Shea		Kilmeadan		MO
John O'Shea	1902	Waterford	plasterer	SA
Paddy O'Sullivan		Dublin	killed 0838	MO, IB, SA

Name	Born	Place	Other Details	Sources
Billy Power		Waterford		MO, SA
Johnny Power		Waterford		MO, SA
Paddy Power		Waterford		MO, SA
Jim Prendergast		Dublin		MO, JM
Maurice Quinlan		Waterford	killed 0237	MO, BA, RS
Sidney Quinn		Lisburn		KJ
Charles Regan			killed 0837	MO
Jim Regan		Cork		MO, SA
John Q. Robinson		Belfast		MO
M. Roe		Athlone		MO
Michael Russell		Ennis	killed 0237	MO
Frank Ryan		Limerick		SC, BA, SA
Maurice Ryan		Tipperary	'executed' 0738	MO, KJ, BA
Paddy Scanlan		Cork		MO
Bill Scott		Dublin	XII Brigade	MO, ER
John P. Simms		Tipperary		MO
Paddy Smith		Dublin		MO
Patrick Stanley		Dublin		MO
James Straney		Belfast	killed 0738	MO
John Tierney		Limerick	missing 0937	MO, SA
Pat Tighe		Mayo		MO
Liam Tumilson		Belfast	killed 0237	MO
Thomas Walsh		Dublin	killed 0237	BA
David Walshe		Ballina	killed 0138	MO
Michael Waters		Cork		MO
Tommy Woods		Dublin	killed 1236	MO
Jim Woulfe		Limerick	killed 0837	MO

Key to sources

BA	Bill Alexander, *British Volunteers*
CC	*Clare Champion*, 211279
DT	*Dublin Tribune*, 111090
EO	Eoin O'Duffy, *Crusade*
ER	Esmond Romilly, *Boadilla*
GK	Gustav Klaus, *Strong Words*
IB	International Brigade Association Archive
IA	Irish Archives
IT	*Irish Times*, 090475 and 290997
JG	John Gerassi, *Premature Antifascists*
JM	Joe Monks, *With the Reds*
KJ	Kate Johnson, *Spanish Collection*
KW	Keith Watson, *Single to Spain*
LC	*Limerick Chronicle*, 271038

MO   Michael O'Riordan, *Connolly Column*
NM   National Museum of Labour History
OB   'Even the Olives are Bleeding', RTE
RS   Robert Stradling, *Brother Against Brother*
SA   Spanish Archives
SC   Sean Cronin, *Frank Ryan*
SP   *Sunday Press*, 290583

The following served in non-International Brigade units:
Tommy Patton (Achill), Madrid Militia
Jack White (Antrim), POUM Militia

The following Irish names (whose owners may have been Irish born) occur in the
    Spanish Archives:
British Battalion: W. Boyce, P. Boyle, F. Butler, R. Burns, W. Byrne, S. Donnell,
    D. J. Doyle, John Gorman, J. Kelly, W. McCartney, G. McDermott,
    J. McGrath, John O'Connell, William O'Hanlon, J. O'Hara, Charles O'Neill,
    J. Riley, M. Sullivan, Bernard Sweeney, D. Walsh

Lincoln Battalion (0637): A. Burke, G. Cunningham, J. McGrath, M. McLaughlin,
    (?Charles) O'Neill, M. Moran, J. Nolan, W. Walsh

Lincoln Battalion (0238): Roe Burke, Vincent Deegan, Bill Donnelly, Joe Mac-
    Kean, Tom McNulty, Patrick Murphy, Charles O'Barr, Joe O'Brien, Patrick
    O'Boyle, Paul O'Dell, Walter O'Kane, Tom O'Malley, John O'Sullivan, Larry
    O'Toole, Joe Walsh

Other XV Brigade Units: Patrick O'Brien (cook at Albacete), Ernest Mahoney
    (postal services)

Sources and bibliography

ARCHIVAL SOURCES

Archivo General Militar (Ávila)
This repository, part of the overall army records organisation (Servicio Histórico Militar), contains the operational records of the nationalist army during the Spanish Civil War, which were transferred to Ávila from the main centre in Madrid at the end of 1994. There are also a large number of captured republican army documents of operational relevance, catalogued as a discrete collection ('Zona Roja'). I have used the following sections:

Cuartel General del Generalísimo – records of Franco's HQ in Salamanca.
Organización – administrative and divisional records, including POW camps.
Estado Mayor, Primera Sección – records of high commands (mainly of the 'army of the centre').

Archivo Histórico Municipal (Cáceres)
Minute books and other records of the Town Council of Cáceres, 1936–37.

Archivo Histórico Nacional (Civil War Department, Salamanca)
This contains most of the material captured from the defeated side, including the (incomplete) records of the International Brigades. I have used the following sections, which are difficult to categorise exclusively, since they contain overlapping material:

Político-Social, Serie 'R' – records of organisation, membership, pay, discipline, routine orders.
Sección Militar – military operations, orders, casualties.

Archivo del Ministerio de Asuntos Exteriores (Madrid)
This archive, in the basement of the old Foreign Ministry building, contains the diplomatic records of both sides in the Spanish Civil War. I have used files from the following sections:

Archivo de Burgos – records of the nationalist foreign office.
Archivo de Barcelona – records of the republican foreign ministry.
Archivo Renovado – this contains mostly republican files organised as a result of an apparently abortive attempt at reclassification.

Imperial War Museum (London)
I have listened to several dozen recorded interviews from the Sound Archive (for further details, see below).

International Brigade Association Archive (Marx Memorial Library, London)
This library contains records of the British Battalion of the XV International Brigade (1936–38) and the subsequent history of the IBA. A printed catalogue is in the process of publication, but the archive will not be complete until copies of complementary original material presently held in the Comintern Archive in Moscow can be consulted in Clerkenwell Green.

Irish National Archives (Dublin)
Original records of the Irish Free State and Republic. I have consulted selected files, mostly in the Department of Foreign Affairs Section.

National Library of Ireland (Dublin)
Unpublished memoirs and other material (for details, see below).

National Museum of Labour History (Manchester)
Records of the CPGB, including organisation of, and propaganda concerning, the British Battalion of the International Brigades. Of particular interest is the correspondence of Harry Pollitt with the party's representatives in Spain. This archive, too, is incomplete, without many original Central Committee papers which were routinely sent to Moscow.

Public Record Office (Kew, London)
Original British State Papers. I have used only selected Foreign Office files.

University College, Dublin
Fine Gael Party Archives.

Working Class Museum and Library (Salford)
Unpublished memoirs and other memorabilia of International Brigaders from the Greater Manchester area.

OTHER UNPUBLISHED MATERIALS

In the public domain

J. McCarthy, 'Adventures with the Irish Brigade', bound typescript, NLI no. 94609 m13.

L. Walsh, 'General O'Duffy: His Life and Battles', microfilm NLI no. P.6539.

A. McCabe, Ms Journal, commonplace-books, correspondence, NLI Ms 61/2.

B. Clark, 'No Boots to my Feet. Experiences of a Britisher in Spain, 1937 to 1938', WCML typescript.

M. Jenkins, 'Prelude to Better Days', WCML typescript.

Copies of official Daily Routine Orders, NCO lists and passwords of the XV *Bandera*, Beckett Collection, Clew Bay Heritage Centre, Westport, Co. Mayo.

Sources and bibliography

In private possession

M. Becket, 'The Irish Brigade' (ms., 9pp.).
M. Fennell, 'Spain, 1936–37' (ms., 30pp.)
T. Hayes, 'Diary ... Irish Brigade of General Franco's Army'.
P. Hickey, Correspondence (six holograph letters from Spain, 1937).

AUDIO AND AUDIO-VISUAL MATERIALS

NB page nos refer to selected extracts from transcripts printed in Johnson, *The Spanish Civil War Collection* (see below).

Taped interviews made by the author in 1994 (copies in the IWM)

B. Boles, No. 14880, p. 281
T. Dalton, No. 14888, p. 279
W. Geraghty, No. 14893, p. 285
A. Hyde, No. 14889, p. 280
D. Reynolds, No. 14892, p. 284
P. Smith, No. 14891, pp. 282–3

Other audio interviews or recollections

Sound Archive IWM
C.S. Bloom, No. 992, pp. 83–4 (1976)
J. Brewer, No. 9963, pp. 173–9 (1987)
B. Collins, No. 9481, pp. 148–9 (1986) and No. 11296, p. 202 (recorded in 1987 by the North Kensington Local History Project)
B. Doyle, No. 806, pp. 38–9 (1976)
J. Dunlop, No. 11355, pp. 225–8 (1990)
M. Economides, No. 10428, pp. 195–7 (1988)
W. Greenhalgh, No. 10356, pp. 185–6 (recorded in 1984 by J. Cook) and No. 11187, pp. 199–201 (1992)
J. Jump, No. 9524, pp. 153–9 (1986)
J. Kavanagh, No. 14894, pp. 286–7 (1992)
P. Kemp, No. 9769, pp. 165–7 (1987)
P. Kerrigan, No. 810, pp. 47–8 (1976)
M. Levine, No. 9722, pp. 162–3 (1987) and No. 10360, p. 191 (recorded in 1984 by J. Cook)
B. McKenna, No. 847, pp. 76–7 (1976)
J. Monks, No. 11303, pp. 211–13 (recorded in 1986 by the North Kensington Local History Project)
B. Williamson, No. 12385, pp. 253–7 (1991)

J. Brewer, South Wales Miners' Library
P. McBride, RTE Radio Interview, 1988

TV documentary

'Even the Olives are Bleeding', directed by C. O'Shannon, RTE 1975. Contains interviews with the following veterans: A. Bustamente, A. Digges, M. Doolan, B. Doyle, F. Edwards, J. Monks, P. O'Daire, M. O'Riordan, P. Quinn, G. Timlin, T. Flanagan.

NEWSPAPERS

Seriatim files of the following for 1936–37 were consulted at the repositories cited in brackets:
El Adelanto de Salamanca (Hemeroteca Municipal de Madrid)
Connacht Tribune (Tuam Public Library)
Cork Examiner (Colindale)
Irish Times (British Library, Colindale)
Irish Press (Colindale)
Irish Independent (Colindale)
Transmisiones (Madrid)
Tuam Herald (Offices of the Tuam Herald, Tuam)
The Universe, Irish edition (Colindale)
Voz del Combatiente (Madrid)

Other newspaper references are from copies in State Paper files in the PRO and INA; or were made available from copies in private possession.

PUBLISHED SOURCES

Abella, R., *La vida cotidiana durante la guerra civil* (2 vols, Barcelona, Planeta, 1973–75).
Acier, M. (ed.), *From Spanish Trenches. Recent Letters from Spain* (New York, Modern Age Books, 1937).
Aguirre Prado, L., *The Church and the Spanish War* (Madrid, Servicio de Información Española, 1965).
Aldgate, A., *Cinema and History: British Newsreels and the Spanish Civil War* (London, Scolar Press, 1979).
Alexander, B., *British Volunteers For Liberty: Spain, 1936–39* (London, Lawrence and Wishart, rev. edn, 1986).
Alpert, M., *El ejército republicano en la guerra civil* (Barcelona, Ibérica de Ediciones, 1977).
Alpert, M., *A New International History of the Spanish Civil War* (London, Macmillan, 1994).
Álvarez, S. *et al.*, *Historia política y militar de las Brigadas Internacionales* (Madrid, Compañía Literaria, 1996).
Alvarez Rodríguez, R. and López Ortega, R., *Poesía Anglo-Norteamericana de la Guerra Civil Española: antología bilingüe* (Salamanca, Junta de Castilla y León, 1986).
Angus, J., *With the International Brigade in Spain* (Loughborough, Loughborough University Dept. of Economics, 1983).

Anon., *In Spain with the International Brigade: A Personal Narrative* (London, Burns Oates and Washborne, 1938).

Azaña, M., *La Velada en Benicarló* (Madrid, Espasa-Calpe, 1981).

Aznar, M., *Historia militar de la Guerra de España* (3 vols, 3rd edn, Madrid, Editorial Nacional, 1958–63).

Beevor, A., *The Spanish Civil War* (London, Orbis, 1982).

Blacam, A. de, *For God and Spain. The Truth about the Spanish War* (Dublin, Irish Messenger Office, 1936).

Bolín, L., *Spain: The Vital Years* (New York, 1967).

Bowyer Bell, J., *Secret Army: A History of the IRA, 1916–1970* (London, Anthony Blond, 1970).

Bowyer Bell, J., Ireland and the Spanish Civil War, in Klaus, *Strong Words*.

Brome, V., *The International Brigades* (London, Heinemann, 1965).

Burgo, J. del, *Conspiración y Guerra Civil* (Madrid, Alfaguara, 1970).

Cairns, D. and Richards, S., *Writing Ireland: Colonialism, Nationalism and Culture* (Manchester, Manchester University Press, 1988).

Cattell, D., *Communism and the Spanish Civil War* (Berkeley and Los Angeles, University of California Press, 1955).

Cardozo, H. G., *The March of a Nation: My Year of Spain's Civil War* (London, Eyre and Spottiswoode, 1937).

Carr, R., *The Civil War in Spain 1936–39* (London, Weidenfeld and Nicolson, 1986).

Carr, R. (ed.), *The Chances of Death: The Spanish Civil War Diary of Priscilla Scott-Ellis* (Norwich, Michael Russell, 1995).

Carroll, P., *The Odyssey of the Abraham Lincoln Brigade: Americans in the Spanish Civil War* (Stanford, Calif., University Press, 1994).

Casas de la Vega, R., *El Terror – Madrid 1936. Investigación histórica y catálogo de víctimas identificadas* (2nd edn, Madridejos, Editorial Fenix, 1994).

Castells, A., *Brigadas Internacionales de la Guerra de España* (Barcelona, Ariel, 1974).

Cierva, R. de la, *Historia esencial de la Guerra Civil Española* (Madridejos, Editorial Fenix, 1996).

Cierva, R. de la, *Brigadas Internacionales 1936–1996: la verdadera historia. Mentira histórica y error de Estado* (Madridejos, Editorial Fenix, 1997).

Cleugh, J., *Spanish Fury. The Story of the Civil War* (London, Harrap, 1962).

Chavez Palacios, J., *La Represion en la Provincia de Cáceres en la guerra civil* (Cáceres, Diputación Provincial de Cáceres, 1992).

Chavez Palacios, J., *Huidos y maquis: la actividad guerrillera en la provincia de Cáceres 1936–1950* (Cáceres, Diputación Provincial de Cáceres, 1994).

Colodny, R., *The Struggle For Madrid: The Central Epic of the Spanish Conflict, 1936–1937* (New York, Paine-Whitman, 1958).

Coogan, T. P., *De Valera: Long Fellow, Long Shadow* (London, Heinemann, 1993).

Cook, J., *Apprentices of Freedom* (London, Quartet Books, 1979).

Copeman, F., *Reason in Revolt* (London, Blandford Books, 1948).

Corkhill, D. and Rawnsley, S., *The Road to Spain* (Dunfermline, Borderline Press, 1981).

Cortada, J. (ed.), *Historical Dictionary of the Spanish Civil War, 1936–1939* (Westport, Conn., Greenwood Press, 1982).

Cronin, M., Blueshirts, Sports and Socials, *History Ireland* (Autumn, 1994), 43–7.

Cronin, M., *The Blueshirts and Irish Politics* (Dublin, Four Courts Press, 1997).

Cronin, S., *Frank Ryan: The Search for the Republic* (Dublin, Repsol, 1980).

Cullingford, E., *Yeats, Ireland and Fascism* (Dublin, Gill and Macmillan, 1981).

Cunningham, V., *British Writers of the Thirties* (Oxford, Oxford University Press, 1988).

Cunningham, V. (ed.), *The Penguin Book of Spanish Civil War Verse* (Harmondsworth, Penguin, 1980).

Davies, N., *Europe: A History* (Oxford, Oxford University Press, 1996).

Davis, T., *The Poems of Thomas Davis* (Dublin and London, James Duffy, 1846; repr. Chadwick-Healey, 1994).

Delperrie de Bayac, J., *Les Brigades Internationales* (Paris, Fayard, 1968).

Díaz-Plaja, F., *La vida cotidiana en la España de la guerra civil* (Madrid, Edaf, 1994).

Eby, C., *Between the Bullet and the Lie: American Volunteers in the Spanish Civil War* (New York, Holt Rinehart and Winston, 1969).

Esenwein, G. and Shubert, A., *Spain at War: The Spanish Civil War in Context 1931–1939* (London, Longman, 1996).

Ellman, R., *Yeats – The Man and the Masks* (Harmondsworth, Penguin, 1987).

Ennis, V., Some 'Catholic Moors', *An Cosantoir: Journal of the Irish Defence Services* (February, 1984), 39–43.

Ford, H., *A Poet's War* (Philadelphia, University of Pennsylvania Press, 1965).

Foss W. and Gerachty, C., *The Spanish Arena* (London, Gifford, 1938).

Francis, H., *Miners Against Fascism: Wales and the Spanish Civil War* (London, Lawrence and Wishart, 1984).

Gárate Córdoba, J. M. (ed.), *Mil días de fuego. Memorias documentadas de la guerra del treinta y seis* (Barcelona, Caralt, 1972).

Gárate Córdoba, J. M. (ed.), *Partes oficiales de la guerra* (2 vols, Madrid, Editorial San Martín for Servicio Histórico Militar, 1977–78).

García, J., *Estructura agraria y conflictos campesinos en Cáceres durante la II República* (Cáceres, Diputación Provincial de Cáceres, 1982).

García Venero, M., *Historia de las Internacionales en España, 1936–1939* (Madrid, Ediciones del Movimiento, 1957).

Gerassi, J., *The Premature Antifascists: North American Volunteers in the Spanish Civil War 1936–39 – An Oral History* (New York, Praeger, 1986).

Gibson, I., *Un irlandés en España* (Madrid, Planeta, 1981).

Graham, F. (ed.), *The Battle of Jarama: The Story of the British Battalion of the International Brigade in Spain* (Newcastle on Tyne, F. Graham, 1987).

Gregory, W., *The Shallow Grave* (London, Gollancz, 1986).

Gurney, J., *Crusade in Spain* (Newton Abbot, Readers Union, 1976).

Herrick, W., ¡*Hermanos!; A Novel about the Spanish Civil War* (London 1969; edn cit. Chance Press, New York, 1983).

Hoar, V., *The Mackenzie-Papineau Battalion: Canadian Participation in the Spanish Civil War* (Canada, Copp Clark Publishing Co., 1969).

Hills, G., *The Battle for Madrid* (London, Vantage, 1976).

Jackson, M., *Fallen Sparrows: The International Brigades in the Spanish Civil War* (Philadelphia, American Philosophical Soc., 1994).

Jellinek, F., *The Civil War in Spain* (London, Gollancz, 1938).

Johnson, K. *et al.* (eds), *The Spanish Civil War Collection: Sound Archive Oral History Recordings* (London, Imperial War Museum, 1996).

Johnston, V. B., *Legions of Babel: The International Brigades in the Spanish Civil War* (London, Pennsylvania University Press, 1967).

Keegan, J., *The Face of Battle* (Harmondsworth, Penguin, 1978).

Kemp, P., *Mine Were of Trouble* (London, Cassel, 1957).

Keogh, D., *Ireland and Europe, 1919–1948* (Dublin, Gill and Macmillan, 1988).

Keogh, D., *Twentieth-Century Ireland: Nation and State* (Dublin, Gill and Macmillan, 1994).

Keogh, D., An Eye Witness to History: Fr. Alexander McCabe and the Spanish Civil War, *Breifne – Journal of the Breifne Historical Society* 8 1996, 445–89.

Kilfeather, T. P., 'Spanish Inferno', series of articles (*Sunday Independent*, 15, 22, 29 May; 5, 12, 19, 26 June; 3 July 1960).

Kindelán, A., *Mis cuadernos de guerra* (Madrid, Ediciones Plus Ultra, 1945).

Kitchen, M., *Europe Between the Wars* (London, Longman, 1988).

Klaus, H. Gustav, The Authorship of the Somhairle Macalastair Ballads, *Irish University Review* 26 (1), 1996, 107–17.

Klaus, H. Gustav (ed.), *Strong Words, Brave Deeds: The Poetry, Life and Times of Thomas O'Brien, Volunteer in the Spanish Civil War* (Dublin, O'Brien Press, 1994).

Landis, A., *The Abraham Lincoln Battalion* (New York, Citadel Press, 1967).

Lee, L., *A Moment of War: A Memoir of the Spanish Civil War* (New York, The New Press, 1991).

Levine, M., *From Cheetham to Cordova: A Manchester Man of the Thirties* (Manchester, 1984).

Lindsay, P., *Memories* (Dublin, Blackwater Press, 1992).

Lister, E., *Memorias de un luchador: los primeros combates* (Madrid, Ediciones Del Toro, 1977).

Litton, H., *The Irish Civil War: An Illustrated History* (Dublin, Wolfhound Press, 1997).

Longo, L., *Le Brigate Internazionali in Spagna* (Rome, Editori Riuniti, 1956).

Lunn, A., *Spanish Rehearsal for World War: An Eyewitness Account of the Spanish Civil War* (London, Sheed and Ward 1937, repr. Old Greenwich, Conn., 1974).

Lyons, D. (ed.), *Land of the Poets – Ireland* (London, Sunburst Books, 1996).

McCullagh, F., *In Franco's Spain. Being the Experiences of an Irish War-Correspondent during the Great Civil War which Began in 1936* (London, Burns and Oates, 1937).

MacDougall, I. (ed.), *Voices from the Spanish Civil War: Personal Recollections of Scottish Volunteers in Republican Spain, 1936–39* (Edinburgh, Polygon Press, 1986).

McInerney, M., *Peader O'Donnell: Irish Social Rebel* (Dublin, O'Brien Press, 1974).

McKee, S., *I Was a Franco Soldier – By an Ex-member of the Irish Brigade* (London, United Editorial, 1938).

MacLysaght, E., *The Surnames of Ireland* (6th edn., Dublin, Irish Academic Press, 1991).

Manning, M., *The Blueshirts* (Dublin, Gill and Macmillan, 1970).

Martínez Bande, M., *La batalla de Teruel* (Madrid, Editorial San Martín, 1974).

Martínez Bande, M., *El Frente de Madrid* (Barcelona, Caralt Editorial, 1976).

Martínez Bande, M., *La marcha sobre Madrid* (Madrid, Editorial San Martín, 1982).

Martínez Bande, M., *La Batalla del Ebro* (Madrid, Editorial San Martín, 1988).

Mayle, B., *Fine Gael, 1923–1987* (Dublin, Blackwater Press, 1993).

Merriman, M. and Lerude, W., *American Commander in Spain: Robert Hale Merriman and the Abraham Lincoln Battalion* (Reno, University of Nevada Press, 1986).

Mezquida y Gené, E., *La Batalla del Ebro* (Tarragona, Diputación Provincial, 1973).

Mitchell, M., *Storm over Spain* (London, Secker and Warburg, 1937).

Moloney, T., *Westminster, Whitehall and the Vatican: The Role of Cardinal Hinsley, 1935–43* (London, Burns and Oates, 1985).

Monks, J., *With the Reds in Andalusia* (London, privately printed, 1985).

Montero Barrado, S., *Paisajes de la guerra: nueve itinerarios por los frentes de Madrid* (Madrid, Comunidad de Madrid, 1987).

Murphy, J. A., *Ireland in the Twentieth Century* (Dublin, Gill and Macmillan, 1975).

Naughton, L. and Watterson, J., *Irish Olympians* (Dublin, Blackwater Press, 1990).

Nelson, C. and Hendricks, J., *Madrid 1937: Letters of the Abraham Lincoln Brigade from the Spanish Civil War* (London, Routledge, 1996).

Nesterenko, I. (ed.), *International Solidarity with the Spanish Republic, 1936–1939* (Moscow, Progress Publishers, 1975).

Ó Cuinneaghán, S., *The War in Spain* (Enniscorthy, Enniscorthy Echo, n.d. but 1975).

Ó Cuinneaghán, S., *Saga of the Irish Brigade to Spain 1936 (November 1936–June 1937)* (Enniscorthy, Donnegan Print, n.d. but 1975).

O'Connor, P., *A Soldier of Liberty: Recollections of a Socialist and Anti-fascist Fighter* (Dublin, MSF, 1996).

O'Donnell, P., *Salud! An Irishman in Spain* (London, Methuen, 1937).

O'Duffy, E., *Crusade in Spain* (Dublin, Browne and Nolan, 1988).

Oram, H., *The Newspaper Book – A History of Newspapers in Ireland, 1649–1983* (Dublin, MO Books, 1983).

O'Riordan, M., *Connolly Column* (Dublin, New Books, 1979).

O'Riordan, M(anus), *Portrait of an Irish Anti-Fascist: Frank Edwards 1907–1983* (Dublin, 1984), pamphlet in IBA Archive, Box A-12 Ed/1.

Pike, D. W., *Conjecture, Propaganda and Deceit and the Spanish Civil War: The International Crisis over Spain, 1936–1939, as seen in the French Press* (Stanford, California Institute of International Studies, 1968).

Preston, P., *The Spanish Civil War, 1936–39* (London, Weidenfeld and Nicolson, 1986).

Preston, P., *Franco – A Biography* (London, Collins, 1993).

Richardson, T. D., *Comintern Army: The International Brigades in the Spanish Civil War* (Lexington, University of Kentucky Press, 1982).

Romilly, E., *Boadilla: A Personal Record of the English Group of the Thaelmann Battalion in Spain* (London, Hamish Hamilton, 1937).

Rosenstone, R., *Crusade of the Left: The Lincoln Battalion in the Spanish Civil War* (New York, University Press of America, 1969, repr. 1980).

Rubio Cabeza, M., *Diccionario de la Guerra Civil Española* (2 vols, Barcelona, Planeta, 1987).

Rust, W., *Britons in Spain: The History of the British Battalion of the XVth International Brigade* (London, Lawrence and Wishart, 1939).

Ryan, F. (ed.), *The Book of the XV Brigade: Records of British, American, Canadian and Irish Volunteers in the XV International Brigade* (Madrid, War Commissariat 1938, repr. Newcastle, Frank Graham, 1975).

Salas Larrazábal, R. *et al.*, *Aproximación histórica a la Guerra Española* (Madrid, Universidad de Madrid, 1970).

Sanchez, J. M., *The Spanish Civil War as Religious Tragedy* (Indiana, University of Notre Dame Press, 1987).

Scheller, K. and Navareño, A., *Cáceres: Everything under the Sun* (London, Harrap-Columbus, 1988).

Shelley, R., *Guide to the Postal History of the Spanish Civil War* (Brighton, privately printed, 1975).

Stephan, E., *Spies in Ireland* (London, Four Square Books, 1965).

Stradling, R. A., History and the Triumph of Art: Manuel Azana's Vision of Spanish Democracy, in Stradling *et al.*(eds), *Conflict and Coexistence: Nationalism and Democracy in Modern Europe – Essays in Honour of Harry Hearder* (Cardiff, University of Wales Press, 1977), 132–58.

Stradling, R. A., The Propaganda of the Deed: History, Hemingway, and Spain, *Textual Practice* 3 (1989), 15–35.

Stradling, R. A., *The Spanish Monarchy and Irish Mercenaries: The Wild Geese in Spain, 1618–68* (Dublin, Irish Academic Press, 1994).

Stradling, R. A., Franco's Irish Volunteers, *History Today* (April, 1995), 40–7.

Stradling, R. A., A War of Ideals?, *Cathair na Mart* 15 (1995), 110–18.

Stradling, R. A., Battleground of Reputations: Ireland and the Spanish Civil War', in Preston, P. and Mackenzie, A. (eds), *The Republic Besieged: Civil War in Spain, 1936–1939* (Edinburgh, Edinburgh University Press, 1996), 103–28.

Stradling, R. A., *Cardiff and the Spanish Civil War* (Cardiff, Butetown History and Arts Centre, 1996).

Stradling, R. A. (ed.), *Brother Against Brother: The Experiences of a Volunteer in the Spanish Civil War* (Stroud, Sutton Publishing, 1998).

Sullivan, R., *Christopher Caudwell* (Beckenham, Croom Helm, 1987).

Thomas, F., *To Tilt at Windmills: A Memoir of the Spanish Civil War* (East Lansing, State University of Michigan Press, 1996).

Thomas, H., *The Spanish Civil War* (3rd edn, Harmondsworth, Penguin, 1977).

Tierney, W., Irish Writers and the Spanish Civil War, *Eire Ireland* 7 (3), 1972, 36–55.

Tisa, J., *Recalling the Good Fight: An Autobiography of the Spanish Civil War* (Mass., Bergin and Garvey, 1985).

Toro y Guisbert, M. de (ed.), *Pequeño Larousse Ilustrado* (4th edn, Paris, Librería Larousse, 1916).

Toynbee, P. (ed.), *The Distant Drum: Reflections on the Spanish Civil War* (London, Book Club edn, 1976).

Trench, C., *Nearly Ninety: Reminiscences* (Ballivor, Co. Meath, The Cannon Press, 1996)

Turnbull, P. and Burn, J., *Men-at-Arms: The Spanish Civil War* (London, Osprey, 1978).

Veiga, M., *Fusilamiento en Navidad. Antonio Canales, tiempo de República* (Mérida, Editorial Regional de Extremadura, 1993).

Walker, G., *The Politics of Frustration – Harry Midgley and the Failure of Labour in Northern Ireland* (Manchester, Manchester University Press, 1980).

Watson, K., *Single to Spain* (London, Arthur Barker, 1937).

Whyte, J., *Church and State in Modern Ireland, 1923–79* (Dublin, Gill and Macmillan, 1980).

Williams, C. et al., *Memorials of the Spanish Civil War* (Stroud, Sutton Publishers, 1996).

Williamson, H. (ed.), *Toolmaking and Politics: The Life of Ted Smallbone – An Oral History* (Birmingham, Linden Books, 1987).

Wintringham, T., *English Captain* (London, Faber and Faber, 1939).

Yeats, W. B., *The Collected Poems of W. B. Yeats* (London, Macmillan, 1982).

Younger, C., *Ireland's Civil War* (London, Collins, 1970).

Zaragoza, C., *Ejército Popular y militares de la República (1936–39)* (Barcelona, Planeta, 1983).

Index

N.B. entries refer to text only. Given names and personal titles are only entered where a possibility of confusion exists.

Index